First World War
and Army of Occupation
War Diary
France, Belgium and Germany

33 DIVISION
98 Infantry Brigade
King's (Liverpool Regiment)
4th Battalion
1 November 1915 - 23 November 1919

WO95/2427/1

The Naval & Military Press Ltd
www.nmarchive.com
Published in association with The National Archives

Published by

The Naval & Military Press Ltd

Unit 10 Ridgewood Industrial Park,

Uckfield, East Sussex,

TN22 5QE England

Tel: +44 (0) 1825 749494

www.naval-military-press.com

www.nmarchive.com

This diary has been reprinted in facsimile from the original. Any imperfections are inevitably reproduced and the quality may fall short of modern type and cartographic standards.

© **Crown Copyright**
Images reproduced by permission of The National Archives, London, England, 2015.

Contents

Document type	Place/Title	Date From	Date To
Heading	WO95/2427-1 4 Bn. King's Liverpool Regt 1915 Nov. 1919 Nov		
Heading	33rd Division 56th Infy Bde 4th Bn (King's) L.Pool Regt 1915 Nov-1919 Nov From Lahore Div		
Heading	Division Infy Bde King's (L'Pools) Nov 1915		
Heading	137th Inf. Bde. 46th Div. Battn. Transferred From Sirhind Bde. Lahore Div. 10.11.15. Battn. Transferred to 56th Inf Bde. 19th Div. 3.12.15 War Diary 4th Battn. The King's (Liverpool Regiment). November 1915		
War Diary	Pont Rochon	01/11/1915	04/11/1915
War Diary	Ind V A	05/11/1915	10/11/1915
War Diary	A Section	10/11/1915	12/11/1915
War Diary	Lorette Road Reserve Billets	14/11/1915	14/11/1915
War Diary	Regnier Le Clerc (Merville)	15/11/1915	21/11/1915
War Diary	Croix Barbee	22/11/1915	30/11/1915
Heading	Appendices.		
Miscellaneous	Not to be published Headquarters Lahore Division	09/11/1915	09/11/1915
Miscellaneous	Routine Order by Lieut Colonel L.W.Y. Campbell Commanding Sirhind Brigade	08/11/1915	08/11/1915
Miscellaneous	4th Bn The Kings (L'pool Regt)		
Miscellaneous	In The Field	06/11/1915	06/11/1915
Miscellaneous			
Miscellaneous	In The Field	13/11/1915	13/11/1915
Miscellaneous	Field Return.		
Miscellaneous	Sheet I In The Field	13/11/1915	13/11/1915
Miscellaneous	4th Bn The King's (L'Pool Regt)	13/11/1915	13/11/1915
Miscellaneous			
Miscellaneous	4th Bn The King's (L'Pool Regt)	20/11/1915	20/11/1915
Miscellaneous	In The Field	20/11/1915	20/11/1915
Miscellaneous			
Miscellaneous	4th Bn The King's (L'Pool Regt)	27/11/1915	27/11/1915
War Diary	In The Field	29/11/1915	29/11/1915
Miscellaneous			
Heading	19th Division 58th Infy Bde 4th Bn King's (L'Pool Regt) Dec 1915-Feb 1916		
Heading	58th Inf. Bde. 19th Div. Battn. transferred from 137th Inf. Bde. 46th Div. to 56th Inf. Bde. 19th Div. 3.12.15. Battn. transferred from 56th Inf. Bde. 19.12.15 War Diary 4th Battn. The King's (Liverpool Regiment). December 1915 Attached: Appendices.		
War Diary	B. Sub Sector S 4.b. 7/4 And Croix Barbee	01/12/1915	04/12/1915
War Diary	Croix Barbee	05/12/1915	07/12/1915
War Diary	Locon	08/12/1915	19/12/1915
War Diary	Hun St + Locon.	20/12/1915	31/12/1915
Heading	Appendices.		
Miscellaneous	4th Bn The King's (L'Pool Regt)	04/12/1915	04/12/1915
Miscellaneous	In The Field	04/12/1915	04/12/1915
Miscellaneous			
Miscellaneous	4th Bn The King's (L'Pool Regt)	11/12/1915	11/12/1915
Miscellaneous	In The Field	11/12/1915	11/12/1915

Miscellaneous			
Miscellaneous	In The Field	17/12/1915	17/12/1915
Miscellaneous			
Miscellaneous	4th Bn The King's (L'Pool Regt)	17/12/1915	17/12/1915
Miscellaneous	In The Field	17/12/1915	17/12/1915
Miscellaneous	Sheet 3 In The Field	17/12/1915	17/12/1915
Miscellaneous			
Miscellaneous	4th Bn The King's (L'Pool Regt)	24/12/1915	24/12/1915
Miscellaneous	In The Field	24/12/1915	24/12/1915
Miscellaneous			
Miscellaneous	4th Bn The King's (L'Pool Regt)	31/12/1915	31/12/1915
Miscellaneous	In The Field	31/12/1915	31/12/1915
Miscellaneous			
Miscellaneous	Sheet 2 In The Field	31/12/1915	31/12/1915
Miscellaneous			
Heading	58 XIX 4 Liverpool Regt Jan Vol III		
War Diary	Trenches S 5. L-10.b. Billets Locon	01/01/1916	04/01/1916
War Diary	Locon	05/01/1916	14/01/1916
War Diary	S. D 14. Central	15/01/1916	21/01/1916
War Diary	Locon & S 14 Central	22/01/1916	23/01/1916
War Diary	Locon	24/01/1916	25/01/1916
War Diary	La Pannerie	26/01/1916	31/01/1916
Miscellaneous	19th Division No. G.a. 906	24/01/1916	24/01/1916
Miscellaneous	4th Bn The King's (L'Pool Regt)	01/01/1916	01/01/1916
Miscellaneous	In The Field	07/01/1916	07/01/1916
Miscellaneous			
Miscellaneous	4th Bn The King's (L'Pool Regt)	14/01/1916	14/01/1916
Miscellaneous	In The Field	14/01/1916	14/01/1916
Miscellaneous			
Miscellaneous	4th Bn The King's (L'Pool Regt)	21/01/1916	21/01/1916
Miscellaneous	In The Field	21/01/1916	21/01/1916
Miscellaneous			
Miscellaneous	In The Field	28/01/1916	28/01/1916
Miscellaneous	4th Bn The King's (L'Pool Regt)	28/01/1916	28/01/1916
Miscellaneous			
War Diary	Le Sart (near Merville)	01/02/1916	13/02/1916
War Diary	Billets Le Sart & Laventie	14/02/1916	16/02/1916
War Diary	Le Drumez	17/02/1916	24/02/1916
War Diary	Croix Marmuse	25/02/1916	26/02/1916
War Diary	Bethune	27/02/1916	27/02/1916
War Diary	Annequin South	28/02/1916	28/02/1916
War Diary	Trenches 21 Section	29/02/1916	29/02/1916
Miscellaneous	Special Order Of The Day. By Major-General G.T.M. Bridges, C.M.G., D.S.O., Commanding 19th Division.	25/02/1916	25/02/1916
Heading	98th Brigade 33rd Division. 4th Battalion The King's Liverpool Regiment March 1916		
War Diary	Trenches 2.1. Sector (Auchy Area)	01/03/1916	04/03/1916
War Diary	Annequin. S	05/03/1916	06/03/1916
War Diary	Trenches 2.0. Sector (Auchy Area)	07/03/1916	09/03/1916
War Diary	Montmorency Barracks Bethune	10/03/1916	16/03/1916
War Diary	Le Quesnoy, Bethune Map 1/40,000 Squsses F.8 & 9.	22/03/1916	24/03/1916
War Diary	Le Quesnoy.	25/03/1916	26/03/1916
War Diary	Trenches Cuinchy Section (Brick Stacks)	27/03/1916	31/03/1916
Miscellaneous	The following messages was received from the Brigade Commander on the 27th March 1916.	27/03/1916	27/03/1916
Miscellaneous	4th Bn The King's (L'Pool Regt)	03/03/1916	03/03/1916

Miscellaneous	In The Field	03/03/1916	03/03/1916
Miscellaneous		03/03/1916	03/03/1916
War Diary	4th Bn The King's (L'Pool Regt)	10/03/1916	10/03/1916
Miscellaneous	Sheet I In The Field	10/03/1916	10/03/1916
Miscellaneous	Sheet 2 In The Field	10/03/1916	10/03/1916
Miscellaneous			
Miscellaneous	4th Bn The King's (Liverpool Regt) 33rd Division. 16th March 1916	10/03/1916	10/03/1916
Miscellaneous	4th Bn The King's (L'Pool Regt)	17/03/1916	17/03/1916
Miscellaneous	In The Field	17/03/1916	17/03/1916
Miscellaneous	4th Bn The King's (L'Pool Regt) 33rd Division	17/03/1916	17/03/1916
Miscellaneous	4th Bn The King's (L'Pool Regt)	24/03/1916	24/03/1916
Miscellaneous	In The Field	24/03/1916	24/03/1916
Miscellaneous	4th Bn The King's (L'Pool Regt) 33rd Division	24/03/1916	24/03/1916
Miscellaneous	4th Bn The King's (L'Pool Regt)	31/03/1916	31/03/1916
Miscellaneous	In The Field	31/03/1916	31/03/1916
Miscellaneous	4th Bn The King's (L'Pool Regt)	31/03/1916	31/03/1916
Heading	98th Brigade 33rd Division 4th Battalion The King's Liverpool Regiment April 1916		
War Diary	Le Quesnoy Bethune Map 1/40,000 Squares F.8.9	01/04/1916	01/04/1916
War Diary	Oblinghem (Squares W 20 & 26.)	02/04/1916	10/04/1916
War Diary	Beuvry	11/04/1916	14/04/1916
War Diary	Trenches (Auchy Left Sub. Sector)	15/04/1916	18/04/1916
War Diary	Beuvry	19/04/1916	22/04/1916
War Diary	Trenches Auchy (Left Sub Section)	23/04/1916	26/04/1916
War Diary	Bethune	27/04/1916	30/04/1916
Miscellaneous	4th Bn The King's (Liver Pool Regt)	07/04/1916	07/04/1916
Miscellaneous	In The Field	07/04/1916	07/04/1916
Miscellaneous	4th Bn The King's (Liverpool Regt)	07/04/1916	07/04/1916
Miscellaneous	4th Bn The King's (Liverpool Regt)	14/04/1916	14/04/1916
Miscellaneous	France	14/04/1916	14/04/1916
Miscellaneous	4th Bn The King's (Liverpool Regt) 33rd Division	14/04/1916	14/04/1916
Miscellaneous	4th Bn The King's (Liverpool Regt) France	21/04/1916	21/04/1916
Miscellaneous	France	21/04/1916	21/04/1916
Miscellaneous			
Miscellaneous	Sheet 2 France	21/04/1916	21/04/1916
Miscellaneous	4th Bn The King's (Liver Pool Regt) 33rd Division	21/04/1916	21/04/1916
Miscellaneous	4th Bn The King's (Liverpool Regt) France	28/04/1916	28/04/1916
Miscellaneous	France	28/04/1916	28/04/1916
Miscellaneous	4th Bn The King's (Liverpool Regt)	28/04/1916	28/04/1916
Heading	98th Brigade. 33rd Division 4th Battalion The King's Liverpool Regiment		
War Diary	Bethune	01/05/1916	03/05/1916
War Diary	Bethune & Trenches Cuinchy (Left Subsection)	04/05/1916	08/05/1916
War Diary	Le Quesnoy (Bethune Sheet F. 8. C)	09/05/1916	09/05/1916
War Diary	Le Quesnoy	10/05/1916	12/05/1916
War Diary	Cuinchy Left Subsection	13/05/1916	16/05/1916
War Diary	Le Quesnoy	17/05/1916	20/05/1916
War Diary	Cuinchy Left Sub Section	21/05/1916	24/05/1916
War Diary	Le Quesnoy	25/05/1916	28/05/1916
War Diary	Bethune	29/05/1916	31/05/1916
Miscellaneous	4th Bn The King's (Liverpool)	31/05/1916	31/05/1916
Miscellaneous	Ac 36/141 Infantry Brigade	31/05/1916	31/05/1916
Miscellaneous	4th Bn The King's (L'pool Regt)	05/05/1916	05/05/1916
Miscellaneous	France	05/05/1916	05/05/1916
Miscellaneous	4th Bn The King's (L'pool Regt) 33rd Division	05/05/1916	05/05/1916

War Diary	4th Bn The King's (Liverpool Regiment)	12/05/1916	12/05/1916
Miscellaneous	France	12/05/1916	12/05/1916
Miscellaneous			
Miscellaneous	4th Bn The King's (Liverpool Regt)	12/05/1916	12/05/1916
Miscellaneous	4th Bn The King's (Liverpool Regt)	19/05/1916	19/05/1916
Miscellaneous	France	19/05/1916	19/05/1916
Miscellaneous	4th Bn The King's (Liverpool Regiment) 33rd Division	19/05/1916	19/05/1916
Miscellaneous	4th Bn The King's (L'Pool Regt)	26/05/1916	26/05/1916
Miscellaneous	France	26/05/1916	26/05/1916
Miscellaneous	4th Bn The King's (Liverpool Regt)	26/05/1916	26/05/1916
Heading	98th Brigade. 33rd Division. 4th Battalion The King's Liverpool Regiment June 1916		
War Diary	Ecole Des Jeunes Filles-Bethune	01/06/1916	10/06/1916
War Diary	Ecole Des Jeunes Filles Bethune & Le Quesnay	11/06/1916	11/06/1916
War Diary	Le Quesnoy	12/06/1916	17/06/1916
War Diary	And Trenchs Rehew Sivenchy Risht Section	17/06/1916	20/06/1916
War Diary	Beuvry	21/06/1916	30/06/1916
Miscellaneous	All Units, 98th Infantry Brigade.	10/06/1916	10/06/1916
Miscellaneous	4th Bn The King's (L'Pool Regt)	02/06/1916	02/06/1916
Miscellaneous			
Miscellaneous	France	02/06/1916	02/06/1916
Miscellaneous			
Miscellaneous	Sheet II France	02/06/1916	02/06/1916
Miscellaneous	Sheet I France	02/06/1916	02/06/1916
Miscellaneous	4th Bn The King's (L'Pool Regt)	02/06/1916	02/06/1916
Miscellaneous	4th Bn The King's (Liverpool Regt) 33rd Division	09/06/1916	09/06/1916
Miscellaneous	4th Bn The King's (Liverpool Regt) France	09/06/1916	09/06/1916
Miscellaneous	France	09/06/1916	09/06/1916
Miscellaneous	4th Bn The King's (Liverpool Regt)	16/06/1916	16/06/1916
Miscellaneous	France	16/06/1916	16/06/1916
Miscellaneous	4th Bn The King's (Liverpool Regt)	16/06/1916	16/06/1916
Miscellaneous	4th Bn The King's (Liverpool Regt)	23/06/1916	23/06/1916
Miscellaneous			
Miscellaneous	Sheet 2 S France	23/06/1916	23/06/1916
Miscellaneous	France	23/06/1916	23/06/1916
Miscellaneous	4th Bn The King's (Liverpool Regt) France	23/06/1916	23/06/1916
Miscellaneous	4th Bn The King's (Liverpool Regt)	30/06/1916	30/06/1916
Miscellaneous	France	30/06/1916	30/06/1916
Miscellaneous	4th Bn The King's (L'Pool Regt)	30/06/1916	30/06/1916
Heading	98th Inf. Bde. 33rd Div. War Diary 4th Battn. The King's (Liverpool Regiment). July 1916		
War Diary	Beuvry	01/07/1916	02/07/1916
War Diary	Guinchy Subsection	03/07/1916	07/07/1916
War Diary	Gonnehem	08/07/1916	08/07/1916
War Diary	Rainneville	09/07/1916	10/07/1916
War Diary	Vaux. Sur. Somme	11/07/1916	12/07/1916
War Diary	Ville-Sous-Corbie	13/07/1916	13/07/1916
War Diary	Meaulte	14/07/1916	15/07/1916
War Diary	Front Line	16/07/1916	17/07/1916
War Diary	Caterpillar Wood	18/07/1916	19/07/1916
Miscellaneous	Front Line	20/07/1916	20/07/1916
War Diary	Caterpillar Wood	21/07/1916	21/07/1916
War Diary	Dernancourt	22/07/1916	31/07/1916
Heading	Appendices.		
Miscellaneous	33rd Division.		
Miscellaneous	4th Bn The King's (Liverpool Regt)	07/07/1916	07/07/1916

Miscellaneous	France	07/07/1916	07/07/1916
Miscellaneous	4th Bn The King's (L'Pool Regt)	14/07/1916	14/07/1916
Miscellaneous	France	14/07/1916	14/07/1916
Miscellaneous	4th Bn The King's (L'Pool Regt)	21/07/1916	21/07/1916
Miscellaneous	France	21/07/1916	21/07/1916
Miscellaneous	4th Bn The King's (L'Pool Regt)	21/07/1916	21/07/1916
Miscellaneous	4th Bn The King's (L'Pool Regt)	23/07/1916	23/07/1916
Miscellaneous	4th Bn The King's (Liverpool Regt)	23/07/1916	23/07/1916
Miscellaneous	4th Bn The King's (Liverpool Regt)	28/07/1916	28/07/1916
Miscellaneous	France	28/07/1916	28/07/1916
Miscellaneous	8th Bn The King's (Liverpool Regt)	28/07/1916	28/07/1916
Miscellaneous			
Miscellaneous	4th Bn The King's (Liverpool Regt)		
Miscellaneous			
Heading	98th Brigade. 33rd Division. 1/4th Battalion The King's Liverpool Regiment August 1916		
War Diary	Dernancourt	01/08/1916	06/08/1916
War Diary	Mametz Wood	07/08/1916	07/08/1916
War Diary	Fricourt Wood	08/08/1916	13/08/1916
War Diary	Trenches	13/08/1916	13/08/1916
War Diary	Bazentin-Le-Grand	04/08/1916	16/08/1916
War Diary	Trenches	17/08/1916	18/08/1916
War Diary	Mametz Wood	19/08/1916	19/08/1916
War Diary	Fricourt Wood	20/08/1916	25/08/1916
War Diary	Carlton French	26/08/1916	27/08/1916
War Diary	Front Line	28/08/1916	31/08/1916
Heading	98th Brigade 33rd Division. 4th Battalion The King's Liverpool Regiment September 1916		
War Diary	Dernancourt	01/09/1916	01/09/1916
War Diary	Cardonette	02/09/1916	02/09/1916
War Diary	Candas	03/09/1916	04/09/1916
War Diary	Nuncq	05/09/1916	07/09/1916
War Diary	Sus St. Leger	08/09/1916	09/09/1916
War Diary	Coullemont	10/09/1916	12/09/1916
War Diary	Humber-Camp	13/09/1916	19/09/1916
War Diary	Bayencourt	20/09/1916	20/09/1916
War Diary	Hebuterne Trenches	21/09/1916	25/09/1916
War Diary	Bayencourt	26/09/1916	30/09/1916
Heading	98th Brigade 33rd Division. 4th Battalion The King's Liverpool Regiment October 1916		
War Diary	Bayencourt	01/10/1916	01/10/1916
War Diary	Ivergny	02/10/1916	16/10/1916
War Diary	Wanquetin	17/10/1916	18/10/1916
War Diary	Ivergny And Daours	19/10/1916	20/10/1916
War Diary	Daours & Meaulte	21/10/1916	21/10/1916
War Diary	Meaulte	22/10/1916	22/10/1916
War Diary	Trones Wood	23/10/1916	23/10/1916
War Diary	Trones Wood & Trenches	24/10/1916	24/10/1916
War Diary	Trenches By Les Boeufs	25/10/1916	28/10/1916
War Diary	Trones Wood Huts Carnoy	29/10/1916	31/10/1916
Miscellaneous	Copy of Message Lieut to 4th Kings G.O.C. XIV Corps. on 28th Oct 1916	28/10/1916	28/10/1916
Miscellaneous	Copy of Message Lieut 4th Kings by G.O.C. 33rd Division on 28th Oct 1916	28/10/1916	28/10/1916
Heading	98th Brigade. 33rd Division. 4th Battalion The King's (Liverpool Regiment) November 1916		

War Diary	Trones Wood & Trenches at Les Boeufs Numbers	01/11/1916	03/11/1916
War Diary	And Bernagay X Roads	04/11/1916	04/11/1916
War Diary	Sand Pits Meaulte	05/11/1916	09/11/1916
War Diary	Huppy (Near Abbeville)	10/11/1916	12/11/1916
War Diary	Huppy	13/11/1916	30/11/1916
Heading	98th Brigade. 33rd Division. 4th Battalion The King's Liverpool Regiment December 1916		
War Diary	Huppy	01/12/1916	04/12/1916
War Diary	On The March	05/12/1916	05/12/1916
War Diary	Sailly Le Sec	06/12/1916	06/12/1916
War Diary	Camp 112	07/12/1916	07/12/1916
War Diary	Coup 112 & 16	08/12/1916	09/12/1916
War Diary	Coup 20 + Branch	10/12/1916	10/12/1916
War Diary	Trenches N Of Bouchavesnes	11/12/1916	14/12/1916
War Diary	Petit Bois	15/12/1916	18/12/1916
War Diary	Camp 17	19/12/1916	21/12/1916
War Diary	Trenches Rancourt	22/12/1916	24/12/1916
War Diary	Mavrepas Ravine	25/12/1916	26/12/1916
War Diary	Camp III	27/12/1916	28/12/1916
War Diary	Camp III And Bethencourt St Oven	29/12/1916	29/12/1916
War Diary	Bethencourt St Ouen	30/12/1916	31/12/1916
War Diary	Bethencourt St Ouen	01/01/1917	31/01/1917
War Diary	In Trenches Front Line Clery	01/02/1917	05/02/1917
War Diary	Support Dugout	06/02/1917	08/02/1917
War Diary	Field Line Cleney	09/02/1917	12/02/1917
War Diary	Support Trenches Clery	13/02/1917	16/02/1917
War Diary	Suzanne	17/02/1917	22/02/1917
War Diary	Support Trenches Road Wood	23/02/1917	24/02/1917
War Diary	Front Trenches List Sub Sector Bethune Rd	25/02/1917	26/02/1917
War Diary	Howitzer Wood	27/02/1917	28/02/1917
War Diary	Left Subsector Perronnero Bouchavesnes	01/03/1917	02/03/1917
War Diary	Road Wood	03/03/1917	04/03/1917
War Diary	Front Line	05/03/1917	07/03/1917
War Diary	Road Wood	08/03/1917	08/03/1917
War Diary	Camp 12	09/03/1917	22/03/1917
War Diary	Sailly Laurette	23/03/1917	01/04/1917
War Diary	Lahoussoye	02/04/1917	02/04/1917
War Diary	Pierregot	03/04/1917	03/04/1917
War Diary	Ficheux	12/04/1917	17/04/1917
War Diary	Hindenbure Support Line Map 5.1.B.S.W N. 34	18/04/1917	24/04/1917
War Diary	Suncken Road T.3.A.	25/04/1917	25/04/1917
War Diary	Beaumetz By Loges	26/04/1917	30/04/1917
War Diary	Beaumetz By Loges	01/05/1917	02/05/1917
War Diary	Douchy By Ayette	03/05/1917	11/05/1917
War Diary	Hindenburg Line	12/05/1917	15/05/1917
War Diary	Boyelles	16/05/1917	19/05/1917
War Diary	Hindenburg Line	20/05/1917	21/05/1917
War Diary	Boyelles	22/05/1917	25/05/1917
War Diary	Hindenburg Line Fontaine By Crossvilles	26/05/1917	28/05/1917
War Diary	Boyelles	29/05/1917	31/05/1917
War Diary	Blaireville	01/06/1917	18/06/1917
War Diary	Boyelles	19/06/1917	19/06/1917
War Diary	Bde Support	20/06/1917	24/06/1917
War Diary	Boyelles	25/01/1917	30/06/1917
War Diary	Bellacourt	01/07/1917	03/07/1917
War Diary	Acheux	04/07/1917	04/07/1917

War Diary	Talmas	05/07/1917	05/07/1917
War Diary	Belloy-Sur-Somme	06/07/1917	06/07/1917
War Diary	Allery (Porthieu)	07/07/1917	15/07/1917
War Diary	Allery	16/07/1917	31/07/1917
War Diary	La Panne	01/08/1917	17/08/1917
War Diary	St Georges Sector	18/08/1917	23/08/1917
War Diary	Queensland Came Dost Dunkerke	24/08/1917	27/08/1917
War Diary	La Panne	28/08/1917	28/08/1917
War Diary	Ghyvelde	29/08/1917	29/08/1917
War Diary	Braydunes	30/08/1917	31/08/1917
War Diary	Serques	01/09/1917	15/09/1917
War Diary	Ochtezeele	16/09/1917	16/09/1917
War Diary	Steenvourde	17/09/1917	17/09/1917
War Diary	Le Coq De Paille	18/09/1917	20/09/1917
War Diary	Ontario Camp Reninghelst	21/09/1917	23/09/1917
War Diary	Kruisstraathoek	24/09/1917	24/09/1917
War Diary	Reutelbeek Sector	25/09/1917	27/09/1917
War Diary	Dickebusch	28/09/1917	28/09/1917
War Diary	Lynde	29/09/1917	30/09/1917
War Diary	Linde	01/10/1917	05/10/1917
War Diary	Ypres	06/10/1917	18/10/1917
War Diary	Neuve Eglise	19/10/1917	22/10/1917
War Diary	Bristol Castle Sector	23/10/1917	26/10/1917
War Diary	In The Line	27/10/1917	27/10/1917
War Diary	Neuve Eglise	31/10/1917	02/11/1917
War Diary	Shankhill Camp Neuve Eglise	03/11/1917	12/11/1917
War Diary	Merris Area	13/11/1917	16/11/1917
War Diary	Camp I.9.A. Sheet 28	17/11/1917	18/11/1917
War Diary	Support Line Seine	19/11/1917	22/11/1917
War Diary	Rt Sub Sector Passehensaiele Sector	23/11/1917	24/11/1917
War Diary	I 9 a Potipje	25/11/1917	25/11/1917
War Diary	Toronto Camp	26/11/1917	30/11/1917
War Diary	Toronto Camp Brandhoek	01/12/1917	01/12/1917
War Diary	Potidje	02/12/1917	05/12/1917
War Diary	Support Framburg	06/12/1917	07/12/1917
War Diary	Hamburg	08/12/1917	09/12/1917
War Diary	Passchendaele Lt Sub Sector	10/12/1917	12/12/1917
War Diary	Camp St Jean	13/12/1917	13/12/1917
War Diary	Eecke Area	14/12/1917	31/12/1917
War Diary	Poperinghe	01/01/1918	03/01/1918
War Diary	Eecke Area	04/01/1918	05/01/1918
War Diary	St Jean Camp	06/01/1918	19/01/1918
War Diary	Support Hamburg	20/01/1918	21/01/1918
War Diary	Right Sub Sector	22/01/1918	23/01/1918
War Diary	St Lawrence Camp Brandhoek	24/01/1918	27/01/1918
War Diary	Right Subsector Passchendaele	28/01/1918	29/01/1918
War Diary	Toronto Camp West Brandhoek	30/01/1918	30/01/1918
War Diary	Boisdinghem	31/01/1918	22/02/1918
War Diary	Brandhoek	23/02/1918	23/02/1918
War Diary	St Jean Camp	24/02/1918	25/02/1918
War Diary	Support Passchendale Sector	26/02/1918	28/02/1918
War Diary	4th Bn The King "S" Order No II		
Miscellaneous	4th Bn The King "S" Order No. 19		
Miscellaneous	4th Bn The King "S" Order No. 18		
War Diary	Hamburg (Support Bn)	01/03/1918	01/03/1918
War Diary	St Jean Camp	02/03/1918	05/03/1918

War Diary	Front Line (Left)	06/03/1918	09/03/1918
War Diary	St Jean Camp	10/03/1918	15/03/1918
War Diary	Front Line Left	16/03/1918	21/03/1918
War Diary	St Lawrence Camp Brandhoek	22/03/1918	31/03/1918
Heading	4th Battalion "The Kings" Liverpool Regt. April 1918		
War Diary	Line	01/04/1918	03/04/1918
War Diary	Brandhoek	04/04/1918	07/04/1918
War Diary	Ambrines	08/04/1918	11/04/1918
War Diary	Ravelsberg	12/04/1918	12/04/1918
War Diary	Bailleul	13/04/1918	13/04/1918
War Diary	Meteren	14/04/1918	18/04/1918
War Diary	Meteren & Boeschede	19/04/1918	19/04/1918
War Diary	Boeschepe	20/04/1918	20/04/1918
War Diary	Bavinchove	21/04/1918	26/04/1918
War Diary	Hondeghem	27/04/1918	30/04/1918
War Diary	98th Infantry Brigade Appendix I	21/04/1918	21/04/1918
Miscellaneous	98th Inf. Bde. Order No. 218	10/04/1918	10/04/1918
Miscellaneous	98th Bde		
War Diary	Hondeghem	01/05/1918	01/05/1918
War Diary	Blaringhem	02/05/1918	02/05/1918
War Diary	Busseboom	03/05/1918	04/05/1918
War Diary	Bickebusch	04/05/1918	12/05/1918
War Diary	27 L. T. D. 5.1.	12/05/1918	17/05/1918
War Diary	Dirty Buckel Camp (27.A.30.d.1.9)	18/05/1918	20/05/1918
War Diary	Dirty Bucket Camp	21/05/1918	30/05/1918
War Diary	Bois St Acaire	31/05/1918	31/05/1918
Miscellaneous	Report on the action taken by the Battalion during the Operations in the vicincty of Dickebusch Lake and Ridge Wood-May 7th to 11th 1918		
Miscellaneous Diagram etc	4th Bn. "The King's"		
Miscellaneous	Brigade Exercise		
Miscellaneous			
Miscellaneous	Narrative Recerence Sheet 27 N.W. 1/20,000		
War Diary	Bois St Acaire	01/06/1918	02/06/1918
War Diary	East Poperinghe (28 G.2.d.7.7.)	03/06/1918	05/06/1918
War Diary	East Poperinghe	06/06/1918	10/06/1918
War Diary	Front Line Right Sub Sector Canal Sector	11/06/1918	15/06/1918
War Diary	Support Line Dickebusch Canal	16/06/1918	20/06/1918
War Diary	Brandhoek	21/06/1919	25/06/1919
War Diary	Front Line Left Rides Sector	26/06/1917	30/06/1918
War Diary		01/07/1918	27/07/1918
War Diary	Left Bn Left Bde Sector	28/07/1918	30/07/1918
War Diary	Left Bn: Left Sub Sector "Canal Sector"	01/08/1918	04/08/1918
War Diary	Knollys Fm:	05/08/1918	05/08/1918
War Diary	Green Line	06/08/1918	09/08/1918
War Diary	Left Bn: Right Sub Sector "Canal Sector"	10/08/1918	16/08/1918
War Diary	St Jan-Ter-Biezen	17/08/1918	20/08/1918
War Diary	Mentque	21/08/1918	27/08/1918
War Diary	Mentque Grouches	28/08/1918	28/08/1918
War Diary	Grouches	29/08/1918	14/09/1918
War Diary	Les Boeufs	15/09/1918	17/09/1918
War Diary	Lechelle	18/09/1918	18/09/1918
War Diary	Equancourt Fins Ridge	19/09/1918	19/09/1918
War Diary	Trenches Near Villers Guislam	20/09/1918	30/09/1918
War Diary	Villers Guislain	01/10/1918	04/10/1918

War Diary	Pigeon Quarry	05/10/1918	07/10/1918
War Diary	Honnecourt	08/10/1918	08/10/1918
War Diary	Honnecourt Clary	09/10/1918	09/10/1918
War Diary	Clary Troisvilles R. Selle	10/10/1918	10/10/1918
War Diary	R. Selle	11/10/1918	11/10/1918
War Diary	Troisvilles	12/10/1918	12/10/1918
War Diary	Clary	13/10/1918	20/10/1918
War Diary	Clary Troisvilles	21/10/1918	21/10/1918
War Diary	Troisvilles	22/10/1918	22/10/1918
War Diary	Montay Area	23/10/1918	23/10/1918
War Diary	Croix	24/10/1918	24/10/1918
War Diary	La Faucette	25/10/1918	25/10/1918
War Diary	Sassegnies	05/11/1918	05/11/1918
War Diary	Engle Fontain	26/10/1918	26/10/1918
War Diary	Montay	27/10/1918	31/10/1918
War Diary	Montay	01/11/1918	04/11/1918
War Diary	Engle Fontaine	05/11/1918	05/11/1918
War Diary	Sart-Bara	06/11/1918	07/11/1918
War Diary	Aulnoye	08/11/1918	08/11/1918
War Diary	Sassegnies	09/11/1918	14/11/1918
War Diary	Vendecies Au Bois	15/11/1918	15/11/1918
War Diary	Caullery	16/11/1918	10/12/1918
War Diary	Masnieres Faureil	11/12/1918	12/12/1918
War Diary	Bapaume	12/12/1918	12/12/1918
War Diary	Albert	13/12/1918	13/12/1918
War Diary	Hilonville	14/12/1918	14/12/1918
War Diary	Ailly Sur Somme	15/12/1918	15/12/1918
War Diary	Camp En Amienois	16/12/1918	16/12/1918
War Diary	Dromesnil	19/12/1918	02/01/1919
War Diary	Poix-du-Nord	03/01/1919	03/01/1919
War Diary	Le Havre Camp 14 Harfleur	04/01/1919	04/01/1919
War Diary	Camp 14-harfleur Le Havre	05/01/1919	07/01/1919
War Diary	Harfleur	08/01/1919	15/01/1919
War Diary	Harfleur Camp 14	16/01/1919	20/01/1919
War Diary	Harfleur Camp 15	20/01/1919	27/01/1919
War Diary	Harfleur	28/01/1919	31/05/1919
War Diary	Havre	01/06/1919	10/06/1919
War Diary	Duisans	11/06/1919	17/06/1919
War Diary	Douai	18/06/1917	04/11/1919
War Diary	Boulogne	05/11/1919	23/11/1919

WO 95 2427/1

4 BN. KING's LIVERPOOL REGT

1915 NOV - 1919 NOV

53RD DIVISION
90TH INFY BDE

4TH BN (KING'S) L.POOL REGT

~~MAR 1915 NOV 1919~~

1915 Nov – 1919 Nov

From LAHORE DIV (NOV

VISION
NFY BDE

KING'S (L'POOLS)

NOV 1915

LAHORE DIV   SIRHIND BDE

DIV from 25 2 16

137th Inf.Bde.
46th Div.

Battn. transferred
from Sirhind Bde.
Lahore Div. 10.11.15.

Battn. transferred
to 56th Inf.Bde. 19th
Div. 3.12.15.

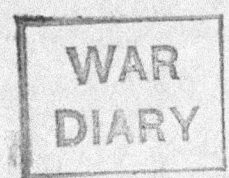

WAR DIARY

4th BATTN. THE KING'S (LIVERPOOL REGIMENT).

N O V E M B E R

1 9 1 5

Attached:

Appendices.

WAR DIARY or INTELLIGENCE SUMMARY

Army Form C. 2118.

4"B" "The King's" (Liverpool Regt.)

Month: November 1915.

Place	Date	Hour	Summary of Events and Information	Remarks and references to Appendices
PONT ROCHON	1 Nov		In billets. Very wet day. 2 Officers + 180 men employed on working parties in front line. Lt Col THARRATT went to hospital. 7 men to hospital. 16 men went to 173rd Coy RE for duty as miners (Tunnelling Coy).	
	2.XI.15		In billets. Very wet day. 1 Officer + 130 men employed on working parties in front line. 2 men from hospital. 6 men to hospital.	
	3.XI.15		In billets. Fine day. 3 men from hospital. 1 man to hospital.	
	4.XI.15		In billets. The battalion moved into the front trenches with supports — Hd Qrs & 2nd & 4th Dbls (2nd Lancashire Brigade) at Sub-Sector 2nd VA. *H.Q.N. ST nunaine. 7 + 1 Suffolks now up. Epelcin Offrs' Suffolks. Relief completed 7.20 pm.	× Map BETHUNE (enclosed) Plate 58 pnn S 4 – 62, not returned.
2nd VA	5.XI.15		On men from hospital. 5 men to hospital. On men wounded. Fine day. In trenches. Showery day. Very wasterly, wet in trenches. Much work on repairing + renewing damage to the trench parapet. He fired field guns. Left unopposed, Strafed our front line supports & PORT ARTHUR KEEP between 4.30 + 5 pm. 3 men from hospital. On men to hospital. He counter in	
"	6.XI.15		In trenches. Usual sniping + patrolling. PORT ARTHUR was again shelled but no damage done. Work or repairs continued in defences. 3 men to hospital and 2nd Lieut H.T. JENKINS. Ne main wounded. (OC DMC H.Mlee.)	
	7.XI.15		In trenches. Various staff officers & Xn Capts. & Lt' Dundas (& OC 139 Brigade) visited the trenches. Sniping carried out and several working parties were employed by Ret Frns. PORT ARTHUR shelled as usual. Work continued on repairs of defences. 3 men from hospital. On men for hospital. 3 men to hospital. On men wounded.	
	8.XI.15		Colonel Alphonse QRAL + Right Dept Major went to CROIX BARBEE to meet G.O.C. LAHORE DIVISION who said good-bye to gunn Coy in which our Battalion he refect at lang la billet + having till tasks for their work during the past 8 months. Enemys Snipers were very active + he given shelled PORT ARTHUR a little areoplane fires over our lines at 3.30 pm. Work + pairs + communication trenches continued. One man from hospital 2 to BED + mores (unfits) sent to Base. On men to hospital. On men wounded.	

Army Form C. 2118.

WAR DIARY
or
INTELLIGENCE SUMMARY. 4'Bn. "The King's" (Liverpool Regt)

(Erase heading not required.)

November 1915.

Instructions regarding War Diaries and Intelligence Summaries are contained in F. S. Regs., Part II. and the Staff Manual respectively. Title pages will be prepared in manuscript.

Place	Date	Hour	Summary of Events and Information	Remarks and references to Appendices
2nd V.A.	9.XI.15		In the trenches - heard sniping + patrolling. On artillery was active in reply to enemy's snipers. Our Snipers claim to have hit 3 Germans who were working behind their trench. Our front line supports were shelled by light field guns PORT ARTHUR was also hit - some damage done - Wire entrained on parapet & communications - 3 men to hospital. 2 Lieut C.O. GREEN invalided to England. Windy day. Wet night.	
Do	10.XI.15		In the trenches. Sniping as usual. Machine gun fire at intervals throughout the night also indirect fire by rifle battery. PORT ARTHUR. Repairs to trenches continued + improvements made. The SIRHIND BRIGADE was relieved by 137 Brigade. 46' NORTH MIDLAND DIVISION to whom we were attached & We remained in the trenches. 1/5" South Staffs Regt relieved 1/1 Gurkhas on our left and 1 Mkts Suth Regt on our right relieved 4' Blackwatch. Very wet night. 5 men to hospital.	
A. Section	11.XI.15		In trenches with 137 Brigade. 3 Officers & 6 NCO 1/6" Sth Staffs Regt were attached for instruction - Indirect fire by our rifle battery. Hostile shell fire shelled PORT ARTHUR - Lieut A.T.S. SUMMNER wounded from 3 asltrs (cel) + cloudy day - 10 men to hospital -	
Do	12.XI.15		In trenches. Very wet night. Our machine guns fires periodically during day + night. Enemy's field guns active on PORT ARTHUR. + scored 2 direct hits: No material damage done. Hostile aeroplane observed over our lines between 9 + 10 A.M. during night in retaliation to our rifle. 3 Hostile aeroplanes observed over our lines between 9/10 AM. 2 men wounded by fall of day - out: 8 men to hospital. One man from hospital. 2 Lieut W.R. IRVING invalided to England -	
Do	13.XI.15		In trenches - Very wet + windy. 2 Officers & 40 men of Lancashire attached for instruction. The battalion was relieved by 1/6 South Staffords. Relief completed 7.20 p.m. The battn moved into billets in LORETTO ROAD - ST VAAST for the night. One man to hospital, 3 men from hospital -	
LORETTO ROAD (Reserve billets)	14.XI.15		The battalion marched via BOUT DEVILLE - L'ESTREM - MERVILLE to billets in REGNIER LE CLERC arriving about 1pm + taking over billets from Guards Brigade - Three men from hospital -	

1577   Wt.W10791/1773   500,000   1/15   D. D. & L.   A.D.S.S./Forms/C. 2118

Army Form C. 2118.

4th Bn "The King's" (Liverpool Regt)

WAR DIARY or INTELLIGENCE SUMMARY

(Erase heading not required.)

November 1915

Places	Date	Hour	Summary of Events and Information	Remarks and references to Appendices
REGNIER LE CLERC (MERVILLE)	15.XI.15		In billets (attached 46th Division 11th Corps.) 4 men to hospital 4 men from hospital — 4 men from hospital.	
Do	16.XI.15		Do.	
Do	17.XI.15		Do. 7 men from hospital. Lieut F.V. Ramsatt invalided to England, drowned in wreck of hospital ship "ANGLIA". Major G.E. HARDIE and Captain W. ODELL 1/23rd OUTRAM'S RIFLES left the battn when general J. LAHORE DIVISION. to join 5th Rifles. Captain F.J. TRUMP, 1st MONMOUTH REGT. took over temporary command of the battalion.	
Do	18.XI.15		In billets — one man to hospital, one man from hospital —	
Do	19.XI.15		Do. Eleven men to hospital.	
Do	20.XI.15		Do. Orders received to join 137th Brigade on 21st.	
Do	21.XI.15		Do. The Battn moved to CROIX BARBEE to receive billets before marching up. Major General the Hon. MONTAGU STUART WORTLEY, C.B, CMG, MVO, DSO, Commdg. 46th Division. inspected the battalion en route, [illegible] before marching up. two men to hospital, one man from hospital.	
CROIX BARBEE	22.XI.15		Two Companies moved into front line trenches "B" Sub Sector (LIVERPOOL ST. to CHURCH ROAD relieving 1/5th South Staffd Regt. The other two companies remained in billets at CROIX BARBEE and HILLS KEEP — Company Hdqrs. for CROIX BARBEE POST. E and RUE DU PUITS POST. (R. LEFT) Battalion H.Q. located (Coys 3 days) 5.ORs to billets 2.ORs in trenches Heavy mist.	
Do	23.XI.15		7 NEUVE CHAPELLE Enemy shrapnelled front line. Heavy howitzer fire. SW Corner. Enemy machine guns active. 2 men wounded. 3 men to hospital.	
Do	24.XI.15		Quiet night. Enemy howitzers active on the "NEB" Artillery active. Wind W.N. patrol A & B Cos. Enemy [illegible] to B & C Cos. in trenches. One man wounded in LA BASSEE ROAD relief completed 7.30 p.m. 3 men to hospital. 1 man from hospital.	
Do	25.XI.15		Quiet night — Strong wind. Enemy gun Private REYNOLDS	

Army Form C. 2118.

WAR DIARY
or
INTELLIGENCE SUMMARY.
(Erase heading not required.)

4 Bn "The King's" (Liverpool Regt)

November 1915

Instructions regarding War Diaries and Intelligence Summaries are contained in F. S. Regs., Part II. and the Staff Manual respectively. Title pages will be prepared in manuscript.

Place	Date	Hour	Summary of Events and Information	Remarks and references to Appendices
CROIX BARBEE	26/XI/15		2 Coys in Brigade Reserve. 2 Coys in trenches – Enemy artillery more than usually active. Ainsley gun Shelled NEUVE CHAPELLE. Quiet night. Some snipers. One man wounded. One man sick to hospital. One man from hospital. 2 L/Cpls & Soden rej unit from England. A draft of 19 other ranks rej unit from base.	Pte Heaps wounded
Do	27/XI/15		Quiet day – Enemy batteries again active. Tramway front line & also dug outs by Head Quarters (2 men wounded). 2 men to hospital – Coys & front – Pte Hutchinson & another man relieved by Lieut Fiddler R.A.M.C.	Lieut Fiddler R.A.M.C.
Do	28/XI/15		B & C Coys relieved A & D Coys in front trenches. C & D Coys & front – HdQtrs light shells from German Saps & dugouts on line from NE to NE of LIVE ROAD ST. Two men wounded. 3 men to hospital.	
Do	29/XI/15		Quiet night. Patrol went out down the Sap opposite The N.E.B. & proceeded as far as German wire to the house about 40 yards they thought not down the walkers about 15 yards along German wire to the right. They heard a German sentry walking up & down & heard 6 turks at him, no retaliation followed. Reserve Brig – n/to Shelled – Artillery & both sides unusually active by JONES relieved Captn TRUMP (in command) by the letter Rej unit from writer Lt HANKIN.) One man to hospital –	
Do	30/XI/15		Fairly quiet night. Heavy Rain. Snow knots of troops on right with M.G. fire & rapid rifle. 27 Rounds battle invitiago fired between LA BASSEE ROAD & NEUVE CHAPELLE mostly along EDGEWARE ROAD. We of these did not explode. Front line was also shelled between 10 AM & 11:30 AM & light Hell from Asphalt for was active throughout the day artillery on both sides active. Wind Slight – One man to hospital, one man from hospital. Lieut A.R.MUNROE R.A.M.C. relieved Lieut F. TIBBLES R.A.M.C. as before. Officer of watch.	

Neil Snow Major
Adjutant 4/The King's

A P P E N D I C E S .

Copy. Not to be published.
Headquarters Lahore Division.

To OC 4 Kings.

On the departure of the Indian Corps from France, & the consequent severance of the 1/8th Kings (Liverpool Rgt) from the Lahore Division, the Divisional Commander wishes to express his thanks to the Regiment for the good work they have done while under his command. Their loyalty & devotion to duty have been worthy of all praise, their bearing in action has left nothing to be desired, & their discipline has been excellent throughout. The thanks of the Divisional Commander are due especially to Lt Colonel J.W. Allen & Major R.C.R. Innes for the manner in which they have maintained the spirit & efficiency of the regiment in most trying vicissitudes, during the time they have been in France. The Divisional Commander regrets he has not been able personally to wish farewell to all ranks but hopes that this may be conveyed to those whom he has not seen, together with his best wishes for every good fortune in the future.

(Signed) H.D. Keary. Major General
Comg Lahore Division.

Certified true copy.
R C R Innes Major
9·XII·15. Adjt. 4/the Kings.

Routine Orders by Lieut Colonel L.W.Y. Campbell.
Commanding Sirhind Brigade.
Dated 8th November, 1915.

Part II
446.

Brigadier-General W.G. Walker, V.C., C.B., wishes the following order to be conveyed to 4th King's:—

"On the departure of the 4th King's, the Brigade Commander wishes to express to Colonel Allen and all ranks of the Battalion his high appreciation of their work, and to thank them for their loyal co-operation under all circumstances. For the last 8 months since they joined the Brigade, whether in action or in the Routine work of the trenches, their behaviour and conduct has been all that could be desired, and they have fully maintained the high reputation of "The King's Regiment". He feels sure that all ranks of the Brigade will join him in expressing great regret at their departure, and in wishing them all good luck in the future."

(sd) R.B. Phayre Captain
Staff Captain, Sirhind Brigade.

True copy

R.C.R. Ince
Major
Adjt 4th Bn The King's Regiment

FIELD RETURN

Army Form B. 213.

No. of Report 25

(To be furnished by all arms, services, and departments (except A.S.C. units) to the A. G.'s Office at the Base in accordance with Field Service Regulations, Part II.)

RETURN showing numbers RATIONED by, and Transport on charge of, 1/5 King's Own (4th Bn. Regt.) at on the field 6th November 1915 Date.

DETAIL	Personnel			Animals							Guns, carriages, and limbers and transport vehicles					Mechanical					REMARKS
	Officers	Other ranks	Natives	Horses Riding	Draught	Heavy Draught	Mules Pack	Large	Small	Camels	Oxen	Guns, carriages and limbers, showing description	Ammunition wagons and limbers	Machine guns	Aircraft, showing description	Horsed 4 Wheeled	2 Wheeled	Motor Cars	Tractors	Lorries, showing description	Trucks, showing description	Trailers	Motor Bicycles	Bicycles	
Effective Strength of Unit	24	893		14	12	23		30						4		19	5								On command Officers Boot Repair 1, Act 3, Gun Sgt 1, Bat armr.k 1, other ranks 14, Act Imbdrys 11, Sgts 14, Act m 11
Details, by Arms attached to unit as in War Establishment:— Army Ordnance Corps R.A.M.C. 123rd Outram's Rifles K.O.K. Lancaster Regt	1 2 1																								M/ service 5, m sentry 52, Trench Morton 10, Base rebet enter cr for Brumbuton 16, — 150
Total	28	893		14	12	23		30						4		19	5								
War Establishment	30	995		14	12	23		30						4		19	5								
Wanting to complete (Detail of Personnel and Horses below)	2	102																								attached interp A.J.M 8, 1, 4, 13
Surplus																										
*Attached (not to include the details shown above)																				Horses H.D. — Riding — Mules					
Civilians:— Employed with the Unit Accompanying the Unit		1																								8, 1, 4, 13
TOTAL RATIONED	22 Brit	13		13	4	15		26																		

R.A.M.C. W/o H. Lieut Colonel   Signature of Commander.

7th November 1915   Date of Despatch.

* In the case of field ambulances, hospitals or depots, the number of patients are to be included here, the names being shown in A. F. A. 36.

For information of the A.G.'s Office at the Base.

Officers and men who have become casuals, been transferred or joined since last report.

Place _In the Field_   Date _6th November 1915_

Regtl. Number	Rank	Name	Corps	Nature of casualty, or name of unit from or to which transferred	Date of being struck off or coming on the ration return	Remarks*
10514	Pte	Gess J.		To Hospital	30-10-15	
8858	-"-	Baldwin J.		-"-	-"-	
9200	a/Lcp	Racliffe		-"-	-"-	
12080	Pte	Maghill T.		-"-	31-10-15	
13540	-"-	McGuirk G.		-"-	-"-	
15140	-"-	Walsh		-"-	-"-	
12394	-"-	Yass R.		-"-	-"-	
8208	-"-	Burton		-"-	30-10-15	
9206	-"-	Henry		-"-	31-10-15	
10074	Cpl	Pickett		-"-	1-11-15	
11820	Pte	Carney W.		-"-	-"-	
10964	-"-	Nearer T.		-"-	-"-	
7675	-"-	Leather H.		-"-	-"-	
13696	-"-	Hughes		-"-	-"-	
11269	-"-	Murphy J.		-"-	-"-	
18224	-"-	Walsh H.		-"-	-"-	
7048	-"-	Ford		-"-	-"-	
8234	-"-	Harris F.		-"-	2-11-15	
13615	-"-	Bates		-"-	-"-	
10481	-"-	Burns R.		-"-	-"-	
20809	-"-	Gibson G.		-"-	3-11-15	
8329	-"-	Denver		-"-	4-11-15	
11314	-"-	Harvey H.		-"-	-"-	
13645	-"-	Hill E.		-"-	-"-	
12158	-"-	Smith		-"-	-"-	
14500	Cpl	Philson R.		-"-	-"-	
281140	Pte	Looney		-"-	1-11-15	
	Lieut	Thapratt C.J.		To Base Depot	31-10-15	For Discharge
7296	Pte	Baker		Merguedina	4-11-15	
10472	Pte	Daley		From Hospital	2-11-15	
10514	-"-	Gess		-"-	-"-	
8208	-"-	Burton		-"-	3-11-15	
12394	-"-	Yass		-"-	-"-	
18224	-"-	Walsh H.		-"-	-"-	
7702	-"-	McGivern		-"-	-"-	
10496	a/Cp	Ramsey		-"-	4-11-15	
8452	Cpl	Temple		-"-	5-11-15	
85131	L/Cp	Tyrer R.		-"-	-"-	
11234	L/Cpl	Owens		-"-	-"-	
7634	Cpl	Jackson R.		To Hospital	5-11-15	
8328	-"-	Leong		-"-	2-11-15	
10209	-"-	Niles		-"-	-"-	

* State whether absence is of a permanent or temporary nature, adding, in the case of casuals from wounds or disease, any available information for communication to the relatives.

Perforated Sheet giving detail of personnel and horses wanting to complete shown on Army Form B. 213.

Number of Report _____

Detail of Wanting to Complete																																																	W.O.s and N.C.O.s (by ranks) not included in trade columns	TOTAL, waiting to agree with complete		Horses			
	Drivers					Gunners	Smith Gunners	Range Takers	Farriers				Cold Shoers	Wheelers			Saddlers or Harness Makers	Blacksmiths	Bricklayers and Masons	Carpenters and Joiners	Fitters & Turners (R.E.)		R.A. Fitters	Wireless	Plumbers	Electricians		Signalmen	Engine Drivers		Air Line Men	Permanent Line Men	Operators, Telegraph	Cablemen	Brigade Section Pioneers	General-duty Pioneers	Signallers	Instrument Repairers	Motor Cyclists	Motor Cyclist Artificers	Telephonists	Clerks	Machine Gunners	Armament Artificers			Armourers	Storemen	Privates		Officers	Other Ranks	Riding	Draught	Heavy Draught	Pack
	R.A.	R.E.	A.S.C.	Car	Lorry	Steam				Sergeants	Corporals	Shoeing, or Shoeing and Carriage Smiths		R.A.	H.T.	M.T.					Wood	Iron				Ordinary	W.T.		Loco.	Field									Fitters						Fitters	Range Finders									
CAVALRY																																																							
R.A.																																																							
R.E.																																																							
INFANTRY																																																			3 94 *Aluminium Pistols*	2 102				
R.A.M.C.																																																							
A.O.C.																																																							
A.V.C.																																																							

Remarks:— New drafts for 75

for Lieut Colonel _____ Signature of Commander.

1st Bn The King's (L'pool Regt) Unit.

Indian Corps Formation to which attached.

9th November 1915 Date of Despatch.

Sheet II

For information of the A.G.'s Office at the Base.

Officers and men who have become casuals, been transferred or joined since last report.

Place On the Field Date 13th November 1915

Regtl. Number	Rank	Name	Corps	Nature of casualty, or name of unit from or to which transferred	Date of being struck off or coming on the ration return	Remarks*
26269	Pte	Bateman J	4th Bn The King's (L'pool Regt)	To Field Amb	12.11.15	
10992	—	Selves J		—"—	—"—	
10365	—	Fogarty J		—"—	—"—	
25245	—	Hardy J		—"—	—"—	
20799	—	Baldwin R		—"—	—"—	
8385	—	Hunt S		—"—	—"—	
13950	—	Prowse W		—"—	—"—	
9228	—	Strong J		From England	12.11.15	
	Lieut	Sunderland				

R H Innes Major
for Lieut Colonel
Comdg 4th Bn The King's (L'pool Regt)

*State whether absence is of a permanent or temporary nature, adding, in the case of casuals from wounds or disease, any available information for communication to the relatives.

Army Form B. 213.

FIELD RETURN.

No. of Report _____

(To be furnished by all arms, services, and departments to the A.G.'s Office at the Base in accordance with Field Service Regulations, Part II.)

Date _____

RETURN showing numbers RATIONED by, and Transport on charge of, _____ at _____

DETAIL.	Personnel			Animals								Guns, carriages, and limbers and transport vehicles												REMARKS
	Officers	Other ranks	Natives	Horses			Mules		Camels	Oxen		Guns, carriages and limbers, showing description	Ammunition wagons and limbers	Machine guns	Aircraft, showing description	Horsed		Motor Cars	Tractors	Mechanical			Motor Bicycles	Bicycles	
				Riding	Draught	Heavy Draught	Pack	Large	Small								4 Wheeled	2 Wheeled			Lorries, showing description	Trucks, showing description	Trailers			
Effective Strength of Unit																									
Details, *by Arms* attached to unit as in War Establishment :—																									
Total																									
War Establishment																									
Wanting to complete																									
Surplus																									
*Attached (not to include the details shown above)																									
Civilians :— Employed with the Unit Accompanying the Unit																									
TOTAL RATIONED ...																									

* In the case of field ambulances, hospitals or depots, the number of patients are to be included here, the names being shown in A. F. A. 36.

Wt.-W. 6005-894 (35047) U. B. Ltd. 500,000 10/14   Forms B. 213 / b

Signature of Commander. _____

Date of Despatch. _____

Sheet I

For information of the A.G.'s Office at the Base.

Officers and men who have become casuals, been transferred or joined since last report.

Place In the Field Date 13th November 1915

Regtl. Number	Rank	Name	Corps	Nature of casualty, or name of unit from or to which transferred	Date of being struck off or coming on the ration return	Remarks*
	Lieut	Jenkins H.T.		To Field Amb	6-11-15	
11016	Sgt	Kneale				
19540	--	Dean A.				
17785	Pte	French				
14666	--	Sealey				
19159	--	O'Neill				
6366	--	O'Donohue				
11014	--	Newnes				
11843	--	Owens		To No 8		
14299	--	Byrne		Infantry		
11104	--	Benson		Base Depot	11-11-15	
9862	--	Sharples		Classified		
18080	--	White		"B X"		
12454	--	Smith				
14360	--	Mangan				
24008	--	McCabe				
9024	--	Lucas				
24899	--	Hake				
13093	--	Winter				
7526	--	Murray				
16208	--	Burton G.A.				
28258	--	Grimshaw		To Field Amb	7-11-15	
14404	--	Whelan		-"-	-"-	
11525	--	McGuire		-"-	-"-	
11281	--	Williams		-"-	8-11-15	
9044	--	Rankin		-"-	-"-	
29018	--	Norris		-"-	-"-	
42010	--	Helan		-"-	-"-	
9640	A/Sgt	Miche		-"-	9-11-15	
11569	Cpl	Williams		-"-	-"-	
14243	Pte	Davies		-"-	-"-	
5269	Cpl	Richardson		-"-	10-11-15	
13292	Pte	Edwards		-"-	-"-	
18650	--	Simpson		-"-	-"-	
9459	--	Walters		-"-	-"-	
12404	--	Brough		-"-	-"-	
12206	C.Q.M.S	Hollis		Wounded in a	6-11-15	
11243	Sgt	McCall		-"-	-"-	
18654	--	Davies		-"-	8-11-15	
15462	--	Hamilton M.J.		-"-	10-11-15	Injured by fall
11551	--	Edwards		-"-	-"-	of dug-out.
28140	--	Looney		From Hospital	7-11-15	
11314	--	Harvey		-"-	-"-	
4448	--	Ford		-"-	-"-	
14500	Cpl	Philson		-"-	8-11-15	
10813	Pte	McGregor		-"-	9-11-15	
14618	--	Milloy		From Prison	7-11-15	
11306	Cpl	Hayes		To Field Amb	11-11-15	
16784	Pte	Brough		-"-	-"-	
25693	L/Cpl	Morton		-"-	-"-	
19102	Pte	Cavanagh		-"-	-"-	
13038	--	Davies		-"-	-"-	
10875	--	Ryan		-"-	-"-	
25950	--	Brogan		-"-	-"-	
12466	--	Firth		-"-	-"-	
13543	--	Wright		-"-	-"-	
12515	Sgt	Woods		-"-	-"-	
12193	Sgt	Leahy		-"-	12-11-15	

* State whether absence is of a permanent or temporary nature, adding, in the case of casuals from wounds or disease, any available information for communication to the relatives.

FIELD RETURN.

Army Form B. 213.

No. of Report **36**   Diary

(To be furnished by all arms, services, and departments (except A.S.C. units) to the A. G.'s Office at the Base in accordance with Field Service Regulations, Part II.)

RETURN showing numbers RATIONED by, and Transport on charge of _4th Bn Rifle Brigade_ at/in the field _13th North'd Bde_ Date.

of _Lt Col L H Beett Regt_

DETAIL	Personnel			Animals							Guns, carriages, and limbers and transport vehicles				Horsed		Mechanical					REMARKS
	Officers	Other ranks	Natives	Horses			Mules		Camels	Oxen	Guns, carriages, limbers, showing description	Ammunition wagons and limbers	Machine guns	Aircraft, showing description	4 Wheeled	2 Wheeled	Tractors	Lorries, showing description	Trucks, showing description	Trailers	Motor Bicycles	Bicycles	
				Riding	Draught	Heavy Draught	Pack	Large	Small														
Effective Strength of Unit	25 841			14	12	23		30						4		19	5							On command Officers
Details, by Arms attached to unit as in War Establishment:—																								Base Depot 4
Army Ordnance Corps		1																						sick 1
R. A. Vet C.	1																							Wounded Bee 4
123rd Outram's Rifles	2																							leave 4
R.O. Royal Lanc Regt	1																							—
																							10
Total	29 842			14	12	23		30						4		19	5							Other ranks
War Establishment	30 995			14	12	23		30								19	5							attached at depot 44
Wanting to complete	1 153							20						1		19	5							leave 6
Surplus														1										atta R.E. 20
*Attached (not to include the details shown above) (Detail of Personnel and Horses below)																								Base depot 1 in Echelon 1
																							45
Civilians:— Employed with the Unit Accompanying the Unit		1																						Divisional Train
TOTAL RATIONED ...	10 948			14	12	15		30																Heavy D Trains 8
																							8

* In the case of field ambulances, hospitals or depots, the number of patients are to be included here, the names being shown in A. F. A. 36.

Ken Jones Major
for _Lieut Colonel_   Signature of Commander.
14th November 1915   Date of Despatch.

Perforated Sheet giving detail of personnel and horses wanting to complete, shown on Army Form B. 213.

Number of Report 36

Detail of Wanting to Complete	Drivers							Gunners	Smith Gunners	Range Takers	Farriers			Wheelers			Saddlers or Harness Makers	Blacksmiths	Bricklayers and Masons	Carpenters and Joiners	Fitters & Turners (R.E.)		Fitters				Electricians				Engine Drivers		Air Line Men	Permanent Line Men	Operators, Telegraph	Cablemen	Brigade Section Pioneers	General-duty Pioneers	Signallers	Instrument Repairers	Motor Cyclists	Motor Cyclist Artificers	Telephonists	Clerks	Machine Gunners	Armament Artificers			Armourers	Storemen	Privates	W.O's. and N.C.O's. (by ranks) not included in trade columns	TOTAL wanting to complete with Other Ranks		Horses			
	R.A.	R.E.	A.S.C.	Car	Lorry	Steam					Sergeants	Corporals	Shoeing, or Shoeing and Carriage Smiths	Cold Shoers	R.A.	H.T.	M.T.					Wood	Iron	R.A.	Wireless	Plumbers	Ordinary	W.T.	Signalmen	Loco.	Field															Fitters	Range Finders						Officers	Other Ranks	Riding	Draught	Heavy Draught	Pack
CAVALRY																																																						1	33				
R.A.																																																										
R.E.																																																										
INFANTRY																																																				Ackering Other Ranks	44					
R.A.M.C.																																																										
A.O.C.																																																										
A.V.C.																																																										

Remarks :—

R C H Joel Major
for Lieut Colonel
C.O. 3rd Bn The King's (Liverpool Regt) Unit
V & Corps Formation to which attached.
18 November 1915 Date of Despatch.

Signature of Commander.

[P.T.O.

FIELD RETURN.

Army Form B. 213.
Army Form B. 213. (Field Service Regulations, Part II.)

No. of Report. 34

(To be furnished by all arms, services, and departments (except A.S.C. units) to the A. G.'s Office at the Base in accordance with Field Service Regulations, Part II.)

RETURN showing numbers RATIONED by, and Transport on charge of, 4th Bn the Kings (Liverpool Regt) at In the field 20th Nov 1915 Date.

DETAIL	Personnel			Animals								Guns, carriages, and limbers and transport vehicles			Horsed		Mechanical					REMARKS
	Officers	Other ranks	Natives	Horses Riding	Draught	Heavy Draught	Mules Pack	Large	Small	Camels	Oxen	Guns, carriages and limbers, showing description	Ammunition wagons and limbers	Machine guns	Aircraft, showing description	4 Wheeled	2 Wheeled	Motor Cars	Tractors	Lorries, showing description	Trucks, showing description	Trailers	Motor Bicycles	Bicycles	
Effective Strength of Unit	27	853		14	12	23		30						4		19	5								Not Returned On Command Officers 1 Base Depot 5 Sick 1 Summer Bas 3 Jean 70
Details, by Arms attached to unit as in War Establishment:— Army Ordnance Corps 1 R.A.M.C. 1 Kgs L Lanc Regt 1 38 Monmouth Regt 1																									
Total	30	854		14	12	23		30																		Other Ranks On Command 38 Sick 4 Wlth R.E's 16
War Establishment	30	995		14	12	23		30						4		19	5								Base Depot 1 3rd Echelon 1 [?] 62
Wanting to complete		145??																							
Surplus																									
*Attached (not to include the details shown above) (Detail of Personnel and Horses below)																									Devouvral[?] view H.D. Horses 8
Civilians:— Employed with the Unit Accompanying the Unit																									
TOTAL RATIONED ...	20??			14	12	15		30																	

* In the case of field ambulances, hospitals or depots, the number of patients are to be included here, the names being shown in A. F. A. 36.

D I Surrey Captain Signature of Commander.
20th Nov 1915 Date of Despatch.

For information of the A.G.'s Office at the Base.

Officers and men who have become casuals, been transferred or joined since last report.

Place In the Field   Date 20th Novr 1915

Regtl. Number	Rank	Name	Corps	Nature of casualty, or name of unit from or to which transferred	Date of being struck off or coming on the ration return	Remarks*
	Major	Hardie G.B.	132nd Outram's Rifles I.A.	Rejoined from Indian bers	17-11-15	
	Captn	Odell W.				
6840	Sgt	Reynolds J.		from Hospl	13-11-15	
11569	C/pl	Williams H.B.		"	"	
12443	Pte	Davies H.		"	"	
26589	"	Denner A.		"	"	
20809	"	Gibson P.		"	"	
17143	Sgt	Leahy P.		"	14-11-15	
20499	Pte	Baldwin R.		"	"	
13543	"	Wright A.		"	"	
26409	"	Bateman J.		"	15-11-15	
10964	"	Weaver W.		"	"	
17202	"	Weeds J.		"	"	
9444	"	Hankin T.		"	"	
18650	"	Simpson J.		"	16-11-15	
19102	"	Cavanagh J.		"	"	
6851	"	Wardle E.		"	"	
15402	"	Hamilton W.J.		"	"	
11306	Cpl	Davis J.		"	17-11-15	
10645	Pte	Fegarty W.		"	"	
10092	"	Dennes T.		"	"	
24954	"	Haynes T.		"	"	
8298	Cpl	Makin J.		"	"	
9459	Pte	Walters B.		"	"	
25134	"	Walsh J.		"	18-11-15	
14004	"	Coppack P.		To	15-11-15	
25243	"	Hardy J.		from	17-11-15	
13146	"	Crabb F.		(affiliated)		
8465	"	Radcliffe J.		to 60 pro N.N.	15-11-15	
9141	"	James J.		P. 109 D of W		
24115	"	Hagan T.		To Hospl	13-11-15	
12491	"	Graham T.			15-11-15	
14260	"	Smith T.			"	
10496	A/Sgt	Ramsey			"	
11229	Pte	Campbell C.			19-11-15	
10846	Sgt	Stewart T.			"	
10472	Pte	Catchwell T.				
	Captn	Trump S.J.	1st Monmouth Regt	for duty	18-11-15	

J.J. Dunn Captain
Comdg 4th Bn The King's Regt

Perforated Sheet giving detail of personnel and horses wanting to complete, shown on Army Form B. 213.

Number of Report __31__

Detail of Wanting to Complete		
CAVALRY		
R.A.		
R.E.		
INFANTRY	W.O's and N.C.O's (by ranks) not included in trade columns: *Regimental Pioneers* — 16	Other Ranks: — 16
R.A.M.C.		
A.O.C.		
A.V.C.		

Remarks:—

Explanation of difference

✕ 16 men required to replace similar number permanently attached 173rd Tunnelling Company

Signature of Commander: **F.J. Smith** Captain

Unit: **4th Bn The King's (Liverpool Regt.)**

Formation to which attached: **6th Division**

Date of Despatch: **1st November 1915**

Army Form B. 213.

FIELD RETURN.

No. of Report 38

(To be furnished by all arms, services, and departments (except A.S.C. units) to the A. G.'s Office at the Base in accordance with Field Service Regulations, Part II.)

RETURN showing numbers RATIONED by, and Transport on charge of 4/J Bn Lucking's at in the field 24th Oct 1915 Date.

DETAIL	Personnel			Animals							Guns, carriages, and limbers and transport vehicles				Horsed		Motor Cars	Tractors	Mechanical		Trailers	Motor Bicycles	Bicycles	REMARKS
	Officers	Other ranks	Natives	Horses			Mules		Camels	Oxen	Guns, carriages and limbers, showing description	Ammunition wagons and limbers	Machine guns	Aircraft, showing description	4 Wheeled	2 Wheeled			Lorries, showing description	Trucks, showing description				
				Riding	Draught	Heavy Draught	Pack	Large	Small															
Effective Strength of Unit	24	859		14	12	23		30						17		19	5								On Command Officers
Details, by Arms attached to unit as in War Establishment:—																									Basic Details 2
Army Ordnance Corps	1																								Sick Reports 1
R.A.M.C.	1																								10th Division Sig 1
K.O. R. Lanc Regt	1																								Leave 4
1st Munster Regt	1																								
N.Z.	1																								Observation
Total	27	859		14	12	23		30						18		19	5								Civil Employ 2
War Establishment	30	995		14	12	23		30						10		19	5								Newd 1 — 15
Wanting to complete	3	139																							Edu — 5
Surplus																									Battle Post 13
*Attached (not to include the details shown above)																									Leave 17
																									Furnishers to 14 field ambulance 35
																									Base depot 2
Civilians:— Employed with the Unit Accompanying the Unit																									gun school 1
TOTAL RATIONED ...	19/55			14	12	15		30																	not carried from 8 I.D. period

* In the case of field ambulances, hospitals or depots, the number of patients are to be included here, the names being shown in A. F. A. 36.

A.J. Ennes Captain Signature of Commander.

24th Novr 1915 Date of Despatch.

For information of the A.G.'s Office at the Base.

Officers and men who have become casuals, been transferred or joined since last report.

Place _In the Field_   Date _24th November 1915_

Regtl. Number	Rank	Name	Corps	Nature of casualty, or name of unit from or to which transferred	Date of being struck off or coming on the ration return	Remarks*
	Lieut	Spring N.P.		joined	12-11-15	
	--	Knott E.D.		do	9-11-15	
	--	Lomas E.J.		England	9-9-15	
	--	Little R.		to hospital	19-11-15	
11645	--	Rice L.				
11410	--	Edwardson				
11755	--	Hamilton				
	L/Cpl	Ashton H				
8540	A/Cpl	Searcy N.H.				
11913	Pte	May H				
	--	Fisher				
20016	--	Buchanan				
	--	Crabbe				
29772	Pte	Anderson H		--	--	
	--	Kinnear				
	Cpl	Hodgson		--	20-11-15	
	--	Haynes				
	--	Brennan				
	--	Walsh		from Hospital	13-11-15	
	--	Beach		do	21-11-15	
	--	Reynolds		killed in a.	21-11-15	
	L/Cpl	Shepherd		w in a.	21-11-15	
	--	Ambrose				
	--	Baldwin				
	--	Bostie				
	--	Doherty				
13253	Cpl	Farmer a			15	
26491	--	Allcock				
24246	--	Owen				
26024	--	Shields				
13175	--	Leechman				
12653	--	Eccleshey				
9400	--	Langfield				
21063	--	Cross				
13631	Cpl	Christie a				
10553	--	McKenna H		from the 8 Infantry		
14740	--	Shields E		Base Depot		
11831	--	Smith R				
12146	--	Henry H				

A. J. Jump, Captain

Comdg 4th Bn The King's (Liverpool Regt)

Perforated Sheet giving detail of personnel and horses wanting to complete, shown on Army Form B. 213.

Number of Report __38__

Detail of Wanting Complete		Drivers					Gunners	Smith Gunners	Range Takers	Farriers			Cold Shoes	Wheelers			Saddlers or Harness Makers	Blacksmiths	Bricklayers and Masons	Carpenters and Joiners	Fitters & Turners (R. E.)		Fitters			Plumbers	Electricians			Signalmen	Engine Drivers		Air Line Men	Permanent Line Men	Operators, Telegraph	Cablemen	Brigade Section Pioneers	General-duty Pioneers	Signallers	Instrument Repairers	Motor Cyclists	Motor Cyclist Artificers	Telephonists	Clerks	Machine Gunners	Armament Artificers			Armourers	Storemen	Privates	W.O.'s and N.C.O.'s (by ranks) not included in trade columns	TOTAL wanting to agree with Other Ranks to complete		Horses			
		R.A.	R.E.	A.S.C.	Car	Lorry	Steam				Sergeants	Corporals	Shoeing, or Shoeing and Carriage Smiths		R.A.	H.T.	M.T.					Wood	Iron	R.A.	Wireless			Ordinary	W.T.		Loco.	Field														Fitters	Range Finders						Officers	Other Ranks	Riding	Draught	Heavy Draught	Pack
CAVALRY																																																									
R.A.																																																			Approved					
R.E.																																																									
INFANTRY																																																			151	19 x				
R.A.M.C.																																																									
A.C.C.																																																									
A.V.C.																																																									

Remarks :— Include 14 men required to replace 19 men attached to 193rd Tunnelling Company, not struck off strength of battalion

T.J. Duert Captain Signature of Commander.

4th Bn. The Bengs (Libera) Regt. Unit.

D. A. Berfer Formation to which attached.

24th November 1915 Date of Despatch.

P.T.O.

19TH DIVISION
58TH INFY BDE

4TH BN KING'S (L'POOL REGT)
DEC 1915   -   FEB 1916

58th Inf.Bde.
19th Div.

Battn. transferred from 137th Inf.Bde. 46th Div. to 56th Inf.Bde. 19th Div. 3.12.15.

Battn. transferred from 56th Inf.Bde. 19.12.15.

WAR DIARY

4th BATTN. THE KING'S (LIVERPOOL REGIMENT).

DECEMBER

1915

Attached:

Appendices.

Army Form C. 2118.

WAR DIARY
or INTELLIGENCE SUMMARY. 4th 18th "The King's" (Liverpool Regt.)

(Erase heading not required.)

December 1915

Place	Date	Hour	Summary of Events and Information	Remarks and references to Appendices
B. Sub. Sector S.4.b. 7/4 and CROIX BARBÉE	1 Dec.		In trenches. ½ Bn in reserve billets CROIX BARBÉE. Jain day. Garrisons for various posts in vicinity. Hostile artillery very active at intervals throughout the day. Heavy thunder storm stopped 2.6 shells seen between Hind Quarters & Pen. Q. Shoot did not complete. Our heavy batteries replied with 4" rounds. Lieut. P.R.F. MASON explodes Max Machine Gun fire. Men worked at drainage damage slight. A & D Cos relieved B & C Cos in front line. Rejoined from England — 2nd Lieut. C.P. GAULTIER joined from 3rd Bn. A & D Cos relieved B & C Cos in front line relief complete 7 pm. 2 men to hospital. Pr. Bateman M.I. rejoined the unit.	
Do	2 XII 15		In trenches. Fine day — Heavy hostile shelling during the morning. Our artillery replied particularly field batteries. Not light. One man wounded. 2 men to hospital. 1 man to base for discharge.	
Do	3 XII 15		In trenches. Wet + muddy day. Very quiet. Trenches were almost impassable through frost, wet & rain OXFORD ST. clear. 8 men to hospital also Capt. G.W.D. ALLEN. 1 man to base to discharge. 2nd Lieut. N.E.M. NELLY Pt. Kings Own (R. Lancaster Regt.) attached left for STOMER L'Isere Royal Flying Corps. Major E.M. BEALL D.S.O. rejoined from England. Tel. No. became attached to 58 Brigade 19 Division in inspection of out billets of Brigade	
Do	4 XII 15		In trenches. Wet day. Very little activity. The battalion was relieved in the trenches by 7 Royal Welsh Lancs Regt. + on completion of relieve about 7 pm the two companies in trenches were moved back to reserve billets at CROIX BARBÉE. 5 men to hospital. 2nd Lieuts J.C. HANNON + V. GRAY joined from 3rd Batt.	
CROIX BARBÉE	5 XII 15		In reserve billets. Garrisons for 8 defensive posts in 2nd line provided by the battn. in addition to the posts already provided near CROIX BARBÉE. Fine day. 2 Lieuts H.T. FISHENDEN + C.P. GAULTER sent to B.H.Q. and so were 2 D.G.T. West R 1175 Territorial Res RE for temporary duty. One Machine Gun was left to garrison front KEEPS. 4 men to hospital. 2 men from hospital.	
Do	6 XII 15		In reserve billets. Fine morning. Wet afternoon. 3 men to hospital. Lieut. E.G. MATHER rejoined from SIRHIND BRIGADE HEAD QUARTERS.	
Do	7 XII 15		In reserve billets. Fine morning. Wet afternoon & night. Garrisons of Posts relieved by units of 56 + 57 Brigades. The Battalion marched via VIEILLE CHAPELLE + ZELOBES to billets at LOCON when it became divisional reserve of 19th Division. On Machine guns relieved by 56 & 94 Brigade MG Cos. The battalion marched via VIEILLE CHAPELLE + ZELOBES to billets at LOCON when it became divisional reserve. 16 men rejoined from 173 Tunnelling Co RE.	
LOCON	8 XII 15		In billets. Wet day. 2nd Lieut D.H. PACK joined on appointment from Cadet School. Capt. G.W.D ALLEN transferred to England Sick. (Divisional Reserve 19th Division.)	
Do	9 XII 15		In billets. Very wet all day. 2 men to hospital. Do	

Army Form C. 2118.

WAR DIARY
or
INTELLIGENCE SUMMARY. 4th Br. "1/2 Kings" (Liverpool Regt.)

(Erase heading not required.)

Instructions regarding War Diaries and Intelligence Summaries are contained in F. S. Regs., Part II. and the Staff Manual respectively. Title pages will be prepared in manuscript.

Month and Year: December 1915

Place	Date	Hour	Summary of Events and Information	Remarks and references to Appendices
LOCON.	10-XII-15		In billets. Damp & showery. Wet night. 2nd Lieuts J.C. HANNON and V. GRAY went to XIX Division Class of Instruction. One man to hospital.	
Do	11-XII-15		In billets - wet day - 2 men from hospital	
Do	12-XII-15		In billets. Fine day. A draft of 52 men joined from Base, under Captain H.F. NAILER. 2nd Northampton Regt. who returned to base next day - 2 men from hospital.	
Do	13-XII-15		In billets. Fine cold day. 9 men to hospital. 1 man from hospital. 2 men to Base for discharge. 4 men from Base.	
Do	14-XII-15		In billets. Fine dull & windy. 3 men to hospital. 2nd Lieut H.G. TRIPP slightly wounded (remains at duty.) A draft of 46 men joined from Base. 2 men to hospital.	
Do	15-XII-15		Do Fine dull day.	
Do	16-XII-15		Do Dull damp & windy. Wet night. 1 man joined from Base.	
Do	17-XII-15		Do Dull damp day. Wet afternoon & night. 5 men from hospital.	
Do	18-XII-15		Do Damp & mildy. One man to hospital.	
Do	19-XII-15		Do Fine day. Half Battalion moved into trenches (in the Sub. Section (HUN ST.) in relief of 7th South Lancs Regt: 9th Welsh Regt on right, 9th R Welsh Fusiliers on left. with 58th Brigade. 4 men to hospital.	
HUN ST + LOCON.	20-XII-15		Half Batt in billets, Half Batt in trenches. Patrolling & sniping as normal. On trenches Guns active throughout the night. Enemy quiet by day but very active with light field guns during the night. Work carried out repairing old portion of front trench. One man killed (K/11353 Pte W.E. SMITH. C Coy Machine Gun Detachment killed. One man wounded. One man from hospital.	

WAR DIARY
INTELLIGENCE SUMMARY. 4th Bn "The King's" (Liverpool Regt.)

Army Form C. 2118.

December 1915

Place	Date	Hour	Summary of Events and Information	Remarks and references to Appendices
HUN ST & LOCON	21 XII 15		½ Battn in trenches : ½ in billets. Wet day. Our trenches were fired periodically & were very effective at night with indirect fire. Enemy's snipers very active. Intermittent shelling of our line by light field guns. Work carried out:- Bailing of trenches, parapet thickened. Parts of bad trench made in part in revenement of line. One man killed (No 11466 Pmte P Kelly B Coy) One man wounded. One man from hospital.	
Do	22 XII 15	Do	Sniping as usual. Our trenches were fired on & enemy's positions during the day & silenced. Hrs of enemy. He fired about 50 shells on our front line - light field guns & 5.9. Between 11 AM & 12 noon & a few more during afternoon without doing any serious damage. Our listening post heard enemy working on his wires & pumping opposite POPES NOSE at 3 AM. 33 gaits & 2 parapets repaired. Dull & showery day. No man wounded.	
Do	23 XII 15	Do	C & D Coys relieved A & B Coys in trenches. 6 Wills Rgt. on our Right & Cheshire Regt. on our left. Fine day. Very wet night. One man from hospital. Hostile [?] gun active with Indirect fire. Enemy M G on opposite POPES NOSE active. Quiet night. No shelling.	
Do	24 XII 15	Do	Dl & cold & showery. Our snipers disposed a battle working party. R C O P 9 Gods Do out. Saw hostile shells (light field guns) at 3 AM & 5.4 P.m & shot 12 to RvH 1st & 11 AM.	
Do	25 XII 15	Do	Windy & showery. 2 men to hospital. 2 ea L/C M S TRIPP to hospital. Quiet day. Enemy aircraft & possibly the trenches a number of lights at night, probably Chinese lanterns. Very little shelling.	
Do	26 XII 15	Do	Showery. A draft of 70 NCOs & men joined from Base. One man killed. (No 3887 L.C Pmte W. MARTIN.) 4 men to hospital. Quiet day in trenches. A few shells fired for high fusion fired at PORT ARTHUR & OXFORD ROAD.	
Do	27 XII 15	Do	On billet & trenches. A & B Coys relieved C & D Coys in trenches. Showery. ? Went up on our right 2 Welsh Fusrs in on left. 4 men to hospital. Lieut E.S. MATHER & 2 Lt GS HOBART joined. Chm of Instruction 1st XIX of Divisional School. Hostile artillery active on our front with light field guns.	
Do	28 XII 15	Do	In billet & trenches. Fine day. Our hostile gun fired during night & indirect fire was good periodically by Mach. trenches (same enemy snipers less active. Enemy lost 50 shells of shell & chiefly shrapnel - light field guns. An officer patrol went out from the trenches & oxford & two O.Ps. during night & listening posts heard no indications of enemy mine work. Our listening posts heard no indications of enemy mine work.	

WAR DIARY or INTELLIGENCE SUMMARY

Army Form C. 2118.

4th Bn "The King's" (Liverpool Regt)

December 1915.

Place	Date	Hour	Summary of Events and Information	Remarks and references to Appendices
LOCON + (Floriston) (HUN 57)	29.XII.15		In billets & trenches. Hostile artillery (both heavy & light guns) active on our intersection & general hostile aircraft flew over our line. Enemy sniper active by night. A patrol went out & found enemy wiring in his line in vicinity S.11.A.1.15 – 2.3. On return 2 patrol on returning was disposed to firstly the squadron met our OXFORD ROAD (name which applies to a small trench in front of the Epinette) & fired by any sentry post should challenged on. He that did not open fire. They reported that the Orchard is held by a German by sentry groups — 2 killed by a German sniper.	
Do.	30.XII.15		In billets & trenches. Hostile aircraft flew active. Enemy shelled our intersection very heavily with guns of all calibres. Some shots were also put into his defences but in his to consolidate these day. Sergt W.T. FISHENDEN wounded to hospital. One man from hospital.	
Do.	31.XII.15		In billets & trenches. Dull morning. Some rain. Enemy heavily shelled ISLES. Enemy rear twenty. Enemy shells fell in vicinity of BERFORD ROAD ZZ which did not explode. Some shots with 33 being shots in fair wind hostile aeroplane on our left. One to hospital. C + D Coy relieved A + B Coy in trenches in front line. B/Welch & R Welch Fusis (300th Bgd? CRUTCHLEY) b/Welch in our night, 6/ Cheshires on our left. — One man to Brilaw & R Welch Fusis (300th Bgd? CRUTCHLEY)	

4th Jany 1916.

Jn. Allen. Lt. Colonel
Comndg 4th Bn. "The King's"
(Liverpool Regt)

A P P E N D I C E S .

Army Form B. 213.

FIELD RETURN.

Diary

No. of Report 39

(To be furnished by all arms, services, and departments (except A.S.C. units) to the A. G.'s Office at the Base in accordance with Field Service Regulations, Part II.)

RETURN showing numbers RATIONED by, and Transport on charge of **Lt Col Tulloch** at **in the field** **4th Decbr 1915**

Tibbet Riot

Detail	Personnel			Animals							Guns, carriages, and limbers and transport vehicles				Horsed		Motor Cars	Tractors	Mechanical		Trailers	Motor Bicycles	Bicycles	REMARKS
	Officers	Other ranks	Natives	Horses Riding	Draught	Heavy Draught	Pack	Mules Large	Mules Small	Camels	Oxen	Guns, carriages, limbers, showing description	Ammunition wagons and limbers	Machine Guns	Aircraft, showing description	4 Wheeled	2 Wheeled			Lorries, showing description	Trucks, showing description				
Effective Strength of Unit	25	893		14	12	23		20						4		19	5								In Command 2 Adjutant Bde 1 adm missed Bde 1 Returns Orderly Room 1 Gun 5
Details, by Arms attached to unit as in War Establishment:— R.A.M.C.	1																									Other Ranks 6 bats Orderly 6
Army Ordnance Corps	1	1																								Driver 12 Gas 11 Under A.P.M. 25
Total	29	939		14	12	23		20						4		19	5									Camp 16 Pioneer R.E. 14 Field ambulance 39 Base detach 1 ests detach 128
War Establishment	30	915		14	12	23		20						4		19	5									
Wanting to complete	1	126 *																								
Surplus																										
*Attached (not to include the details shown above)																										
Civilians:— Employed with the Unit Accompanying the Unit																										With Sup Train Arnolds 440
TOTAL RATIONED …	30	921		14	12	15		20																		

* In the case of field ambulances, hospitals or depots, the number of patients are to be included here, the names being shown in A. F. A. 36.

* Does not include 16 n.c.o.'s and men attached Tunnelling Company. Total: in order to complete 152.

Signature of Commander. **A. Lewis, Lewis Lt Col Major**

Date of Despatch. **4th December 1915**

For information of the A.G.'s Office at the Base.

Officers and men who have become casuals, been transferred or joined since last report.

Place: In the Field   Date: 4th December 1915

Regtl. Number	Rank	Name	Corps	Nature of casualty, or name of unit from or to which transferred	Date of being struck off or coming on the ration return	Remarks*
	Lieut	Soden L.C.			24-11-15	
	Lieut	Mason P.R.F.		} From England	1-12-15	
	Lieut	Gaulter C.P.			—"—	
13994	Pte	Satchwell T		From Hospital	25-11-15	
11913	—"—	Clay H		—"—	26-11-15	
10846	Sgt	Stewart T		—"—	30-11-15	
11529	Pte	Hamilton		—"—	1-12-15	
23333	—"—	Levine A		—"—		
10120	—"—	Hale B				
26340	—"—	Smith E				
13588	—"—	Hodgson				
14988	—"—	Dubberley				
14340	—"—	Quayle A				
10623	—"—	Davison				
12014	—"—	McDonough		B.X. men employed in Corps area taken on strength	1-12-15	
12444	L/Cpl	Jennings T				
14960	Pte	Dykes H				
11284	—"—	Cuton				
11436	—"—	Campbell G				
25892	—"—	Cook G				
11638	—"—	Hughes H				
11899	—"—	Hardman W				
10085	—"—	Yerath				
11245	—"—	Goulbourne M				
17676	L/Cpl	Townsend				
7910	A/Cpl	Maines		To Hospital	Date not known	
11196	Pte	Williams		—"—	25-11-15	
23333	Pte	Levine A		—"—		
11018	—"—	Hargreaves R		—"—	26-11-15	
13061	—"—	Teare J		—"—	24-11-15	
18160	—"—	Holmes		—"—		
17120	—"—	Borsey J		—"—	28-11-15	
13149	—"—	Lyons		—"—		
12113	—"—	Boothman W		—"—		
10230	—"—	Watson W		—"—	29-11-15	
14484	—"—	Stevens J		—"—	30-11-15	
4545	—"—	Fitzsimmons J		—"—		
8945	—"—	Roach W		Wounded in a.	24-11-15	
25343	—"—	Tyson T		—"—	26-11-15	
10429	—"—	Roberts W		—"—	24-11-15	
25121	Cpl	Tyrer R		—"—		
9851	Pte	Miles K		—"—	28-11-15	
20064	—"—	Atcherley D		—"—		
9009	—"—	Hankin P		Killed in a.	24-11-15	
8130	—"—	Santley P		—"—	27-11-15	
8301	Cpl	Ashworth H		To Base Depot for discharge	2-12-15	
8126	Pte	Dean W H			3-12-15	
	Maj	Beall E.W.		From England	3-12-15	
	Capt	Trump F.J.	1st Monmouth	To 1st Monmouth	29-11-15	
	Lieut	Sharlatt G.V.	4th Kings	To England	14-11-15	
7966	Pte	Bateman J	1/4 H.L.I.	To 1st Bn H.L.I.	1-12-15	
	Lieut	Willy H P.S.M.	K.O.R.L. Regt	To R.F.C.	3-12-15	
	—"—	Pack W H	4th Kings	From Cadet Sch	29-12-15	

A. Jervis
Lieut for Major
Comdg 4th Bn The King's (L'pool Regt)

* State whether absence is of a permanent or temporary nature, adding, in the case of casuals from wounds or disease, any available information for communication to the relatives.

Perforated Sheet giving detail of personnel and horses wanting to complete, shown on Army Form B. 213.

Number of Report _37_

Detail of Wanting to Complete			CAVALRY	R.A.	R.E.	INFANTRY	R.A.M.C.	A.O.C.	A.V.C.
Drivers	R.A.								
	R.E.								
	A.S.C.								
	Car								
	Lorry								
	Steam								
	Gunners								
	Smith Gunners								
	Range Takers								
Farriers	Sergeants								
	Corporals								
Shoeing, or Shoeing and Carriage Smiths									
	Cold Shoers								
Wheelers	R.A.								
	H.T.								
	M.T.								
Saddlers or Harness Makers									
Blacksmiths									
Bricklayers and Masons									
Carpenters and Joiners									
Fitters & Turners (R.E.)	Wood								
	Iron								
Fitters	R.A.								
	Wireless								
	Plumbers								
Electricians	Ordinary								
	W.T.								
	Signalmen								
Engine Drivers	Loco.								
	Field								
Air Line Men									
Permanent Line Men									
Operators, Telegraph									
Cablemen									
Brigade Section Pioneers									
General-duty Pioneers									
Signallers									
Instrument Repairers									
Motor Cyclists									
Motor Cyclist Artificers									
Telephonists									
Clerks									
Machine Gunners									
Armament Artificers	Fitters								
	Range Finders								
Armourers									
Storemen									
Privates									
W.O's and N.C.O's (by ranks) not included in trade columns			Officers 12223426			1349			
TOTAL, wanting to agree with complete	Officers		13						
	Other Ranks								
Horses	Riding								
	Draught								
	Heavy Draught								
	Pack								

Remarks:— Kenna Kent for Major
Lt Col in the King's (Liverpool Regt)
XI Corps

Signature of Commander.
Formation to which attached. _The King's (Liverpool Regt)_ Unit.
Date of Despatch _6th December 1915_

FIELD RETURN

Army Form B. 213.

No. of Report 40

(To be furnished by all arms, services, and departments (except A.S.C. units) to the A. G.'s Office at the Base in accordance with Field Service Regulations, Part II.)

RETURN showing numbers RATIONED by, and Transport on charge of 4th Bn. Ty. Corps at in the field 11th Decr. 1915.

DETAIL	Personnel			Animals							Guns, carriages, and limbers and transport vehicles				Horsed		Mechanical					REMARKS
	Officers	Other ranks	Natives	Horses Riding	Draught	Heavy Draught	Mules Pack	Large	Small	Camels	Oxen	Guns, carriages and limbers, showing description	Ammunition wagons and limbers	Machine guns	Aircraft, showing description	4 Wheeled	2 Wheeled	Motor Cars	Tractors	Lorries, showing description	Trucks, showing description	Trailers	Motor Bicycles	Bicycles	
Effective Strength of Unit	30	824		14	12	23		30						4											On command officers 2 Base Depot 5 Pool Zubuna Bn. 1 Leave 2 Sick 7 Tunnelling Coy 10
Details, by Arms attached to unit as in War Establishment:— Amybulance Corb. R.A.M.C.	1	4																							Other Ranks: Corps Gmbly 6 Div. X — 13 Bat — 12 Warden A. S. M. 2 Feens 14 Tunnelling Coy 103 Field Artillery 9 Cag Depot 1 Beafellow 2 R.F.C.
Total	31	828		14	12	23		30						4		19	5								176
War Establishment	30	995		14	12	23		20						4		19	5								
Wanting to complete (Detail of Personnel and Horses below)		167																							
Surplus	1																								
*Attached (not to include the details shown above)																									
Civilians:— Employed with the Unit Accompanying the Unit																									
TOTAL RATIONED	31	828		14	12	23		30																	

* In the case of field ambulances, hospitals or depots, the number of patients are to be included here, the names being shown in A.F.B.36. Div X Tricor & 14 other horses

H.M. Jones Mjr for Lt. Colonel Signature of Commander.

11 December 1915 Date of Despatch.

For information of the A.G.'s Office at the Base.

Officers and men who have become casuals, been transferred or joined since last report.

Place: In the Field   Date: 11th December 1915

Regtl. Number	Rank	Name	Corps	Nature of casualty, or name of unit from or to which transferred	Date of being struck off or coming on the ration return	Remarks*
10540	Pte	Keir A		To Hospl	1-12-15	
11663	"	Malone J		"	"	
9851	"	Wardle B		"	"	
12099	"	Holt		"	"	
8461	"	Curphy G		"	"	
26964	"	Cunningham H		"	"	
10540	"	Goss		"	2-12-15	
12910	LCpl	Jerons E		"	"	
20766	Pte	Law W		"	3-12-15	
14243	"	Davies		"	"	
10088	"	Mitchell J		"	"	
8403	"	Culshaw W		"	"	
8030	"	Dunn F		"	"	
6418	"	Foster T		"	"	
9431	"	Davies G		"	"	
12611	"	Bradshaw W	4A Bn The King's (L'pool Regt)	"	"	
8524 g/15	"	Harrison W		"	4-12-15	
12686	Pte	Lampkin		"	"	
8595	"	Kilgome F		"	"	
12434	"	Sutherland T		"	"	
14536	"	O'Neill H		"	"	
10504	"	Beesley W		"	5-12-15	
5322	"	Griffin W		"	"	
9008	"	Aspinall A		"	"	
11615	"	Smith W		"	"	
26249	"	Linzey J		"	6-12-15	
11116	"	Coffey D		"	"	
9498	"	Brown D		"	"	
	W/Cpl	Allen G.W.D		"	3-12-15	
9798	Pte	Simpson A		Wounded in A	2-12-15	
7411	"	Looney T		To England	21-11-15	
17115	"	Beathman W		From Hospl	5-12-15	
11018	"	Hargreaves R		"	"	
26964	"	Cunningham H		"	9-12-15	
11663	"	Malone J		"	"	
10300	"	Griffiths		To England	29-11-15	
9491	"	Daley P		To Hospl	10-12-15	
9323	"	Gavin		From England	4-12-15	
	Lieut	Gannon H				
		Gray F				

RCR Ime Major
for Lieut Colonel
Comdg 4th Bn The King's (L'pool Regt)

* State whether absence is of a permanent or temporary nature, adding, in the case of casuals from wounds or disease, any available information for communication to the relatives.

Perforated Sheet giving detail of personnel and horses wanting to complete, shown on Army Form B. 213.

Number of Report _____

Detail of Wanting to Complete			CAVALRY	R.A.	R.E.	INFANTRY	R.A.M.C.	A.O.C.	A.V.C.
Drivers	R.A.								
	R.E.								
	A.S.C.								
	Pack								
	Lorry								
	Steam								
Gunners									
Smith Gunners									
Range Takers									
Farriers	Sergeants								
	Corporals								
	Shoeing, or Shoeing and Carriage Smiths								
	Cold Shoers								
Wheelers	R.A.								
	H.T.								
	M.T.								
Saddlers or Harness Makers									
Blacksmiths									
Bricklayers and Masons									
Carpenters and Joiners									
Fitters & Turners (R.E.)	Wood								
	Iron								
Fitters	R.A.								
	Wireless								
Plumbers									
Electricians	Ordinary								
	W.T.								
Signalmen									
Engine Drivers	Loco.								
	Field								
Air Line Men									
Permanent Line Men									
Operators, Telegraph									
Cablemen									
Brigade Section Pioneers									
General-duty Pioneers									
Signallers									
Instrument Repairers									
Motor Cyclists									
Motor Cyclist Artificers									
Telephonists									
Clerks									
Machine Gunners									
Armament Artificers	Fitters								
	Range Finders								
	Armourers								
Storemen									
Privates									

| W.O.'s and N.C.O.'s (by ranks) not included in trade columns | | | | | | 2/3 | | | |

TOTAL to agree with complete	Officers					1/3			
	Other Ranks								
Horses	Riding								
	Draught								
	Heavy Draught								
	Pack								

Remarks:—

N.R. Order for first detail
4th Bn - Tetbury Gloucs Regt
11th Oct 1915
11th December 1915.

Signature of Commander _____

Unit _____

Formation to which attached _____

Date of Despatch _____

Sheet 2

For information of the A.G.'s Office at the Base.

Officers and men who have become casuals, been transferred or joined since last report.

Place: In the Field   Date: 14th December 1915

Regtl. Number	Rank	Name	Corps	Nature of casualty, or name of unit from or to which transferred	Date of being struck off or coming on the ration return	Remarks*
24948	Pte	Haslam J			16-12-15	
30356	--	Swords J			--	
10141	--	Collinson SH			--	
11464	--	Hesketh H			--	
11613	--	Ashbrook G			--	
26982	--	Holland T			--	
24200	--	Burroughs T			--	
26140	--	Storey J.A			--	
24622	--	Featherbairdo G			--	
11833	--	Halsall J			--	
24541	--	Stewart J		Joined Regiment from No 8 Infantry Base Depot	--	
24896	--	Wishnaw			--	
24914	--	Hayes J			--	
14950	--	Cavanagh J			--	
29012	--	Jenkins W			--	
2931-	--	Showcross T			--	
29341	--	Todd A			--	
29390	--	Harrison W			--	
29405	--	Brown T			--	
29861	--	Jameson A			--	
29840	--	Reeves E			--	
26803	--	Webster G			--	
29900	--	Walsh J			--	
29951	--	Thomas J			--	
29952	--	Beasley J			--	
29961	--	Helmes J			--	
29942	--	Maloney W			--	
29994	--	Tonkins EG			--	
30052	--	Lowe W.H			--	
30063	--	McHugh H			--	
30109	--	Penny			--	
30122	--	William M.J			--	
30149	--	Young W.J			--	
30507	--	Payne B			--	
30533	--	Beattie A.P			--	
30610	--	Gallagher R			--	
31744	--	Kirwan J			--	
31146	--	Atwood J.G			--	
3163	--	Green J.G			--	
3192	--	Lea A			--	
3168	--	Christie S.M			--	
9165	--	Reardon			--	
24933	--	Devine W			--	
30454	--	Kelly M			19-12-15	
20466	--	Law J		From Hospl	11-12-15	
14844	--	Stevens J			--	
2864	--	Cunningham H			--	
25249	a/Cpl	Harrison W		--	12-12-15	
5327	Pte	Griffin W		--	--	
8930	--	Dunn J		--	13-12-15	
13162	--	Clayfield F		Absent from	22-6-15	
17496	--	Hughes J		Classified	Not on
18921	--	Mire G		Permanent	ration
8946	Sgt	Mullery P		Base	strength
11466	L/Cpl	Jennings F			--	
5322	Pte	Griffin W		To Base Depot	13-12-15	
8309	--	Tighe T		For Discharge	--	
9151	--	Donovan J		To Hospl	--	

* State whether absence is of a permanent or temporary nature, adding, in the case of casuals from wounds or disease, any available information for communication to the relatives.

Army Form B. 213.

FIELD RETURN.

No. of Report

(To be furnished by all arms, services, and departments to the A.G.'s Office at the Base in accordance with Field Service Regulations, Part II.)

Date

RETURN showing numbers RATIONED by, and Transport on charge of, _____ at _____

DETAIL.	Personnel			Animals							Guns, carriages, and limbers and transport vehicles				Horsed		Motor Cars	Tractors	Mechanical		Trailers	Motor Bicycles	Bicycles	REMARKS
	Officers	Other ranks	Natives	Horses			Mules		Camels	Oxen	Guns, carriages and limbers, showing description	Ammunition wagons and limbers	Machine guns	Aircraft, showing description	4 Wheeled	2 Wheeled			Lorries, showing description	Trucks, showing description				
				Riding	Draught	Heavy Draught	Pack	Large	Small															
Effective Strength of Unit
Details, by Arms attached to unit as in War Establishment :—
Total
War Establishment
Wanting to complete
Surplus
* Attached (not to include the details shown above)
Civilians :—
Employed with the Unit
Accompanying the Unit
TOTAL RATIONED ...

* In the case of field ambulances, hospitals or depots, the number of patients are to be included here, the names being shown in A. F. A. 36.

Wt.-W. 6005-894 (35047) U. B. Ltd. 500,000 10/14   Forms B. 213

Signature of Commander.

Date of Despatch.

Army Form B. 213 — FIELD RETURN

(To be furnished by all arms, services, and departments (except A.S.C. units) to the A. G.'s Office at the Base in accordance with Field Service Regulations, Part II.)

No. of Report 4
Diary
RETURN showing numbers RATIONED by, and Transport on charge of **H.Q. 3rd the King's (Liverpool Regt)** at **in the field** Date **14th Dec 1915**

Detail	Personnel — Officers	Other ranks	Natives	Horses — Riding	Draught	Heavy Draught	Pack	Mules — Large	Small	Camels	Oxen	Guns, carriages, limbers, description	Ammunition wagons and limbers	Machine Guns	Aircraft, description	Horsed 4-Wheeled	Horsed 2-Wheeled	Motor Cars	Tractors	Lorries	Trucks	Trailers	Motor Bicycles	Bicycles	Remarks
Effective Strength of Unit	29	922		14	12	23		30						4		19	5								Commanders Officer 2, Base Depot 6, Sean i 2, actg Turnsllnty 10
Details, by Arms attached to unit as in War Establishment: — R.A.M.C.	1																								Other Ranks— York-Lanc'r 30, San Ending 21, Lance A.P.M's
Army Ordnance Corps	1																								Keane 21, Attd 4/5/7 boy Rb 102, Field Ambulance 13, Orderlies 1, R.F.C. 2, R.E. 2, Absent 1 / 192
Total	30	923		14	12	23		30						4		19	5								
War Establishment	30	995		14	12	23		30						4		19	5								
Wanting to complete	—	72																							
Surplus	—	1																							
*Attached (not to include the details shown above)																									Horses with Civil Train M.B. 8
Civilians:— Employed with the Unit Accompanying the Unit																									
Total Rationed	20	931		14	12	15		30																	

* In the case of field ambulances, hospitals or depots, the number of patients are to be included here, the names being shown in A. F. A. 36.

R. C. Jones, Major for Lt Colonel
Signature of Commander.
14th December 1915 — Date of Despatch.

Sheet I

For information of the A.G.'s Office at the Base.

Officers and men who have become casuals, been transferred or joined since last report.

Place **In the Field**   Date **14th December 1915**

Regtl. Number	Rank	Name	Corps	Nature of casualty, or name of unit from or to which transferred	Date of being struck off or coming on the ration return	Remarks*
23960	Pte	Ellams J.F.H			13-12-15	
11869	--	Murphy J			--	
11256	--	Salter A			--	
9051	--	Wright H			--	
24115	--	Haban			--	
13118	--	Cook A			--	
124540	--	Wilson H			14-12-15	
30406	--	Rowan			14-12-15	
241040	--	Gribben T			14-12-15	
24230	--	Landy C			14-12-15	
30032	--	Conway J			13-12-15	
24129	--	Banks W			--	
24930	--	James W			--	
20336	--	Pitt L			--	
21354	--	Corrin J			--	
3/304	--	James J			--	
29945	--	Nelson J			--	
29534	--	Howard W			--	
31219	--	Rimmer Ro			--	
30469	--	Draper F			--	
30451	--	Ainsworth J			--	
30432	--	Davies W			--	
1856	--	Goodsall	Reinforcements from No 8 Infantry Base Depot	4 A.Bn Training (Liverpool Regiment)	--	
9341	--	Needham P			--	
29008	--	Smith H			--	
31409	--	Sooley			--	
12191	--	Graham J			--	
29461	--	Fee C			--	
31282	--	Evans J			--	
9006	--	Hannon H			--	
9093	--	Brown J			--	
14985	--	Gilbert J			--	
9043	--	Doran J			--	
8844	--	Conning J			--	
14819	--	Turton A			--	
8902	--	Taylor A			--	
30380	--	Freeman J			--	
30398	--	Flanaghan J			--	
30423	--	Parry H			--	
24812	--	Glasgow A			--	
30399	--	Morris R			--	
29306	--	Draper R.J			--	
29939	--	Hughes J			--	
8855	--	Girard			--	
30400	--	Phipps R			--	
20326	--	Kinrade C			--	
26413	--	Finn C			--	
26448	--	Higham H			--	
30205	--	Pennington D			--	
20391	--	Fry H			--	
304040	--	Higgins R			--	
24414	--	Pomfret A			--	
29140	--	Harker J			--	
29965	--	McCusker M			--	
10499	--	Willcox H			--	
10454	--	Williams H			--	
14830	Sgt	Watson J			16-12-15	
29067	LCpl	Richardson J				

*State whether absence is of a permanent or temporary nature, adding, in the case of casuals from wounds or disease, any available information for communication to the relatives.

For information of the A.G.'s Office at the Base.

Officers and men who have become casuals, been transferred or joined since last report.

Place: In the field   Date: 14th December 1915

Regtl. Number	Rank	Name	Corps	Nature of casualty, or name of unit from or to which transferred	Date of being struck off or coming on the ration return	Remarks*
7905	Pte	Tonge A		To Hospital	13-12-15	
23333	—	Levine A		—	—	
11383	—	Dempsey P		—	14-12-15	
12575	—	Ashworth W		—	—	
20856	—	Atherton J		—	—	
10011	—	Dowd J		Base Depot	14-12-15	
	2/Lieut	Allen G.W.D.		To England	8-12-15	

REM Ives Major
for Lieut Colonel
Comdg 4th Bn The King's (L'pool Regt)

* State whether absence is of a permanent or temporary nature, adding, in the case of casuals from wounds or disease, any available information for communication to the relatives.

Army Form B. 213.

FIELD RETURN.

No. of Report ————

(To be furnished by all arms, services, and departments to the A.G.'s Office at the Base in accordance with Field Service Regulations, Part II.)

Date. ————

RETURN showing numbers RATIONED by, and Transport on charge of, ———————— at ————————

DETAIL.	Personnel			Animals								Guns, carriages, and limbers and transport vehicles						Mechanical				
	Officers	Other ranks	Natives	Horses				Mules		Camels	Oxen	Guns, carriages and limbers, showing description	Ammunition wagons and limbers	Machine guns	Aircraft, showing description	Horsed		Motor Cars	Tractors	Lorries, showing description	Trucks, showing description	Trailers	Motor Bicycles	Bicycles	REMARKS
				Riding	Draught	Heavy Draught	Pack	Large	Small							4 Wheeled	2 Wheeled								
Effective Strength of Unit																									
Details, *by Arms* attached to unit as in War Establishment:—																									
Total																									
War Establishment																									
Wanting to complete																									
Surplus																									
² Attached (not to include the details shown above)																									
Civilians:—																									
Employed with the Unit																									
Accompanying the Unit																									
TOTAL RATIONED ...																									

* In the case of field ambulances, hospitals or depots, the number of patients are to be included here, the names being shown in A. F. A. 36.

Signature of Commander. ————

Date of Despatch. ————

Wt.W. 6005-894. (35047) U. B. Ltd. 500,000 10/14   Forms B. 213

Perforated Sheet giving detail of personnel and horses wanting to complete, shown on Army Form B. 213.

Number of Report _____ #1

Detail of Wanting to Complete	Drivers						Gunners	Smith Gunners	Range Takers	Farriers			Wheelers			Saddlers or Harness Makers	Blacksmiths	Bricklayers and Masons	Carpenters and Joiners	Fitters & Turners (R.E.)		Fitters				Plumbers	Electricians			Signalmen	Engine Drivers		Air Line Men	Permanent Line Men	Operators, Telegraph	Cablemen	Brigade Section Pioneers	General-duty Pioneers	Signallers	Instrument Repairers	Motor Cyclists	Motor Cyclist Artificers	Telephonists	Clerks	Machine Gunners	Armament Artificers			Armourers	Storemen	Privates	W.O.s and N.C.O.s (by rank) not included in trade columns	TOTAL to agree with wanting to complete		Horses			
	R.A.	R.E.	A.S.C.	Car	Lorry	Steam				Sergeants	Corporals	Shoeing, or Shoeing and Carriage Smiths	Cold Shoers	R.A.	H.T.	M.T.						Wood	Iron	R.A.	Wireless			Ordinary	W.T.		Loco.	Field													Fitters	Range Finders						Officers	Other Ranks	Riding	Draught	Heavy Draught	Pack
CAVALRY																																																									
R.A.																																																									
R.E.																																																									
INFANTRY																																																				541 (Communical other Ranks)		42				
R.A.M.C.																																																									
A.O.C.																																																									
A.V.C.																																																									

Remarks :— A.R. Jones

Signature of Commander. Major for Lt Col
4th Bn The King's (Liverpool Regt) Unit.
XIX Division Formation to which attached.
XI Corps 17th Oct 1915 Date of Despatch.

[P.T.O.]

No. of Report 42

Army Form B. 213.

FIELD RETURN.

(To be furnished by all arms, services, and departments (except A.S.C. units) to the A. G.'s Office at the Base in accordance with Field Service Regulations, Part II.)

RETURN showing numbers RATIONED by, and Transport on charge of, 4 Bn Thetford at In the field 24 Decr 1915 Date.
(Final Report)

Diary

Detail	Personnel			Animals							Guns, carriages and transport vehicles				Mechanical				Remarks
	Officers	Other ranks	Natives	Horses Riding	Draught	Heavy Draught	Pack	Mules Large	Small	Camels	Oxen	Guns, carriages	Ammunition wagons	Machine guns	Aircraft	Horsed 4 Wheeled	2 Wheeled	Motor Cars	Tractors	Lorries	Trucks	Trailers	Motor Bicycles	Bicycles	
Effective Strength of Unit	29	915		14	12	23		30						4		19	5								On Command Officers 2, 4, 2, 1, 9 Base Depot, Leave acct 139 T&I, sick
Details, by Arms attached to unit as in War Establishment:— R.A.M.C. Army Ordnance Corps	1	1																							Other Ranks Base-sick 29, See Embkt
Total	30	916		14	12	23		30						4		19	5								Under A.P.M. 24
War Establishment	30	995		14	12	23		30						4		19	5								Leave Pates 139 T.Boy 98, Field Ambulance 16
Wanting to complete (Detail of Personnel and Horses below)		-79																							Conductor 1, R.F.C. 2, R.E. 1, absent
Surplus																									
*Attached (not to include the details shown above)																									
Civilians:— Employed with the Unit Accompanying the Unit													1												Animals 197
Total Rationed	21	919		14	12	15		30						4		19	5								40 Horses actt with Divl Train

* In the case of field ambulances, hospitals or depots, the number of patients are to be included here, the names being shown in A. F. A. 36.

Signature of Commander __Von Owen Major 4 Bn__

Date of Despatch __24th December 1915__

For information of the A.G.'s Office at the Base.

Officers and men who have become casuals, been transferred or joined since last report.

Place: In the Field Date: 24th December 1915

Regtl. Number	Rank	Name	Corps	Nature of casualty, or name of unit from or to which transferred	Date of being struck off or coming on the ration return	Remarks*
12466	Pte	Firth T.	✓	To Hosptl	10-11-15	
26093	L.Cpl	Merton C	✓	—"—	11-11-15	
24141	Pte	McNeill T	✓	—"—	21-11-15	
14584	—"—	Halliday W	✓	—"—	15-12-15	
6283	—"—	Nightingale C	✓	—"—	—"—	
11306	Cpl	Hayes J	✓	—"—	18-12-15	
12545	Pte	Smith J.T.	✓	—"—	19-12-15	
9033	—"—	Eyre J	✓	—"—	—"—	
7900	—"—	Quinn P	✓	—"—	—"—	
4868	—"—	McDonald J	✓	—"—	—"—	
11353	—"—	Smith W.E.	✓	Killed in a	20-12-15	
11468	—"—	Kenny P	✓	—"—	21-12-15	
9142	Sgt	Jones T	✓	Wounded in a	20-12-15	
24246	Pte	Owens H	✓	—"—	21-12-15	
8886	—"—	Oliver J	✓	—"—	22-12-15	
23333	—"—	Levine A	✓	From Hosptl	20-12-15	
6418	—"—	Lester T	✓	—"—	21-12-15	
~~3640~~	~~—"—~~	~~Saunders H~~	~~✓~~	~~—"—~~	~~—"—~~	
14584	—"—	Halliday W		—"—	23-12-15	
13914	L.Cpl	Jerons	✓	—"—	19-12-15	
8596	Pte	Kilcoyne	✓	—"—	—"—	
12680	—"—	Lamkin J	✓	—"—	—"—	
8761	—"—	Murphy C	✓	—"—	—"—	
9498	—"—	Brown H	✓	—"—	—"—	

R C M Ime

Major for Lt.Col

Comdg 4th Bn The King's (Lpool) Regt

* State whether absence is of a permanent or temporary nature, adding, in the case of casuals from wounds or disease, any available information for communication to the relatives.

Perforated Sheet giving detail of personnel and horses wanting to complete, shown on Army Form B. 213.

Number of Report 42

Detail of Wanting to Complete	Drivers						Gunners	Smith Gunners	Range Takers	Farriers			Shoeing, or Shoeing and Carriage Smiths	Cold Shoers	Wheelers			Saddlers or Harness Makers	Blacksmiths	Bricklayers and Masons	Carpenters and Joiners	Fitters & Turners (R. E.)		Fitters			Electricians			Signalmen	Engine Drivers		Air Line Men	Permanent Line Men	Operators, Telegraph	Cablemen	Brigade Section Pioneers	General-duty Pioneers	Signallers	Instrument Repairers	Motor Cyclists	Motor Cyclist Artificers	Telephonists	Clerks	Machine Gunners	Armament Artificers			Armourers	Storemen	Privates	W.O's and N.C.O's. (by rank) not included in trade columns	TOTAL wanting to agree with Other Ranks to complete		Horses				
	R.A.	R.E.	A.S.C.	Car	Lorry	Steam				Sergeants	Corporals				H.T.	M.T.	A.					Wood	Iron	R.A.	Wireless	Plumbers	Ordinary	W.T.		Loco.	Field														Fitters	Range Finders					Officers	Other Ranks	Riding	Draught	Heavy Draught	Pack
CAVALRY																																																								
R.A.																																																								
R.E.																																																				Armourer Ch. Ranks	1	79				
INFANTRY																																																					5/4					
R.A.M.C.																																																									
A.O.C.																																																									
A.V.C.																																																									

Remarks:— Res. Res — Infantry.

Signature of Commander 4Bn the King's (Liverpool Regt) **Unit.**

Formation to which attached XI Corps

Date of Despatch 4th December 1915

Army Form B. 213

FIELD RETURN.

(To be furnished by all arms, services, and departments (except A.S.C. units) to the A. G.'s Office at the Base in accordance with Field Service Regulations, Part II.)
RETURN showing numbers RATIONED by, and Transport on charge of 4th Bn. The King's (Lpool Regt) at In the Field. Date 31st December 1915.

No. of Report 43   Army

| DETAIL | Personnel | | | Animals | | | | | | | Guns, carriages, and limbers and transport vehicles | | | | Horsed | | Motor Cars | Tractors | Mechanical | | | Motor Bicycles | Bicycles | REMARKS |
	Officers	Other ranks	Natives	Horses Riding	Draught	Heavy Draught	Pack	Mules Large	Small	Camels	Oxen	Guns, carriages and limbers, showing description	Ammunition wagons and limbers	Machine guns	Aircraft, showing description	4 Wheeled	2 Wheeled			Lorries, showing description	Trucks, showing description	Trailers			
Effective Strength of Unit	29	968		14	12	23		30						4		19	5								On Command
Details, by Arms attached to unit as in War Establishment:—																									Officers
																									Knee Report
																									Leave 4
																									Sick 1
R.A.M.C.	1																								Attd 1/2nd T by 2
Army Ordnance Corps		1																							Other Ranks
																									Corps Employ 11
																									Sick 10
																									Bde —
Total	30	969		14	12	23		30						4		19	5								Attd R.E. 94
War Establishment	30	995		14	12	23		30						4		19	5								" R.F.C. 1
Wanting to complete	—	26																							On Command 4
Surplus																									Leave 31
(Detail of Personnel and Horses below)																									Absent 2
*Attached (not to include the details shown above)																									Under A.P.M. 26
Civilians:— Employed with the Unit Accompanying the Unit																									Field Ambulance 29
																									3rd Echelon 1
TOTAL RATIONED	21	757		14	12	15		30																	212
																									Animals
																									H.Q. Horses Attd Kub. Train B

* In the case of field ambulances, hospitals or depots, the number of patients are to be included here, the names being shown in A.F.A. 36.

Kendall Major for O.C. Signature of Commander.
31st December 1915. Date of Despatch.

For information of the A.G.'s Office at the Base.

Officers and men who have become casuals, been transferred or joined since last report.

Place: In the Field.   Date: 31st December 1915.

Regtl. Number	Rank	Name	Corps	Nature of casualty, or name of unit from or to which transferred	Date of being struck off or coming on the ration return	Remarks*
8320	Sgt	Honan M.				
25178	L/Cpl	Houghton J.				
27935	-"-	Heard J.				
10000	Pte	Simpson J.				
25043	-"-	Mackie J.				
11994	-"-	Mooney J.				
11281	-"-	Nicholson J.				
11143	-"-	McGrale J.				
18558	-"-	Burke G.				
30642	-"-	Connor P.				
10598	-"-	Rimmer C.				
30094	-"-	Warburton J.				
30482	-"-	Walker D.				
31228	-"-	Shelly J.				
29350	-"-	Gerrard J.				
27469	-"-	Hornes J.		4th Bn The King's (Liverpool Regiment.)	Reinforcements from No 8 Infantry Base Depot.	
27449	-"-	Lord C.			24-1-12-15.	
37832	-"-	Baker W.				
27638	-"-	Beardsworth R.				
27959	-"-	Almond C.				
29884	-"-	Paul C.				
29920	-"-	Wade J.				
27610	-"-	Kemp J.				
13514	-"-	Hoggarth T.				
27118	-"-	Smith J.				
27728	-"-	Jones J.				
29073	-"-	McFarlin W.				
27053	-"-	Moran J.				
10097	-"-	Murphy M.				
27632	-"-	Pepper J.				
27416	-"-	Daley J.				
29811	-"-	Rogers J.				
29874	-"-	Pilsbury P.				
27686	-"-	Rennie A.				
30000	-"-	Lea J.				
30056	-"-	Taylor J.				
29933	-"-	Vaney J.				
29852	-"-	Roberts W.				
29017	-"-	Baldwin A.				
30345	-"-	Pye J.				
29999	-"-	Riding J.				
27295	-"-	Sullivan A.				
27834	-"-	Doyle A.				
27448	-"-	Miller A.				
29074	-"-	Hughes W.				
30519	-"-	Pearse G.				
27117	-"-	Smith W.				
30074	-"-	Orrington R.				
30557	-"-	Ginley A.				
8804	-"-	Bower A.				
10793	-"-	O'Halloran J.				
27170	-"-	Dugdale J.				
29063	-"-	Stansfield F.				
30019	-"-	Wright J.				
29344	-"-	Butler J.H.				
30016	-"-	Seddon H.				
27720	-"-	Holyard W.				
31760	-"-	Harley J.				

* State whether absence is of a permanent or temporary nature, adding, in the case of casuals from wounds or disease, any available information for communication to the relatives.

Army Form B. 213.

FIELD RETURN.

No. of Report _____

(To be furnished by all arms, services, and departments to the A.G.'s Office at the Base in accordance with Field Service Regulations, Part II.)

Date _____

RETURN showing numbers RATIONED by, and Transport on charge of, _____ at _____

DETAIL.	Personnel			Animals								Guns, carriages, and limbers and transport vehicles						Mechanical				REMARKS
	Officers	Other ranks	Natives	Horses				Mules		Camels	Oxen	Guns, carriages and limbers, showing description	Ammunition wagons and limbers	Machine guns	Aircraft, showing description	Horsed		Motor Cars	Tractors	Lorries, showing description	Trucks, showing description	Trailers	Motor Bicycles	Bicycles	
				Riding	Draught	Heavy Draught	Pack	Large	Small							4 Wheeled	2 Wheeled								
Effective Strength of Unit																									
Details, *by Arms* attached to unit as in War Establishment :—																									
Total																									
War Establishment																									
Wanting to complete																									
Surplus																									
*Attached (not to include the details shown above)																									
Civilians :— Employed with the Unit Accompanying the Unit																									
TOTAL RATIONED ...																									

* In the case of field ambulances, hospitals or depots, the number of patients are to be included here, the names being shown in A. F. A. 36.

Wt.-W. 6005-894 (3047) U. B. Ltd. 500,000 10/14 Forms $\frac{\text{B. 213}}{5}$

Signature of Commander, _____

Date of Despatch. _____

Sheet 2

For information of the A.G.'s Office at the Base.

Officers and men who have become casuals, been transferred or joined since last report.

Place: In the Field   Date: 31st December 1915

Regtl. Number	Rank	Name	Corps	Nature of casualty, or name of unit from or to which transferred	Date of being struck off or coming on the ration return	Remarks*
26994	Pte	Riley R.		Reinforcements from No 6 Infantry Base Depot	24-12-15	
27628	"	Gerling R.				
27263	"	Palomo S.				
8951	"	Barlow E.				
27475	"	Doyle J.				
26265	"	Kearney J.				
27799	"	Sharrocks J.P.				
29882	"	Bleasdale J.P.				
29913	"	Winstanley W.				
30355	"	Lewis J.				
27235	"	Hack J.				
29854	"	Healing J.H.				
10502	"	Presley J.		To no Hospital	30-12-15	
11722	"	Martin W.		Killed in A.	26-12-15	
30055	L/Cpl	Crutchley		To England	30-12-15	
12653	Pte	Eckersley E.		To Hospital	31-12-15	
25148	"	Martin J.		"	29-12-15	
13213	Cpl	Grace J.		"	"	
24622	Pte	Leatherbarrow		"	"	
9402	"	McGuern E.		"	26-12-15	
9228	"	Strong J.		"	"	
18059	"	Harrison J.		"	"	
30304	"	Wilkinson J.		"	"	
13378	"	Barrington J.		"	25-12-15	
24127	"	Banks W.		"	"	
9216	L/Cpl	Clark W.		"	27-12-15	
13573	Pte	Wright S.		"	"	
10169	"	Bather J.		"	"	
25951	"	Gibbons J.P.		"	"	
12917	L/Cpl	Baines J.		"	"	
19483	Pte	Millen A.		"	"	
	Lieut	Tripp R.B.		"	25-12-15	

Mitchell Major for O.C.
4th Bn The King's (Liverpool) Regt

* State whether absence is of a permanent or temporary nature, adding, in the case of casuals from wounds or disease, any available information for communication to the relatives.

Perforated Sheet giving detail of personnel and horses wanting to complete, shown on Army Form B. 213.

Number of Report 43.

Detail of Wanting to Complete				CAVALRY	R.A.	R.E.	INFANTRY	R.A.M.C.	A.O.C.	A.V.C.
Drivers	R.A.									
	R.E.									
	A.S.C.									
	Car									
	Lorry									
	Steam									
Gunners										
Smith Gunners										
Range Takers										
Farriers	Serjeants									
	Corporals									
Shoeing, or Shoeing and Carriage Smiths										
Cold Shoers										
Wheelers	R.A.									
	H.T.									
	M.T.									
Saddlers or Harness Makers										
Blacksmiths										
Bricklayers and Masons										
Carpenters and Joiners										
Fitters & Turners (R.E.)	Wood									
	Iron									
Fitters	R.A.									
	Wireless									
	Plumbers									
Electricians	Ordinary									
	W.T.									
Blacksmiths										
Engine Drivers	Loco.									
	Field									
Air Line Men										
Permanent Line Men										
Operators, Telegraph										
Cablemen										
Brigade Section Pioneers										
General-duty Pioneers										
Signallers										
Instrument Repairers										
Motor Cyclists										
Motor Cyclist Artificers										
Telephonists										
Clerks										
Machine Gunners										
Armament Artificers	Fitters									
	Range Finders									
Armourers										
Storemen										
Privates										
W.O's and N.C.O's, (by ranks) not included in trade columns					Gunners Privates		521			
TOTAL wanting to agree with	Officers									
	Other Ranks						26			
Horses	Riding									
	Draught									
	Heavy Draught									
	Pack									

Remarks:—

Mitchell Major for O.C. Signature of Commander.
4th Bn The King's (Liverpool Regt.) Unit.
XI Corps Formation to which attached.
31st December 1915 Date of Despatch.

58 XIX

+ Liverpool Regt
Jan
Vol III

9.

Vol XI.

Army Form C. 2118.

WAR DIARY
or
INTELLIGENCE SUMMARY.   4th Bn "The King's (Liverpool Regt)"
(Erase heading not required.)

Vol XI.

JANUARY 1916

Instructions regarding War Diaries and Intelligence Summaries are contained in F. S. Regs., Part II. and the Staff Manual respectively. Title pages will be prepared in manuscript.

Place	Date	Hour	Summary of Events and Information	Remarks and references to Appendices
TRENCHES S5L–10L. Billets LOCON.	1-1-16		In trenches & billets. Fine day. Occasional showers. Very windy. Enemy Machine Guns active about night. Enemy quiet by day. Our Machine Guns in action at night. A hostile working party was sniped M.G. Emplacements. Patrols went out by night as usual. One hostile light field Gun was located at S.11.c.5/2. Much work done & different improvements. In hostile shelling chiefly light field guns on PORT ARTHUR, OXFORD ROAD & LA BASSEE ROAD. 6/Billets got a ringle g/shell-burst in air. One man from hospital.	
Do	2-1-16		In trenches + billets. Windy + showery. Hostile artillery more active. OXFORD ROAD were shelled & our front line heavily shelled by light field guns especially in vicinity of PIPES NOSE when our shell burst through a M.G. emplacement doing much damage. An attempt was made to destroy an Enemy listening post behind Barricade in OXFORD ROAD by Captain the Sanderson, but they were found to have escaped the main defences as in the trenches further back which is strongly patrolled & wired – One man killed (M25793 Private R. GORST.) 4 men wounded.	
Do	3-1-16		In trenches & billets. Enemy very quiet all day + night. Our front line was shelled by light field guns between 11.30 AM & 12 AM but without result. Windy + cloudy. One man died of wounds (M.15402 Private M. HAMILTON.) 2 men from hospital. One man to base to discharge.	
Do	4-1-16		In trenches & billets. Showery day. Quiet in trenches. C & D Companies were relieved by patrons g 10 Worcester Regt + 8th Gloucester + a completion of relief reported Battn Headquarters at LOCON. One man to hospital.	
LOCON. Do	5-1-16 6-1-16		Fine day. In billets. 11 men to hospital. One man from hospital. Fine + windy. In billets. (N9305 Private G. TAPP. found drowned in LA BASSEE CANAL. 2 men to hospital.	
Do	7-1-16		Windy + showery. In billets. One man from hospital. One man wounded.	
Do	8-1-16		Fine day. In billets. One man to hospital. 2/Lieut H.T. JENKINS (3rd Bn) invalided to England.	
Do	9-1-16		Fine day. Rain at night. In billets. One man to hospital. One man from hospital. One man wounded.	

Army Form C. 2118.

WAR DIARY
or
INTELLIGENCE SUMMARY.

4th Bt "The King's" (Liverpool Regt)

JANUARY 1916

(Erase heading not required.)

Instructions regarding War Diaries and Intelligence Summaries are contained in F.S. Regs., Part II. and the Staff Manual respectively. Title pages will be prepared in manuscript.

Place	Date	Hour	Summary of Events and Information	Remarks and references to Appendices
LOCON	10.1.16	-	In billets. Fine day. One man to hospital.	
Do	11.1.16		Dull day. Some rain. Front at night. In billets.	
Do	12.1.16		Do. Windy. In billets. Officers inspected trenches prior to going into the line on night of 14/15th inst. Two men to hospital. Two men from hospital.	
Do	13.1.16		Very windy with frequent showers. In billets.	
Do	14.1.16		In billets. Fine day. A draft of 35 NCOs & men arrived from Base. Two companies (A & B) with C.O. and Adjutant went into trenches SOUTH of RUE DU BOIS (LA QUINQUE RUE) with head quarters at S.14 Central. BETHUNE contoured Sheet 36c. NW. Two men to hospital - 6 E KENT Regt in on right & 9 which Regt in on left. 3 which Regt on right. One man wounded.	2nd Lieut P.T. FISHENDEN invalided through illness to England.
Do. & 14.Central	15.1.16		In billets & trenches. Fine day. Nothing of importance occurred. Two men from hospital.	
Do.	16.1.16		Do. Two men to hospital. One man from hospital.	
Do.	17.1.16		Do. Usual sniping & M.G. fire in vicinity of TUBE STATION & PRINCES ROAD.	
Do.	18.1.16		Do. One man wounded. German Communication trench opposite centre of our line destroyed by our shell fire. Dull & showery.	
Do.			Do - C & D Companies relieved A & B Coys in trenches. One man from hospital.	1st R Berks in our right & on left.
Do.	19.1.16		Do. Fine day. One man wounded. 2nd Lieut J.W. LAWRENCE joined from 17th Bttn. Nothing of importance to report. Enemy quiet.	
Do	20.1.16		In billets & trenches. Misty & showery. Enemy working party seen getting into position at S.22.c.3/8. after using till they were all over. rifle & M.G. fire was opened about 11pm. One man to base for discharge.	
Do	21.1.16		In billets & trenches. Occasional bursts of rifle & M.G. fire during night. A patrol of 7 Gransdiers Guards was out reconnaissance. Enemy wire got hung up which too slowly cut & was challenged by enemy who opened fire. One man Pt SIMMONS was badly hit Shot still in the wire & in the enemy was with Nurses & Pt SIMMONS appeared to have been still fast in the wire. The party had to withdraw without him. A further search was made for him later in the night but any to the absence of moon it was not possible to see enough to pierce fire. From 6.30 very windy. A draft of 25 NCOs & men joined from base. No 8870 Pte SIMMONS missing believed killed whilst on a patrol duty.	

1577 Wt. W10791/1773 50,000 1/15 D.D. & L. A.D.S.S./Forms/C. 2118

Army Form C. 2118.

WAR DIARY
or
INTELLIGENCE SUMMARY.
(Erase heading not required.)

4th Bn. "The King's" (Liverpool Regt)

Instructions regarding War Diaries and Intelligence Summaries are contained in F.S. Regs., Part II. and the Staff Manual respectively. Title pages will be prepared in manuscript.

Place	Date	Hour	Summary of Events and Information	Remarks and references to Appendices
LOCON S.14 Central	22.1.16		In billets & trenches. Fine day. Enemy rather more active & our retaliation in our necessity accordingly. One man to hospital. W.25239 Pte Wardle C E MAISM W accidentally wounded. Died in 23rd unit.	
Do	23.1.16		Do. Most of night, fine day. Aircraft active, both ours & enemys. In our vicinity during day C & D Coys were relieved from trenches by 13th R Welsh Fusiliers – 113th Brigade 38th Division – on having Bn. H.Q. at Locon on completion of relief.	Copy of letter re satisfactory work of troops in the trenches attached 4.22.1.16.
LOCON	24.1.16		In billets. Dull day. Some showers.	
Do	25.1.16		Do. Fine cold day. Battalion moved to billets at LA PANNERIE (Q.28.d – Q.34.b.c – W.4.a.) 2 men to hospital.	
LA PANNERIE	26.1.16		Do. Fine day. Lecture by G.O.C. XIth Corps to all officers of XIX Division at ST VENANT. 1 man from hospital.	
Do	27.1.16		Do. Dull day. 2 men from hospital.	
Do	28.1.16		Do. Dull day. One man from hospital. 2 men to hospital.	
Do	29.1.16		Do. Dull day. One man to England for discharge. 2nd Lieut H.T. JENKINS wounded, struck by shrapnel of bullet.	
Do	30.1.16		Do. Fine cold day. Pte 7959	
Do	31.1.16		Do. Fine cold day. The Battalion moved to new billets at LE SART (West of MERVILLE) arriving in 58th Brigade area. Lieut P.A.F. MASON & 2 Serjts went to Divisional School of Instruction. 2 men went to 1st Army Anti-Gas School.	

J.W. Allen Lt Colonel
Commanding 4th Bn "The King's"
(Liverpool Regt)

2-2-16

19th Division No. G.a. 906

Officer Commanding
4th Bn. The King's (L'pool Regt)

The Divisional Commander wishes me to say that he visited the front line trenches held by one of your Companies on the 19th instant and was much struck by the good organization of the defence, as also by the alertness of all ranks.

H.Q. 19th Division (sd) R.W. Johnson Lt Col G.S.
22nd Jan'y 1916.   19th Division

Certified True Copy –

R C A Innes Major
Adjt 4 / The King's

24-1-16.

Army Form B. 213.

FIELD RETURN.

No. of Report 144 Diary

(To be furnished by all arms, services, and departments (except A.S.C. units) to the A. G.'s Office at the Base in accordance with Field Service Regulations, Part II.)

RETURN showing numbers RATIONED by, and Transport on charge of, 144 Bty the King's at On the field 14 January 1916 Date.

Detail	Personnel			Animals							Guns, carriages, and limbers and transport vehicles			Horsed		Mechanical					Remarks
	Officers	Other ranks	Natives	Horses			Mules		Camels	Oxen	Guns, carriages, limbers, showing description	Ammunition wagons and limbers	Machine guns	Aircraft, showing description	4 Wheeled	2 Wheeled	Motor Cars	Tractors	Lorries, showing description	Trucks, showing description	Trailers	Motor Bicycles	Bicycles	
				Riding	Draught	Heavy Draught	Pack	Large	Small															
Effective Strength of Unit	29	941		14	12	23		30					4		19	5								Air Expedition: Officers 2, Base Depot 3, Leave 2, Sick 1, Attd N.3 T bay 1, M.G. Section 11
Details, by Arms attached to unit as in War Establishment:—																									Other Ranks 11, Corps Employ 10, Sick 4
RAMC 1																									
Army Ordnance Corps 1																									
Total	30	942		14	12	23		30					4		19	5								Personnel — Attd R.E. 1, R.F.C. 703, On Command 15, Leave 13, Field Ambulance 13, 3rd Echelon 1, Horses 1 to his 25, M.G. bay 58 — 256
War Establishment	30	995		14	12	23		30					4		19	5								
Wanting to complete	—	53																							
Surplus																									
*Attached (not to include the details shown above)																									
Civilians:— Employed with the Unit																									With M.T. sect.
Accompanying the Unit																									Animals Rein Horses 1, 2 Draughts 8, Heavy 4
Total Rationed	19	686		113	141	185		36																	Saddles 5

* In the case of field ambulances, hospitals or depots the number of patients are to be included here, the names being shown in A. F. A. 36.

W. Jones Major ?? Col. Signature of Commander.
7th January 1916. Date of Despatch.

For information of the A.G.'s Office at the Base.

Officers and men who have become casuals, been transferred or joined since last report.

Place **In the Field**   Date **7th January 1916**

Regtl. Number	Rank	Name	Corps	Nature of casualty, or name of unit from or to which transferred	Date of being struck off or coming on the ration return	Remarks*
12653	Pte	Eckersley E		From Hospl	1-1-16	
8856	-"-	Oliver J		-"-	3-1-16	
9223	-"-	Gavin		-"-	-"-	
12717	L/Cpl	Baines L		-"-	4-1-16	
11726	-"-	Geary W		-"-	5-1-16	
5172	Pte	Waugh G		To Hospl	31-12-15	
11251	-"-	Morris		-"-	-"-	
11381	-"-	Nicholson J		-"-	29-12-15	
8748	-"-	Winn W		-"-	-"-	
11677	-"-	Ready E		-"-	-"-	
8139	-"-	Hill		-"-	-"-	
9932	-"-	Clegg W		-"-	5-1-16	
9457	-"-	Walters A		-"-	-"-	
25119	Cpl	Bushell J		-"-	-"-	
6936	Sgt	Burton J		-"-	-"-	
8193	Pte	Stokes A		-"-	-"-	
27534	-"-	Doyle J		-"-	-"-	
26971	-"-	Dinkerley J		-"-	-"-	
9093	-"-	Brown		-"-	-"-	
25493	-"-	Ernst R		Killed in Action	2-1-16	
15402	-"-	Hamilton W		Died of Wounds	3-1-16	
11726	L/Cpl	Geary W		Wounded in Action	2-1-16	
9117	Pte	Roberts		-"-	-"-	
10675	-"-	Fogarty		-"-	-"-	
12643	-"-	Garrett		-"-	-"-	
26463	-"-	Carless J		To Base	13-12-15	
9434	-"-	Brown W		for discharge	31-12-15	
7076	L/Cpl	Cunningham J			3-1-16	
	Lieut	Fishenden A.J.		To F. Ambulance	30-12-15	
30409	Pte	Penn J		To Hospital	4-1-16	
8106	-"-	Wilcox		-"-	5-1-16	
9250	-"-	McNamara P		-"-	-"-	
29534	-"-	Howarth		-"-	-"-	
26491	-"-	Adcock J		-"-	6-1-16	
9079	Cpl	Stinchcomb F		-"-	-"-	
9204	Pte	Carr W		Declared a Deserter	1-1-16	
9308	-"-	Tapp G		Found Drowned	6-1-16	
13583	-"-	Hopkin L		To England	24-12-15	

Corps column (bracketed): 4th Bn The King's (L'pool Regt)

RCH Ines
Major for Lt Colonel.
Com'd'g 4th Bn The King's (L'pool Regt)

* State whether absence is of a permanent or temporary nature, adding, in the case of casuals from wounds or disease, any available information for communication to the relatives.

Perforated Sheet giving detail of personnel and horses wanting to complete, shown on Army Form B. 213.

Number of Report ____

Detail of Wanting to Complete	Drivers					Gunners	Smith Gunners	Range Takers	Farriers			Shoeing, or Shoeing and Carriage Smiths	Cold Shoers	Wheelers			Saddlers or Harness Makers	Blacksmiths	Bricklayers and Masons	Carpenters and Joiners	Fitters & Turners (H.E.)		Fitters			Plumbers	Electricians		Signalmen	Engine Drivers		Air Line Men	Permanent Line Men	Operators, Telegraph	Cablemen	Brigade Section Pioneers	General-duty Pioneers	Signallers	Instrument Repairers	Motor Cyclists	Motor Cyclist Artificers	Telephonists	Clerks	Machine Gunners	Armament Artificers			Storemen	Privates	W.Os. and N.C.Os. (by ranks) not included in trade columns		TOTAL to agree with wanting to complete		Horses				
	R.A.	R.E.	A.S.C.	Car	Lorry	Steam				Sergeants	Corporals			P.A.	H.T.	M.T.					Wood	Iron	R.A.	Wireless			Ordinary	W.T.		Loco.	Field														Fitters	Range Finders	Armourers				Officers	Other Ranks		Riding	Draught	Heavy Draught	Pack
CAVALRY																																																				43				
R.A.																																																							
R.E.																																																							
INFANTRY																																																				6 48	Lewisgun privates				
R.A.M.C.																																																							
A.O.C.																																																							
A.V.C.																																																							

Remarks:—

Signature of Commander. McIlnes Major for Lt Col
4th Bn The Kings (L'pool Regt.) Unit.
XI Corps Formation to which attached.
9th January 1916 Date of Despatch.

[P.T.O.]

No. of Report 45   Army Form B. 213.

FIELD RETURN.

(To be furnished by all arms, services, and departments (except A.S.C. units) to the A. G.'s Office at the Base in accordance with Field Service Regulations, Part II.)

RETURN showing numbers RATIONED by, and Transport on charge of, 4th Bn The King's (Xi'port Regt) at In the field   Date 14th January 1916

Diary

DETAIL	Personnel			Animals — Horses				Mules		Camels	Oxen	Guns, carriages, limbers, showing description	Ammunition wagons and limbers	Machine guns	Aircraft, showing description	Horsed 4-Wheeled	Horsed 2-Wheeled	Motor Cars	Tractors	Mechanical Lorries, showing description	Mechanical Trucks, showing description	Trailers	Motor Bicycles	Bicycles	REMARKS
	Officers	Other ranks	Natives	Riding	Draught	Heavy Draught	Pack	Large	Small																
Effective Strength of Unit	28,976			14	12	23		30						4			19	5								New Commander Officers Base Report 1 Leave 5 Sick 2 Attd 173 T Bn 1 M.G. Section 2 Stretcher bearers 11 Corps Employ 11 Div 10 Attd R.E's 100 R.F.C. 4 By Command 21 Leave 19 Field Ambulance 19 3rd Echelon 2 Wesley X.P.M. 68 N.G. toy 90 Animals 261 Sick New 6
Details, by Arms attached to unit as in War Establishment:—																										
R.A.M.C.	1																									
Army Ordnance Corps		1																								
Total	28,977			14	12	23		30						4			19	5								
War Establishment	30	995		14	12	23		30						4			19	5								
Wanting to complete	1	18																								
Surplus																										
*Attached (not to include the details shown above)																										Riding Horse 1 H.D. — 1 M.G. boy — 8
Civilians:— Employed with the Unit Accompanying the Unit																										
TOTAL RATIONED	18	710		13	14	15		26																		Mules 4

* In the case of field ambulances, hospitals or depots, the number of patients are to be included here, the names being shown in A. F. A. 36.

× Two Officers/Captn Rea and Lieut Hutchings on sick leave in England, included, not yet struck off Batt strength

N C Young Major & Lt Col   Signature of Commander.

14th January 1916 Date of Despatch.

For information of the A.G.'s Office at the Base.

Officers and men who have become casuals, been transferred or joined since last report.

Place **In the Field**   Date **14th January 1916**

Regtl. Number	Rank	Name	Corps	Nature of casualty, or name of unit from or to which transferred	Date of being struck off or coming on the ration return	Remarks*
9228	Pte	Strong J.	4th Bn The King's (Liverpool Regt)	From Hosptl	7-1-16	
14285	-"-	Harris		-"-	8-1-16	
11306	Cpl	Hayes J.J.		-"-	9-1-16	
13573	Pte	Wright S.		-"-	-"-	
13215	Cpl	Grace J.		-"-	12-1-16	
27834	Pte	Doyle J.		-"-	-"-	
11237	Cpl	Owens J.		To Hospital	8-1-16	
11559	Pte	Hamilton J.		-"-	9-1-16	
4228	Sgt	Cairns W.		-"-	10-1-16	
9226	Pte	Rogers W.		Wounded in A.	7-1-16	
10236	-"-	Evans D.		-"-	9-1-16	
	Lieut	Jenkins A.J.		To England	8-1-16	
11677	Pte	Ready		From Hosptl	13-1-16	
29913	-"-	Winstanley D		To Hosptl	-"-	
13680	-"-	Lampkin		-"-	-"-	
8891	Sgt	Devling W.H.		Reinforcements from No 8 Infantry Base Depot.	14-1-16	
8951	Cpl	Butler G				
14956	-"-	Slack W.				
29369	-"-	Smith C.				
27127	S/Sgt	Appleby J.A.				
10609	Pte	McNally J.				
27409	-"-	Rochester W.				
27205	-"-	Malone W.				
29021	-"-	Miller A.				
11439	-"-	Lewis J.				
29978	-"-	Cowan J.				
29991	-"-	Mitchell A.				
29360	-"-	Lawley G.				

* State whether absence is of a permanent or temporary nature, adding, in the case of casuals from wounds or disease, any available information for communication to the relatives.

For information of the A.G.'s Office at the Base.

Officers and men who have become casuals, been transferred or joined since last report.

Place __In the Field__   Date __14th January 1916__

Regtl. Number	Rank	Name	Corps	Nature of casualty, or name of unit from or to which transferred	Date of being struck off or coming on the ration return	Remarks*
25878	Pte	Warren G				
30066	-"-	Eaves W				
27288	-"-	Wellman G				
30852	-"-	Jones J				
27236	-"-	Aspden J R				
26479	-"-	Eadie H				
29867	-"-	Miller J				
27888	-"-	Johnson B	The King's (L'pool Regt)	Reinforcements from No 8 Infantry Base Depot	14-1-16	
29010	-"-	Rush W				
29032	-"-	Garlington W				
20056	-"-	Taylor W				
29088	-"-	Conner J				
29094	-"-	Ockleshaw W				
29362	-"-	Baldwin H				
29878	-"-	Beattie E				
30007	-"-	Simcock R				
30457	-"-	Tabern J				
30583	-"-	Organ H				
30666	-"-	Kenrick J W				
31233	-"-	Cruikshank J				
31285	-"-	Newell J				
30308	-"-	Draper J				

RCA Jones
Major for Lieut Colonel
Comdg 4th Bn. The King's (Liverpool Regt)

* State whether absence is of a permanent or temporary nature, adding, in the case of casuals from wounds or disease, any available information for communication to the relatives.

Army Form B. 213.

FIELD RETURN.

No. of Report _____   Date _____

(To be furnished by all arms, services, and departments to the A.G.'s Office at the Base in accordance with Field Service Regulations, Part II.)

RETURN showing numbers RATIONED by, and Transport on charge of, _____ at _____

DETAIL.	Personnel			Animals								Guns, carriages, and limbers and transport vehicles				Horsed		Motor Cars	Tractors	Mechanical		Trailers	Motor Bicycles	Bicycles	REMARKS.
	Officers	Other ranks	Natives	Horses			Mules		Camels	Oxen		Guns, carriages and limbers, showing description	Ammunition wagons and limbers	Machine guns	Aircraft, showing description	4 Wheeled	2 Wheeled			Lorries, showing description	Trucks, showing description				
				Riding	Draught	Heavy Draught	Pack	Large	Small																
Effective Strength of Unit Details, by *Arms* attached to unit as in War Establishment:—																									
Total																									
War Establishment																									
Wanting to complete																									
Surplus																									
* Attached (not to include the details shown above)																									
Civilians :— Employed with the Unit Accompanying the Unit																									
TOTAL RATIONED ...																									

* In the case of field ambulances, hospitals or depots, the number of patients are to be included here, the names being shown in A. F. A. 36.

Wt.W. 6005-864 (33047) U. B. Ltd. 500,000 10/14   Forms B. 213/b

_____ Signature of Commander.

_____ Date of Despatch.

Perforated Sheet giving detail of personnel and horses wanting to complete, shown on Army Form B. 213.

Number of Report 45

Detail of Wanting to Complete			R.A.	A.S.C.	Car	Lorry	Steam	Gunners	Smith Gunners	Range Takers	Farriers – Serjeants	Corporals	Shoeing, or Shoeing and Carriage Smiths	Cold Shoers	Wheelers R.A.	H.T.	M.T.	Saddlers or Harness Makers	Blacksmiths	Bricklayers and Masons	Carpenters and Joiners	Fitters & Turners (R.E.) Wood	Iron	Fitters R.A.	Wireless	Plumbers	Electricians Ordinary	W.T.	Signalmen	Engine Drivers Loco.	Field	Air Line Men	Permanent Line Men	Operators, Telegraph	Cablemen	Brigade Section Pioneers	General-duty Pioneers	Signallers	Instrument Repairers	Motor Cyclists	Motor Cyclist Artificers	Telephonists	Clerks	Machine Gunners	Armament Artificers Fitters	Range Finders	Armourers	Storemen	Privates	W.O's. and N.C.O's. (by ranks) not included in trade columns	TOTAL, to agree with wanting to complete Officers	Other Ranks	Horses Riding	Draught	Heavy Draught	Pack
CAVALRY																																																								
R.A.																																																								
R.E.																																																								
INFANTRY																																																			513 Ammunition Privates		1	18				
R.A.M.C.																																																								
A.O.C.																																																								
A.V.C.																																																								

Remarks:—

Signature of Commander. Rev Jones Major to Lt Col

Unit. 4th Bn The King's (L'pool Regt)

Formation to which attached. XI Corps

Date of Despatch. 14th January 1916

(82434.) Wt. 4394/2217. 500,000. 6/15. B.M.&S. Forms/B. 213/6.

[P.T.O.

No. of Report 46

FIELD RETURN.

Army Form B. 213.

(To be furnished by all arms, services, and departments (except A.S.C. units) to the A. G.'s Office at the Base in accordance with Field Service Regulations, Part II.)

RETURN showing numbers RATIONED by, and Transport on charge of, H.Q. 1st Bn The King's (L'pool Regt) at In the Field 21st January 1916 Date.

DETAIL	Personnel			Animals								Guns, carriages, and limbers and transport vehicles										REMARKS
	Officers	Other ranks	Natives	Horses Riding	Horses Draught	Horses Heavy Draught	Pack	Mules Large	Mules Small	Camels	Oxen	Guns, carriages and limbers, showing description	Ammunition wagons and limbers	Machine guns	Aircraft, showing description	Horsed 4 Wheeled	Horsed 2 Wheeled	Motor Cars	Tractors	Lorries, Mechanical showing description	Trucks, Mechanical showing description	Trailers	Motor Bicycles	Bicycles	
Effective Strength of Unit	29	969		14	12	23		30						4			5								Officers On Command 1 Base Depôt Leave 3 Sick Leave 2 Sick 1 Attd 13rd T boy 2 N.Y Section ― 10 Other Ranks On Command 4 Corps Employ 6 Sick 13 Bde ― 9 Attd 13rd T boy Rta 101 Attd R F C 1 Leave 16 Field Ambulance 11 Under X P Ms 23 3rd Echelon 1 M.G. Coy 61 Rest Station 4 250
Details, by Arms attached to unit as, in War Establishment:— R.A.M.C. Army Ordnance Corps	1 1	1																							
Total	30	970		14	12	23		30						4			19	5								
War Establishment	30	995		14	12	23		30						4			19	5								
Wanting to complete	1	25						1																		
Surplus (Detail of Personnel and Horses below)																										
*Attached (not to include the details shown above)																										
Civilians:— Employed with the Unit Accompanying the Unit																										
TOTAL RATIONED ...	20	920		13	4	15		26																		Females With Avid Serv 1 HDs 8 Rates 4 Mules 1

NCN Ones

* In the case of field ambulances, hospitals or depots, the number of patients are to be included here, the names being shown in A.F.A. 36.

Major Superintendent Col Signature of Commander.

21st January 1916 Date of Despatch.

For information of the A.G.'s Office at the Base.

Officers and men who have become casuals, been transferred or joined since last report.

Place In the Field   Date 21st January 1916

Regti. Number	Rank	Name	Corps	Nature of casualty, or name of unit from or to which transferred	Date of being struck off or coming on the ration return	Remarks*
11251	Pte	Morris J.	4th Bn The King's (L'pool Regt)	From Hospital	15-1-16	
30409	-"-	Penn J.		-"-	-"-	
14536 (17143)	-"-	O'Neill J.		-"-	16-1-16	
8106	-"-	Wilson G.		-"-	18-1-16	
9207	-"-	Carr W.		From Deserter	-"-	
31709	-"-	Dooley J.		To Hospital	14-1-16	
10720	-"-	Cosgrove V.		-"-	-"-	
14288	Sgt	Leaver J.		-"-	12-1-16	
11639	Cpl	Lister J.		-"-	-"-	
11574	-"-	Williamson E.		-"-	14-1-16	
25095	Pte	Lewin A.J.		-"-	-"-	
10787	-"-	Greensmith J.W.		-"-	16-1-16	
26297	-"-	Lyons H.		-"-	-"-	
8179	-"-	May J.J.		To Base for Discharge	20-1-16	
11677	-"-	Ready E.		Wounded in Action	15-1-16	
6287	Cpl	Wilson W.		-"-	17-1-16	
26964	Pte	Cunningham H.		-"-	19-1-16	
	T/2 Lieut	Lawrence J.W.		Transferred from 19th Bn The King's (L'pool Regt)	19-1-16	

R C M Ince
Major for Lieut Colonel
Comdg 4th Bn The King's (L'pool Regt)

*State whether absence is of a permanent or temporary nature, adding, in the case of casuals from wounds or disease, any available information for communication to the relatives.

Perforated Sheet giving detail of personnel and horses wanting to complete, shown on Army Form B. 213.

Number of Report __46__

Detail of Wanting to Complete	Drivers					Gunners	Smith Gunners	Range Takers	Farriers		Shoeing or Shoeing and Carriage Smiths	Cold Shoers	Wheelers			Saddlers or Harness Makers	Blacksmiths	Bricklayers and Masons	Carpenters and Joiners	Fitters & Turners (R. E.)		Fitters			Plumbers	Electricians		Signalmen	Engine Drivers		Air Line Men	Permanent Line Men	Operators, Telegraph	Cablemen	Brigade Section Pioneers	General-duty Pioneers	Signallers	Instrument Repairers	Motor Cyclists	Motor Cyclist Artificers	Telephonists	Clerks	Machine Gunners	Armament Artificers		Armourers	Storemen	Privates	W.O.'s and N.C.O.'s (by rank) not included in trade columns	TOTAL wanting to complete with to agree		Horses			
	R. A.	R. E.	A. S. C.	Cat	Lorry	Steam				Sergeants	Corporals			R. A.	H. T.	M. T.					Wood	Iron	R. A.	Wireless			Ordinary	W. T.			Loco.	Field													Fitters	Range Finders					Officers	Other Ranks	Riding	Draught	Heavy Draught	Pack
CAVALRY																																																						
R.A.																																												*signature*										
R.E.																																																					
INFANTRY																																													5 20						25			
R.A.M.C.																																																					
A.O.C.																																																					
A.V.C.																																																					

Remarks:—

Signature of Commander. Major for Lieut Col

4th By The King's (L'pool Regt) Unit.

XI th Corps Formation to which attached.

21st January 1916 Date of Despatch.

For information of the A.G.'s Office at the Base.

Officers and men who have become casuals, been transferred or joined since last report.

Place **In the Field** Date **28th January 1916.**

Regti. Number	Rank	Name	Corps	Nature of casualty, or name of unit from or to which transferred	Date of being struck off or coming on the ration return	Remarks*
25076	Cpl	Middleton R.	} 4th Bn The King's (Liverpool Regt)	} Reinforcements from No 8. Infantry Base Depot.	} 22-1-16	
18041	L Cpl	Teare J.				
28031	Pte	Eadron A.H.				
31288	-"-	Gaughran J.				
31287	-"-	Harley R.				
30051	-"-	McDermott A.				
27268	-"-	Dunn J.				
27175	-"-	Follett G.				
30899	-"-	Bowden G.				
27898	-"-	Lawler J.				
30567	-"-	Battersby J.				
11281	-"-	Williams E.				
30505	-"-	Moore A.				
27759	-"-	Bale A.				
24223	-"-	Sherrington J.				
26350	-"-	Scott J.				
27862	-"-	Brasier A.				
24424	-"-	McGowan W.				
27752	-"-	Mullen W.				
24445	-"-	Watmough R.G.				
26266	-"-	Hayes G.				
26305	-"-	Moss J.				
27860	-"-	Broderick J.				
27892	-"-	Robinson J.				
26723	-"-	McCardle J.H.				
14288	Sgt	Leaver J.H.		From Hospital	26-1-16	
4228	-"-	Cairns W.		-"-	27-1-16	
11369	Cpl	Lister G.		To Hospital	22-1-16	
8402	Pte	Rommer N.		-"-	25-1-16	
10492	-"-	Horan N.		-"-	"	
10084	-"-	Costello G.		Wounded	22-1-16	Accidental
25239	-"-	Comaish W.		Missing	21-1-16	Believed Killed
8870	Lieut	Simmonds				
		Hutchings K.L.		To England. Sick.	28-1-16	

R C N Jones
Major for Lieut Colonel.

Comdg 4th Bn The King's (Liverpool Regt.)

* State whether absence is of a permanent or temporary nature, adding, in the case of casuals from wounds or disease, any available information for communication to the relatives.

Army Form B. 213.

FIELD RETURN.

No. of Report __4.7__

(To be furnished by all arms, services, and departments (except A.S.C. units) to the A. G.'s Office at the Base in accordance with Field Service Regulations, Part II.)

RETURN showing numbers RATIONED by, and Transport on charge of, _H.Q. 1st The King's (Liverpool Regt.) of_ at _In the Field_ __28th January 1916__ Date.

DETAIL	Personnel			Animals							Guns, carriages, and limbers and transport vehicles			Horsed		Mechanical					REMARKS
	Officers	Other ranks	Natives	Horses Riding	Horses Draught	Horses Heavy Draught	Pack	Mules Large	Mules Small	Camels	Oxen	Guns, carriages and Limbers, showing description	Ammunition wagons and limbers	Machine Guns	Aircraft, showing description	4 Wheeled	2 Wheeled	Motor Cars	Tractors	Lorries, showing description	Trucks, showing description	Trailers	Motor Bicycles	Bicycles	
Effective Strength of Unit	28	992		14	12	23		30						4		19	5							9	On Command Officers 1 Base Depot 2 Sick 1 Attd R to 2 M' Gun Coy 2 Sick leave to England 8 Other Ranks Corps Employ 9 Sick 14 Ride 4 Attd R.E's 105 " R.F.C. 1 Command 7 Under A.P.M. 26 Field Ambulance 13 3rd Echelon 1 Corps Rest Sta. 1 M'Gun Coy 59 Leave 4 244
Details, by Arms attached to unit, as in War Establishment:—																										
R.A.M.C.	1																									
Army Ordnance Corps.		1																								
Total	29	993		14	12	23		30						4		19	5							9	
War Establishment	30	995		14	12	23		30						4		19	5							9	
Wanting to complete	1	2																							
Surplus																									
*Attached (not to include the details shown above)																									Animals With M.G. Coy Riding Horses 3 H.D. " 4 Mules 8
Civilians:— Employed with the Unit Accompanying the Unit																									
TOTAL RATIONED	21	149		13	4	15		26																	

* In the case of field ambulances, hospitals or depots, the number of patients are to be included here, the names being shown in A. F. A. 36.

Ken Jones Signature of Commander. Major for Lieut Col

__28th January 1916__ Date of Despatch.

Perforated Sheet giving detail of personnel and horses wanting to complete, shown on Army Form B. 213.

Number of Report 47

Detail of Wanting to Complete	Drivers					Gunners	Smith Gunners	Range Takers	Farriers			Wheelers			Saddlers or Harness Makers	Blacksmiths	Bricklayers and Masons	Carpenters and Joiners	Fitters & Turners (R. E.)		Fitters			Plumbers	Electricians		Signalmen	Engine Drivers			Air Line Men	Permanent Line Men	Operators, Telegraph	Cablemen	Brigade Section Pioneers	General-duty Pioneers	Signallers	Instrument Repairers	Motor Cyclists	Motor Cyclist Artificers	Telephonists	Clerks	Machine Gunners	Armament Artificers				Privates	W.O's. and N.C.O's. (by ranks) not included in trade columns	TOTAL, to agree with wanting to complete		Horses			
	R.A.	A.S.C.	Car	Lorry	Steam				Sergeants	Corporals	Shoeing, or Carriage Smiths	Cold Shoers	R.A.	H.T.	M.T.					Wood	Iron	R.A.	Wireless		Ordinary	W.T.		Loco.	Field														Fitters	Range Finders	Armourers	Storemen			Officers	Other Ranks	Riding	Draught	Heavy Draught	Pack
CAVALRY																																																						
R.A.																																																					
R.E.																																																					
INFANTRY																																																	Surplus	5		×5				
R.A.M.C.																																																					
A.O.C.																																																					
A.V.C.																																																					

Remarks:— × Three Privates Surplus.

Nil Return Signature of Commander. Appendicent &c
4th Bn the King's (Liverpool Regt) Unit.
XIth Corps. Formation to which attached.
28th January 1916. Date of Despatch.

WAR DIARY or INTELLIGENCE SUMMARY

Army Form C. 2118.

Vol XII

February 1916.

4th Br "The King's" (Liverpool Regt)

Place	Date	Hour	Summary of Events and Information	Remarks and references to Appendices
LE SART (nr MERVILLE)	1-2-16		In Billets. Fine day. Company Training.	
	2-2-16		In Billets. Fine cold day. Training & Musketry on Rifle Range. One man to hospital.	
D°	3.2.16		D° Very windy. Some men at work. Company Training. One man to Base for discharge.	
D°	4-2-16		D° Dull & windy, rain at night. Company Training – Lecture by O.C. 55th Airports at 9th West Regt Instrl' School.	
D°	5-2-16		Fine day. 2nd Lieut H.A. TRIPP rejoined from hospital & home. Company Training.	
D°	6.2.16.		Fine day. Wet evening. C.O. went to Divisional Conference afternoon – Church Parade. One man evacuated (attached 2/2/5 Lowland Fd R.E.)	
D°	7.2.16		Windy & showery. Afternoon & Specialist Officers went to a Bomb attack demonstration by 3rd Canadian Infantry Brigade. Reg't Concert evening – one man to hospital	
D°	8-2-16		Showery day. Wet evening. (Training continued).	
D°	9.2.16		Fine cold day. Training. One man to hospital.	
D°	10.2.16		Fine day. Training as usual	
D°	11.2.16		Very wet all day. Lecture by O.C. 55th Division to all Officers morning. Brigade were inspected by Field Marshal Lord KITCHENER at 3 pm. One man to hospital	Officer attached.
D°	12.2.16		Fine dull day. Training carried on. One man to Base for duty.	
D°	13-2-16		Dull day. Some rain. Captain J.E. ROSS. Lieutenant J.S. HUTCHINGS & 2 Lieut J.H. LOMAS joined from England. A & B Companies (fewer) to LAVENTIE for attachment to 2555 C° R.E. for duty. Trenchdigs. One man to hospital. One man from hospital.	

Army Form C. 2118.

WAR DIARY
or
INTELLIGENCE SUMMARY.
4 Bn. "The King's" (Liverpool Regt.)

February 1916.

(Erase heading not required.)

Instructions regarding War Diaries and Intelligence Summaries are contained in F.S. Regs., Part II. and the Staff Manual respectively. Title pages will be prepared in manuscript.

Place	Date	Hour	Summary of Events and Information	Remarks and references to Appendices
Billets LE PART	14.2.16		In billets. 2 Coys at LAVENTIE. Machine Gun Detachment rejoined from Brigade Machine Gun Company. Usual parades & "Training". One man to hospital.	
LAVENTIE	15.2.16		In billets. 2 Coys at LAVENTIE. 30 NCOs & men of C. Coy joined Detachment with Trenchdigging Company. Fine day. Wet evening. Parades & Training carried on. One man to hospital. One man to base for discharge. One man to Hospital in England.	
Do	16.2.16		In billets at LAVENTIE. Head Quarters & C & D Coys with A & B Sections moved to billets near LA GASSEE Road LE DRUMEZ & took over billets from A/13x Brigade. M.G. Section rejoined M.G. Company with Superintent.	
LE DRUMEZ	17.2.16		In reserve billets. Detachment with Trenchdigging Coy remained in Pots. Fine day & windy. On man wounded. In Brigade Reserve.	
Do	18.2.16		Am 17. Very wet day. Windy. One man to hospital.	
Do	19.2.16		In Brigade Reserve. Cloudy. Some rain. About 11pm. Hostile aeroplane dropped 2 bombs near Battn. H.Q. one failed to explode. No damage done. Shot at. might 2 men to hospital 3 men wounded.	
Do	20.2.16		In Brigade Reserve. Cloudy but fine. One man killed (No.9698 Private P. Summerskill.) 10 men joined from base.	
Do	21.2.16		In Brigade Reserve. Col's & fine. Orders received that Battn. would join 33rd Division a 25th inst. Heavy bombardment South for day. Hostile aeroplane active.	
Do	22.2.16		Very cold. Snow all morning. In Brigade Reserve. C.O. visited 33rd Division. 2 men to hospital.	
Do	23.2.16		In Brigade Reserve. Snow. C & D Coys & Trs.H.Q. 3 Officers of Pots released by 10th R. Warwicks Rgt & 9th Cheshire B Coy rejoined from Trenchdigging Coy R.E.	
Do	24.2.16		The Battalion moved to CROIX MARMEUSE. Cols & Trs.H.Q. A Coy rejoined from Trenchdigging Coy R.E. also part of D Coy men under 2. GAULTER from 253rd Coy R.E. M.G. dns. of gun Section rejoined Battn. 2 Pots & Officers relieved by 8th Worts Staffors Rgt. Col & Trs.H.Q. & Batt transferred to 98th Brigade 33rd Division. 8 men rejoined from Corps Employment.	※ Special orders attached.
CROIX MARMEUSE	25.2.16			
Do	26.2.16		The Battn. moved to BETHUNE & billeted. Col with shows a ground. Very heavy frost for transport & slippery.	

1577 Wt. W10791/1773 50,000 1/15 D. D. & L. A.D.S.S./Forms/C. 2118.

Army Form C. 2118.

WAR DIARY
or
INTELLIGENCE SUMMARY. 4th Bn "The King's" (Liverpool Regt) February 1916

(Erase heading not required.)

Place	Date	Hour	Summary of Events and Information	Remarks and references to Appendices
BETHUNE	27.2.16		In billets. Very cold. Batt. marched to ANNEQUIN SOUTH wh reserve billets. C.O. Adjutant & Commanders of Coys visited trenches.	
ANNEQUIN SOUTH	28.2.16		In reserve billets. The Batt. moved into trenches (near CAMBRIN) & 2 Sector. in relief of 19th Batt Royal Fusiliers. Hostile aeroplane over our billets during morning. Wet + muddy.	
Trenches 2.1 Sector	29.2.16		Snow + cold. In trenches. one man wounded. 4 men joined from base. Working parties under R.E. employed daily, about 100 men, from 19h to 22h & on 29/02/29. X 19th Batt R. Fus.	

J.W. McRea Lt Colonel
Comnd'g 4th Bn "The King's"
(Liverpool Regt)

SPECIAL ORDER OF THE DAY.
by
Major-General G.T.M. Bridges, C.M.G., D.S.O., Commanding 19th Division.

15/2/16.

On the occasion of the 4th Battalion King's (Liverpool) Regiment leaving the Division, the Major-General Commanding requests the Officer Commanding the battalion to convey to all ranks his appreciation of the fine discipline and soldierly spirit displayed by Officers, N.C.O's and men of the Battalion during the time they have been with the 19th Division, and to wish them good luck on his behalf.

P.M. Davies, Lieut-Colonel,
A.A. & Q.M.G., 19th Division.

98th Brigade

33rd Division.

4th BATTALION THE KING'S LIVERPOOL REGIMENT

MARCH 1 9 1 6.

Volume XIII.

Army Form C. 2118.

WAR DIARY
or
INTELLIGENCE SUMMARY. 4 Bn. "The King's" (Liverpool Regt.)

MARCH 1916.

(Erase heading not required.)

Instructions regarding War Diaries and Intelligence Summaries are contained in F. S. Regs., Part II. and the Staff Manual respectively. Title pages will be prepared in manuscript.

Place	Date	Hour	Summary of Events and Information	Remarks and references to Appendices
Trenches 2.1. Sector (AUCHY Area)	1.3.16		Cold & Windy. In trenches. One man killed (No 2825 Pte H. SWAIN.) Trenches in a bad state owing to bad weather. Transport & Details at BEUVRY.	
	2.3.16		Wet day. In trenches. 2 men wounded. Snow at night.	
	3.3.16		Wet day. Snow at times. In trenches. One man to hospital. 3 men wounded. One man killed. A draft of 23 NCOs & men joined from Base. (No 2932 Pte R. KINRADE)	
	4.3.16		Snow & rain. In trenches. Batt'n relieved in front line by 2nd Argyll & Sutherland Highlanders & went into reserve billets at ANNEQUIN SOUTH. One man to hospital. One man wounded. One man (mine eye) to base to discharge.	
ANNEQUIN S.	5.3.16		In reserve billets. Officers visited trenches in sector. Three later ways & men in R.E. A large number of men employed & working parties in front line. Snow at night. 5 men to hospital.	
Do	6.3.16		In reserve billets. Day working parties employed. One man to hospital. One man from hospital. One man from AUCHY SECTOR (2.0 Sub Sector) in relief of 1st 8th Middlesex Regt (1st Suffolk Regt went on our left & East Surrey Regt on our right) Threw at night. One man to hospital. No man from hospital. No man to "Permanent Base".	
Trenches 2.0 Sector (AUCHY AREA)	7.3.16		In trenches. Snow & sleet all day. Frost at night. One man to hospital. One man wounded.	
Do	8.3.16		Do. Cold & snowy. Frost at night. 3 men to hospital & 6 men wounded. 2 men killed. No 9240 Pte G. GRIFFITHS 8695 Sergt. M. VINCENT	
Do	9.3.16		Do. Cold day. Snow & frost at night. Battalion was relieved by 2nd Worcester Regt. & marched back to BETHUNE arriving about 2 AM. One man from hospital. 2 men to hospital.	
MONTMORENCY BARRACKS BETHUNE	10.3.16		In billets & Barracks. This to CO. The Battalion paraded for presentation of medals to some men of 2nd active trenches. Got 1st Bn ropes. A draft of 53 NCOs & men joined from base.	
	11.3.16		In billets & Barracks. CO's & showery Inspection by G.O.C. 98th Inf. Brigade. morning. C.O. & other Officers visited Reserve trenches afternoon. 2 Officers & 172 NCOs & men employed in working parties in front area. One man to hospital. One man "Permanent Base".	

WAR DIARY or INTELLIGENCE SUMMARY

Army Form C. 2118.

4th Bn "The Kings" (Liverpool Regt)

March 1916

Place	Date	Hour	Summary of Events and Information	Remarks and references to Appendices
MONTMORENCY BARRACKS BETHUNE	12.3.16		Fine day. Warmer. In Barracks & billets. G.O.C. 33rd Division saw all Officers. One man from hospital.	
Do	13.3.16		Fine hot day. 2 Barracks & billets. G.O.C. 98th Bnge inspected Officers drift afternoon. (Reorganisation evening of Officers & 286 men employed on working parties in front area. One man to hospital. 2 men from hospital.	
Do	14.3.16		Fine day. In Barracks & billets. G.O.C. 98th Brigade inspected Regtl Transport. Seven Officers & 373 other ranks employed on working parties in front area.	
Do	15.3.16		Fine day. In Barracks & billets. Two men to hospital. Two men "Permanent Base".	
Do	16.3.16		Dull but fine. Do. The Battalion moved to Windies – Left C & B section Cuinchy Section in relief of 2nd R.W.F. Fusiliers (19th Brigade) – Relief completed 7.40 p.m. One man to hospital. Two men "Permanent Base".	
Trenches CUINCHY SECTION (BRICKSTACKS)	17.3.16		In Trenches. Fine day. Lieut H.C. SODEN & Lieut F. GRAY went to course of Instruction at LEWIS GUN SCHOOL. One man to hospital. Two men wounded.	
Do	18.3.16		In Trenches. Fine day. One man from hospital. No. 10609 Pte J. McNALLY killed.	
Do	19.3.16		In Trenches. Fine day. One man wounded.	
Do	20.3.16		Do. 2nd Lieut D.H. PACK wounded.	
Do	21.3.16		Do. Showery. Battalion relieved in trenches by 2nd Bn Argyll & Sutherland Highlanders. Relief completed 10 p.m. The Battn moved to Reserve billets LE QUESNOY.	
LE QUESNOY BETHUNE MAP 1/20000 Square F.8.9.	22.3.16		In Reserve billets. Wet day. Captain J.E. ROSS to Hospital Sick. Lieut J.W. LAWRENCE to STOKES MORTAR course. One man to hospital. One man from hospital. 3 Officers & 283 men employed on working parties in front.	
Do	23.3.16		In reserve billets. Dull day. Lieut W.V.T. ROSSHAWE rejoined from Gunnery class. 2 Officers & 114 other ranks employed on working parties. Snow at night. Cold.	
Do	24.3.16		In Reserve billets. Cold & snow almost all day. 2 Officers 118 other ranks employed on working parties. One man to "Permanent Base". Lieut D.S. JONES R.A.M.C. from 101st Field Ambulance relieved Lieut A.R. MUNROE as Battn Medical Officer. Lieut E.G. Mather rejoined from Signal Course. R.A.M.C.	

Army Form C. 2118.

WAR DIARY
or
INTELLIGENCE SUMMARY. 4th Bn "The King's" (Liverpool Regt.)

(Erase heading not required.)

Instructions regarding War Diaries and Intelligence Summaries are contained in F. S. Regs., Part II. and the Staff Manual respectively. Title pages will be prepared in manuscript.

Month: March 1916.

Place	Date	Hour	Summary of Events and Information	Remarks and references to Appendices
LE QUESNOY	25.3.16		In reserve Billets. Showery day but bright. Captain R.G. DAVIES (15th Bn) and 2nd Lieut W.R. IRVING joined from Base. 166 NCOs & men employed in working parties in front line. One man to hospital, one man to base for dodgery.	Copy of Message re Raid attached.
Do	26.3.16		In reserve Billets. Wet & windy. Lieut W.C. SODEN & 2nd Lieut K. GRAY rejoined from leave from Germ. The Battalion moved to trenches CUINCHY SECTOR (Brickstacks) in relief of 2nd Argyll & Sutherland Highlanders. A raid was carried out on enemy trenches by a party under Lieut B. BECK & Lieut H.B. TRIPP. A gap was cut in enemy wire & the party entered his trenches targeting a German Officer. 2nd Lieut TRIPP injured (wounded at duty) & one man wounded - Sgt 3098 Pte J. FLANAGAN who died next day. One man to hospital.	
Trenches CUINCHY SECTION (Brickstacks)	27.3.16		In trenches. Wet day, very windy. BRICKSTACKS heavily shelled by hostile artillery. 3 men killed - (No 7605 Sergt G. R. ALLISTER, No 8201 Sergt F. FRASER and No 12087 Lcpl F.G. SPENCER.)	
Do	28.3.16		In trenches, fine but windy. Nothing unusual occurred. Two men to hospital.	
Do	29.3.16		In trenches. Fine day. Two Companies (A & D) were relieved in front line by 2 Companies 9/16th Rifle Brigade attached for instruction. Company Commanders & selected NCOs remained with them to give advice & instruct. Major R. BRIDGES 2nd in Command & Medical Officer were also attached to Bn Hd Qrs. B & D Companies moved into Brigade Reserve at ANNEQUIN N. whilst Bn remained until 31st providing working parties by day & night in front line - Nothing unusual happened. Three men to hospital.	
Do	30.3.16		In trenches. Fine day. 16th Rifle Brigade still in front line under instruction.	
Do	31.3.16		In trenches. Fine day. Relieved by 2nd Bn Argyll & Sutherland Highlanders in the trenches. Relief completed 9.15 p.m. 2 Coys 16th Rifle Brigade moved to ANNEQUIN N. The Battn moved to reserve billets LE QUESNOY. One man to hospital, two men wounded. 2nd Lieut J.H. LOMAS rejoined from DIVISIONAL SCHOOL. 2nd Lieut J.W. LAWRENCE rejoined from STOKES MORTAR CLASS.	

7-4-16 -

J.W. Allen
Lt. Colonel
Comnd 4th Bn "The King's"
(Liverpool Regt.)

The following message was received from the Brigade Commander on the 27th March 1916.

"G.O.C. wishes to express to you his keen admiration of the work of the raiding party last night under LIEUTS BECK and TRIPP aaa. The condition as to weather rendered the work very difficult and G.O.C. considers the wire cutting a particularly fine piece of work, and the party deserves very great credit for their coolness and determination aaa.
Please convey his congratulations to whole party on their work."

True copy
R.C.R. Jones - Major
Adjt 2th Bn The Kings Regt

Army Form B. 213.

FIELD RETURN.

N of Report. 52

Diary

(To be furnished by all arms, services, and departments (except A.S.C. units) to the A. G.'s Office at the Base in accordance with Field Service Regulations, Part II.)

RETURN showing numbers RATIONED by, and Transport on charge of, 4th Bn. Buffs (E.Kent Regt) at In the Field Date 2nd March 1916.

DETAIL	Personnel			Animals									Guns, carriages, and limbers and transport vehicles									REMARKS
	Officers	Other ranks	Natives	Horses Riding	Horses Draught	Horses Heavy Draught	Pack	Mules Large	Mules Small	Camels	Oxen	Guns, carriages and limbers, showing description	Ammunition wagons and limbers	Machine guns	Aircraft, showing description	Horsed 4 Wheeled	Horsed 2 Wheeled	Motor Cars	Tractors	Mechanical Lorries, showing description	Mechanical Trucks, showing description	Trailers	Motor Bicycles	Bicycles	
Effective Strength of Unit	29	1006		14	16	14	2	31						4		19	5							9	Not Rationed Officers Base Depot 1 Inst. of Instruction 1 Leave 22
Details, by Arms attached to unit as in War Establishment:— R.A.M.C. Army Ordnance Corps	1 1																								Other Ranks On Command 79
Total	30	1008		14	16	14	2	31						4		19	5							9	Base Employed 4
War Establishment	25	995		14	16	14	2	31						4		19	5							9	of Instruction 30
Wanting to complete (Detail of Personnel and Horses below)	5																								In Field Amb 1
																									Leave 29
Surplus		12																							Duty Employed 6
*Attached (not to include the details shown above)																									156
Civilians:— Employed with the Unit Accompanying the Unit																									Div'l train H.O. doms 8
TOTAL RATIONED	X 30	1090		14	16	9	2	31																	

* In the case of field ambulances, hospitals or depots, the number of patients are to be included here, the names being shown in A.F.A. 36.

N McGrath Major Signature of Commander.

2nd March 1916 Date of Despatch.

For information of the A.G.'s Office at the Base.

Officers and men who have become casuals, been transferred or joined since last report.

Place _In the Field_ Date _3rd March, 1916_

Regtl. Number	Rank	Name	Corps	Nature of casualty, or name of unit from or to which transferred	Date of being struck off or coming on the ration return	Remarks*
16963	Cpl	Roberts W		Wounded in A	29-2-16	
28385	Pte	Swain H		Killed in A	1-3-16	
18441		Holt R		Wounded	2-3-16	
26046/29362		Baldwin R		"	"	
8306		Johnson W			29-2-16	
10797		Georgenson A				
8601		Rimmer T				
8980	Cpl	Sanderson J				
X145	Sgt	Charlesworth G				
9049	Cpl	Stinchcomb J				
9852	Pte	Tunney J				
25968		McNeill H				
29608		Luna L				
26208		Burton		4th Bn The King's (Lpool Regt)	From No 8 Infantry Base Depot	
20124		Banks W				
13615		Bates G				
2303		Berman S.A.				
16590		Kerr a				
11383		Sembrey Y			3-3-16	
13971		Atkinson M				
21699		Booth A				
21955		Esplick J.H				
52561		Fees				
11568		Gilbertson J				
11203		Harrison				
28959		Morris				
29018		O'Brien R				
21925		Lepton T				
30601		Layefordt Ta				
11920		Wiggins a				
18145		Lyons L				
13054		Warren W				
15950		Prouse W				

RCR Jones

Major
Comdg 4 Bn The King's (Lpool Regt)

* State whether absence is of a permanent or temporary nature, adding, in the case of casuals from wounds or disease, any available information for communication to the relatives.

Perforated Sheet giving detail of personnel and horses wanting to complete, shown on Army Form B. 213.

Number of Report 52

Detail of Wanting to Complete			CAVALRY	R.A.	R.E.	INFANTRY	R.A.M.C.	A.O.C.	A.V.C.
Drivers	R.A.								
	R.E.								
	A.S.C.								
	Car								
	Lorry								
	Steam								
Gunners									
Smith Gunners									
Range Takers									
Farriers	Sergeants								
	Corporals								
Shoeing, or Shoeing and Carriage Smiths									
Cold Shoers									
Wheelers	R.A.								
	H.T.								
	M.T.								
Saddlers or Harness Makers									
Blacksmiths									
Bricklayers and Masons									
Carpenters and Joiners									
Fitters & Turners (R.E.)	Wood								
	Iron								
Fitters	R.A.								
	Wireless								
Plumbers									
Electricians	Ordinary								
	W.T.								
Signalmen									
Engine Drivers	Loco.								
	Field								
Air Line Men									
Permanent Line Men									
Operators, Telegraph									
Cablemen									
Brigade Section Pioneers									
General-duty Pioneers									
Signallers									
Instrument Repairers									
Motor Cyclists									
Motor Cyclist Artificers									
Telephonists									
Clerks									
Machine Gunners									
Armament Artificers	Fitters								
	Range Finders								
	Armourers								
Storemen									
Privates									
W.O's. and N.C.O's. (by ranks) not included in trade columns									
TOTAL to agree with wanting to complete	Officers					5			
	Other Ranks								
Horses	Riding								
	Draught								
	Heavy Draught								
	Pack								

Remarks :—

Signature of Commander. A.C.H.L.— Major

Formation to which attached. 4 Bn Sherwood (Spec. Res.) Regt 33rd Division

Date of Despatch. 2nd March 1916

[P.T.O.

FIELD RETURN.

Army Form B. 213.

No. of Report 53

(To be furnished by all arms, services, and departments (except A.S.C. units) to the A. G.'s Office at the Base in accordance with Field Service Regulations, Part II.)

RETURN showing numbers RATIONED by, and Transport on charge of, 4th Bn The King's (Liverpool Regt) at In the Field Date 10th March 1916.

DETAIL	Personnel			Animals								Guns, carriages, and limbers and transport vehicles										REMARKS
	Officers	Other ranks	Natives	Horses Riding	Horses Draught	Horses Heavy Draught	Mules Pack	Mules Large	Mules Small	Camels	Oxen	Guns, carriages and limbers, showing description	Ammunition wagons and limbers	Machine Guns	Aircraft, showing description	Horsed 4 Wheeled	Horsed 2 Wheeled	Motor Cars	Tractors	Mechanical Lorries	Mechanical Trucks	Trailers	Motor Bicycles	Bicycles	
Effective Strength of Unit	29	1035		14	16	17	2	31						8 *	4 Vickers 4 Lewis	19	5							9	Not Rationed — Officers 1, Base Depot 2, C of Instruction 1, Hosp'l England 1, Leave 5
Details, by Arms attached to unit as in War Establishment:— R.A.M.C. 1 Army Ordnance Corps 1																									Other Ranks — On Command 19, C of Instruction 24, 9 Field Amb 25, Leave 3, Civil Train 0, Bde Employ 5, Sur 1 / 83
Total	30	1036		14	16	17	2	31						8		19	5						9	9	
War Establishment	35	995		14	16	17	2	31						4		19	5								
Wanting to complete	5																								
Surplus		41												4											
Civilians:— Employed with the Unit Accompanying the Unit																									with Divisional train 8 Heavy Draught Horses
TOTAL RATIONED	25	953		14	16	9	2	31																	

* In the case of field ambulances, hospitals or depots, the number of patients are to be included here, the names being shown in A. F. A. 36.

NCM Owen Maj'r for Lieut Colonel Signature of Commander.

10th March 1916 Date of Despatch.

Sheet 1

For information of the A.G.'s Office at the Base.

Officers and men who have become casuals, been transferred or joined since last report.

Place: In the Field   Date: 10th March 1916

Regtl. Number	Rank	Name	Corps	Nature of casualty, or name of unit from or to which transferred	Date of being struck off or coming on the ration return	Remarks*
5469	Cpl	Richardson	J			
25134	-"-	Tyrer	B			
25160	-"-	Bushell				
12009	L/Sgt	Baines	W			
12696	Pte	McGough	N			
6697	L/Cpl	Heber	J			
24602	-"-	Wright	J			
28149	L/Cpl	Brady	J			
7910	L/Cpl	Naines	J			
10945	-"-	Conroy	R			
11261	Drm	Claridge	E	4th Bn the King's (Liverpool Regiment)	Reinforcements from No 1 Entrenching Battalion	
11372	-"-	Richardson	W			
16424	-"-	Wilson	W			
7897	-"-	Wilson	H			
9069	-"-	Stopforth	J			
9279	-"-	Walsh	M		3-1-16	
9040	Pte	Withe	J			
25956	Pte	Broady	J			
27698	-"-	Beresford	H			
7575	-"-	Fitzsimmons	J			
29925	-"-	Cooper	R			
25158	-"-	Carter	C			
30893	-"-	Aspinall	W			
25856	-"-	Baldwin	J			
27729	-"-	Convey			3-1-16	
30413	-"-	Smith	R			
27452	-"-	Ashworth	J			
11159	-"-	McCauley	J			
27798	-"-	Heighton	J			
27409	-"-	Myers	R			
21206	-"-	Thomas	W			
7721	-"-	Haslam	H		10-1-16	
13645	-"-	Hill	J			
9366	-"-	Donohoe	J			
9008	-"-	Aspinall	J			
8633	-"-	Day	J			
26283	-"-	Nightengale	E			
20913	-"-	Winstanley	E			
29534	-"-	Howarth	W			
9820	-"-	Adams	H			
30494	-"-	Ball	J			
29993	-"-	Bullows	J			
29085	-"-	Brewer	M			
24179	-"-	Finnegan	E			
27115	-"-	Morgan	J			
27751	-"-	Riley	M			
11458	-"-	Reilly	M			
30348	-"-	Riley	J			
8713	-"-	Wynn	J			
1116	-"-	Bulgayne	R			
26945	-"-	Halford	R			
10318	-"-	Timmer	E			
30496	-"-	Topping	R			
12653	-"-	Eckersley	E		From Hosptl	6-3-16	
29362	-"-	Baldwin	H	"	9-3-16	
9240	-"-	Griffiths	G	Killed in A	8-3-16	
8695	Sgt	Vincent	M	"	"	
10979	Pte	Quinn	W	Wounded in A	4-3-16	

* State whether absence is of a permanent or temporary nature, adding, in the case of casuals from wounds or disease, any available information for communication to the relatives.

Sheet 2

For information of the Officer i/c of a Base Record Office.

Officers and men who have left or joined since last report.

Place: In the Field   Date: 10th March 1916

Regtl. Number	Rank	Name	Corps	Name of unit from or to which transferred	Date of being struck off or coming on the ration return	Remarks *
10932	Pte	Moore G.		Wounded in A.	8-3-16	
10813	-"-	McGregor J.		-"-	-"-	
18197	-"-	Lyons J.		-"-	-"-	
23182	-"-	Connor J.		-"-	-"-	
8809	-"-	Scholefield J.		-"-	-"-	
29975	-"-	Nelson J.		-"-	-"-	
11240	-"-	Hampton W.		-"-	9-3-16	
12177	-"-	Jennings R.		P.B.	6-3-16	
27170	-"-	Dugdale J.		To Base	4-3-16	
9932	-"-	Clegg W.		To England for Munitions Work	29-2-16	
12681	A/Cpl	Townsend J.	4th Bn The King's (Liverpool Regt.)			
25342	Pte	Cook J.				
12085	-"-	Horath C.		B X	25-2-16	
11426	-"-	Campbell J.				
11399	-"-	Hardman J.				
11484	-"-	Couton J.				
10603	-"-	Done J.		To Hosptl.	4-3-16	
12402	-"-	Woods J.		-"-	25-2-16	
29326	-"-	Kinrade R.		Killed in A.	3-2-16	
29362	-"-	Baldwin A.		Wounded in A.	-"-	
30469	-"-	Draper F.		-"-	-"-	
30451	-"-	Ainsworth J.		-"-	-"-	
9071	-"-	Bailey A.		To Hosptl, Seaforth England		

Lieut Colonel
Comd'g 4th Bn The King's (Liverpool Regt)

* State whether absence is of a permanent or temporary nature.

Army Form B. 213.

FIELD RETURN.

(To be furnished by all arms, services, and departments to the Base Record Office in accordance with Field Service Regulations, Part II.)

No. of Report _____

Date _____

RETURN showing numbers RATIONED by, and Transport on charge of, _____ at _____

DETAIL.	Personnel			Animals							Transport Vehicles		Guns, carriages, and limbers, showing description	Ammunition wagons and limbers	Machine guns	REMARKS
	Officers	Other ranks	Natives	Horses			Mules		Camels	Oxen	4 Wheeled	2 Wheeled				
				Riding	Draught	Pack	Large	Small								
Effective Strength of Unit																
Details, *by Arms* attached to Unit as in War Establishment:—																
Total																
War Establishment																
Wanting to complete																
Surplus																
*Attached (not to include the details shown above)																
Civilians :— Employed with the Unit																
Accompanying the Unit																
TOTAL RATIONED ...																

* In the case of field ambulances, hospitals or depôts, the number of patients are to be included here, the names being shown in A. F. A. 36.

_____ Signature of Commander.

_____ Date of Despatch.

(5674e) Wt. 2141, 2190 35000 8-09 W B & L   Forms B. 213/2

Perforated Sheet giving detail of personnel and horses wanting to complete, shown on Army Form B. 213.

Number of Report 53

Detail of Wanting to Complete	Drivers						Gunners	Smith Gunners	Range Takers	Farriers			Shoeing or Carriage Smiths	Cold Shoers	Wheelers			Saddlers or Harness Makers	Blacksmiths	Bricklayers and Masons	Carpenters and Joiners	Fitters & Turners (R.S.)		Fitters				Electricians			Engine Drivers		Air Line Men	Permanent Line Men	Operators, Telegraph	Cablemen	Brigade Section Pioneers	General-duty Pioneers	Signallers	Instrument Repairers	Motor Cyclists	Motor Cyclist Artificers	Telephonists	Clerks	Machine Gunners	Armament Artificers			Armourers	Stretchermen	Privates	W.O.'s and N.C.O.'s (by ranks) not included in trade columns	TOTAL wanting to complete			Horses			
	R.A.	R.E.	A.S.C.	Car	Lorry	Steam				Sergeants	Corporals				R.A.	H.T.	M.T.					Wood	Iron	R.A.	Wireless	Plumbers	Ordinary	W.T.	Signalmen	Loco.	Field														Fitters	Range Finders						Officers	Other Ranks	Riding	Draught	Heavy Draught	Pack
CAVALRY																																																			5					
R.A.																																																								
R.E.																																																								
INFANTRY																																																								
R.A.M.C.																																																								
A.O.C.																																																								
A.V.C.																																																								

Remarks:—

Signature of Commander. A.M.Ogee Major
for Lieut Colonel.
Unit. 4th Bn The King's (Liverpool Regt)
Formation to which attached. 33rd Division
Date of Despatch. 10th March 1916

Army Form B. 213.

FIELD RETURN.

No. of Report 54

Diary

(To be furnished by all arms, services, and departments (except A.S.C. units) to the A. G.'s Office at the Base in accordance with Field Service Regulations, Part II.)

RETURN showing numbers RATIONED by, and Transport on charge of, 4th Bn The Loyal N. Lancs Regt at Kemmel on the field. Date 14th March 1916

DETAIL	Personnel			Animals								Guns, carriages, and limbers and transport vehicles					Horsed		Mechanical					REMARKS
	Officers	Other ranks	Natives	Horses Riding	Horses Draught	Horses Heavy Draught	Pack	Mules Large	Mules Small	Camels	Oxen	Guns, carriages and limbers, showing description	Ammunition wagons and limbers	Machine guns	Aircraft, showing description	4 Wheeled	2 Wheeled	Motor Cars	Tractors	Lorries, showing description	Trucks, showing description	Trailers	Motor Bicycles	Bicycles	
Effective Strength of Unit	29	1109		14	16	14	2	31						4			19 5							9	Officers not Rationed Boot Repairer Sent to England course of about 5/4
Details, by Arms attached to unit as in War Establishment:— R.A.M.C. Army Ordnance Corps	1	1																								
Total	30	1020		14	16	14	2	31						4			19 5							9	Other Ranks on command 19 9 W.O. Barber 1
War Establishment	25	995		14	16	14	2	31						4			19 5							9	9 Sec — 1 9 pick train field amb balance 16
Wanting to complete (Detail of Personnel and Horses below)	5																								Bearer officers to be watch 15/8Y
Surplus		108																							With W.O.E. Theure 3 H.D. Horses
Civilians:— Employed with the Unit Accompanying the Unit																									
TOTAL RATIONED ...	23	933		14	16	14	2	31																	

* In the case of field ambulances, hospitals or depots, the number of patients are to be included here, the names being shown in A. F. A. 36.

× 15 men permanently attached 25/2/16 Tunnelling Coy. R.E.

Col J.M. Allen Lt Colonel   Signature of Commander.

14 March 1916   Date of Despatch.

For information of the A.G.'s Office at the Base.

Officers and men who have become casuals, been transferred or joined since last report.

Place In the Field   Date 14th March 1916

Regtl. Number	Rank	Name	Corps	Nature of casualty, or name of unit from or to which transferred	Date of being struck off or coming on the ration return	Remarks*
16942	Pte	Hell A		To Hospital	5-3-16	
19018	--	O'Brien R		--	8-3-16	
24468	--	Miller H		--	5-3-16	
16996	--	Riley R		--	--	
25603	--	Mackie J		--	--	
11853	--	Wood J	4th Bn The King's (L'pool Regt)	--	--	
9881	--	Corcoran		--	3-3-16	
14213	--	Whitfield E		--	7-3-16	
11984	--	Tunney B		--	8-3-16	
30066	--	Eares W.		--	6-3-16	
10214	--	Smith G.A		--	8-3-16	
30564	--	Battersby		--	13-3-16	
14988	--	Dubberley G		To Base Depot	11-3-16	
11681	--	Malone J		--	15-3-16	
12014	--	McDonough H		--	--	
2254	--	Richardson G		--	16-3-16	
30622	--	Wilson		--	--	
10813	--	McGregor R		From Hospl	12-3-16	
9041	--	Bailey H		--	13-3-16	
11984	--	Tunney T. H		--	--	
9698	--	Brown D		Wounded in a	9-3-16	
35856	--	Baldwin J		Taken on strength last week in error. Was not struck off on admission to field ambulance 30-12-15		

(sd) J.W. Allen Lieut Colonel
Comdg. 4th Bn The King's (L'pool Regt)

* State whether absence is of a permanent or temporary nature, adding, in the case of casuals from wounds or disease, any available information for communication to the relatives.

Perforated Sheet giving detail of personnel and horses wanting to complete, shown on Army Form B. 213.

Number of Report 54

Detail of Wanting to Complete	Drivers						Farriers				Wheelers			Saddlers or Harness Makers	Blacksmiths	Bricklayers and Masons	Carpenters and Joiners	Fitters & Turners (R.E.)		Fitters			Electricians		Signalmen	Engine Drivers		Air Line Men	Permanent Line Men	Operators, Telegraph	Cablemen	Brigade Section Pioneers	General-duty Pioneers	Signallers	Instrument Repairers	Motor Cyclists	Motor Cyclist Artificers	Telephonists	Clerks	Machine Gunners	Armament Artificers		Armourers	Storemen	Privates	W.O.'s and N.C.O.'s, (by ranks) not included in trade columns	TOTAL, to agree with wanting to complete		Horses				
	R.A.	R.E.	A.S.C.	Pack	Lorry	Steam	Gunners	Smith Gunners	Range Takers	Sergeants	Corporals	Shoeing, or Shoeing and Carriage Smiths	Cold Shoers	R.A.	H.T.	M.T.					Wood	Iron	H.A.	Wireless	Ordinary	W.T.		Loco.	Field												Fitters	Range Finders						Officers	Other Ranks	Riding	Draught	Heavy Draught	Pack
CAVALRY																																																	5					
R. A.																																																						
R. E.																																																						
INFANTRY																																																						
R. A. M. C.																																																						
A. O. C.																																																						
A. V. C.																																																						

Remarks:—

(sd) J Mullin Lieut Colonel Signature of Commander.

4th Bn Sherwood Foresters Regt Unit.

39rd Division Formation to which attached.

14th March 1916 Date of Despatch.

Army Form B. 213.

N⁰ of Report 55 — **FIELD RETURN.** — Diary

(To be furnished by all arms, services, and departments (except A.S.C. units) to the A. G.'s Office at the Base in accordance with Field Service Regulations, Part II.)

RETURN showing numbers RATIONED by, and Transport on charge of, 4th B. the King's __ own __ Regt. at __ In the Field __ Date __ 24th March 16 __

Detail	Personnel			Horses			Mules		Camels	Oxen	Guns, carriages and limbers, showing description	Ammunition wagons and limbers	Machine Guns	Aircraft, showing description	Horsed		Motor Cars	Tractors	Mechanical			Trailers	Motor Bicycles	Bicycles	REMARKS
	Officers	Other ranks	Natives	Riding	Draught	Heavy Draught	Pack	Large	Small							4 Wheeled	2 Wheeled			Lorries, showing description	Trucks, showing description				
Effective Strength of Unit	28	1012		14	16	17	2	31						4		19	5								9	Not Rationed Officers 1 Base Depot 5 Hospital in England 1 Course of Instruction 6 Field Ambulance __ 14 Leave
Details, by Arms attached to unit as in War Establishment:— R.A.M.C. Army Ordnance Corps		1 1																								
Total	29	1013		14	16	17	2	31						4		19	5								9	Other Ranks An Command 16 Duty Employ 1 Sick 6 Corps 1 Duty Train 6 Field Ambulance 9
War Establishment	35	995		14	16	17	2	31						4		19	5								9	
Wanting to complete	6																									Course of Instr. 28 Attd 25th & Coy R.E. 15 Leave __ 121
Surplus		3ˣ																								203
*Attached (not to include the details shown above) Civilians:— Employed with the Unit Accompanying the Unit																										4th Suppl Train 8 H.D. Horses
Total Rationed ...	15	810		14	16	9	2	31																		

* In the case of field ambulances, hospitals or depots, the number of patients are to be included here, the names being shown in A. F. A. 36.

ˣ 15 Men permanently attached to 251st Tunnelling Coy. R. E.

R. H— Lieut Colonel. Signature of Commander.

24th March 1916. Date of Despatch.

For information of the A.G.'s Office at the Base.

Officers and men who have become casuals, been transferred or joined since last report.

Place **In the Field**   Date **24th March 1916**

Regtl. Number	Rank	Name	Corps	Nature of casualty, or name of unit from or to which transferred	Date of being struck off or coming on the ration return	Remarks*
10328	Pte	Cassidy J.	4th Bn The King's (L'pool Regt.)	To Hospital	15-3-16	
13615	"	Bates C.		-"-	-"-	
29027	"	Shields J.		-"-	16-3-16	
29861	"	Jamieson A.		-"-	17-3-16	
25167	"	Lord J.		-"-	11-3-16	
10609	"	McNally J.		Killed in A.	18-3-16	
11366	Sgt	Seymour		Wounded in A.	14-3-16	
31207	Pte	James J.		-"-	-"-	
27104	"	Gubbins J.		-"-	19-3-16	
	Lieut	Pack D.H.		-"-	20-3-16	
18217	Pte	Smith G.		From Hospl	22-3-16	
	Captn	Ross J.E.		To Field Amb.	22-3-16	
29027	Pte	Shields J.		From Hospl	18-3-16	

Admissions to and Discharges from Field Ambulance.

29861	Pte	Jamieson A.		To Field Amb.	16-3-16	
29027	"	Shields J.		-"-	-"-	
28073	L/Cpl	Winfield E.		-"-	-"-	
14940	Pte	Dykes W.		-"-	19-3-16	
5722	Sgt	Beard L.		-"-	-"-	
11536	Pte	Greenthwaite R.		-"-	20-3-16	
9207	"	Carr W.		From Field Amb.	16-3-16	
10816	"	Ruscoe N.		-"-	-"-	
28073	L/Cpl	Winfield E.		-"-	21-3-16	
11611	Pte	Carroll P.		-"-	16-3-16	
29027	"	Shields J.		-"-	18-3-16	
10729	Drmr	Jones J.		-"-	-"-	
13687	Pte	Doston W.E.		-"-	20-3-16	
12368	"	Gallagher J.		-"-	21-3-16	
11604	"	Foster G.		-"-	23-3-16	

J.W. Allen Lieut Colonel
Comdg 4th Bn The King's (Liverpool Regt).

* State whether absence is of a permanent or temporary nature, adding, in the case of casuals from wounds or disease, any available information for communication to the relatives.

Perforated Sheet giving detail of personnel and horses wanting to complete, shown on Army Form B. 213.

Number of Report 55

Detail of Wanting to Complete			CAVALRY	R.A.	R.E.	INFANTRY	R.A.M.C.	A.O.C.	A.V.C.
Drivers	R.A.								
	R.E.								
	A.S.C.								
	Car								
	Lorry								
	Steam								
Gunners									
Smith Gunners									
Range Takers									
Farriers	Serjeants								
	Corporals								
	Shoeing, or Shoeing and Carriage Smiths								
	Cold Shoers								
Wheelers	R.A.								
	H.T.								
	M.T.								
Saddlers or Harness Makers									
Blacksmiths									
Bricklayers and Masons									
Carpenters and Joiners									
Fitters & Turners (R.E.)	Wood								
	Iron								
Fitters	R.A.								
	Wireless								
	Plumbers								
Electricians	Ordinary								
	W.T.								
	Signalmen								
Engine Drivers	Loco.								
	Field								
Air Line Men									
Permanent Line Men									
Operators, Telegraph									
Cablemen									
Brigade Section Pioneers									
General-duty Pioneers									
Signallers									
Instrument Repairers									
Motor Cyclists									
Motor Cyclist Artificers									
Telephonists									
Clerks									
Machine Gunners									
Armament Artificers	Fitters								
	Range Finders								
Armourers									
Storemen									
Privates									
W.Os. and N.C.O's. (by ranks not included in trade columns)									
TOTAL to agree with wanting to complete	Officers				6				
	Other Ranks								
Horses	Riding								
	Draught								
	Heavy Draught								
	Pack								

Remarks :—

Tho. Allen Lieut-Colonel Signature of Commander.

4th Bn. the King's (Liverpool Regt.) Unit.

33rd Division Formation to which attached.

24th March 1916. Date of Despatch.

Army Form B. 213.

FIELD RETURN.

(Army Form B. 213 — Part II, Field Service Regulations)

(To be furnished by all arms, services, and departments (except A.S.C. units) to the A. G.'s Office at the Base in accordance with Field Service Regulations, Part II.)

RETURN showing numbers RATIONED by, and Transport on charge of, 4th Bn Highlanders at the Field. Date 31 March 1916.

N° of Report 56

Detail	Personnel			Animals								Guns, carriages, and limbers and transport vehicles				Horsed		Mechanical					Remarks
	Officers	Other ranks	Natives	Horses Riding	Draught	Heavy Draught	Pack	Mules Large	Small	Camels	Oxen	Guns, carriages, limbers, showing description	Ammunition wagons and limbers	Machine Guns	Aircraft, showing description	4 Wheeled	2 Wheeled	Motor Cars	Tractors	Lorries, showing description	Tracks, showing description	Trailers	Motor Bicycles	Bicycles	
Effective Strength of Unit	29	998		14	16	14	2	31						4		19	5							9	Nil returns Officers Bicycles leave Bowers of men Fild Amb
Details, by Arms attached to unit as in War Establishment:																									
R.A.M.C.																									Other Ranks
Army Ordnance Corps	1	1																							on command 16 Dis' Emplmt 1
Total	30	999		14	16	14	2	31						4		19	5							9	330 6
War Establishment	35	985		7	16	14	2	31						4		19	5							9	Colour 1
Wanting to complete (Detail of Personnel and Horses below)	5	14*																							Amm' Train Siege Amb 6– Bowers 15–
Surplus																									Bowers 24 70
*Attached (not to include the details shown above)																									Leave atd 29 & 30 th 15
Civilians:— Employed with the Unit Accompanying the Unit																									*Am'n Train Rovers 8*
TOTAL RATIONED	22	986		14	16	9	2	31																	

* In the case of field ambulances, hospitals or depots, the number of patients are to be included here, the names being shown in A. F. A. 36.

* & men permanently attached 2nd Lt Tannatt from R.E.

M. Ar Lieut Colonel Signature of Commander.

31 March 1916 Date of Despatch.

For information of the A.G.'s Office at the Base.

Officers and men who have become casuals, been transferred or joined since last report.

Place _In the Field_   Date _31st March 1916_

Regtl. Number	Rank	Name	Corps	Nature of casualty, or name of unit from or to which transferred	Date of being struck off or coming on the ration return	Remarks*
	Lieut	Jervis A.C.		Sick	14-1-16	On leave Eng Land
	Capt	Davies R.G.		} From } England	25-3-16	
	Lieut	Irving W.R.				
	—	Pack A.H.		~~Wounded~~		
	—	Tiss H.B.		Wounded in a	26-3-16	Slight Remained at Duty
8351	Sgt	Fraser J	4th Bn The King's (Liverpool Regt)	} Killed } in action	28-3-16	
4605	—	McAllister G				
13064	Cpl	Spencer L.G.				
20398	Pte	Flanagan J		Wounded in a	26-3-16	
7940	—	Kirwen D		—"—	4-3-16	
14940	—	Dykes G		To Hospital	22-3-16	
9292	—	Manning E		—"—	26-3-16	
9820	—	Adams J		—"—	28-3-16	
12260	—	Lindenburg S		—"—	—"—	
11306	Cpl	Hayes J		—"—	29-3-16	
9304	Pte	Carr W		—"—	—"—	
11422	—	Morgan W		—"—	—"—	
12366	—	Gallagher J		To Base P.B.	24-3-16	
8234	—	Mellor J		To Base en route to England	25-3-16	
		Admittances to and Discharges from F.A.				
9292	Pte	Manning E		To F.A.	25-3-16	
9820	—	Adams J		—"—	—"—	
11306	Cpl	Hayes J		—"—	26-3-16	
9304	Pte	Carr W		—"—	—"—	
12260	—	Lindenburg S		—"—	28-3-16	
11422	—	Morgan W		—"—	—"—	
24686	—	Taylor T		From F.A.	24-3-16	
1802	—	Hampson H		—"—	25-3-16	

J.W. Allen Lieut Colonel
Comdg 4th Bn The Kings (Liverpool Regt)

* State whether absence is of a permanent or temporary nature, adding, in the case of casuals from wounds or disease, any available information for communication to the relatives.

Perforated Sheet giving detail of personnel and horses wanting to complete, shown on Army Form B. 213.

Number of Report 3[?]

Detail of Wanting to Complete		Drivers						Gunners	Smith Gunners	Range Takers	Farriers		Shoeing, or Shoeing and Carriage Smiths	Cold Shoers	Wheelers			Saddlers or Harness Makers	Blacksmiths	Bricklayers and Masons	Carpenters and Joiners	Fitters & Turners (R. E.)		Fitters			Electricians			Signalmen	Engine Drivers		Air Line Men	Permanent Line Men	Operators, Telegraph	Cablemen	Brigade Section Pioneers	General-duty Pioneers	Signallers	Instrument Repairers	Motor Cyclists	Motor Cyclist Artificers	Telephonists	Clerks	Machine Gunners	Armament Artificers		Armourers	Storemen	Privates	W.O's and N.C.O's. (by ranks) not included in trade columns			TOTAL, to agree with wanting to complete		Horses			
	R.A.	R.E.	A.S.C.	Car	Lorry	Steam				Sergeants	Corporals			R.A.	H.T.	M.T.					Wood	Iron	R.A.	Wireless	Plumbers	Ordinary	W.T.		Loco.	Field														Fitters	Range Finders								Officers	Other Ranks	Riding	Draught	Heavy Draught	Pack
CAVALRY																																																								
R.A.																																																								
R.E.																																																			Bhindia		14		5/14			
INFANTRY																																																								
R.A.M.C.																																																								
A.O.C.																																																								
A.V.C.																																																								

Remarks :—

M. Allen Lieut Colonel Signature of Commander.
Comdg 4 1/3 Bn. the King's (Liverpool) Unit.
33rd Division Formation to which attached.
21st March 1916 Date of Despatch.

98th Brigade
33rd Division

4th BATTALION

THE KING'S LIVERPOOL REGIMENT

APRIL 1916

Army Form C. 2118.

Volume XIV.   Original

WAR DIARY or INTELLIGENCE SUMMARY.   4 'B' 1/L King's (Liverpool Regt)

APRIL 1916.

(Erase heading not required.)

Instructions regarding War Diaries and Intelligence Summaries are contained in F.S. Regs., Part II. and the Staff Manual respectively. Title pages will be prepared in manuscript.

Place	Date	Hour	Summary of Events and Information	Remarks and references to Appendices
LE QUESNOY BETHUNE MAP 1:40,000 Square F.9.9.	1-4-16		In reserve Billets. Fine day. On arrival of 1/6 Bn K.R.R.C. at 3pm the Battalion marched via BETHUNE to billets at OBLINGHEM. Reaching billets 6 pm. (DIVISIONAL RESERVE.)	
OBLINGHEM. (Square N 20-26.)	2-4-16		In billets. Fine day. (Battalion attached to 108th Brigade until completion of Brigade reshuffle on night of 2nd/3rd April.) 1 man to hospital for discharge.	
Do	3-4-16		In billets. Fine day. Lieut L.C. SODEN & 2nd Lieut T.H. IRVING went to Divisional School - 2nd Lieut J.H. LOMAS to Physical Training Course. 2nd Lieut C.D. REES joined on appointment from C.O.C.T. School & 2/Lieut Davis three. 4 men to hospital.	
Do	4-4-16		In billets. Fine day. Companies and Transport inspected by G.O.C. 98th Inf. Brigade. 2 men from hospital.	
Do	5-4-16		Do Do Usual training carried out - one man from hospital.	
Do	6-4-16		Do Do Lectures at Béthune for all officers by G.O.C. XI Corps 5pm. 2nd Lieut W.R. IRVING rejoined from Lewis Gun Course. Lieut C.D. REES joined Grenade School. Wet night. One man to hospital. One man "Permanent Base".	
Do	7-4-16		In billets. Fine day. 2nd Lieut R. McCRAE to Lewis Gun Class.	
Do	8-4-16		In billets. Fine day. 2 men from hospital.	
Do	9-4-16		In billets. Fine day. Church Parade - 2/Lieut J.H. LOMAS rejoined from Physical Training Course. Lieut L.C. SODEN and 2nd Lieut T.H. IRVING rejoined from Sniping Class. 2nd Lieut G.S. HARBURY & LEWIS GUN COURSE. Lieut H.J. BOWER R.A.M.C. joined as medical officer during absence on leave of Lieut D.S. JONES. R.A.M.C. One man wounded. (M.G. Sec.)	
Do	10-4-16		In billets. Fine day. The B.Att marched at 1pm to reserve billets BEUVRY. One officer & 70 men employed on working parties in front line - One man to hospital.	
BEUVRY.	11-4-16		In reserve Billets. Showery. 2 officers & 164 other ranks employed on working parties.	
Do	12-4-16		In reserve Billets. Wet day. 3 officers & 275 other ranks employed on working parties. 2nd Lieut J.W. LAWRENCE joined 98/1 Trench Mortar Battery. C/M on A.T.S. SIMMANCE to hospital - One man to hospital.	

1577 Wt. W10791/1773 50,000 1/15 D.D.&L. A.D.S.S./Forms/C. 2118.

Army Form C. 2118.

WAR DIARY
or
INTELLIGENCE SUMMARY.   4th Bn "The Kings" (Liverpool Regt)

April 1916.

(Erase heading not required.)

Place	Date	Hour	Summary of Events and Information	Remarks and references to Appendices
BEUVRY	13.4.16		In reserve billets. Windy & showery. C.O. Adjt & Coy Commanders visited trenches. 1 Officer & 220 other ranks employed on working parties in front line.	
Do	14.4.16		In reserve billets. Dull day with heavy showers. Very wet evening. The Battn. moved into trenches - Left Sub Section AUCHY SECTION in relief of 7/Argyll & Sutherland Highlanders. Relief completed 9.40 p.m. Six men wounded.	
Trenches (AUCHY Left Sub-Section)	15.4.16		In trenches. Fine day. 2 Officers & 90 men employed on working parties with Trench Mortar Battery. Two mines were exploded between MINE POINT CRATER and R.W.F. CRATER by the enemy. These were followed by our artillery & Trench Mortar fire, to which enemy retaliated. Following the explosions two working parties of 7/Argylls went out & relieved enemy's trenches, where they found 3 men who tried to identify position. Our casualties 2 trenches confiscated in the retaliation, but were not called on to march. 2 men from hospital. Lieut E.C. SODEN & 4 men wounded. One man killed (N.14062 Pte J. KELLY.)	
Do	16.4.16		In trenches. Fine day. 1 Officer & 80 men employed with Trench Mortar Battery, laterally wounded received. Lieut R. McCRAE rejoined from LEWIS GUN COURSE. One man killed (No.11587 Pte J. BROWNING) 4 men wounded.	
Do	17.4.16		In trenches. Dull, windy & showery. Lieut J.S. HUTCHINGS went to LEWIS GUN COURSE. Lieut G.S. HORBURY rejoined from LEWIS GUN COURSE. CAMIERS. Lieut A.H. SHARPE and D.M. BANGHAM from leave. 2 men to hospital. 3 men wounded. Enemy fired heavy salvoes on our support & reserve lines, doing little damage. Hostile machine guns active at night.	
Do	18.4.16		In trenches. Wet day. 1 Officer & 21 other ranks employed on working party with T.M. Battery. The battalion was relieved by 2/Argylls - relief completed 10.30 p.m. Battn. moved to reserve billets BEUVRY at 12 M.N. One man to hospital. One man from base. On landing field in Rugetoke, M.G. emplacement by POPE'S NOSE being considerable damage. Heavy rain which washed rain & rain in working parties in front line.	
BEUVRY	19.4.16		In reserve billets. Wet day. 2 Officers & 284 other ranks employed on working parties in front line. Two men from hospital.	
Do	20.4.16		In reserve billets. Fine day. Slight showers, windy. 1st Lieut H.D. ROBERTS joined from Base. Lieut C.D. REES. rejoined from Grenade School. Lieut H.C. SODEN joined Grenade School. Lieut D.S JONES. R.A.M.C. rejoined & Lieut H.T. BOWER. R.A.M.C. returns to 101st Field Ambulance. One Officer & 384 other ranks employed on working parties in front line. One man to hospital. One man from hospital on one Man Killed (8362670 Pte J. DICKENSON. whilst accompanying the R.E.)	
Do	21.4.16		In reserve billets. Fine morning. Very wet evening & at night. 1 Officer & 195 other ranks employed on working parties in front line. Lieut C.P.GAWTER rejoined from Divisional School.	

WAR DIARY or INTELLIGENCE SUMMARY

Army Form C. 2118.

4th Bn "The Kings" (Liverpool Regt)

April 1916

Place	Date	Hour	Summary of Events and Information	Remarks and references to Appendices
BEUVRY	22-4-16		In reserve billets. The Battn moved to trenches - Left Sub Section - AUCHY Section in relief of 2/Argyll & Sutherland Highrs. Relief completed 11-10 pm. Very wet night & day. Trenches in a bad state. 3 other ranks wounded. Working parties with training for R.E. at night.	
Trenches AUCHY (Left Subsection)	23-4-16		Fine day. In trenches. At 6.10 pm we exploded a mine near TWIN CRATER & occupied & consolidated crater. Hostile machine guns active at night. One man to hospital. 7 men wounded.	
Do	24-4-16		Fine dull day. Some shelling of our support by day. Much rifle grenade activity. We put out a wire entanglement in front of the wire. Capt J.E. ROSS & 2nd Lieut M.A. TRIPP wounded during night. One man 11882 Pte DAVIES one man wounded.	
Do	25-4-16		Fine hot day. A raid was carried out by 1/Middlesex Regt on our right at 10pm. They had considerable success further west & was carried out as our left by Yorks. Also entered enemy trenches but was not so successful. Aircraft active. Two prisoners were sent from RWF Regt by our Brigadier. Capt J.E. ROSS died in hospital 9.15am. Our other men to hospital. One man killed (M/2232 Pte RICHARDS) 3 men wounded.	
Do	26-4-16		Fine hot day. In trenches. Battn was relieved by 1st Queens. Relief completed 10.20 pm. On relief the trench trenches to billets at BETHUNE & reached MONTMORENCY Barracks. Lieut J.S. HUTCHINGS returned from leave. Officer casualties Capt J.E. ROSS and Sergt H. ROSE were buried at BETHUNE.	
BETHUNE	27-4-16		In billets & barracks. Fine hot day. Lieut J.L. WARING went to Bayard Hoishing House. Lieut MASON & Lewis Gun Corpl. Capt A.J.S. SIMMANCE rejoined from hospital.	
Do	28-4-16		In billets & barracks. Fine hot day. Training carried out by Companies - 2 men to hospital, 2 men from Base.	
Do	29-4-16		In billets & barracks. Fine hot day. Training carried out & Right Anchors. (Outposts)	
Do	30-4-16		In billets & barracks. Fine hot day. Church Parades. 2nd Lieut W.V. Tradshaw & 1 man to hospital.	

No. Allen
Lt Colonel
Comdg 4/ "The Kings"
1-5-16

Army Form B. 213.

FIELD RETURN.

Diary

No. _____ Report 57

(To be furnished by all arms, services, and departments (except A.S.C. units) to the A. G.'s Office at the Base in accordance with Field Service Regulations, Part II.)

RETURN showing numbers RATIONED by, and Transport on charge of, _N° 11 Bn the Kings (Liverpool R.R.)_ at _In the Field_ 7th April 19__ Date.

Detail	Personnel			Animals								Guns, carriages, and limbers and transport vehicles			Horsed		Mechanical					Remarks
	Officers	Other ranks	Natives	Horses Riding	Draught	Heavy Draught	Pack	Mules Large	Small	Camels	Oxen	Guns, carriages and limbers, showing description	Ammunition wagons and limbers	Machine guns	Aircraft, showing description	4 Wheeled	2 Wheeled	Motor Cars	Tractors	Lorries, showing description	Trucks, showing description	Trailers	Motor Bicycles	Bicycles	
Effective Strength of Unit	30	986		14	16	19	2	31						4			19	5								Not Rationed Officers 1 Base Depot 2 Leave 6 Course of Instr 9
Details, by Arms attached to unit as in War Establishment :— R.A.M.C. 1 Army Ordnance Corps 1																										Other Ranks 16 (In Command) 6 Sick Empty 5 Base 1 9 horses 7 bull teams 5 9 field arty 38 Course of Instr 26 Leave 27 Wild 25 2nd by R.E. 13
Total	31	987		14	16	19	2	31						4			19	5								
War Establishment	35	945		14	16	19	2	31						4			19	5								
Wanting to complete (Detail of Personnel and Horses below)	4	35 X																								
Surplus																										
*Attached (not to include the details shown above)																										Lieut Piggen R.A. Moss 8
Civilians:— Employed with the Unit Accompanying the Unit																										
Total Rationed ...	32	856	14	16	19	2	31																			

* In the case of field ambulances, hospitals or depots, the number of patients are to be included here, the names being shown in A.F.A. 36.

X 24 Nov permanently attached Ken Joe _____ Major or Lieut Colonel Signature of Commander.

251st Inumbling bn R.E. _____ 7th April 1916. Date of Despatch.

For information of the A.G.'s Office at the Base.

Officers and men who have become casuals, been transferred or joined since last report.

Place __In the Field__   Date __7th April 1916__

Regtl. Number	Rank	Name		Corps	Nature of casualty, or name of unit from or to which transferred	Date of being struck off or coming on the ration return	Remarks*
11439	Pte	Lewis	J.		To Hospital	31-3-16	
23242	"	Sawhurst	W.		" "	3-4-16	
25160	"	Bushell	J.		" "	" "	
30301	"	Jayforth	E.		" "	" "	
30610	"	Gallagher	P.	4th Bn the King's (Liverpool Regt)	" "	" "	
13115	"	Boothman	J.		" "	4-4-16	
11565	A/Cpl	Westwell	W.		" "	" "	
1142	Cpl	Murphy	J.		Wounded in A.	31-3-16	
8684	Sgt	Reynolds	J.E.		" "	" "	
8468	Pte	Booth	J.		To Base for discharge	2-4-16	
12153	"	Morton	W.		P.B.	6-4-16	
11569	Cpl	Williams	M.E.		" "	24-2-16	
26413	Pte	Linn	J.		To England	28-3-16	
8969	"	Hill	W.		From Hospital	5-4-16	
~~	Lieut	C.D. Rees			From Base	3-4-16	
	Lieut	Munroe	A.R.	R.A.M.C	To 101st Field Ambulance for duty		
	"	Jones	D.S.		From 101st Field Ambulance for duty		

__Admittances to and Discharges from Field Ambulance__

13115	Pte	Boothman	J.		To Field Amb	31-3-16	
31768	"	Christie	J.		"	1-4-16	
23242	"	Sawhurst			"	1-4-16	
11565	A/Cpl	Westwell	W.		"	2-4-16	
30601	Pte	Jayforth	E.		"	"	
25160	"	Bushell	J.		"	"	
12153	"	Morton			"	"	
30610	"	Gallagher	P.		"	"	
18217	"	Smith	G.		"	5-4-16	
13997	Capt	Stainstreet Ross	J.E.		From Field Amb	1-4-16	

RCR Innes
Major for Lieut Colonel.
Comd'g 4th Bn The King's (Liverpool Regiment)

* State whether absence is of a permanent or temporary nature, adding, in the case of casuals from wounds or disease, any available information for communication to the relatives.

Perforated Sheet giving detail of personnel and horses wanting to complete, shown on Army Form B. 213.

Number of Report 51.

Detail of Wanting to Complete			
CAVALRY			
R.A.			
R.E.			
INFANTRY	Riding Horses	35	
	Other Ranks	35	
R.A.M.C.			
A.O.C.			
A.V.C.			

Remarks:—

H. H. Grier, Major & Lieut. Colonel, Signature of Commander.

4th Bn The King's (Liverpool Regt) Unit.

33rd Division Formation to which attached.

9th April 1916. Date of Despatch.

[P.T.O.

Army Form B. 213.

FIELD RETURN

N° of Report 58

(To be furnished by all arms, services, and departments (except A.S.C. units) to the A. G.'s Office at the Base in accordance with Field Service Regulations, Part II.)

RETURN showing numbers RATIONED by, and Transport on charge of, _4th By of Flying Kings_ at _France_. Date _14th April 1916_.

DETAIL	Personnel			Animals.							Guns, carriages, and limbers and transport vehicles				Mechanical				REMARKS
	Officers	Other ranks	Natives	Horses			Mules		Camels	Oxen	Guns, carriages and limbers, showing description	Ammunition wagons and limbers	Machine guns	Aircraft, showing description	4 Wheeled	2 Wheeled	Motor Cars	Tractors	
				Riding	Draught	Heavy Draught	Pack	Large	Small											
Effective Strength of Unit	30	983		14	16	17	2	31					4		17	5				9 Base Depot Not Rationed effective
Details, by Arms attached to unit as in War Establishment:—																					Guard Details
R.A.M.C.	1																				Hospital 2
Army Veterinary Corps		1																			Leave
																					Not Joined Motors 1
																					Other Ranks
																					Command 18
																					Civil Employ 2
Total	31	984		14	16	17	2	31					4		17	5				9 Depo Bureau of Truth 30
War Establishment	36	995		14	16	17	2	31					4		17	5				9 Add 2 Sqd at Bay H.E. 26
Wanting to complete	4	87 X																			Field Arty 10
Surplus																					Depot Establ
(Detail of Personnel and Horses below)																					Mascot 2
																					Nat Sick Horses 1
*Attached (not to include the details shown above)																					Sundr Motor City 11
																					Leave 16
Civilians:— Employed with the Unit Accompanying the Unit																					Base Employ 4
																					13 2
TOTAL RATIONED	22	926		10	14	9	2	31													April Strain
																					6. H.D. Amos

* In the case of field ambulances, hospitals or depots, the number of patients are to be included here, the names being shown in A.F.A. 36.

X 26 men permanently attached MCM Jones Mgr for Lieut Colonel Signature of Commander.

257st Tunnelling Coy R.E. 14th April 1916 Date of Despatch.

For information of the A.G.'s Office at the Base.

Officers and men who have become casuals, been transferred or joined since last report.

Place _France_   Date _14th April 1916._

Regtl. Number	Rank	Name	Corps	Nature of casualty, or name of unit from or to which transferred	Date of being struck off or coming on the ration return	Remarks*
7942	Cpl	Murphy J.		From Hosptl.	8-4-16	
20799	Pte	Baldwin R.		—"—	—"—	
29414	—"—	Pomfret A.		Wounded in A	9-4-16	
14254	—"—	Skelhorn J.		To Hosptl	26-3-16	
27721	—"—	Haslam H.		—"—	10-4-16	
8401	—"—	Rimmer N.		—"—	12-4-16	
13●97	—"—	Stanistreet J.		—"—	6-4-16	
	Captn	Simmance A.J.S.		—"—	13-4-16	

Admittances to and Discharges from Field Ambulance

26406	Pte	Montheath E		To Field Amb	4-4-16	
8976	—"—	McGregor E		—"—	9-4-16	
27721	—"—	Haslam H.		—"—	—"—	
8401	—"—	Rimmer N.		—"—	10-4-16	
27892	—"—	Robinson J.		—"—	—"—	
30094	—"—	Warburton J		—"—	12-4-16	
	Captn	Simmance A.J.S.		—"—	—"—	
11674	Pte	Williams		—"—	13-4-16	
12397	—"—	Vass O		—"—	13-4-16	
10458	—"—	Lyons J.		From Field Amb	7-4-16	
18217	—"—	Smith J.		—"—	—"—	
18457	—"—	Warren W.		—"—	12-4-16	

H C R Innes

Major for Lieut Colonel

Comdg 4th Bn The King's (Liverpool Regt)

* State whether absence is of a permanent or temporary nature, adding, in the case of casuals from wounds or disease, any available information for communication to the relatives.

Perforated Sheet giving detail of personnel and horses wanting to complete, shown on Army Form B. 213.

Number of Report 58

Detail of Wanting to Complete			Drivers					Gunners	Smith Gunners	Range Takers	Farriers			Wheelers			Saddlers or Harness Makers	Blacksmiths	Bricklayers and Masons	Carpenters and Joiners	Fitters & Turners (R.E.)		Fitters R.A.	Wireless	Electricians			Signalmen	Engine Drivers		Air Line Men	Permanent Line Men	Operators, Telegraph	Cablemen	Brigade Section Pioneers	General-duty Pioneers	Signallers	Instrument Repairers	Motor Cyclists	Motor Cyclist Artificers	Telephonists	Clerks	Machine Gunners	Armament Artificers			Armourers	Storemen	Privates	W.O's. and N.C.O's. (by ranks) not included in trade columns	TOTAL wanting to complete		Horses			
	R.A.	R.E.	A.S.C.	Car	Lorry	Steam					Sergeants	Corporals	Shoeing, or Shoeing and Carriage Smiths	Cold Shoers	R.A.	H.T.	M.T.					Wood	Iron			Ordinary	W.T.			Loco.	Field														Fitters	Range Finders						Officers	Other Ranks	Riding	Draught	Heavy Draught	Pack
CAVALRY																																																							
R.A.																																																							
R.E.																																																							
INFANTRY																																																		37		4+37				
R.A.M.C.																																																							
A.O.C.																																																							
A.V.C.																																																							

Remarks:— Eureka

Signature of Commander. Agn for Lieut Colonel
Formation to which attached. 4th Bn The King's (Liverpool Regt) Unit.
33rd Division
Date of Despatch. 14th April 1916

Army Form B. 213.

FIELD RETURN. (Army Form B. 213, in accordance with Field Service Regulations, Part II.)

No. of Report 59. Diary

(To be furnished by all arms, services, and departments (except A.S.C. units) to the A. G.'s Office at the Base in accordance with Field Service Regulations, Part II.)

RETURN showing numbers RATIONED by, and Transport on charge of, 4th Bn The King's (Liverpool Regt) at France Date 21st April 1916

[Stamp: 4TH BATTALION THE KING'S (LIVERPOOL) REGT. 21. APR 1916 ORDERLY ROOM]

DETAIL	Personnel			Animals							Guns, carriages, limbers and transport vehicles				Horsed		Mechanical					REMARKS
	Officers	Other ranks	Natives	Horses Riding	Horses Draught	Horses Heavy Draught	Mules Pack	Mules Large	Mules Small	Camels	Oxen	Guns, carriages limbers, showing description	Ammunition wagons and limbers	Machine guns	Aircraft, showing description	4 Wheeled	2 Wheeled	Motor Cars	Tractors	Lorries, showing description	Trucks, showing description	Trailers	Motor Bicycles	Bicycles	
Effective Strength of Unit	32	964		14	10	9		24						4			16 6								Not Rationed Officers: Base Depot 1, 2nd T.M. Bty 1, Hospital 1½, Command of Inst 3½ = 5
Details, by Arms attached to unit as in War Establishment:— R.A.M.C. 1 Army Ordnance Corps 1																									Other Ranks: On Command 17, Bde Employ 6, Attd 251st Tunnelling Coy 26 ; Commd Instr 26 ; Attd Trench Mortar Bty 11 ; Corps Employ 6 ; Field Ambulance 26 ; Absent 1 ; Base Employ 13 ; Hospital England 2/13 = 131¼ ; With Ruil Train 8 HD Horses
Total	33	965		14	10	9		24						4			16 6								
War Establishment	35	995		14	10	9		24						4			16 6								
Wanting to complete	2	56 x																							
Surplus																									
(Detail of Personnel and Horses below)																									
*Attached (not to include the details shown above)																									
Civilians:— Employed with the Unit Accompanying the Unit																									
TOTAL RATIONED	33	931		14	10	1		24																	

* In the case of field ambulances, hospitals or depots, the number of patients are to be included here, the ranks being shown in A.F.A. 36.

x 26 Men permanently attached 251st Tunnelling Coy. R.E.

Signature of Commander. A.W. St Colonel

Date of Despatch. 21st April 1916

For information of the A.G.'s Office at the Base.

Officers and men who have become casuals, been transferred or joined since last report.

Place France.   Date 21st April 1916

Regtl. Number	Rank	Name	Corps	Nature of casualty, or name of unit from or to which transferred	Date of being struck off or coming on the ration return	Remarks*
11565	Pte	Westwell W.		From Hospital	15-4-16	
30610	-"-	Gallagher P.		-"-	-"-	
10547	-"-	Healey J.		-"-	19-4-16	
14681	-"-	Foster J.		-"-	-"-	
9018	-"-	Mitchell H.			20-4-16	
	Lieut	Sharpe R.H.		} From Base	17-4-16	
	Lieut	Bingham R.H.			-"-	
	Lieut	Roberts H.D.			20-4-16	
6740	CSM	Townley A.H.		From Base	18-4-16	
29839	Pte	Hughes J.	The King's (Liverpool Regiment)	Wounded in A	14-4-16	Accidental
9018	-"-	Mitchell H.		-"-	-"-	
9644	Sgt	Arden		-"-	-"-	
14500	-"-	Philson L.		-"-	-"-	
1449	Pte	Lord C.		-"-	15-4-16	
13975	-"-	Stinchcomb H.		-"-	14-4-16	
25074	Sgt	Rose J.H.		-"-	-"-	
8845	Pte	Douglas F.		-"-	10-4-16	
11342	Dmr	Richardson W.		-"-	-"-	
18022	L/Cpl	Hadwen		-"-	-"-	
	Lieut	Soden L.J.		-"-	-"-	
24053	Pte	Moran J.		-"-	16-4-16	
28409	-"-	Bateman J.		-"-	-"-	
30852	-"-	Jones J.		-"-	-"-	
12653	-"-	Eckersley		-"-	-"-	Shell Shock
8843	-"-	Newall H.		-"-	19-4-16	
10024	-"-	O'Hare J.		-"-	-"-	
10708	-"-	Adams J.		-"-	-"-	
14062	-"-	Kelly		Killed in A	15-4-16	
11587	-"-	Liptonhill J.		-"-	16-4-16	
10691	-"-	Shinners		To Hospital	17-4-16	
30305	-"-	Blackhurst		-"-	18-4-16	
10912	-"-	Welsby W.		-"-	17-4-16	
14487	-"-	Dickinson		} On strength of 2nd Auth P.B.	2-4-16	
10198	-"-	Nelson				
12108	-"-	Hampson			20-4-16	

Admittances to and Discharges from Field Ambulance

25134	Pte	Walsh L.		To Field Amb	14-4-16	
10967	-"-	Weaver G.		-"-	-"-	
26964	-"-	Tomlinson		-"-	-"-	
30413	-"-	Smith R.	11th Bn	-"-	-"-	
12108	-"-	Hampson H.		-"-	-"-	
4533	-"-	Roberts H.		-"-	-"-	
25190	-"-	Whittaker B.		-"-	-"-	
30434	-"-	Kelly H.		-"-	-"-	
25178	-"-	Houghton J.		-"-	-"-	
10691	-"-	Shinners J.		-"-	-"-	
8623	-"-	Bollinger		-"-	-"-	
25856	-"-	Baldwin		-"-	16-4-16	
29063	-"-	Stansfield		-"-	-"-	
10912	-"-	Welsby P.		-"-	17-4-16	
13369	-"-	Dunn G.		-"-	19-4-16	
29854	-"-	Keating H.		-"-	20-4-16	

* State whether absence is of a permanent or temporary nature, adding, in the case of casuals from wounds or disease, any available information for communication to the relatives.

Army Form B. 213.

FIELD RETURN.

No. of Report _____

(To be furnished by all arms, services, and departments to the Base Record Office in accordance with Field Service Regulations, Part II.)

Date. _____

RETURN showing numbers RATIONED by, and Transport on charge of, _____ at _____

DETAIL.	Personnel			Animals							Transport Vehicles		Guns, carriages, and limbers, showing description	Ammunition wagons and limbers	Machine guns	REMARKS
	Officers	Other ranks	Natives	Horses			Mules		Camels	Oxen	4 Wheeled	2 Wheeled				
				Riding	Draught	Pack	Large	Small								
Effective Strength of Unit Details, *by Arms* attached to Unit as in War Establishment:—																
Total																
War Establishment																
Wanting to complete																
Surplus																
*Attached (not to include the details shown above)																
Civilians:— Employed with the Unit Accompanying the Unit																
TOTAL RATIONED ...																

* In the case of field ambulances, hospitals or depôts, the number of patients are to be included here, the names being shown in A. F. A. 36.

_____ Signature of Commander.

_____ Date of Despatch.

(56616a) Wt. 1066/1860 35000 6-09 W B & L   Forms B. 213

Sheet 2

For information of the Officer i/c of a Base Record Office.

Officers and men who have left or joined since last report.

Place: France Date: 21st April 1916

Regtl. Number	Rank	Name	Corps	Name of unit from or to which transferred	Date of being struck off or coming on the ration return	Remarks *
27608	L/Cpl	Wright J.		To Field Amb	20-4-16	
10977	Pte	Drake H.	4th Bn	-,,-	-,,-	
29952	-,,-	Beesly J.	The King's	-,,-	-,,-	
25243	-,,-	McNeill J.		-,,-	-,,-	
11646	-,,-	Power J.	(Liverpool	From Field Amb	14-4-16	
26706	-,,-	Monheather S.	Regt)	-,,-	-,,-	
30094	-,,-	Warburton J.		-,,-	-,,-	
12108	-,,-	Hampson H.		-,,-	19-4-16	
25190	-,,-	Whittaker T.		-,,-	-,,-	
25856	-,,-	Baldwin J.		-,,-	20-4-16	

Lieut Colonel
Comdg 4th Bn The King's (L'pool Regt)

* State whether absence is of a permanent or temporary nature.

Perforated Sheet giving detail of personnel and horses wanting to complete, shown on Army Form B. 213.

Number of Report 59

Detail of Wanting to Complete	Drivers: R.A.	R.E.	A.S.C.	Car	Lorry	Steam	Gunners	Smith Gunners	Range Takers	Farriers: Sergeants	Corporals	Shoeing, or Shoeing and Carriage Smiths	Cold Shoers	Wheelers: R.A.	H.T.	M.T.	Saddlers or Harness Makers	Blacksmiths	Bricklayers and Masons	Carpenters and Joiners	Fitters & Turners (R.E.): Wood	Iron	Fitters: R.A.	Wireless	Electricians: Ordinary	W.T.	Signalmen	Engine Drivers: Loco.	Field	Air Line Men	Permanent Line Men	Operators, Telegraph	Cablemen	Brigade Section Pioneers	General-duty Pioneers	Signallers	Instrument Repairers	Motor Cyclists	Motor Cyclist Artificers	Telephonists	Clerks	Machine Gunners	Armament Artificers: Fitters	Range Finders	Armourers	Storemen	Privates	W.O's and N.C.O's (by ranks) not included in trade columns	TOTAL wanting to complete with Officers	Other Ranks	Horses: Riding	Draught	Heavy Draught	Pack
CAVALRY																																																							
R.A.																																																						
R.E.																																																						
INFANTRY																																																	56	Privates	2	56				
R.A.M.C.																																																						
A.O.C.																																																						
A.V.C.																																																						

Remarks:—

R. M. Allen Lt Colonel Signature of Commander.
4th Bn The King's (Liverpool Regt) Unit.
33rd Division Formation to which attached.
21st April 1916 Date of Despatch.

[P.T.O.

No. of Report 60.

Army Form B. 213.

Diary

FIELD RETURN.

(Army Form Service Regulations, Part II.)

(To be furnished by all arms, services, and departments (except A.S.C. units) to the A. G.'s Office at the Base in accordance with Field Service Regulations, Part II.)

RETURN showing numbers RATIONED by, and Transport on charge of H.A. for the Army at Havre. Date 28th April 1916.
(Guns, carriages, limbers and transport vehicles)

DETAIL.	Personnel			Animals.								Guns, carriages, limbers, showing description	Ammunition wagons and limbers	Machine guns	Aircraft, showing description	Horsed		Motor Cars	Tractors	Mechanical			Motor Bicycles	Bicycles	REMARKS
	Officers	Other ranks	Natives	Riding	Horses Draught	Heavy Draught	Pack	Mules Large	Small	Camels	Oxen					4 Wheeled	2 Wheeled			Lorries, showing description	Trucks, showing description	Trailers			
Effective Strength of Unit	30	949		14	10	9		24						4		16	6								Not Rationed (Officers) Shoe Maker 1, Mtd T.M. Btty 1, Corpes of train 3, Leave 1 —6
Details, by Arms attached to unit as in War Establishment:—																									Other Ranks On Command 16, Rate Employ 4, Attd 251st Coy R.E. 25
R.A.M.C.	1																								
Army Ordnance Corps		1																							
Total	31	949		14	10	9		24						4		16	6								Innes of train 30, Mtd T.M. Btty 11, Corps Employ 6, Field Ambulance 20, Sick Employ 14, Absent 1, Leave 9
War Establishment	35	995		14	10	9		24						4		16	6								
Wanting to complete (Detail of Personnel and Horses below)	4	71 x																							Hosplt England 3
Surplus						5																			With SW Chases 8 H.D. Horses 139
*Attached (not to include the details shown above)																									
Civilians:— Employed with the Unit Accompanying the Unit																									
TOTAL RATIONED	25	810		14	10	1		24																	

* In the case of field ambulances, hospitals or depots, the number of patients are to be included here, the names being shown in A. F. A. 36.

x 25 men permanently attached 237st Tunnelling Coy. R.E.

_____ Signature of Commander.

26th April 1916. Date of Despatch.

For information of the A.G.'s Office at the Base.

Officers and men who have become casuals, been transferred or joined since last report.

Place France.   Date 28th April 1916

Regtl. Number	Rank	Name	Corps	Nature of casualty, or name of unit from or to which transferred	Date of being struck off or coming on the ration return	Remarks*
	Captn	Simmance A.J.S.		From Hospital	27-4-16	
14940	Pte	Sykes W			25-4-16	
9018	"	Mitchell M.		To Hospital	20-4-16	
27724	"	McGowan		"	22-4-16	
28079	"	Gill H		"	23-4-16	
	Captn	Ross J.G.		Wounded in Action	25-4-16	
	Lieut	Tripp A.B.		"		
9090	Pte	Jones J		"	23-4-16	
4776	"	Sweeney		"		
8905	"	Frankland A		"		
26969	"	Cunningham W		"		
27894	"	Brompton J		"		
13687	"	Foster W.E.		"		
11981	"	Grierson J		"		
585	"	Webster J		"	23-4-16	
11633	"	Gallagher J		"	"	
26175	Cpl	Charlesworth J		"	"	
25454	Pte	Marsh H		"	24-4-16	
9658	"	Dickenson J		Killed in Action	20-4-16	
11981	"	Davies J		"	24-4-16	
12432	"	Richards J		"	25-4-16	

Admittances to and Discharges from Field Ambulance

25288	LCpl	Hall A		To Field Amb.	21-4-16	
29063	Pte	Stansfield J		"	"	
27892	"	Robinson J		"		
12615	"	Connelly H		"	22-4-16	
28079	"	Gill A		"		
6505	"	Moore A		"		
9213	"	Woods		"	26-4-16	
9025	Sgt	Randles J		"	27-4-16	
25956	Pte	Brady J		"		
11334	"	McKenna J		"		
10097	"	Murphy J		"		
25734	"	Walsh L		From Field Amb	21-4-16	
11674	"	Williams		"		
13573	"	Wright		"		
10967	"	Weaver G		"	24-4-16	
8623	"	Bollinger G		"		
23273	"	McNeill J		"	25-4-16	
4646	"	Power J		"		
12615	"	Connelly H		"	26-4-16	
10977	"	Drake J		"		
9163	"	Reardon		"		
26964	"	Tomlinson J		"	27-4-16	

Jno Allen Lieut Colonel

Comdg 4th Bn The King's (Liverpool Regt)

* State whether absence is of a permanent or temporary nature, adding, in the case of casuals from wounds or disease, any available information for communication to the relatives.

Perforated Sheet giving detail of personnel and horses wanting to complete, shown on Army Form B. 213.

Number of Report: 60

Detail of Wanting to Complete			
CAVALRY			
R.A.	Drivers	R.A.	
		R.E.	
		A.S.C.	
		Car	
		Lorry	
		Steam	
	Gunners		
	Smith Gunners		
	Range Takers		
	Farriers	Sergeants	
		Corporals	
		Shoeing, or Shoeing and Carriage Smiths	
		Cold Shoers	
	Wheelers	R.A.	
		H.T.	
		M.T.	
	Saddlers or Harness Makers		
R.E.	Blacksmiths		
	Bricklayers and Masons		
	Carpenters and Joiners		
	Fitters & Turners (R.E.)	Wood	
		Iron	
	Fitters	R.A.	
		Wireless	
	Plumbers		
	Electricians	Ordinary	
		W.T.	
	Signalmen		
	Engine Drivers	Loco.	
		Field	
	Air Line Men		
	Permanent Line Men		
	Operators, Telegraph		
	Cablemen		
	Brigade Section Pioneers		
	General-duty Pioneers		
	Signallers		
	Instrument Repairers		
	Motor Cyclists		
	Motor Cyclist Artificers		
	Telephonists		
	Clerks		
INFANTRY	Machine Gunners		
	Armament Artificers	Fitters	
		Range Finders	
	Armourers		
	Storemen		
	Privates		
R.A.M.C.			
A.O.C.			
A.V.C.			

		W.O's. and N.C.O's. (by ranks) not included in trade columns	TOTAL, to agree with wanting to complete		Horses			
			Officers	Other Ranks	Riding	Draught	Heavy Draught	Pack
		Buglers	4					
			4	4				

Remarks:—

Signature of Commander: R. Alex Lieut Colonel

Unit: 4th Bn the King's (Liverpool Regt)

Formation to which attached: 33rd Division

Date of Despatch: 28th April 1916.

[P.T.O.]

98th Brigade.
33rd division

4th BATTALION

THE KING'S LIVERPOOL REGIMENT

M A Y   1 9 1 6

WAR DIARY or INTELLIGENCE SUMMARY

Army Form C. 2118.

Volume XV
MAY 1916
4th Bn. The Kings (Liverpool Regt.)
Vol 4

Place	Date	Hour	Summary of Events and Information	Remarks and references to Appendices
BETHUNE	1-5-16		In Divisional Reserve Billets. Fine day, very hot. Brigade Route March at 8 A.M.	
"	2-5-16		In billets. Very hot day. Ten men to hospital.	
"	3-5-16		In billets. Major Bsall, C.O. Commanding. We went to look at trenches at Cuinchy (left subsection). Cloudy day. Lecture by S.O.C. 33rd Division on Gas. Matel's at 6 p.m. to Officers Mobile Bethune. Ten men to hospital. No men sent to Base classified P.B.	
BETHUNE → TRENCHES CUINCHY (left subsection)	4-5-16		In billets. Very hot day. At hot dogs. At 4 pm orders from Brigade Clear to join 20th Royal Fusiliers in trenches Cuinchy No1 (left subsector) (Brickstacks). Moved off by Companies at 6 pm. Guides from P.O.W. 20 to the Canal. Lt Col Allinson & Adjutant, Major R.S.P.S.Maj, Do reconnaissance Bethune. Relief Complete 10 pm. C.O. Major Bsall took on command of Battalion - Allinson being appointed	
"	5-5-16		In trenches. Very hot day. Rain in evening. Quiet day. No casualties. Lt Col Allinson & Major for reptile risk.	
"	6-5-16		In trenches. Dull + windy. Trench shooting. At Major reports from Lewis Gun Course. Draft of 39 men arrived from Base + were retained at Depot - Beuvry. Quiet day + night - no casualties.	13D
"	7-5-16		In trenches. Dull + showery. 9/Lt Waring + 2/Lt Atkin proceeded on leave. 2/Lt Roberts went to Lewis Gun Course. C.O. Commanders of 18s and 5th A.I.H. visited trenches. Enquired into trenches. Quiet day. 2 casualties for rifle grenade. Draft of 58 (on man reported sick) came up to trenches.	
"	8-5-16		In trenches. Fine with showers. 9/Lt Irving T.H. McLean. Again Quiet. Relieved by 2nd Bn A & S.H. Guides Point Fixe 8.15 pm. relief complete 10.15 pm. Battalion moved	
LE QUESNOY (Bethune Sheet F.8.6.)	9-5-16		to Le Quesnoy (Bethune map F.8.6.) on relief. In Brigade Reserve billets. Rained all day. 9/Lt Trublaine rejoins from hospital. Captain Boniface went on leave. 250 hewn working party to trenches + wiring near Beuvry. Mine exploded by Germans in trench near Bethune keep. District & Place. About 20 casualties in Bat. Buttalion.	

1577 Wt.W10791/1773 50,000 1/15 D. D. & L. A.D.S.S./Forms/C. 2118.

WAR DIARY
or
INTELLIGENCE SUMMARY.
(Erase heading not required.)

Army Form C. 2118.

Instructions regarding War Diaries and Intelligence Summaries are contained in F. S. Regs., Part II. and the Staff Manual respectively. Title pages will be prepared in manuscript.

Place	Date	Hour	Summary of Events and Information	Remarks and references to Appendices
LE QUESNOY	10-5-16		Dull day. 2 men on wiring party. 250 men on working party. 1 man to hospital. 1 man from hospital. 1 man killed.	
"	11-5-16		Fine. 1 Stunt. 2 men were killed. 210 men on working party. 2 Companies (A+B) moved up to No 4 & 5 R/LINE between CAMEL & BLUECOW STREET in support of 2nd R.H. Mns M.Hall 9:10 P.M. 1 man to hospital, 1 man to Base.	
"	12-5-16		Fine. 2 Wells + trenches. Relieved 2nd R.H. in CUINCHY. Left Subsection. 2 Companies report from NUSOFE LINE & went into front trenches with SUB. Battalion. 2/Lt McCrae from Divisional School rejoined. 1 man to hospital. 1 man wounded. 1 man killed.	
CUINCHY Left Subsection	13-5-16		Heavy rain. 2 trenches. Raid by 4/Norfolks on our right starting from No 4 Bay - hostile shell battalion in trenches with fire in support. Lieut. Brock (T/Captain) injured. 1 man on leave. 1 man to hospital.	
"	14-5-16		Dull. 12 men. Dull. In trenches. 6:15 P.M. Enemy mine blown. Trying to our right in L/R Halt line. After Rees to Divisional School. 1 man to hospital. 6 men wounded. 4 men killed. T.M. bombarded. 1 Ripe Company.	
"	15-5-16		In fine. Wet + cold. 2 mine in right J Brigade front at 10 P.M. 1 man to hospital. 2 men wounded. 2 men killed. 1 man to Base.	
"	16-5-16		Very fine. 3 P.M. we blew a mine opposite Sap 16 in crater. Australian Artillery. Brooks came to German trenches + from snipe. We stood off + threw + confining out the new crater. Relieved by 2nd R.H. relief complete 10:15 P.M. 1 man to Base. 2/Lt Gaultz went to leave. 2/Lt McCrae to leave.	
LE QUESNOY	17-5-16		Very fine. 2/Lt Willets 250 men on working party. 2/Lt Sharpe went on leave. to Lewis Gun Course.	
"	18-5-16		Very fine. 2 men were killed. 250 men on working party. 2/Lt Sharpe went to hospital. Brigade Commander Lt Mallen + 16 men to Private Bombing School. 1 man to hospital. 1 man to Base. Wheaton Draft of 12 men on arrival at 3 ratrick.	
"	19-5-16		Very fine. 240 men on working party. 1 man to Base for Discharge.	
"	20-5-16		Very fine. hot. 85 men on working party. Relieved 2nd R.H. CUINCHY Left Subsection. Relief complete 10:10 P.M. Night quiet up to 12 P.M. 1 man to hospital.	

WAR DIARY or INTELLIGENCE SUMMARY

Army Form C. 2118.

4 Bn The King's Liverpool Regt.

May 1916

Place	Date	Hour	Summary of Events and Information	Remarks and references to Appendices
CUINCHY Left subsection	21-5-16	2.8 AM	Mine blown by us at No 7 Sap. A.21.b.95/4. Artillery + T.M retaliation damaged revetts in neighbourhood highly. 6.30 AM Enemy artillery + T.M active. 2/Lt G.S. HORBURY killed by rifle grenade. Observing effect of lachrymatory shells fell sharply; enemy having met them further South. Very hot + fine. Mine blown by us at 9.56 PM by No 5 Sap. A.21.b.9/4. Heavy T.M. retaliation in neighbourhood. C.S.M. Rogers killed. 2/Lt W. Gray wounded.	
"	22-5-16		Fine day very hot. Lieut A.C. SODEN (O.C. A Coy.) killed by rifle grenade. 2/Lt W.V. TRUBSHAWE wounded. Artillery (bombards) Enemy's Trenches pt S. of 4A BASSEE ROAD at 4 PM. 10.30 PM. 2/Lt F. WHITE, 2/Lt A. BACK 2/30 AM. 3 men killed + 6 men wounded 1 man to Base for discharge. 2/Lt E.P. NICKALLS, 2/Lt F. WHITE, 2/Lt A. BACK joined for duty.	
"	24-5-16		Fine but dull. Morning quiet. B. Coy. (in ESPERANTO TERRACE) and 2 Platoon A. Coy. were relieved at 1.30 PM by men of 2/6 A + J.H. who has finished working party. Rest of Battalion relieved by 2/6 A.F.H. by 10.30 p.m. 2/Lt BACK to hospital. One blew a mine by No 16 Sap. 12 M.N.	
LE QUESNOY	25/5/16		Dull + Showers. Lieut J.S. HUTCHINS went on leave. 2/Lt J.C. MANNON to Anti San school. 2/Lt W.R. IRVING to hospital. Capt A.N. BOUMPHREY, 2/Lt T.H. IRVING, 2/Lt R. McCRAE returned from leave. 200 men on working party.	
"	26/5/16		Dull. 300 men on working parties. 2/Lt I. McCORKINDALE joined for duty. 2/Lt SAWSTER (R.W.F.) from Lewis Gun School. Lt Staples appointed adjutant vice Major Read from 30 Gordon Highlanders.	
"	27/5/16		Fine. Cooler. 350 men on working parties. Lieut J. HARPE returned from leave. 2/Lt J.H. LOMAS went on leave. 2/Lt E.P. NICKALLS to Lewis Gun School. 2 men killed + 1 man wounded. C.O. & Adjutant to R.J. major 1 Coy S/L major to Bayonet Fighting School at Divisional School W. 28 C. 2.2.	
"	28/5/16		Fine - warm. 98 A.B wide relief by 100th Bde cancelled. Starting his afternoon - Orders to move to GOLF STS. Jeunes Filles received 6 PM. 9.30 PM. relieved by 11th Royal Sussex Regt - 116 Brigade - all men to hospital - C.O. ret. C. & 2 Coys. marched to reserve line of 15th Division.	
BETHUNE	29/5/16		Fine. Marching to billets ready to move at short notice. Bn. A + C. Coys. marched to huts of Anti San School.	

Army Form C. 2118.

Volume XV

WAR DIARY
or
INTELLIGENCE SUMMARY.

(Erase heading not required.)

4th Bn. The Kings own Liverpool Regt.

May 1916

Instructions regarding War Diaries and Intelligence Summaries are contained in F. S. Regs., Part II. and the Staff Manual respectively. Title pages will be prepared in manuscript.

Place	Date	Hour	Summary of Events and Information	Remarks and references to Appendices
BETHUNE	30/5/16		Rain during morning. Fine afternoon — C.O. & O.C. C & D Coys reconnoitred the reserve line of 11th & 1st Divisions. Standing to at 2 hours notice. Sgt T.H. Irving to Boulogne Typhoid Course. One man to Base to transfer R.E. Two men to hospital.	
"	31/5/16		Fine. O.C. A & B Coy reconnoitred reserve lines of 16th & 1st Divisions. Still standing to. Period of warning lengthened to 4 hours. 2 ~/~ Sgts rejoined from hospital.	

Ian Campbell D.S.O. Colonel
Comdg 4th Bn. The King's Lpool Regt.

1577 Wt. W10791/1773 500,000 1/15 D. D. & L. A.D.S.S./Forms/C. 2118.

4th Kings (Liverpool)

The Brigadier wishes to convey to you and all ranks his hearty congratulations on the mention of your battalion in the Commander in Chief's Despatches, which has been so well deserved.

31/5/16 (Sd) R M Watson Captn.
Brigade Major
98th Infantry Brigade

Certified true copy

[signature] Lieut.
31/5/16 Adjt 1/4th Bn The Kings Regt.

Ac 36/141

98th Infantry Brigade

Out of 65 Battalions mentioned in the Commander-in-Chief's Despatches for good work in carrying out raids there are no fewer than six belonging to the 33rd Division.

19th Brigade. 2nd Bn. Royal Welsh Fus.

98th Brigade. 1st Middlesex Regt.
2nd Bn. A & S Highlanders
4th Bn. King's (Liverpool) Regt.
1/4th Bn. Suffolk Regt.

100th Brigade 1st Bn. Queens (R.W.S.) Regt.

I warmly congratulate these battalions on the distinction they have thus gained.

The success achieved in raids carried out in the Division has been materially assisted by the skilful co-operation of the Divisional Artillery, Royal Engineers, Trench Mortar Batteries, and Machine Gun Companies, and to them I wish to express my acknowledgment of their good work.

With so fine a fighting spirit in the Division there can be no doubt as to the share it will have in bringing about the final victory over the enemy.

31/3/16   (Sd) H. J. S. Landon, Major General
            Commanding 33rd Division

4th Bn. King's (Liverpool) Regt.

For information.

            (Sd) T. P. Clarke, Major
            & Staff Captain, 98th Infy. Brigade

Certified true copy
J W Stephes
Lieut
Adjt. 4th Bn. The King's Regt.

Army Form B. 213

FIELD RETURN.

(To be furnished by all arms, services, and departments (except A.S.C. units) to the A. G.'s Office at the Base in accordance with Field Service Regulations, Part II.)

RETURN showing numbers RATIONED by, and Transport on charge of, 4th Infantry Bde (4th Bn Royal Scots) at France 5th May 1916 Date.

No. of Report 61.

DETAIL	Personnel			Animals								Guns, carriages, and limbers and transport vehicles				Horsed		Mechanical					REMARKS
	Officers	Other ranks	Natives	Horses Riding	Draught	Heavy Draught	Pack	Mules Large	Small	Camels	Oxen	Guns, carriages and limbers, showing description	Ammunition wagons and limbers	Machine guns	Aircraft, showing description	4 Wheeled	2 Wheeled	Motor Cars	Tractors	Lorries	Trucks	Trailers	Motor Bicycles	Bicycles	
Effective Strength of Unit	30	943		14	10	9		24						4		16	6							9	Base Depot 1 — Not Returned Officer 1 Att T.M. By 1 Course of Instr 2 Leave 1 Hospital 4/5
Details, by Arms attached to unit as in War Establishment:—																									
R.A.M.C.		7/5																							Other Ranks 31 On Command 21 Base Employ 4
Army Ordnance Corps	1																								
Total	31	944		14	10	9		24						4		16	6							9	Atts 25+6+4+R5 = 34 9 Course of Instr 30
War Establishment	30	992		14	10	9		24						4		16	6								Att T.M. By 1 Employment 6 Field ambulance 25
Wanting to complete		4	82*																						Wks Y Employ 15 Leave 114 Hospital Emp 2
Surplus	1																								762
Attached (not to include the details shown above)																									
Civilians:— Employed with the Unit Accompanying the Unit																									
TOTAL RATIONED	25+32	14	10	1		24																			Not Dest Trans No Horses 7

* In the case of field ambulances, hospitals or depots, the number of patients are to be included here, the names being shown in A. F. A. 36.

* 21 New Service ranks attached 253rd Tunnelling Company R.E.

Signature of Commander Turnbull Major 5 May 1916

Date of Despatch

For information of the A.G.'s Office at the Base.

Officers and men who have become casuals, been transferred or joined since last report.

Place: France   Date: 5th May 1916

Regtl. Number	Rank	Name	Corps	Nature of casualty, or name of unit from or to which transferred	Date of being struck off or coming on the ration return	Remarks*
11234	Cpl	Owens J		From No 8. Infy	28-4-16	
12652	Pte	Leonardi A				
31801	--	Hulse C		Base Depot		
24422	--	McGowan W		From Hospl	--	
29952	--	Busby J		To Hosptl	21-4-16	
30409	--	Phipps A		--	29-4-16	
13420	Cpl	Scott S		--	30-4-16	
	2/Lt	Trubshawe W		--	--	
18454	Pte	Warren W		--	--	
12615	--	Connelly H		--	2-5-16	
11834	--	McKenna J		To Base Depot PB	3-5-16	
9256	--	Rice T		To Hosptl	--	
8593	--	Fenton J			2-5-16	
8259	--	Wilson J		To Base for Discharge	30-4-16	
9242	Pte	Coyne T		To F.A.	29-4-16	
30409	--	Phipps A		--	--	
18454	--	Warren W		--	--	
10648	--	Davidson C		--	--	
13420	Cpl	Scott S		--	--	
31468	Pte	Christie S		--	--	
12652	--	Leonardi A		--	--	
14956	LCpl	Hack W		--	1-5-16	
12615	Pte	Connelly H		--	--	
9256	--	Rice T		--	--	
27935	--	Devine W		--	2-5-16	
8159	Cpl	Gale G		--	--	
8593	Pte	Fenton J		--	1-5-16	
10370	--	Sullivan		--	2-5-16	
12482	--	Kelly Jas		--	3-5-16	
30040	--	Errington R		--	--	
12939	--	Hughes T		--	--	
24858	--	Williams J		--	--	
29369	--	Smith J		--	4-5-16	
3915	--	Kelly J		--	--	
44060	--	Upton J		--	--	
8946	--	McGregor W		From F.A.	29-4-16	
24602	LCpl	McColl J		--	--	
10413	Pte	Smith J		--	30-4-16	
14956	LCpl	Hack W		--	--	
20298	Cpl	Hall J		--	1-5-16	
10648	Pte	Davidson J		--	2-5-16	
11834	--	McKenna J		--	3-5-16	
10094	--	Murphy A		--	--	
12482	--	Kelly Jas		--	4-5-16	

* State whether absence is of a permanent or temporary nature, adding, in the case of casuals from wounds or disease, any available information for communication to the relatives.

Marshall Major
Comdg 4th Bn The King's (L'pool) Regt

Perforated Sheet giving detail of personnel and horses wanting to complete, shown on Army Form B. 213.

Number of Report 6

Detail of Wanting to Complete	Drivers						Gunners	Smith Gunners	Range Takers	Farriers				Wheelers			Saddlers or Harness Makers	Blacksmiths	Bricklayers and Masons	Carpenters and Joiners	Fitters & Turners (R. E.)		Fitters			Electricians			Signalmen	Engine Drivers		Air Line Men	Permanent Line Men	Operators, Telegraph	Cablemen	Brigade Section Pioneers	General-duty Pioneers	Signallers	Instrument Repairers	Motor Cyclists	Motor Cyclist Artificers	Telephonists	Clerks	Machine Gunners	Armament Artificers			Storemen	Privates	W.O.'s and N.C.O.'s (by ranks) not included in trade columns				TOTAL wanting to agree with complete		Horses				
	R.A.	R.E.	A.S.C.	Car	Lorry	Steam				Sergeants	Corporals	Shoeing, or Shoeing and Carriage Smiths	Cold Shoers	R.A.	H.T.	M.T.					Wood	Iron	R.A.	Wireless	Plumbers	Ordinary	W.T.		Loco.	Field														Fitters	Range Finders	Armourers							Officers	Other Ranks	Riding	Draught	Heavy Draught	Pack
CAVALRY																																																			Pinata					4.2				
R.A.																																																											
E.E.																																																											
INFANTRY																																																			2					4.2				
R.A.M.C.																																																											
A.O.C.																																																											
A.V.C.																																																											

Remarks:—

Mitchell Major Signature of Commander.
4th Br. the Kings (Liverpool Regt) Unit.
33rd Division Formation to which attached.
5th May 1916 Date of Despatch.

Army Form B. 213.

FIELD RETURN.

To be made up to and for Sunday in each week.

No. of Report 6h

(To be furnished by all arms, services, and departments (except A.S.C. units) to the A. G.'s Office at the Base in accordance with Field Service Regulations, Part II.)

RETURN showing numbers
(a) Effective strength of Unit. 1st Bn. The King's (Liverpool Regiment) at France
(b) Rationed by Unit. Date 12th May 1916.

DETAIL	Personnel			Animals							Guns, carriages, and limbers and transport vehicles			Horsed		Motor Cars	Tractors	Mechanical		Trailers	Motor Bicycles	Bicycles	REMARKS
	Officers	Other ranks	Natives	Horses Riding	Draught	Heavy Draught	Pack	Mules Large	Small	Camels	Oxen	Guns, carriages, limbers showing description	Ammunition wagons and limbers	Machine guns	Aircraft showing description	4 wheeled	2 wheeled			Lorries, showing description	Trucks, showing description			
Effective Strength of Unit	24	993		11	9	8	9	27						4		16	6							Officers / Not Rationed 1 / Base Depot 5 / Leave 1 / C.O.S. 2 / Hospital 9
Details, by Arms attached to unit as in War Establishment:—																								
R.A.M.C.	1																							
Army Cyclist Corps.		1																						Other Ranks 2x / On command 21 / On Employ 6 / With 2nd Sect 33rd R.E. 33 / L.G.S. 9 / Med T.M. Batty 11 / Corps Employ 6 / Div Employ 8 / Bde Employ 8 / Brit Employ 15 / Leave 136 / Depot Coy 2 / Neft & Tolsford 265
Total	30	994		11	9	8	9	27						4		16	6							
War Establishment	35	1015		12	26	9	9	27						4		16	6							
Wanting to complete (Detail of Personnel and Horses below)	5	62½		1	17	1																		
Surplus																								
*Attached (not to include the details shown above)																								
Civilians:— Employed with the Unit Accompanying the Unit																								
TOTAL RATIONED...	21	709		11	9			27															8 H.D. Stores

* In the case of field ambulances, hospitals or depots, the number of patients are to be included here, the names being shown in A. F. A. 36.

x Indicates men permanently attached to :-
Tunnelling Company and French Mortar Battery

Kendall Lieut Colonel Signature of Commander.
12th May 1916. Date of Despatch.

For information of the A.G.'s Office at the Base.

Officers and men who have become casuals, been transferred or joined since last report.

Place France. Date 12th May 1916.

Regtl. Number	Rank	Name	Corps	Nature of casualty, or name of unit from or to which transferred	Date of being struck off or coming on the ration return	Remarks
10693	Pte	Mulligan J.				
7621	-"-	Baker S.J.				
21327	-"-	Gledhill J.				
31310	-"-	Howell J.				
31311	-"-	Leatherbarrow J.				
26238	-"-	Riley J.				
27884	-"-	Robinson J.				
6132	L/Cpl	McAlley R.				
20089	Pte	Buchanan J.				
23272	-"-	Fairhurst J.W.				
11559	-"-	Hamilton J.	The Kings (Liverpool Regt)	Reinforcements from the Infantry Base Depot.		
12167	-"-	Sanderson F.				
12151	-"-	Thornley J.				
13680	-"-	Lampkin J.				
18059	-"-	Harrison J.				
11500	-"-	Hoey G.			5-1-16	
31244	-"-	Kerruish J.				
8882	-"-	Moore W.				
7816	-"-	Pauline A.				
26350	-"-	Henry H.L.				
9973	-"-	Hughes R.				
25095	-"-	Lewin S.J.			5-1-16	
27278	-"-	Booth R.				
31479	-"-	Halliday G.				
30091	-"-	Johnson A.				
33067	-"-	McManus J.				
27625	-"-	Parker J.				
30613	-"-	Young F.				
30960	-"-	Darlington W.				
11574	Cpl	Williamson G.				
13240	L/Cpl	McCabe J.				
27136	Pte	Boardman			8-1-16	
9881	-"-	Corcoran J.				
25213	-"-	Ellis J.				
13570	-"-	McGuirk J.				
~~1733~~	-"-	~~Jones J.~~				
18440	-"-	Stephenson R.				
7681	-"-	Dolan E.				
12643	-"-	Barrett W.				
20175	Cpl	Charlesworth G.	4th Bn The Kings (Liverpool Regt)	From Hospital	6-5-16	
13831	Pte	Fitzpatrick A.		"	8-5-16	
31768	Pte	Christie S.M.		To Hospital	3-5-16	
9274	-"-	Coyne B.		"	29-4-16	
9213	-"-	Woods		"	4-5-16	
26787	-"-	Brough J.		"	8-5-16	
9124	-"-	Smith J.		"	10-5-16	
9907	Sgt	Cooke G.		"		
10977	Pte	Inches H.		To Base P.B.	9-5-16	
8298	Sgt	Makin J.		Wounded in Action	7-5-16	
11379	Pte	Campbell L.		To England	24-4-16	
9552	-"-	Sullivan P.		Transferred to R.E.	5-4-16	
27774	-"-	Ryan J.		From Hospital	9-5-16	
8005	-"-	Frankland A.		"	10-5-16	
13724	Cpl	Scott S.		"	9-5-16	
	Lieut	Rubshawe W.T.				
6438	Pte	Holcroft A.		To Base for Hearings	11-5-16	
	Lieut	Lawrence J.W.		To 95/2 Trench Mortar Battery	8-5-16	

* State whether absence is of a permanent or temporary nature, adding, in the case of casuals from wounds or disease, any available information for communication to the relatives.

For information of the Officer i/c of a Base Record Office.

Officers and men who have left or joined since last report.

Place _____   Date _____

Regtl. Number	Rank	Name	Corps	Name of unit from or to which transferred	Date of being struck off or coming on the ration return	Remarks *
	2Lt	Allen	J.W.L.R.	To Hospital	6-5-16	
	Major	Jones	R.E.R.L.O	—"—	—"—	
Admittances to and Discharges from Field Ambulance						
29965	Pte	McCusker	G	To Field Amb	5-5-16	
29882	"	Bleasdale	R	—"—	7-5-16	
9907	Sgt	Cooke	G	—"—	9-5-16	
9105	LCpl	Peters	S	—"—	—"—	
12043	Pte	Barreto	D	—"—	—"—	
11509	"	Hoey	G	—"—	10-5-16	
9025	Sgt	Randles	S	From Field Amb	6-5-16	
12939	Pte	Hughes	R	—"—	6-5-16	
27258	"	Hillman	G	—"—	—"—	
29965	"	McCusker	G	—"—	7-5-16	
8598	Cpl	Higgins	R	—"—	8-5-16	
9159	"	Little	G	—"—	—"—	
11382	Pte	Jones	D	—"—	—"—	
12397	"	Vose	D	—"—	9-5-16	
30464	"	Riley	K	—"—	—"—	
10345	"	Sullivan		—"—	11-5-16	

McBeale Lieut Colonel
comdg 4th Bn The King's (Liverpool Regt)

* State whether absence is of a permanent or temporary nature.

Army Form B. 213.

FIELD RETURN.

(To be furnished by all arms, services, and departments to the Base Record Office in accordance with Field Service Regulations, Part II.)

No. of Report _____
Date _____

RETURN showing numbers RATIONED by, and Transport on charge of, _____ at _____

| DETAIL. | Personnel ||| Animals |||||||| Transport Vehicles || Guns, carriages, and limbers, showing description | Ammunition wagons and limbers | Machine guns | REMARKS |
| | Officers | Other ranks | Natives | Horses ||| Mules || Camels | Oxen | 4 Wheeled | 2 Wheeled | | | | |
				Riding	Draught	Pack	Large	Small								
Effective Strength of Unit																
Details, *by Arms* attached to Unit as in War Establishment:—																
Total																
War Establishment																
Wanting to complete																
Surplus																
*Attached (not to include the details shown above)																
Civilians:—																
Employed with the Unit																
Accompanying the Unit																
TOTAL RATIONED …																

* In the case of field ambulances, hospitals or depots, the number of patients are to be included here, the names being shown in A. F. A. 36.

Signature of Commander _____

Date of Despatch _____

(54010a) Wt. 1005/1860 50000 6-09 W B & L   Forms B. 213

Perforated Sheet giving detail of personnel and horses wanting to complete, shown on Army Form B. 213.

Number of Report 62

Detail of Wanting to Complete	Drivers						Gunners	Smith Gunners	Range Takers	Farriers				Cold Shoers	Wheelers			Saddlers or Harness Makers	Blacksmiths	Bricklayers and Masons	Carpenters and Joiners	Fitters & Turners (R. E.)		Fitters			Plumbers	Electricians			Signalman	Engine Drivers		Air Line Men	Permanent Line Men	Operators, Telegraph	Cablemen	Brigade Section Pioneers	General-duty Pioneers	Signalers	Instrument Repairers	Motor Cyclists	Motor Cyclist Artificers	Telephonists	Clerks	Machine Gunners	Armament Artificers			Armourers	Storemen	Privates	W.O's. and N.C.O's. (by ranks) not included in trade columns	TOTAL to agree with waiting to complete		Horses			
	R.A.	R.E.	A.S.C.	Car	Lorry	Steam				Sergeants	Corporals	Shoeing, or Shoeing and Carriage Smiths			R.A.	T.H.	M.T.					Wood	Iron	R.A.	Wireless			Ordinary	W.T.		Loco.	Field														Fitters	Range Finders						Officers	Other Ranks	Riding	Draught	Heavy Draught	Pack
CAVALRY																																																							
R.A.																																																							
R.E.																																																							
INFANTRY																																																			62	Infantry	5	62				
R.A.M.C.																																																							
A.O.C.																																																							
A.V.C.																																																							

Remarks :—

Turnbull Lieut Colonel, Signature of Commander.

4th Bn the King's (Liverpool Regt) Unit.

33rd Division Formation to which attached.

12th May 1916. Date of Despatch.

FIELD RETURN.

To be made up to and for Sunday in each week.

No. of Report 63

Army Form B. 213.

(To be furnished by all arms, services, and departments (except A.S.C. units) to the A. G.'s Office at the Base in accordance with Field Service Regulations, Part II.)

RETURN showing numbers (a) Effective strength of Unit. H.H. the Royal Devonport Regt(?) at France
(b) Rationed by Unit.   Date 19th May 1916.

Detail	Personnel			Animals							Guns, carriages, and limbers and transport vehicles				Mechanical			Motor Bicycles	Bicycles	Remarks
	Officers	Other ranks	Natives	Horses Riding	Horses Draught	Horses Heavy Draught	Mules Pack	Mules Large	Mules Small	Camels	Oxen	Guns, carriages and limbers, showing description	Ammunition wagons and limbers	Machine guns	Aircraft, showing description	Horsed 4 wheeled	Horsed 2 wheeled	Motor Cars	Tractors	Lorries, showing description	Trucks, showing description	Trailers			
Effective Strength of Unit	27	960		11	9	8		24						4		16	6							9	Horse Depot / Leave / Horses Destruction — Officers — Not Rationed 16 4 6 3 6 8
Details, by Arms attached to unit as in War Establishment:— R.A.M.C.																										
Any Ordnance Corps	1	1																								
Total	28	961		11	9	8		24						4		16	6							9	On Command / Corps Employ 16 / Rest — in 2 / Trench Mortar Bty 6 11 / Field Ambulance 9 / Leave 38 / 409 35Siege(?) Inc(?)tillery(?) 6 31
War Establishment	44	1105		12	26	9																		9	Course/Instruction 30 / Sick Employ 15
Wanting to complete	16	73		1	17	1	9																			Hospital 2 / England 3
Surplus								24																	Absent 3
																									Att 99th Bn A.B. 346 / 741
*Attached (not to include the details shown above)																									With Civil Employ / S.H.D. Horses
Civilians:— Employed with the Unit Accompanying the Unit																									
Total Rationed...	20	1		11	9			24																	

* In the case of field ambulances, hospitals or depots, the number of patients are to be included here, the names being shown in A. F. A. 36.

Inverell Lieut Colonel Signature of Commander.
19th May 1916. Date of Despatch.

x Includes 39 Men permanently attached to Inverell
Including Bty and French Mortar Battery.

For information of the A.G.'s Office at the Base.

Officers and men who have become casuals, been transferred or joined since last report.

Place France   Date 19th May 1916

Regtl. Number	Rank	Name	Corps	Nature of casualty, or name of unit from or to which transferred	Date of being struck off or coming on the ration return	Remarks
30709	Pte	Phipps	R			
10081	-"-	Brennand	J			
29939	-"-	Hughes	J			
26379	-"-	Lousey	W	From Base	1-5-16	
11734	-"-	Morgan	M			
9272	-"-	Coyne				
13402	-"-	Woods	J			
8739	-"-	Hill	J			
31709	-"-	Sorley	J			
10236	-"-	Evans	H			
9802	-"-	Sharples	W		13-5-16	
26468	-"-	Jackson	J			
14928	Pte	Wright	H	From Hospital	15-5-16	
8423	-"-	Crimmins	J	Wounded in Action	14-5-16	
27819	-"-	Glasgow	J			
11462	LCpl	Elmer	W			
7621	Pte	Baker	J			
11129	-"-	Woods	J			
14928	-"-	Wright	H			
27444	Pte	Wilcocks	J		15-5-16	
27632	-"-	Pepper				
8855	-"-	Gerard	S	Killed in Action	14-5-16	
21327	-"-	Gledhill	JW			
11888	-"-	Humphries				
14506	-"-	Radcliffe	J			
10959	LCpl	Pearson	L		15-5-16	
30519	Pte	Pearse	G			
11726	2Cpl	Geary	J	To Hospital	13-5-16	
9434	Pte	Davies	J	-"-	12-5-16	
12640	-"-	Barrett	J	-"-	11-5-16	
9502	-"-	Newbury	J	To Base for Discharge	15-5-16	
8266	-"-	Munsey	JW	-"-	19-5-16	
25098	-"-	Bowes	JW	To Military Prison	1-5-16	
13543	-"-	Wright	S	-"-	-"-	
7583	-"-	Parry	G	-"-	-"-	
12191	-"-	Graham	J	-"-	-"-	
12717	-"-	Baines	J			
10691	-"-	Shinners	H	From Hospital	18-5-16	
26987	-"-	Brough	H	-"-	14-5-16	
10619	-"-	Smith	A	Transferred to R.E.	22-2-16	
12658	-"-	Loftus	M	Killed in Action	10-5-16	
30288	LCpl	Hall	H	Wounded in Action	12-5-16	
30496	Pte	Topping	R	Killed in Action	-"-	
	Lt Col	Allen J.W.C.M.G.		To England	9-5-16	
	Major	Jones	R.F.R.S.O.			

Admittances to and Discharges from Field Ambulance

11574	LCpl	Williamson		To Field Amb	12-5-16	
9434	Pte	Davies	J	-"-	13-5-16	
21383	-"-	Dempsey	P	-"-	18-5-16	
25950	-"-	Brady	J	From Field Amb	14-5-16	
11809	-"-	Hoey	J	-"-	13-5-16	
30385	-"-	Moore	H	-"-	15-5-16	
12652	-"-	Leonard	J	-"-	16-5-16	

Turnbull Lieut Colonel
Comdg 4th Bn The King's (Liverpool Regt)

* State whether absence is of a permanent or temporary nature, adding, in the case of casuals from wounds or disease, any available information for communication to the relatives.

Perforated Sheet giving detail of personnel and horses wanting to complete, shown on Army Form B. 213.

Number of Report 63

Detail of Wanting to Complete	Drivers						Gunners	Smith Gunners	Range Takers	Farriers				Wheelers			Saddlers or Harness Makers	Blacksmiths	Bricklayers and Masons	Carpenters and Joiners	Fitters & Turners (R. E.)		Fitters			Plumbers	Electricians		Signalmen	Engine Drivers		Air Line Men	Permanent Line Men	Operators, Telegraph	Cablemen	Brigade Section Pioneers	General-duty Pioneers	Signallers	Instrument Repairers	Motor Cyclists	Motor Cyclist Artificers	Telephonists	Clerks	Machine Gunners	Armament Artificers				Storemen	Privates	W.O.s and N.C.O.s (by ranks) not included in trade columns	TOTAL to agree with wanting to complete		Horses				
	R.A.	R.E.	A.S.C.	Car	Lorry	Steam				Sergeants	Corporals	Shoeing, or Shoeing and Carriage Smiths	Cold Shoers	R.A.	H.T.	M.T.					Wood	Iron	R.A.	Wireless			Ordinary	W.T.		Loco.	Field														Fitters	Range Finders	Armourers				Officers	Other Ranks	Riding	Draught	Heavy Draught	Pack
CAVALRY																																																									
R.A.																																																									
R.E.																																																					16	73				
INFANTRY																																																		73							
R.A.M.C.																																																									
A.O.C.																																																									
A.V.C.																																																									

Remarks:—

Burdett Lieut. Colonel Signature of Commander.

4th Bn. The King's (Liverpool Regiment) Unit.

33rd Division Formation to which attached.

19th May 1916 Date of Despatch.

[P.T.O.

FIELD RETURN.

Army Form B. 213.

To be made up to and for Sunday in each week.

No. of Report 64 Diary

(To be furnished by all arms, services, and departments (except A.S.C. units) to the A. G.'s Office at the Base in accordance with Field Service Regulations, Part II.)

RETURN showing numbers (a) Effective strength of Unit. 2th An. M. Regt (Depot Cadre) at France   Date.
(b) Rationed by Unit.

Detail	Personnel			Animals							Guns, carriages, and limbers and transport vehicles										Remarks
	Officers	Other ranks	Natives	Horses			Mules		Camels	Oxen	Guns, carriages and limbers, showing description	Ammunition wagons and limbers	Machine guns	Aircraft, showing description	Horsed		Motor Cars	Tractors	Mechanical			
				Riding	Draught	Heavy Draught	Pack	Large	Small							4 wheeled	2 wheeled			Lorries, showing description	Trucks, showing description	Trailers	Motor Bicycles	Bicycles	
Effective Strength of Unit	39	402		11	9	8		21						4											Not likely dept
Details, by Arms attached to unit as in War Establishment:—																										9 Aust Lt horse
R.A.M.C	1																								1 Lancashire Hospital
Army Veterinary Corps																										Horse Master
Total	28 W3			11	9	8		21						4											Armoured
War Establishment	41	495		12	25	9	9									11	6								16	Field Arty
Wanting to complete	16	89		1	17	1	9									16	6								6	31
Surplus								21																	45	32
*Attached (not to include the details shown above)																									3	6
Civilians:— Employed with the Unit Accompanying the Unit																									32	17
Total Rationed...	12 W3			11	9	9		21																	129	

* In the case of field ambulances, hospitals or depots, the number of patients are to be included here, the names being shown in A. F. A. 36.

× Personally 39 men permanently attached to ___ Turnbull ___ Signature of Commander.

___ 2th May 1916 ___ Date of Despatch.

For information of the A.G.'s Office at the Base.

Officers and men who have become casuals, been transferred or joined since last report.

Place: France   Date: 26th May 1916

Regtl. Number	Rank	Name	Corps	Nature of casualty, or name of unit from or to which transferred	Date of being struck off or coming on the ration return	Remarks
	Lieut	Nichalls E.P.			24/5/16	
	"	White F.		From Base	24/5/16	
	"	Back A.			24/5/16	
	Lieut	Horbury G.B.		Killed in Action	21/5/16	
	Lieut	Soden A.C.		"	22-5-16	
	Lieut	Trutshawe W.V.		Wounded in Action		
	"	Gray V.		"	23-5-16	
	"	Irving W.P.		To Hospital	25-5-16	
	"	Back A.			24-5-16	
14616	Pte	Halliday K.		Hosptl in England	24-3-16	
9640	L/Cpl	McGuire W.		"	3-4-16	
8915	Pte	Kelly J.		To England	12-5-16	
29920	"	Wate L.		Wounded in Action	22-5-16	
26749	"	Evans W.		"	23-5-16	
30642	"	Connor P.		"	"	
29633	"	Halsall J.		"	"	
10913	"	Rose J.		"	"	
7816	"	Pauline R.		"	"	
8824	"	McDermott A.		"	"	
6524	C.S.M.	Rogers J.		Killed in Action	"	
11018	Pte	Hargreaves R.		"	"	
11250	"	Harmon P.		"	"	
20994	"	Tompkins G.		"	"	
8241	"	Williams A.		To Base for Discharge	23-5-16	
8596	"	Kilcoyne J.		"	25-5-16	
27395	"	Sullivan P.		To Hospital	22-5-16	
14835	"	Squires		"	20-5-16	
	Lieut	McCorkindale J.		From Base	26-5-16	

Admittances to and Discharges from Field Ambulance.

18835	Pte	Squires F.A.		To field Amb.	19-5-16	
14928	"	Wright A.		"	20-5-16	
27475	"	Doyle		"	22-5-16	
29882	"	Bleasdale R.		"	23-5-16	

Ansdell Lieut Colonel
Comdg 11th Bn The King's (Liverpool Regt)

* State whether absence is of a permanent or temporary nature, adding, in the case of casuals from wounds or disease, any available information for communication to the relatives.

Perforated Sheet giving detail of personnel and horses wanting to complete, shown on Army Form B. 213.

Number of Report _64_

Detail of Wanting to Complete	Drivers					Gunners	Smith Gunners	Range Takers	Farriers			Cold Shoers	Wheelers			Saddlers or Harness Makers	Blacksmiths	Bricklayers and Masons	Carpenters and Joiners	Fitters & Turners (H.K.)		Fitters			Plumbers	Electricians			Signalmen	Engine Drivers		Air Line Men	Permanent Line Men	Operators, Telegraph	Cablemen	Brigade Section Pioneers	General-duty Pioneers	Signallers	Instrument Repairers	Motor Cyclists	Motor Cyclist Orderlies	Telephonists	Clerks	Machine Gunners	Armament Artificers				Armourers	Storemen	Privates	W.O.s and N.C.O.s (by ranks) not included in trade columns	TOTAL wanting to agree with complete		Horses				
	R.A.	R.E.	A.S.C.	Car	Lorry	Steam				Sergeants	Corporals	Shoeing, or Carriage Smiths		B.A.	H.T.	M.T.					Wood	Iron	B.A.	Wireless			Ordinary	W.T.		Loco.	Field													Fitters	Range Finders					Officers	Other Ranks	Riding	Draught	Heavy Draught	Pack
CAVALRY																																																			1 34					
R.A.																																																	34						
R.E.																																																							
INFANTRY																																																							
R.A.M.C.																																																							
A.O.C.																																																							
A.V.C.																																																							

Remarks:—

Signature of Commander _Mitchell Lee Col_

1st Durham Light Infantry

Unit _3rd Division_

Formation to which attached

Date of Despatch _24th May 1916_

[P.T.O.

98th Brigade.

33rd Division.

4th BATTALION

THE KING'S LIVERPOOL REGIMENT

J U N E   1 9 1 6

WAR DIARY or INTELLIGENCE SUMMARY

Army Form C. 2118.

Volume XVI

June 1916

2 Bn The King's (Liverpool Regt)

Place	Date	Hour	Summary of Events and Information	Remarks and references to Appendices
ECOLE DES JEUNES FILLES – BETHUNE	1-6-16		Lieut MATHER from Grenade School. 2nd Dist WHITE to Grenade School. Battalion to hot baths.	
"	2-6-16		Lieut A R NICHOLS and 35 men joined from Base. 59 NCOs + men joined from N/Combending Battalion efficient Regt rejoined from Brigade School	
"	3-6-16		Lieut J. HUTCHINGS from leave. C.S.M. E. SPENCER appointed to Regtl S/M. Battalion King's Lpool Regt. 2/Lt SPENCER posted to D Company 1 man to hospital – 1 man from hospital	
"	4-6-16		Church Parades at BETHUNE CATHEDRAL + MUNICIPAL THEATRE. 1 ill at the other thee.	
"	5-6-16		Shavers. 2nd Lieut LOMAS rejoined from leave. Battalion Swimming Sports in Bethune baths. 2 men to hospital.	
"	6-6-16		Shavers. 2nd Lieut NICKALLS reported from Curse. 2 men to hospital	
"	7-6-16		Showery and much Cooler. Lewis Gun Drill, bayonet fighting especially. Hoisted on firing all the period. Battalion sports. Brigade Cricket in MUNICIPAL THEATRE	
"	8-6-16		Lieut BAN SHAW + Lewis Gun Curse. Brigade Boxing Tournament in MUNICIPAL THEATRE. 1 men from hospital. 2 men to hospital.	
"	9-6-16		Showery. Battalion allotted ANNEZIN SHOOTING RANGE. 2nd Lieut F R MILLIGAN joined from Base. 2 men to hospital	
"	10-6-16		Showery + wet in afternoon. All Officers + NCOs went to rent hotel of German Trenches of AUCHY + CUINCHY Sectors, to view in Garden opposite MUNICIPAL THEATRE. Brigadier General STRICKLAND C.M.G. D.S.O. appointed to 1st Division. He gave his Command of 98th Brigade – He bade Goodbye to C.O. Adjutant + Company Commanders at Bn HQ 6.2.pm.	Farewell Dinner when attended
ECOLE DES JEUNES FILLES BETHUNE + LETRETENOY	11-6-16		Fine morning. Wet afternoon. Battalion paraded at 2 pm, + marched to Brigade Reserve Billets at LETRETENOY, arriving 2.45pm, relieved 12 Royal Sussex Regt–116 Bde. Night very wet. 1 man to hospital.	

WAR DIARY or INTELLIGENCE SUMMARY

Army Form C. 2118.

Volume XVI 4th Bn. The King's (Liverpool Regt)

June 1916

Place	Date	Hour	Summary of Events and Information	Remarks and references to Appendices
LE QUESNOY	12-6-16		In Brigade Reserve. Wet – 280 men on working party to the trenches. Lt. Col. BEALL to hospital with mixed shrubs. Captain R.E. DAVIES temporarily in command. Very bad weather.	
"	13-6-16		Wet & windy. 2/Lt ATKIN to Divisional School. 280 men working party to trenches. Engineer man-ages. 1 man to hospital. F.R. INCE to Home. Transferred 8/9 g Cay. 9th Minn. West & very windy. Captain J.C.P. O'BRION joined from 1st Royal Irish Rifles. 2nd Lieut VARNDELL joined. Trench for base – 5 men to hospital. 280 men working parties.	
"	14-6-16		Wet. C.O. Coy Commanders &c went to look at line No. 1 canal where it was proposed to attach over. 2nd Lieut ROBERTS Sheffield sick. 1 man to hospital. 280 men working party.	
"	15-6-16		Dull but fine. 2nd Dist. G.S.M. SALLOWAY and 2nd Lieut S.H. JOHNSON joined from plate. 2/Lt WHITE rejoined from Grenade Class. 300 men on working parties.	
" and trenches between GIVENCHY RIGHT Subsection	17-6-16		Fine. Draft 120 men from base. Moves in trenches. 6 P.m relieved the 1/6 Cheshire Regt. in I/2 Canal and 1/2 P.m relieved 2/4 TA + S.H. So of the Canal. 100 yards on our right. 1/6 Suffolk Regt on our left. Captain O'BRIEN assumed duties of 2nd in Command of Battalion. The bombardment + observation he reports held by the men charged. Battalion was well taken &c much greater than before. Saw about 1000 yards. Relief complete 12.57 a.m. Sent HUSITES upon to hospital. 2 men draft from base. 4.20 men to Hospital.	
"	18-6-16		Fine. 2 trenches. Quiet day. 2/Lt SHARPE &2 g. School. 2 men to hospital.	
"	19-6-16		C.O. Apt. & Coy. Commanders of 1/20th Royal Irish Rifles came to look at trenches preparatory to taking over. Enemy rifle on artillery bombards No North trench at 12.30 A.M. 2/Lt IRVING T.H. slightly wounded. 3 men wounded.	
"	20-6-16		Fire. Relieved by 20th Royal Irish Rifles – relief complete 12.25 A.M. Battalion marched into Divisional Reserve at BETHUNE. Divisional Horse Show 1st day – Battalion won 1 first prize + 2 second prizes (pack mules & jungle transport) 5 men wounded, 1 killed. 1 man to hospital – 2 men from hospital.	

Army Form C. 2118.

WAR DIARY
or
INTELLIGENCE SUMMARY.
(Erase heading not required.)

Volume XVI
June 1916

4 M.G. Kings (Liverpool) Regt

Place	Date	Hour	Summary of Events and Information	Remarks and references to Appendices
BEUVRY	21-6-16		Fine & hot. General cleaning up. Divisional strafe thro' 2nd Day. Germans raided our trenches for 150 yds section between LONE & 26th inst, repulsed by 2nd R.W.F. & Divisional Reserve.	
"	22-6-16		Dri & hot. Billets. Drill as usual in K occur. 250 men on working parties. 1 man to Base. Church P.P.	
"	23-6-16		Showers heavy day. Usual parades. Draft of 40 O.R. from Base. 1 man from hospital.	
"	24-6-16		Showers. Usual parades. Companies on aero attack. 2/Lt SPENCER returned from leave. 1 man from hospital.	
"	25-6-16		Fine. Church Parade. 300 men on working party. Lt.-Col. Regli D.S.O. went on leave. Capt R. S. DAVIES assumed temporary Command of the Battalion. 1 man to hospital.	
"	26-6-16		Wet. Usual parades.	
"	27-6-16		Showery. Private R. L. HARER. Battalion paraded 9 a.m. + marched past the G.O.C. 33rd Division at ESSARS crossroads. 2nd Lieut MILLIGAN to hospital. 2 men to hospital. 2 men from hospital.	
"	28-6-16		Fog. Wet. 477 men on working parties. All leave cancelled. usual parades.	
"	29-6-16		Wet. 2nd Lieut JOHNSON J.H. to T.M. Course. 2nd Lieut MILLIGAN from hospital. 1 man from hospital in England. 1 man from military Prison.	
"	30-6-16		Showers. Fine in Evening. Usual parades.	

H.G. Warren Capt.
Comdg. 4th Kings (Liverpool) Regt.

All Units, 98th Infantry Brigade.

      It is with much regret that I am about to sever my connection with the 98th Infantry Brigade on being appointed to command the 1st Division. Since I took over command on November 16th, 1915, there have been many changes, and none of the original Battalions are left. The Brigade and Battalion Staffs have also been considerably changed; but in spite of these changes there has been a remarkable cohesion and co-operation between all Units, which, added to a fine Esprit de Corps in each of the Units of the Brigade, a marked devotion to duty, the cultivation of a great offensive spirit, and last but not least the steady attention to discipline and smartness has brought the Brigade to the high fighting and disciplined state of efficiency that it has now reached, as proved by the mention of all Units in the Commander-in-Chief's Despatch. I fully realise that this state could not have been reached without the closest cooperation and willing help that has been freely given me by all ranks in the Brigade.

      I wish to express my deepest gratitude to my Brigade Staff who have worked with unceasing energy for the welfare of the Brigade. To Commanding Officers, Company and Platoon Commanders and all the N.C.O's and men of the Brigade.

      Although we have been engaged in no large operations we have carried out continuous harrassing operations day and night, the effect of which has been most marked on the enemy in front of us.

      I am full of admiration of the soldierly and cheerful manner in which you have borne some of the most trying conditions of the war, both as regards hostile fire and mines, and climatic conditions.

      It is a matter of great regret that I have not had the opportunity to command you as a Brigade in action, but I have the fullest confidence that when the time comes, as it will, no Brigade in the Army will give a better account of itself.

      I shall always watch, and take the greatest interest in your welfare. I bid all ranks Good-bye.

      With my best wishes for your welfare during the War, and after.

                                    Major-General.

10th June, 1916.

Perforated Sheet giving detail of personnel and horses wanting to complete, shown on Army Form B. 213.

Number of Report 65

Detail of Wanting to Complete		Drivers						Gunners	Smith Gunners	Range Takers	Farriers			Cold Shoes	Wheelers			Saddlers or Harness Makers	Blacksmiths	Bricklayers and Masons	Carpenters and Joiners	Fitters & Turners (R.E.)		Fitters			Plumbers	Electricians		Signalmen	Engine Drivers		Air Line Men	Permanent Line Men	Operators, Telegraph	Cablemen	Brigade Section Pioneers	General-duty Pioneers	Signallers	Instrument Repairers	Motor Cyclists	Motor Cyclist Artificers	Telephonists	Clerks	Machine Gunners	Armament Artificers			Storemen	Privates	W.O's. and N.C.O's (by ranks) not included in trade columns				TOTAL to agree with wanting to complete		Horses			
	R.A.	R.E.	A.S.C.	Car	Lorry	Steam				Sergeants	Corporals	Smiths Shoeing, or Shoeing and Carriage		R.A.	H.T.	M.T.					Wood	Iron	R.A.	Wireless			Ordinary	W.T.		Loco.	Field														Fitters	Range Finders	Armourers							Officers	Other Ranks		Riding	Draught	Heavy Draught	Pack
CAVALRY																																																								4				
R.A.	1																																																										
R.E.																																																										
INFANTRY																																																			1							
R.A.M.C.																																																										
A.O.C.																																																										
A.V.C.																																																										

Remarks:— Theo. Neo Lefroy Lieut Colonel Signature of Commander.
4th Bn. The Kings (Lpool) Regt Unit.
33rd Division Formation to which attached.
2nd June 1916 Date of Despatch.

[P.T.O.

Army Form B. 213.

FIELD RETURN.

No. of Report _____

(To be furnished by all arms, services, and departments to the A.G.'s Office at the Base in accordance with Field Service Regulations, Part II.)

Date. _____

RETURN showing numbers RATIONED by, and Transport on charge of, _____ at _____

DETAIL.	Personnel			Animals								Guns, carriages, and limbers and transport vehicles						Horsed		Motor Cars	Tractors	Mechanical		Trailers	Motor Bicycles	Bicycles	REMARKS
	Officers	Other ranks	Natives	Horses			Mules		Camels	Oxen	Guns, carriages and limbers, showing description	Ammunition wagons and limbers	Machine guns	Aircraft, showing description	4 Wheeled	2 Wheeled			Lorries, showing description	Trucks, showing description				
				Riding	Draught	Heavy Draught	Pack	Large	Small														
Effective Strength of Unit Details, *by Arms* attached to unit as in War Establishment:—																							
Total																							
War Establishment																							
Wanting to complete																							
Surplus																							
* Attached (not to include the details shown above)																							
Civilians:— Employed with the Unit Accompanying the Unit																							
TOTAL RATIONED ...																							

_____ Signature of Commander.

_____ Date of Despatch.

* In the case of field ambulances, hospitals or depots, the number of patients are to be included here, the names being shown in A. F. A. 26.

Wt.W.G05-894 (3547) U. B. Ltd. 500,000 10/14 Forms B. 213.

Sheet 3

For information of the A.G.'s Office at the Base.

Officers and men who have become casuals, been transferred or joined since last report.

Place: France   Date: 2nd June 1916

Regtl. Number	Rank	Name	Corps	Nature of casualty, or name of unit from or to which transferred	Date of being struck off or coming on the ration return	Remarks*
33109	Pte	Waterhouse A	King's (Regt.)	Reinforcements from	2-6-16	
30325	"	Burns M		1st Entrenching Bn	"	
		Admittances to and	Discharges	from Field Ambulance		
25731	Cpl	Tyrer	4th Bn (L'pool Regt) The King's	To Field Amb.	28-5-16	
26706	Pte	Montheath		"		
11130	"	Stewart		"	1-6-16	
1959	Dmr	Steele R V		"	"	
13421	Pte	Burns		"	29-5-16	
9223	"	Gavin		"	"	
4228	Sgt	Cairns		"	"	
25731	Cpl	Tyrer		From Field Amb.	30-5-16	
14928	Pte	Wright A		"	"	
33576	"	Tyles		"	1-6-16	
11897	Dmr	Wilson A		"	29-5-16	

A E Stephens Lt for Lieut Colonel
Comdg 4th Bn The King's (L'pool Regt)

Army Form B. 213.

FIELD RETURN.

No. of Report _____

(To be furnished by all arms, services, and departments to the A.G.'s Office at the Base in accordance with Field Service Regulations, Part II.)

Date. _____

RETURN showing numbers RATIONED by, and Transport on charge of, _____ at _____

DETAIL.	Personnel			Animals							Guns, carriages, and limbers and transport vehicles											REMARKS
	Officers	Other ranks	Natives	Horses			Mules		Camels	Oxen	Guns, carriages and limbers, showing description	Ammunition wagons and limbers	Machine guns	Aircraft, showing description	Horsed		Motor Cars	Tractors	Mechanical			
				Riding	Draught	Heavy Draught	Pack	Large	Small							4 Wheeled	2 Wheeled			Lorries, showing description	Trucks, showing description	Trailers	Motor Bicycles	Bicycles	
Effective Strength of Unit Details, *by Arms* attached to unit as in War Establishment:—																						
Total																						
War Establishment																						
Wanting to complete																						
Surplus																						
ª Attached (not to include the details shown above)																						
Civilians:— Employed with the Unit Accompanying the Unit																						
TOTAL RATIONED ...																						

_____ Signature of Commander.

_____ Date of Despatch.

* In the case of field ambulances, hospitals or depots, the number of patients are to be included here, the names being shown in A. F. A. 36.

Wt.W. 6005-894 (32047) U. B. Ltd. 500,000 10/14 Forms B. 213/5

Sheet II.

For information of the A.G.'s Office at the Base.

Officers and men who have become casuals, been transferred or joined since last report.

Place France   Date June 2nd 1916

Regtl. Number	Rank	Name	Corps	Nature of casualty, or name of unit from or to which transferred	Date of being struck off or coming on the ration return	Remarks*
19570	Sgt	Dean	G			
10018	L/Sgt	McHugh	A			
5748	L/Cpl	Ninn	W			
25943		West	J			
27837	Pte	Boardman	J			
30619	"	Lucy				
8432	"	Farrell	G			
8638	"	Hutson	J A			
27947	"	Aspinall	G			
30834	"	Bell	J			
34458	"	Brierlow	W			
33471	"	Bratton	J			
31279	"	Barker	J	King's (Liverpool Regiment)	1st Entrenching Battalion	6
3040	"	Gillard	E			
33023	"	Cahill	A			
34664	"	Cosgrave				
31214	"	Dooley	J			
34163	"	Dewhurst				
27933	"	Devine	W			
29353	"	Davies	W			
1099	"	Durrant	D			
10682	"	Ellis	A			
33126	"	Green	A			
32959	"	Gilroy	G			
33129	"	Glennan	P			
32641	"	Hamlin	W			
30998	"	Howell	J		6	
33025	"	Hutchinson	J G			
32920	"	Hughes	J			
10517	"	Jacques	G			
31751	"	Kay	G			
10934	"	Keegan	J	Bn The King's (Liverpool Regiment) Reinforcements from 1st Entrenching Battalion	1	
34461	"	Kelly	W			
10534	"	Lee	J			
32984	"	Lee	J			
34501	"	Lyall	J			
10946	"	Lockwood	P			
30858	"	Loftus	G			
31854	"	McNish	W			
9250	"	McNamara	J			
34948	"	Marsden	J			
31632	"	McNeil	J			
9326	"	Naylor	J		2	
31344	"	Kennedy	J			
32393	"	Moore	G			
12522	"	Middleton	J			
27977	"	Redman	A			
8935	"	Sherrington	G			
32445	"	Smith	J G			
31828	"	Smith	J			
34341	"	Reid	A			
14428	"	Walmsley	G			
28072	"	Watson	J			
31283	"	Wade	G			
50486	"	Williams	J			
33127	"	Wright	J			
32559	"	Wells	J			

* State whether absence is of a permanent or temporary nature, adding, in the case of casuals from wounds or disease, any available information for communication to the relatives.

Sheet I

For information of the A.G.'s Office at the Base.

Officers and men who have become casuals, been transferred or joined since last report.

Place France   Date 2nd June 1916

Regtl. Number	Rank	Name	Corps	Nature of casualty, or name of unit from or to which transferred	Date of being struck off or coming on the ration return	Remarks
	Lieut	Gray	V	From Wounded	31-5-16	
		Backs	A	From Hospital	29-5-16	
10644	Pte	Connor	L	"	28-5-16	
10913		Rose	G	"	30-5-16	
9256		Rice	G	"	1-6-16	
27444		Wilcocks	G	"	17-5-16	
10046		Morrisey	J	Killed in Action	27-5-16	
13831		Fitzpatrick	A	"		
29882		Bloasdale	R	Wounded in A.	7-5-16	Shell Shock
12482		Kelly		"	27-5-16	
9221	L/Cpl	Gurrie	G	To Hospital	28-5-16	
9808	Pte	Crisp	R	"	"	
30074		Ovington	R	"	4-5-16	
20706		Monteath	E	"	30-5-16	
13421		Lyons	E	"	"	
4225	Sgt	Cairns	J	"	31-5-16	
9223	Pte	Gavin	J	"	"	
29095		Woods	J	"	25-5-16	
7404		Upton	J	To England	13-5-16	
27699		Booth	G	Transferred to No 6	30-5-16	
12399		Hardman	J	D.B.	1-5-16	
12824		Eustance	J	"	10-2-16	
	Lieut	Nichols	A.R.			
9771	L/Cpl	Bamblett	W			
4460		Gibson	W			
27006		Soth	S			
28009		Young	S			
29924	Pte	Bateson	B			
30468		Baker	W			
18305		Cronin	J			
13303		Suney	J			
6884		Griffen	J			
26740		Gaskill	J			
27154		Hodkinson	W			
20337		Gilberry	P			
31780		Hirst	A			
31883		Handley	A			
27597		Haynes	J			
27890		Irving	P			
33004		Jones	J			
31510		Jones	J			
32952		Lowe	R			
29941		Lowry	W			
30385		Brayton	G			
8969		McMans	J			
30529		Musgrave	W			
10534		Murphy	J			
30329		Pendlebury	H			
30784		Mitchell	S			
25440		Owens	W			
30626		Roberts	G			
11176		Smith	C			
27493		Shutt	C			
29932		Turner	C			
25160		Bushel	J			
30601		Taylforth	R			
10501		Cairney	A			
34539		Johnson	A			

Diagonal annotation across rows: "4th Bn. The King's (Liverpool Regt.) Reinforcements from No 8 Infantry Base Depot   2-6-16"

* State whether absence is of a permanent or temporary nature, adding, in the case of casuals from wounds or disease, any available information for communication to the relatives.

Army Form B. 213.

FIELD RETURN.

To be made up to and for Sunday in each week.

No. of Report 65

(To be furnished by all arms, services, and departments (except A.S.C. units) to the A. G.'s Office at the Base in accordance with Field Service Regulations, Part II.

RETURN showing numbers {(a) Effective strength of Unit. 1st Bn the King's (Liverpool Regt) at France
(b) Rationed by Unit.} — Date 2nd June 1916.

Staff

Detail	Personnel			Animals							Guns, carriages, and limbers			Horsed		Mechanical				Motor Bicycles	Bicycles	Remarks
	Officers	Other ranks	Natives	Riding	Draught	Heavy Draught	Pack	Large Mules	Small Mules	Camels	Oxen	Guns, carriages and limbers, showing description	Ammunition wagons and limbers	Machine guns	Aircraft, showing description	4 wheeled	2 wheeled	Motor Cars	Tractors	Lorries, showing description	Trucks, showing description	Trailers			
Effective Strength of Unit	29	1024		11	9	8		27						4		16	6							9	Not Rationed Officers 1, Base Depot 2, Leave 2, Courses of Instr 1, Sick at Hospital 6
Details, by Arms attached to unit as in War Establishment:—																										
R.A.M.C.	1																									Other Ranks 15, In Command, Attd 2 33rd Inniskilling Bn 32, Syl Employ 14, T M Bty 6, 9/3/2 T M Bty 11, Courses of Instr 30, Leave 29, Field Ambulance 96, Ride Employ 22, Machine Gun Coy, Absent 1 = 175
Army Ordnance Corps		1																								
Total	30	1025x		11	9	8		27						4		16	6							9	
War Establishment	14	995		12	26	9	9								4		16	6							9	
Wanting to complete (Detail of Personnel and Horses below)	14	7		1	17	1	9																			
Surplus								27																		W.H. Sut Shaw A D Shaw
*Attached (not to include the details shown above)																										
Civilians :— Employed with the Unit Accompanying the Unit																										
Total, Rationed...	24	830		11	9			27																		

* In the case of field ambulances, hospitals or depots, the number of patients are to be included here, the names being shown in A. F. A. 36.

x Includes 39 men permanently attached to Christopher ____ for Lieut Colonel Signature of Commander.
Tunnelling Coy + Trench Mortar Bty 2nd June 1916 Date of Despatch.

Perforated Sheet giving detail of personnel and horses wanting to complete, shown on Army Form B. 213.

Number of Report __66__

Detail of Wanting to Complete	Drivers							Farriers				Wheelers			Saddlers or Harness Makers	Blacksmiths	Bricklayers and Masons	Carpenters and Joiners	Fitters & Turners (R.E.)		Fitters			Plumbers	Electricians		Signalmen	Engine Drivers		Air Line Men	Permanent Line Men	Operators, Telegraph	Cablemen	Brigade Section Pioneers	General-duty Pioneers	Signallers	Instrument Repairers	Motor Cyclists	Motor Cyclist Artificers	Telephonists	Clerks	Machine Gunners	Armament Artificers				Storemen	Privates	W.O.s and N.C.O's (by rank) not included in trade columns	TOTAL wanting to agree with complete		Horses			
	R.A.	R.E.	A.S.C.	Car	Lorry	Steam	Gunners	Smith Gunners	Range Takers	Sergeants	Corporals	Shoeing, or Shoeing and Carriage Smiths	Cold Shoers	R.A.	H.T.	M.T.					Wood	Iron	R.A.	Wireless		Ordinary	W.T.		Loco.	Field														Fitters	Range Finders	Armourers				Officers	Other Ranks	Riding	Draught	Heavy Draught	Pack
CAVALRY																																																						
R.A.																																																			12	16				
R.E.																																																						
INFANTRY																																																16						
R.A.M.C.																																																						
A.O.C.																																																						
A.V.C.																																																						

Remarks:—

Mitchell Lieut Colonel Signature of Commander.
Comdg 1st Bn The King's (Liverpool Regt) Unit.
33rd Division Formation to which attached.
9th June 1916 Date of Despatch.

[P.T.O.

FIELD RETURN.

Army Form B. 213.

To be made up to and for Sunday in each week.
No. of Report 66
(To be furnished by all arms, services, and departments (except A.S.C. units) to the A. G.'s Office at the Base in accordance with Field Service Regulations, Part II.)
RETURN showing numbers { (a) Effective strength of Unit. 4 Bn The Kings (Liverpool) Regt France
{ (b) Rationed by Unit. Date 9th June 1916

DETAIL.	Personnel			Animals.							Guns, carriages, and limbers and transport vehicles			Horsed		Mechanical				Motor Bicycles	Bicycles	REMARKS
	Officers	Other ranks	Natives	Horses Riding	Horses Draught	Horses Heavy Draught	Mules Pack	Mules Large	Mules Small	Camels	Oxen	Guns, carriages and limbers, showing description	Ammunition wagons and limbers	Machine guns	Aircraft, showing description	4 wheeled	2 wheeled	Motor Cars	Tractors	Lorries, showing description	Trucks, showing description	Trailers			
Effective Strength of Unit	31	1103		11	9	8	9	24						4		16	6							9	Not Rationed Officers 1 Base Hospl 2 Tempy Inclu dets in Hospl 4
Details, by Arms attached to unit as in War Establish- ment :—																										Other Ranks
R.A.M.C.	1																									On Command 14
Army Ordnance Corps		1																								1/1st 2/1st Coy R.E. 30
																										Lieut Employ 14
																										Corps 6
Total	32	1104*		11	9	8	9	24						4		16	6							9	9/12 Toys of the Bty 11 Lovacaef Studio 25
War Establishment	24	995		12	26	9	9							4		16	6							9	Law 7 Field Amb. 8 Bde Employ 6 23 R. Fus M. Gy 23
Wanting to complete	12	16		1	17	1																			144
Surplus									24																W.A. Supt Train
*Attached (not to include the details shown above)																									8 H.D. Horses
Civilians:— Employed with the Unit Accompanying the Unit																									
TOTAL RATIONED...	28	970		11	9	—	—	24																	

— 11 — 8 — 1 6 — — — —
— — — — — — — 9½ Lunch Mortar Btty —

* In the case of field ambulances, hospitals or depots, the number of patients are to be included here, the names being shown in A. F. A. 36.

× Includes 24 May permanently attd Lancaster Regt — Tunbridge Lieut Colonel. Signature of Commander.
" 9½ Lunch Mortar Btty 9th June 1916 Date of Despatch.

For information of the A.G.'s Office at the Base.

Officers and men who have become casuals, been transferred or joined since last report.

Place: France   Date: June 9th 1916

Regtl. Number	Rank	Name	Corps	Nature of casualty, or name of unit from or to which transferred	Date of being struck off or coming on the ration return	Remarks
	Lieut	Milligan	J.R.	From Base	9-6-16	
		Spencer	E	Appointed to a Regular Commission	3-6-16	
26975	Pte	Halford	R	From Hospital	26-5-16	Attd 257st Sun Coy
27295		Sullivan	A	"	3-6-16	
29882		Bleasdale	R	"	8-6-16	
9105	L/Cpl	Peters	J	To England	26-5-16	
27268	Pte	Lynn	R	Wounded in Action	21-5-16	Attd 251st Sun Coy
26975		Halford	A	"		
30482		Walker		To Hospital	23-5-16	
11821		Whittaker	W	"	3-6-16	
11939	Dmr	Steele	R.V.	"	5-6-16	
12106	Pte	Henshall	W	"		
8633	"	Joy	C.W.	"	6-6-16	
27884		Robinson		"		
8043	C.S.M.	Spencer	E	Appointed to a Regular Commission	3-6-16	
13873	Pte	Stephenson	J	To Hospital, England		
8640		Hordern	J	Attd HQ 46th Division		
2475		Baxter	C	Declared a Deserter	4-6-16	
11978		Hughes	J	Attd HQ 2nd Ind Bde		

Admittances to and Discharges from Field Ambulance

12106	Pte	Henshall	W	To Field Amb.	2-6-16	
11821		Whittaker	W	"	4-6-16	
6719	Cpl	Pugh		"	"	
34752	Pte	McNeill		"	"	
9250		McNamara		"	"	
29939	"	Hughes	J	"		
25672	"	Baxter		"	31-5-16	
27884	"	Robinson	J	"	6-6-16	
8633	"	Joy	C.W.	"		
27475	Pte	Doyle	J	From Field Amb.	3-6-16	
6719	Cpl	Pugh		"	5-6-16	
34752	Pte	McNeill	J	"	7-6-16	
9250		McNamara		"	5-6-16	
29939		Hughes	J	"	7-6-16	

McBeall Lieut Colonel
Comdg 4th Bn The King's (Liverpool Regt)

*State whether absence is of a permanent or temporary nature, adding, in the case of casuals from wounds or disease, any available information for communication to the relatives.

Perforated Sheet giving detail of personnel and horses wanting to complete, shown on Army Form B. 213.

Number of Report 67

Detail of Wanting to Complete	Drivers					Gunners	Smith Gunners	Range Takers	Farriers			Cold Shoers	Wheelers			Saddlers or Harness Makers	Blacksmiths	Bricklayers and Masons	Carpenters and Joiners	Fitters & Turners (R.E.)		Fitters			Electricians			Signalman	Engine Drivers			Air Line Men	Permanent Line Men	Operators, Telegraph	Cableman	Brigade Section Pioneers	General-duty Pioneers	Signallers	Instrument Repairers	Motor Cyclists	Motor Cyclist Artificers	Telephonists	Clerks	Machine Gunners	Armament Artificers				Storemen	Privates	W.O.s and N.C.O.s (by rank) not included in trade columns	TOTAL wanting to agree with complete		Horses			
	R.A.	R.E.	A.S.C.	Car	Lorry	Steam				Sergeants	Corporals	Shoeing, or Shoeing and Carriage Smiths		R.A.	R.T.	M.T.						Wood	Iron	R.A.	Wireless		Plumbers	Ordinary	W.T.		Loco.	Field														Fitters	Range Finders	Armourers				Officers	Other Ranks	Riding	Draught	Heavy Draught	Pack
CAVALRY																																																								
R.A.																																																					8			
R.E.																																																								
INFANTRY																																																				41						
R.A.M.C.																																																								
A.O.C.																																																								
A.V.C.																																																								

Remarks:—

R.C. Marshall Capt. Signature of Commander.
4th Bn the Kings (Liverpool Regt.) Unit.
33rd Division Formation to which attached.
16th June 1916 Date of Despatch.

[P.T.O.

For information of the A.G.'s Office at the Base.

Officers and men who have become casuals, been transferred or joined since last report.

Place: France   Date: 16th June 1916

Regtl. Number	Rank	Name	Corps	Nature of casualty, or name of unit from or to which transferred	Date of being struck off or coming on the ration return	Remarks
	Captn	O'Brien J.C.P	Royal Irish Fusiliers	From Base	14-6-16	
	Lieut	Varndell L.J.		"	16-6-16	
	"	Galloway G.W.		"	"	
	"	Johnson S.J.		"	"	
2720	Pte	Daly		To Hospital	8-6-16	
7578	"	Gillow		"	"	
30619	L/Cpl	Lucy		"	9-6-16	
10884	Pte	Fairway		"	"	
11994	"	Mooney		"	11-6-16	
8777	"	Langfield		"	14-6-16	
14844	"	Stevens		"	"	
26725	"	Parker		"	"	
9341	"	Needham P.		"	"	
30634	"	Bell		"	"	
8941	"	Ross		"	15-6-16	
	Lt Col	Beall E. V.D. DSO		"	"	
	Lieut	Roberts		"	"	
3300A	Pte	Jones J.		To Base for transfer to	13-6-16	Under age
11794	"	Cleavely		A.P.M.T.P. P of W	"	
5722	Sgt	Beard				
10141	Pte	Collinson				
11561	"	Campbell				
14277	"	Clarke J.		Transferred to 98th Bde Machine Gun Coy	13-6-16	
8620	"	Corlett				
24408	"	Haslam				
18695	"	Colville				
25705	"	Clarke				
10648	"	Nugent				
14285	"	Harris W.				
18538	"	Burke				
10357	"	Owens				

Admittances to and Discharges from Field Ambulance

10884	Pte	Fairway		To Field Amb	8-6-16	
7578	"	Gillow		"	"	
8941	"	Ross		"	11-6-16	
10967	"	Weaver		"	"	
11994	"	Mooney		"	10-6-16	
9009	"	Smith		"	11-6-16	
27296	"	Booth		"	"	
18095	"	Harrison		"	"	
14844	"	Stevens		"	"	
26725	"	Parker		"	"	
30364	"	Bell		"	"	
8777	"	Langfield		"	"	
13645	"	Hill		"	"	
30619	L/Cpl	Lucy		"	8-6-16	
18062	Pte	Webb		"	7-6-16	
9341	"	Needham		"	11-6-16	
	Lt Col	Beall E. V.D. DSO		"	14-6-16	
	Lieut	Roberts		"	"	
14130	Pte	Stewart		From Field Amb	15-6-16	
11967	"	Weaver		"	12-6-16	
18062	"	Webb		"	"	

Captn.
Comdg. 4th Bn The King's (Liverpool Regt)

* State whether absence is of a permanent or temporary nature, adding, in the case of casuals from wounds or disease, any available information for communication to the relatives.

Army Form B. 213.

FIELD RETURN.

To be made up to and for Sunday in each week.

No. of Report 64.

(To be furnished by all arms, services, and departments (except A.S.G. units) to the A. G.'s Office at the Base in accordance with Field Service Regulations, Part II.)

RETURN showing numbers 1/4 Battn. Kings (Liverpool Regt) at France.
(a) Effective strength of Unit.
(b) Rationed by Unit. Date 11th June 1916.

Detail	Personnel			Animals								Guns, carriages, and limbers and transport vehicles				Horsed		Mechanical					Bicycles	Remarks
	Officers	Other ranks	Natives	Horses			Mules		Camels	Oxen		Guns, carriages and limbers, showing description	Ammunition wagons and limbers	Machine guns	Aircraft, showing description	4 wheeled	2 wheeled	Motor Cars	Tractors	Lorries, showing description	Trucks, showing description	Trailers	Motor Bicycles	
				Riding	Draught	Heavy Draught	Pack	Large	Small															
Effective Strength of Unit	34	968		12	8	9		24						4		16	5						9	Not Rationed
Details, by Arms attached to unit as in War Establishment:—																									Officers
																								1 Base Depot
																								2 Courses of Instr
R.A.M.C.	1																							3 Sick in Hospl
Royal Irish Fusiliers	1																							1 Leave
Army Ordnance Corps		1																							7
																								Other Ranks
																								14 Comd
Total	36	989		12	8	9		24						4		16	5						9	Attd 251st Coy R.E. 30
War Establishment	44	995		12	26	9																			Sick Employ 14
Wanting to complete (Detail of Personnel and Horses below)	8	6		-	18	-		9																	Leave 6
Surplus								24																9	Depot 14
																								9/2 T.M. Battery 12
																								Course of Instr 1
																								Field Amb 14
																								Base Employ 6
																								9/3 Bde MGC 13
																								Absent 1
*Attached (not to include the details shown above)																									121
Civilians:— Employed with the Unit Accompanying the Unit																									With Drafts
Total Rationed	29	862		12	8	1		24																	8-H.D. Stores

* In the case of field ambulances, hospitals or depots, the number of patients are to be included here, the names being shown in A. F. A. 36.

× Include 24 men permanently attached travelling by ...... J.R. [signature] Lt Col. Signature of Commander.
 " " 8 " — " — 9 8/2 French Mortar Battery 11th June 1916. Date of Despatch.

Perforated Sheet giving detail of personnel and horses wanting to complete, shown on Army Form B. 213.

Number of Report _68_

Detail of Wanting to Complete	Drivers						Farriers					Wheelers							Fitters & Turners			Electricians				Engine Drivers											Armament Artificers					W.O.s and N.C.O.s (by ranks) not included in trade columns	TOTAL wanting to complete to agree with Other Ranks		Horses			
	R.A.	R.E.	A.S.C.	Car	Lorry	Steam	Gunners	Smith Gunners	Range Takers	Sergeants	Corporals	Shoeing, or Shoeing and Carriage Smiths	Cold Shoers	R.A.	H.T.	M.T.	Saddlers or Harness Makers	Blacksmiths	Bricklayers and Masons	Carpenters and Joiners	Wood	Iron (R.E.)	R.A. Wireless	Plumbers	Ordinary	W.T.	Steamen	Loco.	Field	Air Line Men	Permanent Line Men	Operators, Telegraph	Cableman	Brigade Section Pioneers	General-duty Pioneers	Signallers	Instrument Repairers	Motor Cyclists	Motor Cyclist Artificers	Telephonists	Clerks	Machine Gunners	Fitters	Range Finders	Armourers	Storemen	Privates		Officers	Other Ranks	Riding	Draught	Heavy Draught	Pack
CAVALRY																																																						
R.A.																																																		8				
R.E.																																																						
INFANTRY																																																1						
R.A.M.C.																																																						
A.O.C.																																																						
A.V.C.																																																						

Remarks:—

(Sd) E. M. Beall Lieut Colonel Signature of Commander.
11th Bn The King's (Liverpool Regt) Unit.
33rd Division Formation to which attached.
23rd June 1916 Date of Despatch.

[P.T.O.

Army Form B. 213.

FIELD RETURN.

No. of Report _____

(To be furnished by all arms, services, and departments to the A.G.'s Office at the Base in accordance with Field Service Regulations, Part II.)

Date _____

RETURN showing numbers RATIONED by, and Transport on charge of, _____ at _____

DETAIL.	Personnel			Animals								Guns, carriages, and limbers and transport vehicles										REMARKS
	Officers	Other ranks	Natives	Horses			Mules		Camels	Oxen	Guns, carriages and limbers, showing description	Ammunition wagons and limbers	Machine guns	Aircraft, showing description	Horsed		Motor Cars	Tractors	Mechanical		Trailers	Motor Bicycles	Bicycles
				Riding	Draught	Heavy Draught	Pack	Large	Small							4 Wheeled	2 Wheeled			Lorries, showing description	Trucks, showing description			
Effective Strength of Unit																							
Details, *by Arms* attached to unit as in War Establishment:—																							
Total																							
War Establishment																							
Wanting to complete																							
Surplus																							
° Attached (not to include the details shown above)																							
Civilians:— Employed with the Unit Accompanying the Unit																							
TOTAL RATIONED ...																							

* In the case of field ambulances, hospitals or depots, the number of patients are to be included here, the names being shown in A.F.A. 36.

_____
Signature of Commander.

_____
Date of Despatch.

Wt.-W. 6005-894 (35047) U. B. Ltd. 500,000 10/14   Forms B. 213/5

Sheet 2

For information of the A.G.'s Office at the Base.

Officers and men who have become casuals, been transferred or joined since last report.

Place France   Date June 23rd 1916

Regtl. Number	Rank	Name	Corps	Nature of casualty, or name of unit from or to which transferred	Date of being struck off or coming on the ration return	Remarks*
29930	Pte	Hougland A				
30338	"	Sayers J				
30624	"	Mahon J				
31800	"	Parker J				
32955	"	Ledger W.H.				
32981	"	Gillow C	King's (Liverpool Regt)	Reinforcements from No 6 Infantry Base depot	6-16	
32999	"	Benson J				
23180	"	Parry J				
33106	"	Clegg J				
33148	"	Walton C				
33467	"	Christian W				
34470	"	Monaghan W			6-16	
34678	"	Flanagan W				
34685	"	Pratt J.S.				
34705	"	Buxton				
34741	"	Franklin T				
34747	"	Waddington J				
8816	"	Duddy J				
9135	"	Wigglesworth J.G.				
20810	"	Stevenson J				
27293	"	Slater J			23	
8648	"	Christie H.				
15469	"	Redmond L				
30753	"	Clarke E				

Admittances to and Discharges from Field Ambulance

9862	Pte	Sharples W		To Field Amb	17-6-16	
6019	Sgt	Hagan W		"	19-6-16	
10967	Pte	Weaver J		"	"	
18003	"	Mackenzie J		"	"	
9043	"	Doran J		"	20-6-16	
12413	Dmr	Wilson A		"	17-6-16	
13914	Cpl	Jerons C		"	"	
20498	Pte	Wilkinson J		From Field Amb	17-6-16	
29369	"	Smith J		"	"	
9862	Pte	Sharples W		"	20-6-16	
11574	Cpl	Williamson E		"	17-6-16	

(Sd) E. M. Beall   Lieut Colonel
Comdg 4th Bn The King's (Liverpool Regt)

* State whether absence is of a permanent or temporary nature, adding, in the case of casuals from wounds or disease, any available information for communication to the relatives.

For information of the A.G.'s Office at the Base.

Officers and men who have become casuals, been transferred or joined since last report.

Place: France   Date: June 23rd/1916

Regtl. Number	Rank	Name	Corps	Nature of casualty, or name of unit from or to which transferred	Date of being struck off or coming on the ration return	Remarks*
	Lt Col	Beall E.M. BD		From Hospl	17-6-16	
5469	Cpl	Richardson S		"	20-6-16	
26265	Pte	Kearney				
4228	Sgt	Cairns W				
8585	Cpl	Dawson J				
1726	L/Cpl	Geary W				
32547	Pte	Grossmith W				
11525	-"-	McGuire H				
25931	-"-	Gibbons R				
29952	-"-	Beesley J				
13997	-"-	Stansheet H				
8596	-"-	Kilcoyne J				
36326	-"-	Sagui J			17-6-16	
25240	-"-	Corth H				
11399	-"-	Hardman M				
14260	-"-	Mangan R				
13704	-"-	Murphy R				
9734	-"-	Davies G				
12653	-"-	Eckersley E				
21178	-"-	Anderson R				
24163	-"-	Kirby L				
5469	Cpl	Richardson S		Wounded in A.	18-6-16	
13820	Pte	Hanlow		"		
26265	-"-	Kearney		"		
29505	-"-	Brown		"		
11663	-"-	Malone		"		
10729	Drmr	Jones H		"		
11142	Pte	Baker J		"	19-6-16	
14503	-"-	Sinclair		"	20-6-16	
9008	-"-	Aspinall H		"		
30497	-"-	Ball		"		
18440	-"-	Stephenson R		"		
33007	-"-	McManus		"		
11399	-"-	Hardman M		"		
10542	-"-	Healey		"	19-6-16	
31214	-"-	Dooley M		Killed in Action	18-6-16	
31851	-"-	McKish W		"	20-6-16	
27084	-"-	Mullins J		Transferred to R.E.	1-5-16	
12628	-"-	Finch J		"	"	
12413	Drmr	Wilson F		To Hospital	18-6-16	
1273	Cpl	Leahy		"		
18003	Pte	Mackenzie F		"	20-6-16	
982	-"-	Sharples W		P.B.	22-6-16	
10835	Cpl	Ashcroft J				
31307	A/Cpl	Johnson J				
8832	Pte	Welsh J				
11781	-"-	Gold J				
11993	-"-	Coundley H				
27100	-"-	Snowden G				
31922	-"-	Nowlan S				
9753	-"-	Wilson S				
16944	-"-	Letters R				
11054	-"-	Russell				
14075	-"-	Webb R			23-6-16	
20832	-"-	Atherton J				
20981	-"-	Cawley J				
29088	-"-	Rattigan R				
29392	-"-	Everett W				

* State whether absence is of a permanent or temporary nature, adding, in the case of casuals from wounds or disease, any available information for communication to the relatives.

FIELD RETURN.

Army Form B. 213.

To be made up to and for Sunday in each week.

No. of Report __68__

(To be furnished by all arms, services, and departments (except A.S.C. units) to the A. G.'s Office at the Base in accordance with Field Service Regulations, Part II.)

RETURN showing numbers (a) Effective strength of Unit __1st/1st the Kings (Liverpool Regt)__ at __France__.
(b) Rationed by Unit.

Date __23rd June 1916__

Diary

DETAIL	Personnel			Animals							Guns, carriages, and limbers and transport vehicles			Horsed		Mechanical				REMARKS
	Officers	Other ranks	Natives	Horses Riding	Horses Draught	Horses Heavy Draught	Pack	Mules Large	Mules Small	Camels	Oxen	Guns, carriages and limbers, showing description	Ammunition wagons and limbers	Machine guns	Aircraft, showing description	4 wheeled	2 wheeled	Motor Cars	Tractors	Lorries	Trucks	Trailers	Motor Bicycles	Bicycles	
Effective Strength of Unit	34	1026		12	8	9		24						4		16	5							9	Not Rationed Officers 1 Base depot 1 Leave 1 With 98/1 TMB 4 Sources of labor 5 sick in hospital 9 — Other Ranks 14 On Command 28 4th/257 Bgy R.E. 14 Field Amb 32 Army of Dublin 11 French Mortar Bttys 5 3rd Corps Employ 7 Ride 12 — 15 Attache Soc M Bty 1 Civil Employ 14 5 With Brit Divn 8 — HD Horses
Details, by Arms attached to unit as in War Establishment:—																										
R.A.M.C. Royal Inniskillen	1																									
Army Ordnance Corps	1																									
Total	36	1024		12	8	9		24						4		16	5							9	
War Establishment	44	995		12	26	9	9							4		16	5							9	
Wanting to complete (Detail of Personnel and Horses below)	8	1		.	18	.	9																		
Surplus								24																	
*Attached (not to include the details shown above)																									
Civilians:— Employed with the Unit Accompanying the Unit																									
TOTAL RATIONED...	24	882		12	8	1	.	24																	

* In the case of field ambulances, hospitals or depots, the number of patients are to be included here, the names being shown in A. F. A. 36.

✗ Included 25 men attached Tunnelling Coy
— 8 — — — French Mortar Btty.

(Sd) E. M. Beall Lieut Colonel Signature of Commander.

23rd June 1916 Date of Despatch.

Perforated Sheet giving detail of personnel and horses wanting to complete, shown on Army Form B. 213.

Number of Report __69__

Detail of Wanting to Complete	Drivers						Gunners	Smith Gunners	Range Takers	Farriers			Cold Shoers	Wheelers			Saddlers or Harness Makers	Blacksmiths	Bricklayers and Masons	Carpenters and Joiners	Fitters & Turners (R.H.)		Fitters			Plumbers	Electricians		Signalmen	Engine Drivers		Air Line Men	Permanent Line Men	Operators, Telegraph	Cablemen	Brigade Section Pioneers	General-duty Pioneers	Signallers	Instrument Repairers	Motor Cyclists	Motor Cyclist Artificers	Telephonists	Clerks	Machine Gunners	Armament Artificers			Armourers	Storemen	Privates	W.O's. and N.C.O's. (by rank(s) not included in trade columns)		TOTAL wanting to complete to agree with Other Ranks on Army Form B. 213.		Horses			
	R.A.	R.E.	A.S.C.	Car	Lorry	Steam				Serjeants	Corporals	Shoeing, or Shoeing and Carriage Smiths		R.A.	H.T.	M.T.					Wood	Iron	R.A.	Wireless			Ordinary	W.T.		Loco.	Field												Fitters	Range Finders							Officers	Other Ranks	Riding	Draught	Heavy Draught	Pack
CAVALRY																																																				8				
R.A.																																																							
R.E.																																																							
INFANTRY																																																							
R.A.M.C.																																																							
A.O.C.																																																							
A.V.C.																																																							

Remarks:—

McDowell Capt. Signature of Commander.

4th Bn. The Kings (Liverpool Regt.) Unit.

32nd Division Formation to which attached.

30th June 1916 Date of Despatch.

[P.T.O.

For information of the A.G.'s Office at the Base.

Officers and men who have become casuals, been transferred or joined since last report.

Place France   Date June 30th 1916.

Regtl. Number	Rank	Name	Corps	Nature of casualty, or name of unit from or to which transferred	Date of being struck off or coming on the ration return	Remarks
10236	Pte	Evans A		from Hospital	23-6-16	
27832	"	Baker W		"	24-6-16	
9213	"	Woods J		"	27-6-16	
26706	"	Montheath E		"	27-6-16	
12252	"	Riley P		from M'tary Prison	29-6-16	
12143	"	Leahy		from Hospital	"	
11970	Drm	Claridge E J		To Hospital	14-6-16	
25095	Pte	Lewin A J		"	25-6-16	
11574	Cpl	Williamson E		"	27-6-16	
25934	Pte	West J M		"	"	
5469	Cpl	Richardson J		"	28-6-16	
20737	Pte	Burns W		"	"	
	Lieut	Milligan F R		"	28-6-16	
	"	Milligan F R		from Hospital	30-6-16	

Admittances to and Discharges from Field Ambulance

11574	Cpl	Williamson E		To Field Amb	23-6-16	
12009	Sgt	Baines J		"	25-6-16	
25095	Pte	Lewin A J		"	23-6-16	
5469	Cpl	Richardson J		"	26-6-16	
10801	Pte	Barr A		"	9-6-16	
11970	Drm	Claridge E		"	16-6-16	
25934	Pte	West J M		"	25-6-16	
34732	"	McNeill J		"	28-6-16	
20737	"	Burns W		"	26-6-16	
	Lieut	Milligan F R		"	27-6-16	
9019	Sgt	Hagan J		from Field Amb	28-6-16	
10967	Pte	Weaver J		"	27-6-16	
9043	"	Doran J		"	28-6-16	
13914	Cpl	Perons E		"	26-6-16	
10801	Pte	Barr A		"	27-6-16	
34732	"	McNeill J		"	30-6-16	

Captn.
Comdg 4th Bn The King's (Liverpool Regt)

* State whether absence is of a permanent or temporary nature, adding, in the case of casuals from wounds or disease, any available information for communication to the relatives.

FIELD RETURN.

Army Form B. 213.

To be made up to and for Sunday in each week.

No. of Report 69

(To be furnished by all arms, services, and departments (except A.S.C. units) to the A. G.'s Office at the Base in accordance with Field Service Regulations, Part II.)

RETURN showing numbers — (a) Effective strength of Unit. 4th Bn. the Royal Scots Regt. France.
(b) Rationed by Unit. Date. 30th June 1916.

DETAIL.	Personnel			Animals.								Guns, carriages, and limbers and transport vehicles										
	Officers	Other ranks	Natives	Horses				Mules		Camels	Oxen	Guns, carriages, limbers, showing description	Ammunition wagons and limbers	Machine guns	Aircraft, showing description	Horsed		Motor Cars	Tractors	Mechanical			Motor Bicycles	Bicycles	REMARKS
				Riding	Draught	Heavy Draught	Pack	Large	Small							4 wheeled	2 wheeled			Lorries, showing description	Trucks, showing description	Trailers			
Effective Strength of Unit	34	1028		12	8	9	–	27						4		16	5							9	Base Depot 1 – Leave 1 Attd 9th/7 T.M. Bty 3 Somerset Inf'try 2 Sick. Hospital 8 Other Ranks 13
Details, by Arms attached to unit as in War Establishment:—																									
R.A.M.C.	1																								One Commdt Attd 23rd Bgd. R.E. 28
Royal Irish Fusiliers	1																								
Army Ordnance Corps		1																							Field Ambulance 8 Course of Instr'n 13
Total	36	1029		12	8	9	–	27						4		16	5							9	Signal Section 11 Course Empty 5
War Establishment	44	995		12	26	9	9									16	5							9	Base 7 M.T. per Ret'n & top left Empty 18 Leave 18 1
Wanting to complete (Detail of Personnel and Horses below)	8	–		–	18	–	9																		
Surplus		1						27																	With Mil. Grave 1 8 – H.D. horses 122
*Attached (not to include the details shown above)																									
Civilians:— Employed with the Unit Accompanying the Unit																									
TOTAL RATIONED...	28	904		12	6	1	–	24																	

* In the case of field ambulances, hospitals or depots, the number of patients are to be included, the names being shown in A. F. A. 36.

× Includes 25 men permanently Attached Unwillingly to — 9th M. Bde. T.M. Bty

— 8 — — — — — — — — — —

Signature of Commander M. Dawes Capt'n

Date of Despatch 30th June 1916.

98th Inf.Bde.
33rd Div.

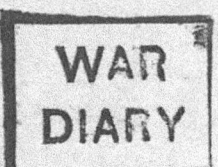

4th BATTN. THE KING'S (LIVERPOOL REGIMENT).

J U L Y

1 9 1 6

Attached:

Appendices.

WAR DIARY or INTELLIGENCE SUMMARY

4th The Kings (Liverpool Reg)

July 1916

Army Form C. 2118

Place	Date	Hour	Summary of Events and Information	Remarks and references to Appendices
BEUVRY	1-7-16		Fine - CO & Coy Commanders visits Beuvry. 500 men working party. 2/Lt JOHNSON from T.M. course. 2/Lt ATKIN from Divl. School. 2/Lt MILLIGAN to Grenade course.	
"	2-7-16		Fine. Capt. SIMMANCE to 1st Army School. 2/Lt MATHER commands B.Coy. 2/Lt REES bombing officer. 2/Lt BACK to Divl. School. Relieved 2nd Worcesters in CUINCHY RIGHT SUBSECTION. Complete 11.30 p.m.	
CUINCHY R.T. SUBSECTION	3-7-16		C.O. from leave on duty. 2/Lt GALLOWAY Killed. 2 A.M. Heavy bombardment on our right.	
"	4-7-16		Wet. C.O. in trench. General in trench - B.Coy lines bombed but trenches all day. 2 bombers on hospital.	
"	5-7-16		About 2 A.M. small party of enemy reached B Coys line - Heavy barrage - 2 men wounded	
"	6-7-16		Wet - C.O. & Coy Commanders 11th Royal Sussex round trenches. One man killed one wounded	
"	7-7-16		Wet - Relieved by 11th Royal Sussex - relief took all night. 2/Lt JOHNSON to hospital. 2/Lt REES 4 men wounded. 2/Lt MILLIGAN from Grenade course.	
GONNEHEM	8-7-16		Relief complete 2 A.M. Companies marched to BETHUNE independently - Tea 4.30 A.M. Rested GONNEHEM. Arrives GONNEHEM 7.30 A.M. No men fell out - 12 miles march - one man wounded. Left for CHOCQUES 10.15 p.m. - entrained by 1 A.M.	
RAINNEVILLE	9-7-16		Rev Lot. 7.30 A.M. detrained LONGEAU (2 miles from AMIENS.) Breakfast at AMIENS Left AMIENS 11.20 A.M. arrives RAINNEVILLE 2.30 p.m. (10 miles march) no men fell out	
"	10-7-16		Fine. Lot. resting.	
VAUX-SUR-SOMME	11-7-16		Fine - moves 6 A.M. Left starting point at head of Brigade 7 A.M. Arrives VAUX-SUR-SOMME 12.15 p.m. no one fell out. In huts with 4/Suffolks. Remainder of Bde at CORBIE. Lewis Guns increased to 6.	
"	12-7-16		Left VAUX 2 p.m. - Arrives VILLE-SOUS-CORBIE 5.15 p.m. (7½ miles) no one fell out. Lewis guns to 8. Steel caps issued.	15.

Army Form C. 2118.

WAR DIARY
or
INTELLIGENCE SUMMARY.

4th B[attalio]n. The King's (Liverpool Reg[iment].)

July 1916

Instructions regarding War Diaries and Intelligence Summaries are contained in F. S. Regs., Part II. and the Staff Manual respectively. Title pages will be prepared in manuscript.

(Erase heading not required.)

Place	Date	Hour	Summary of Events and Information	Remarks and references to Appendices
VILLE-SOUS-CORBIE	13-7-16		Fine – resting. Left for MEAULTE 10.30pm (3 mils) arriving 11.15pm. In billets – Issue of Landsturm No. 12.	
MEAULTE	14-7-16		At 4 hrs notice from 3.45am. Moved 9am 1½ mls East – lulles dinner – more 5pm to old German front line, S of FRICOURT. Arrived 7pm. "Cooper" 10.30pm. Lieut NICHOLS 2nd WARING in front. One man from hospital. Capt. O'BRIEN.	
	15-7-16		Moved 5am. In reserve just W. of BESANTIN-LE-PETIT Wood – dug in. German cataul [casual?] line between HIGH Wood & MARTIN PUICH – heavy shelling. 1st Middlesex attacked & 1 company of 1st MIDDLESEX in front line 11am. Our line from cross roads N of BESANTIN E.P. to 400 yds S. 2 Coys front line 1/2 in reserve to left. 2/L WARING from transport returned 2 men killed. Lieut TAYLR. HUGHES & 2/Lt ATKIN & 25 men wounded. one missing.	Relieved & supports
FRONT LINE	16-7-16		Dull-rain dug new line cross roads to cemetery & occupied it – shelling enemy. Lieut 2/L ATKIN died of wounds. One man killed. 5 wounded.	
"	17-7-16		Fine. 1st MIDDLESEX Coy. Commander round trenches 3pm. This relief cancelled – Relieved by 2nd R.W.F. 5 men killed. 15 wounded & 2 shell shock.	
CATERPILLAR WOOD	18-7-16		Relief complete 3am. Moved to bivouac in Valley E of CATERPILLAR Wood – dug in – direct day. 2.30pm moved into support (enemy counter attacked) dug in FLATIRON Copse to SABOT Copse. 2/Lt WHITE, 2/Lt SPENCER & 14 men wounded. R.S.M. SIBLY. Returned to bivouac 8pm. 1 man to R.F.A. base. 1 man under age.	
"	19-7-16		Fine. C.O. & Coy. Commanders reconnoitred ground in vicinity of BESANTIN LE P. (wood) & village. Coy. Commander round trenches 3pm. Relieved 2nd R.W.F. & 20th R.F. in front line. Relief complete 10.15pm. 4 Coys in front line from cross roads N. of BESANTIN L.P. to Quarry. Lieut HUTCHINGS & 22 men wounded. Bombardment during night.	

WAR DIARY
or
INTELLIGENCE SUMMARY. 4th Bn. The King's (Liverpool Regt)

Army Form C. 2118.

July 1916

Place	Date	Hour	Summary of Events and Information	Remarks and references to Appendices
Front line	20-7-16		Fine. 3.35 A.M. HIGH WOOD attacked by 19th Brigade. Heavy shelling all day. 12.30 p.m. Capt BECK orders to establish liaison between HIGH WOOD + 98th Bgde HQr (through C.O.B. & Across). This effects 1.30 p.m. 2 A.T.S. Hill dug in to find 2 on night too long. Relieves by 7th Loyal N. Lanc + GLOUCESTERS about 11AM. Complete 2AM. Enemy put over gas shells 11pm to 12 h.h. Moved to bivouac at CATERPILLAR WOOD. Died MARTIN + BLACK. HUBBLE COOK, STYRING, BUCHAN, REID from gas. LIEUTS MATHER & MARTIN 15th Captains. PW man killed, 26 wounded + 3 missing.	
CATERPILLAR WOOD	21-7-16		In bivouac - fine bivouac - Heavy shelled with Lachrymatory shells between 9.30 p.m + 11 p.m. Relieves by 7th Gordons about 11.15 p.m. Marches to DERNANCOURT (huts) arriving 3.45 A.M. No one fell out. Officers in tents - men billets. 3 killed, 17 wounded, 5 gassed.	
DERNANCOURT	22-7-16		Fine - In hut. From 4pm at 1 pm notice.	
"	23-7-16		Fine - dull. Still at 2 hrs notice to move.	
"	24-7-16		Fine - dull. Brigadier met new officers at 10AM. 5.00 at 2 hrs notice to men BATHED. 2/Bach from Divl. School WD	
"	25-7-16		Fine. Training. 2/Lt McRAE to Lewis gun camp for training duties. 2/Rees from Hospital (wounded). 2/L GOODYEAR	
"	26-7-16		Dull. Fine Training. Hrs. notice removed. 2/Lt notice removed. WD	
			From Base. 2/Lt to Lewis Gun Camp for training duties. WD	
"	27-7-16		Fine. Hot- Training. Tug of war Scheme - Scouting - R.C's Church 10am. Gymnastic Sq. bayon. Instructing NCO's. Bayonet fighting. Draft 100. 12 from 7th King's, 88 from 8th (Irish) King's Bn.	
			Concert 6 p.m. WD	
"	28-7-16		Fine - hot - Training - Contest by "Shrapnel". 6p.m. than taken to HQr establishment 7th Divn.	
"	29-7-16		Fine - hot - STYRING one day F.M. Court.	
"	30-7-16		Fine - hot - R.C. at Church. C.O. inspected new Draft 11AM Draft parades for holiday Mass 2H. STYRING. 10 P.W. WD	
			Distribution 3-15 A.M. Sports 5.50 p.m.	
"	31-7-16		Fine - hot - ATD Corps Scheme in bow tactics - Lewis Guns Lectures to 270. Turnbull Lieut Colonel Comdg 4. Bn. King's L'pool Regt	

APPENDICES.

G.6. 33rd Division

A.11
33rd Division

XI Corps. R.H.S. 1134

[stamp: 4TH BATTALION THE KING'S (LIVERPOOL REGT) No. 2 - AUG. 1916]

I wish you to convey to all ranks in your Division my great appreciation of the successful operations they have carried out during the time they have been in the Corps, operations which have received frequently the appreciation of the General Officer Commanding the First Army, and of the Commander-in-Chief.

The many raids that have been undertaken by the 33rd Division have furnished models for other Divisions newly arrived from England to join the Corps; and the two recently carried out by the Glasgow Highlanders and the Royal Welsh Fusiliers, respectively, have shewn a brilliance in design and gallantry in execution which could not be surpassed.

I have to thank all ranks for the ready response that they have made whenever I called upon them to undertake any offensive operations. I have found a fine fighting spirit throughout the Division at all times, and it is with the greatest regret that I have to say "Good-bye".

I have seen and spoken to nearly all the officers, and to many of the N.C.O.s and men of the Division, and I shall regret your departure more than any of the sixteen Divisions that have been in my Corps since it was formed, because you are all such fine fighting soldiers.

I wish you "God speed and victory" and I hope before the end of the war that I may again have the high honour of including the 33rd Division in the XI Corps under my command.

(sd) R. Haking. Lt. General
9th July '16.   Comdg XI Corps

All Units, 33rd Division.

It gives the G.O.C. great pleasure to forward to you, for communication to all ranks the above copy of a letter received from Lieut. General Sir R. Haking, Commanding XI Corps.

(sd) R. Cumming. Lt. Colonel
10th July '16.   A.A. & Q.M.G. 33rd Division

True copy
at dawn 4th Bn. The King's Regt.
K Irving Lieut

To be made up to and for Sunday in each week.

No. of Report 70

RETURN showing numbers.

(a) Effective strength of Unit.
(b) Rationed by Unit.

Diary

Army Form B. 213.

(To be furnished by all arms, services, and departments (except A.S.C. units) to the A.G.'s Office at the Base in accordance with Field Service Regulations, Part II.)

1st Bn The King's (Liverpool Regt) at France. Date 4th July 1916.

FIELD RETURN.

Detail	Personnel			Animals								Guns, carriages, and limbers and transport vehicles										Remarks
	Officers	Other ranks	Natives	Horses Riding	Horses Draught	Horses Heavy Draught	Pack	Mules Large	Mules Small	Camels	Oxen	Guns, carriages and limbers, showing description	Ammunition wagons and limbers	Machine guns	Aircraft, showing description	Horsed 4 wheeled	Horsed 2 wheeled	Motor Cars	Tractors	Lorries	Trucks	Trailers	Motor Bicycles	Bicycles	
Effective Strength of Unit	33	1022		12	8	9	9	2						4		16	5							9	1 Not Rationed officers
Details, by Arms attached to unit as in War Establishment:—																										9 Base Depot
R.A.M.C.	1																									Sick
Royal Irish Fusiliers	1																									Synod of Truks atts 91st Bde TM Bty
Army Ordnance Corps		1																								6 Other Ranks
																										In command atts 251st Bde. R.E. 14
																										Field Ambulance 9 31
Total	35	1123*		12	8	9	9	2						4		16	5							9	5 Synod of Truks
War Establishment	44	995		12	26	9	9							4		16	5							9	12 1 M. Battery
Wanting to complete	9	15		-	18	-	9																		5 Anglos Employ
Surplus									2																6 Bde
																									18 attd 9 M. Bde. M.G Coy
*Attached (not to include the details shown above)																									19 Not Employ
Civilians:— Employed with the Unit Accompanying the Unit																									123 With Divl. Trains 6 - H.D. Horses
Total Rationed	29	900		12	8	1	-	2																	

* In the case of field ambulances, hospitals or depots, the number of patients are to be included here, the names being shown in A.F.A. 36.

X Includes 34 now permanently attd 251st Bde R.E. (Sd.) E. M. Beall Lieut Colonel Signature of Commander.

9 - " - " - 90th Bde T.M Battery 4th July 1916 Date of Despatch.

For information of the A.G.'s Office at the Base.

Officers and men who have become casuals, been transferred or joined since last report.

Place France Date July 7th 1916

Regtl. Number	Rank	Name	Corps	Nature of casualty, or name of unit from or to which transferred	Date of being struck off or coming on the ration return	Remarks
6454	Pte	McDonough J		From Hospital	29-6-16	
9223	-"-	Gavin		-"-	-"-	
	Lieut	Galloway G S R		Killed in Action	4-7-16	
10690	Sgt	Ivory J		-"-	6-7-16	
25072	Pte	Carter J C		To Hospital	29-6-16	
12603	-"-	Gosling W		Wounded in Action	4-7-16	
12096	L/Cpl	Nevers W		-"-	-"-	
9228	Pte	Strong		-"-	5-7-16	
27063	-"-	Croft J G		-"-	-"-	
10620	-"-	Bourke F		-"-	6-7-16	
31922	-"-	Moylan J		-"-	3-7-16	Remains at duty
20498	-"-	Wilkinson J		To Hospital	3-7-16	

Admittances to and Discharges from Field Ambulance

Regtl. Number	Rank	Name	Corps	Nature of casualty, or name of unit from or to which transferred	Date of being struck off or coming on the ration return	Remarks
10908	Pte	Ure J		To Field Amb	19-6-16	
30709	-"-	Phipps W		-"-	30-6-16	
14288	-"-	Leaver J		-"-	-"-	
20498	-"-	Wilkinson J		-"-	2-7-16	
25856	-"-	Baldwin J		-"-	-"-	
9223	-"-	Gavin J		-"-	-"-	
7478	-"-	Lord		-"-	29-6-16	
10645	-"-	Goldman L P		-"-	5-7-16	
12009	Sgt	Barnes J		From Field Amb	4-7-16	
10908	Pte	Ure J		-"-	30-6-16	
25856	-"-	Baldwin J		-"-	5-7-16	
7478	-"-	Lord		-"-	4-7-16	
11583	-"-	Dempsey R		-"-	29-6-16	

(Sd) E. Re Beals Lieut Colonel

Comdg 4th Bn The Kings (Liverpool Regt)

* State whether absence is of a permanent or temporary nature, adding, in the case of casuals from wounds or disease, any available information for communication to the relatives.

Diary

To be made up to and for Sunday in each week.

Army Form 'B. 213.

FIELD RETURN.

No. of Report 1/-

(To be furnished by all arms, services, and departments (except A.S.C. units) to the A. G.'s Office at the Base in accordance with Field Service Regulations, Part II.)

RETURN showing numbers (a) Effective strength of Unit. (b) Rationed by Unit.

11th Bn. The King's (Liverpool) Regt. France. Date 14th July 1916.

DETAIL	Personnel			Animals							Guns, carriages, and limbers and transport vehicles			Horsed		Mechanical					REMARKS
	Officers	Other ranks	Natives	Horses Riding	Horses Draught	Horses Heavy Draught	Pack	Mules Large	Mules Small	Camels	Oxen	Guns, carriages and limbers, showing description	Ammunition wagons and limbers	Machine guns	Aircraft, showing description	4 wheeled	2 wheeled	Motor Cars	Tractors	Lorries, showing description	Trucks, showing description	Trailers	Motor Bicycles	Bicycles	
Effective Strength of Unit	32	1014		12	8	9		21						8		16	5								Not Rationed
Details, by Arms attached to unit as in War Establishment :—																									Officers
R.A.M.C.	1																								Base depot sick
Royal Irish Fusiliers	1																								Journal of Instr.
Army Ordnance Corps		1																							Attd 98th Bde T.M.
																									Other ranks
																									On command
																									Attd 251st Coy R.E. 16
																									Field ambulance 10
																									9
Total	34	1015		12	8	9		27						8		16	5								Courses of Instr. 3
War Establishment	44	995		12	26	9		-						8		16	5								98th Bde T.M. Bty 19
Wanting to complete (Detail of Personnel and Horses below)	10				18			9																	Brigade Employ 8
Surplus		20							27																	Attd 98th Bde M.G.C. 18
																									Civil Employ 38
																									111
*Attached (not to include the details shown above)																									With Div. Train
Civilians :— Employed with the Unit Accompanying the Unit																									8 - H.D. Horses
TOTAL RATIONED...	12	1004		12	8	1		27																	

* In the case of field ambulances, hospitals or depots, the number of patients are to be included here, the names being shown in A. F. A. 36.

× Includes 10 men permanently attached 251st Coy R.E. [signature] Lt Colonel Signature of Commander.
         9 " " " " — 98th Bde T.M. Bty
         19

14th July 1916 Date of Despatch.

For information of the A.G.'s Office at the Base.

Officers and men who have become casuals, been transferred or joined since last report.

Place France   Date July 14th 1916

Regtl. Number	Rank	Name	Corps	Nature of casualty, or name of unit from or to which transferred	Date of being struck off or coming on the ration return	Remarks
	Lieut	Rees G.D.	The King's (Liverpool Regiment)	Wounded in A	7-7-16	
11269	Pte	Murphy J.		—"—	—"—	
29369	—"—	Smith C		—"—	—"—	
26305	—"—	Moss J		—"—	—"—	Shock
27118	—"—	Smith J		—"—	—"—	
11537	—"—	Hamilton J		—"—	8-7-16	
27115	—"—	Morgan J		Transferred to R.E.	27-5-16	
29882	—"—	Bleasdale R.		To Hospital	4-7-16	
10645	—"—	Goldman H.		—"—	6-7-16	
30709	—"—	Phipps R		—"—	2-7-16	
10620	—"—	Bourke J.		From Hospital	14-7-16	

Admittances to and Discharges from Field Ambulance

25858	Pte	Baldwin J	4th Bn The King's (Liverpool Regt)	To Field Amb	7-7-16	
34732	—"—	McNeill J		—"—	—"—	
11592	—"—	Maney J		—"—	—"—	
10813	—"—	McGregor J		—"—	—"—	
	—"—	Bateson J		—"—	8-7-16	
13631	Sgt	Christie M		—"—	10-7-16	
12454	Pte	Wilson M		From Field Amb	—"—	
14288	—"—	Leaver J.W		—"—	7-7-16	

Comdg 4th Bn The King's (Liverpool Regt)

* State whether absence is of a permanent or temporary nature, adding, in the case of casuals from wounds or disease, any available information for communication to the relatives.

FIELD RETURN.

Army Form B. 213.

Diary

To be made up to and for Sunday in each week.
No. of Report _____
(To be furnished by all arms, services, and departments (except A.S.C. units) to the A. G.'s Office at the Base in accordance with Field Service Regulations, Part II.)
RETURN showing numbers (a) Effective strength of Unit. #Br the King at France 27 July 1916. Date.
(b) Rationed by Unit. of Brookelets

Detail	Personnel			Animals.								Guns, carriages, and limbers and transport vehicles				Mechanical				Remarks
	Officers	Other ranks	Natives	Horses Riding	Horses Draught	Horses Heavy Draught	Mules Pack	Mules Large	Mules Small	Camels	Oxen	Guns, carriages and limbers, showing description	Ammunition wagons and limbers	Machine guns	Aircraft, showing description	Horsed 4 wheeled	Horsed 2 wheeled	Motor Cars	Tractors	Lorries	Trucks	Trailers	Motor Bicycles	Bicycles	
Effective Strength of Unit		391		12	5	9		29								16	5							9	Not Returned Chicago Base Report Sick Horses of 2nd Rusts were sent in Rly
Details, by Arms attached to unit as in War Establishment:—																									Eden Rents Monegraph Monogramme with system
Royal West Surrey's	1																									
R.G. R.E.	1																									
Army Reserves Corps	1																									9 FM Jor 19
Total		200		12	5	9		29						8		16	5								9 Foot can mine 15
War Establishment		925		15	25	9		25						4		16	5								9 Source of India 3
Wanting to complete (Detail of Personnel and Horses below)		92½		15	5																					Cigdig London 8 War Country 23
Surplus																										Acc as 4 in F Bn 19
*Attached (not to include the details shown above)																										not in over thru
Civilians: Employed with the Unit Accompanying the Unit																										B. I.D. Recto
Total Rationed...																									

* In the case of field ambulances, hospitals or depots, the number of patients are to be included here, the names being shown in A. F. A. 36.

Permanently attached 4/ER 10 .... A.C.B.O. Sunderland ------ Signature of Commander.
5/M 399 27 July 1916 Date of Despatch.
19

Sheet I

For information of the A.G.'s Office at the Base.

Officers and men who have become casuals, been transferred or joined since last report.

Place France   Date 21st July 1916

Regtl. Number	Rank	Name	Corps	Nature of casualty, or name of unit from or to which transferred	Date of being struck off or coming on the ration return	Remarks*
		Officers				
Lieut + Adjt		Hughes J.L.		Wounded	15-7-16	
	2 Lt	Askew J.O.H.		—	—"—	
	"	White S.		—	17-7-16	
	"	Spencer E.		—	—"—	
	Lieut	Hutchings J.		—	19-7-16	
		Other Ranks				
11000	Pt	Morris a.		Killed	15-7-16	
9010	"	Davies H.		—	—"—	
16534	"	Hutchinson J.		—	—"—	
2032	"	Burns M.		—	16-7-16	
3876	"	Oliver R.		—	14-7-16	
X-956	"	Brodie J.		—	—"—	
8710	Cpl	Pugh		—	—"—	
1063	Pt	Smith R.		—	—"—	
11481	"	Cephton E.		—	—"—	
4732	"	Craig J.		Wounded	15-7-16	
X-693	"	Parker R.		—	—"—	
18830	"	Lang B.		—	—"—	
1311	"	Featherbarrow		—	—"—	
9260	"	Raiford J.		—	—"—	
1854	"	Pierce H.		—	—"—	
10992	"	Delves T.		—	—"—	
9364	Cpl	Hanlon T.		—	—"—	
23903	Pt	Thompson A.		—	—"—	
3185	"	Newell J.		—	—"—	
24479	"	Myers R.		—	—"—	
19095	"	Brewer M.		—	—"—	
2727	"	Booth P.		—	—"—	
13060	"	Jackson S.		—	—"—	
31344	"	Berriman J.		—	—"—	
12413	Sgt	Sweeney R.		—	—"—	
11293	Pt	Nightingale E.		—	—"—	
16420	CQMS	West T.		—	—"—	
10264	Pt	Williams T.		—	—"—	
8891	Cpl	Berling H.		—	—"—	
14299	Pt	Brown H.		—	—"—	
4631	"	Allen H.		—	16-7-16	
18544	"	Heggarth S.		—	—"—	
2149	"	Lady R.		—	—"—	
9853	"	Smith R.		—	—"—	
29334	"	Gilherne T.		—	14-7-16	
8705	"	Lund N.		—	—"—	
2961	"	Tomlinson A.		—	—"—	
13468	Sgt	Conlon		—	—"—	
34264	Pt	Carsaram T.		—	—"—	
10554	"	Hobson W.		—	—"—	
860	"	Cook E.		—	—"—	
10323	"	Cague J.		—	—"—	
8871	"	Brown H.		—	—"—	
21416	"	Cullen H.		—	—"—	
29342	"	Everett H.		—	—"—	
20893	"	Aspinall H.		—	—"—	
27610	"	Kent J.		—	—"—	
1932	Cpl	Morton J.		—	—"—	

* State whether absence is of a permanent or temporary nature, adding, in the case of casuals from wounds or disease, any available information for communication to the relatives.

Sheet II

For information of the A.G.'s Office at the Base.

Officers and men who have become casuals, been transferred or joined since last report.

Place: France   Date: 21st July 1916

Regtl. Number	Rank	Name	Corps	Nature of casualty, or name of unit from or to which transferred	Date of being struck off or coming on the ration return	Remarks*
18913	Pte	Ashbrooke		Wounded	14-7-16	
1316		Naylor T		Shell Shock	-do-	
915		Wigglesworth G		-do-		
14454		Wilson H		Wounded	15-7-16	
3293		Moore C		-do-		
31283		Wade E M				
13041		Atkinson M		Missing	15-7-16	B Coy To England Wounded
39403		Saunders H		-do-	14-7-16	B Coy To England Wounded
16250		Henry H		-do-		C
8950		Turner E J		-do-		C
15160		Bushell J		-do-		C To England 22/9/16
9046		Egan F		Wounded	16-7-16	
1869	L.Cpl	Preston A		-do-	14-7-16	
10632		Garland J		-do-	19-7-16	
18620	Cpl	Dunford		-do-		
		Pilsbury		-do-		
31091	L.Cpl	Young J		-do-		
14929	Pte	Wright H		-do-		
		Welsh		-do-		
		Gaskill A		-do-		
6134	C.S.M.	McLaughlin T		-do-	19-7-16	
1440	L.Cpl	Wilson H		-do-		
2573	R.S.M.	Hatton A H		-do-	19-7-16	Slight. Remains at Duty
9939	Pte	Halsall M		-do-	19-7-16	
8064		Holmes		-do-		
11580		Donovan P		-do-		
30458		Buslow M		-do-		
17458		Aden G		-do-		
8909		Morris		-do-		
13892		Williams T		-do-		
		Brown		-do-		
10630		Farrell		-do-		
1294		Whelan J		-do-		
4391		Fitzsimmons J		-do-		
10190		Ewart		-do-		
9034		Shields C		-do-		
1592		Galway		-do-		
1242		Garrett H		-do-		
1247		Morrison J		-do-		
29088		Conran		-do-		
2243	L.Cpl	Richardson J		-do-		
2972	Pte	McDonough H		-do-		
8324	Pte	Green A		Shell shock		
8744		Greenery		Missing		
2007		Thomas J		Wounded	2-7-16	
1801		Orrell				
		Howard				
	Lieut	Martin A				
	2Lt	Gubble G A				
		Dyson E H		Home	20-7-16	
		Cook A J		Base		
		Reid				
		Buchan H E				

J.C.P. O'Brien Capt & O.C.
"B" Co The King's (L'pool Regt)

* State whether absence is of a permanent or temporary nature, adding, in the case of casuals from wounds or disease, any available information for communication to the relatives.

Army Form B. 213.

Sheet II

FIELD RETURN.

To be made up to and for Sunday in each week.

No. of Report _____

(To be furnished by all arms, services, and departments (except A.S.G. units) to the A. G.'s Office at the Base in accordance with Field Service Regulations, Part II.)

RETURN showing numbers (a) Effective strength of Unit.
(b) Rationed by Unit.

at France ___ 28 July 1915 Date.

DETAIL.	Personnel			Animals.								Guns, carriages, and limbers and transport vehicles			Horsed		Mechanical					REMARKS
	Officers	Other ranks	Natives	Horses			Mules		Camels	Oxen		Guns, carriages and limbers, showing description	Ammunition wagons and limbers	Machine guns	Aircraft, showing description	4 wheeled	2 wheeled	Motor Cars.	Tractors	Lorries, showing description	Trucks, showing description	Trailers	Motor Bicycles	Bicycles	
				Riding	Draught	Heavy Draught	Pack	Large	Small																

Effective Strength of Unit

Details, by *Arms* attached to unit as in War Establishment:—

Total

War Establishment

Wanting to complete
(Detail of Personnel and Horses below)

Surplus

*Attached (not to include the details shown above)

Civilians:—
Employed with the Unit Accompanying the Unit

TOTAL RATIONED...

* In the case of field ambulances, hospitals or depots, the number of patients are to be included here, the names being shown in A. F. A. 36.

_____ Signature of Commander.

_____ Date of Despatch.

Diary

FIELD RETURN.

Army Form B. 213.

No. of Report 43

(To be furnished by all arms, services, and departments (except A.S.C. units) to the A. G.'s Office at the Base in accordance with Field Service Regulations, Part II.)

RETURN showing numbers
(a) Effective strength of Unit.
(b) Rationed by Unit.

Date 23rd July 1916

4th Bn. The Kings at France
(Chool Regt)

To be made up to and for Sunday in each week.

Detail	Personnel			Animals								Guns, carriages, and limbers and transport vehicles										Remarks
	Officers	Other ranks	Natives	Horses				Mules		Camels	Oxen	Guns, carriages and limbers, showing description	Ammunition wagons and limbers	Machine guns	Aircraft, showing description	Horsed		Motor Cars	Tractors	Mechanical			
				Riding	Draught	Heavy Draught	Pack	Large	Small							4 wheeled	2 wheeled			Lorries, showing description	Trucks, showing description	Trailers	Motor Bicycles	Bicycles	

Effective Strength of Unit

Details, *by Arms* attached to unit as in War Establishment:—

Total

War Establishment

Wanting to complete
(Detail of Personnel and Horses below)

Surplus

*Attached (not to include the details shown above)

Civilians:—
Employed with the Unit
Accompanying the Unit

Total, Rationed...

* In the case of field ambulances, hospitals or depots, the number of patients are to be included here, the names being shown in A. F. A. 36.

Signature of Commander.

Date of Despatch.

4th Bn The King's (Liverpool Regt)

For information of the A.G.'s Office at the Base.

Officers and men who have become casuals, been transferred or joined since last report.

Place: France   Date: 23rd July 1916

Regtl. Number	Rank	Name	Corps	Nature of casualty, or name of unit from or to which transferred	Date of being struck off or coming on the ration return	Remarks
11525	Pte	McGuire A	The King's (Liverpool Regt) 4th Bn	Killed in Action	20-7-16	
24295	-"-	Sullivan H		-"-	21-7-16	
10304	-"-	Moran J		-"-	-"-	
7448	-"-	Ford J		-"-	-"-	
8023	Sgt	Starkey J		Wounded in Action	20-7-16	
20981	Pte	Gauley J		-"-	-"-	
30557	-"-	Ginley J		-"-	-"-	
26265	-"-	Kearney J		-"-	-"-	
11689	-"-	Hagan J		-"-	-"-	
13522	-"-	Middleton J		-"-	-"-	
10015	L-Cpl	McHugh J		-"-	-"-	
34468	Pte	Baker W		-"-	-"-	
14370	-"-	Quail T H		-"-	-"-	
12252	-"-	Riley J		-"-	-"-	
21293	-"-	Stabler J		-"-	-"-	
29360	-"-	Lawley G		-"-	-"-	
12488	-"-	Andrews W		-"-	-"-	
9001	-"-	Cooper J		-"-	-"-	
12494	-"-	Brides J		-"-	-"-	Shell shock
11425	Cpl	Maxwell W		-"-	-"-	
24120	-"-	Clarke J		-"-	-"-	
29098	Pte	Smith J		-"-	-"-	
14075	-"-	Webb W		-"-	-"-	
9881	-"-	Corcoran J		-"-	-"-	
11332	-"-	Jones J		-"-	-"-	
10600	-"-	Sampson J		-"-	-"-	
30642	-"-	Conol P		-"-	-"-	
30784	-"-	Marsden F		-"-	-"-	
30960	-"-	Darlington W		Missing	-"-	
30539	-"-	Johnson J		-"-	-"-	
11458	-"-	Riley M		-"-	-"-	
25148	-"-	Boughton J		Wounded in Action	21-7-16	
29993	-"-	Bullows J		-"-	-"-	
25126	L/Cpl	Williams A		-"-	-"-	
14249	Pte	Burton H		-"-	-"-	
28042	-"-	Watson J		-"-	-"-	
8715	-"-	Bache W		-"-	-"-	
8332	-"-	Draper R		-"-	-"-	
13422	-"-	Smith R		-"-	-"-	
27442	-"-	Mather A		-"-	-"-	
10908	-"-	Ure A		-"-	-"-	
31233	-"-	Cruickshank J		-"-	-"-	
18811	-"-	Richards J		-"-	-"-	Gassed
30549	Cpl	Powderley J		-"-	-"-	
12353	Pte	Schofield J		-"-	-"-	
25649	-"-	Owens W		-"-	-"-	
11209	-"-	Jones R		-"-	-"-	
15869	-"-	Henshaw J		-"-	-"-	
8749	-"-	Jones J		-"-	-"-	Gassed
26426	-"-	King W		-"-	-"-	
29048	-"-	Luna J		-"-	-"-	
30810	-"-	Parker J		-"-	-"-	
9019	-"-	Jones J		-"-	-"-	

Lieut. Colonel
Comdg 4th Bn The King's Regt

* State whether absence is of a permanent or temporary nature, adding, in the case of casuals from wounds or disease, any available information for communication to the relatives.

Army Form B. 213.

FIELD RETURN.

To be made up to and for Sunday in each week.

No. of Report 14

(To be furnished by all arms, services, and departments (except A.S.C. units) to the A.G.'s Office at the Base in accordance with Field Service Regulations, Part II.)

RETURN showing numbers (a) Effective strength of Unit. 4th (Bn) The King's (Liverpool Regt) — France
(b) Rationed by Unit. Date 28th July 1916

Diary

DETAIL	Personnel			Horses			Mules		Camels	Oxen	Guns, carriages, limbers, showing description	Ammunition wagons and limbers	Machine guns	Aircraft, showing description	4 wheeled	2 wheeled	Motor Cars	Tractors	Lorries, showing description	Trucks, showing description	Trailers	Motor Bicycles	Bicycles	REMARKS
	Officers	Other ranks	Natives	Riding	Draught	Heavy Draught	Pack	Large	Small															
Effective Strength of Unit	34	951		12	8	9	—	24					8			16	5							9	Not Rationed — Officers 1, sick depot 2, house of instrn 4, attd T.M. Btty — Other Ranks — J.M. Battery 19, Bde M.G. Coy 19, attd 251st Bgy T.E. 9
Details, by Arms attached to unit as in War Establishment:—																									
Royal Irish Fusiliers	1																								
R.A.M.C.	1																								
Army Ordnance Corps		1																							
Total	36	958		12	8	9	—	24					8			16	5							9	Command 24
War Establishment	44	995		12	26	9	9	—					8			16	5							9	Duty Employ 22
Wanting to complete (Detail of Personnel and Horses below)	8	55*		—	18	—	9	—																	Bde — 8 Field Ambulance 11 — 103
Surplus							24																		
*Attached (not to include the details shown above)																									With Civil chairs
Civilians:— Employed with the Unit Accompanying the Unit																									8 – 7 D. Horses
TOTAL RATIONED	30	855		12	8	1	—	24																	

* In the case of field ambulances, hospitals or depots, the number of patients are to be included here, the names being shown in A.F.A. 36.

* Permanently attached 251st Bgy T.E. 9
98th T.M. Btty 9
— 18

(Sd) E. M. Beall Lieut Col Signature of Commander.
28th July 1916 Date of Despatch.

For information of the A.G.'s Office at the Base.

Officers and men who have become casuals, been transferred or joined since last report.

Place: France   Date: July 28/1916

Regtl. Number	Rank	Name	Corps	Nature of casualty, or name of unit from or to which transferred	Date of being struck off or coming on the ration return	Remarks*
6256	L/Cpl	Winrow B				
4081	-"-	Johnstone A				
6033	Pte	Gabbott J.G				
5986	-"-	Horley H	7th Bn The King's (Liverpool Regt)			
6054	-"-	Flanagan J				
4944	-"-	Lloyd W				
4929	-"-	Williams K				
6053	-"-	Doyle J				
5092	-"-	Thorne G				
6007	-"-	Marsh R				
4121	-"-	Hogan				
4120	-"-	O'Riley J				
4943	-"-	Austin H				
3902	-"-	Apden H				
5518	-"-	Anderson H				
5219	-"-	Boyan		Reinforcements from No 24 Infantry Base Depot.	/6	
5474	-"-	Broughton R				
5006	-"-	Brown E.W				
3621	-"-	Brennan P.S				
5429	-"-	Byrne J				
5516	-"-	Burton H				
5319	-"-	Butterly P				
5222	-"-	Broughton				
5424	-"-	Barrett L				
3150	-"-	Benwell				
4096	-"-	Ballantine J.G				
4911	-"-	Corcoran				
5288	-"-	Goulbourne W				
5524	-"-	Cunningham A			/-	
5202	-"-	Costello C				
5198	-"-	Corcoran P				
4323	-"-	Cowan J				
5039	-"-	Connolly H				
5023	-"-	Cadogen P				
4586	-"-	Coughlin K				
5120	-"-	Colman J				
3464	-"-	Comerford J				
3544	-"-	Cornell				
5126	-"-	Dempsey			/-	
5493	-"-	Davies J.W				
5711	-"-	Dunne J.G				
2880	-"-	Edwards D.J				
5205	-"-	Fitzgerald J				
5328	-"-	Folly J.G				
3948	-"-	Flintoff J				
5485	-"-	Iverson				
2890	-"-	Freckleton J				
5476	L/Cpl	Garnett	8th Bn The King's (Liverpool Regt)	Reinforcements	28	
5507	Pte	Gallagher R				
5014	-"-	Grace				
5434	-"-	Hewlett P				
5569	-"-	Hynes J.F				
5540	-"-	Jackson J				
3088	-"-	Blakely J				
5013	-"-	Baines E.P				
3303	-"-	Woodruff J				
2283	-"-	Hilton J				

* State whether absence is of a permanent or temporary nature, adding, in the case of casuals from wounds or disease, any available information for communication to the relatives.

For information of the Officer i/c of a Base Record Office.

Officers and men who have left or joined since last report.

Place _____   Date _____

Regtl. Number	Rank	Name	Corps	Name of unit from or to which transferred	Date of being struck off or coming on the ration return	Remarks *
3954	Pte	Lucroft T.				
4942	-"-	Lafontaine H.G.				
5304	-"-	Leatherbarrow E.			16	
5425	-"-	Larkin P.				
5487	-"-	Murphy P.				
3857	L/Cpl	Marcus E.				
2170	Pte	Makinson J.				
5325	-"-	Mercer E.				
5488	Pte					
5484	-"-	Murphy J.	8th Bn The King's (Liverpool Regt)	Reinforcements from No 24 Infantry Base Depot		
2444	-"-	Marsden W.				
2616	-"-	Nicholson G.				
5012	-"-	Noonan P.			1	
5375	-"-	Nugent J.				
2558	-"-	Ogden J.P.				
5038	-"-	Oakes P.				
3636	-"-	Oram W.				
5496	-"-	O'Hare J.				
4757	-"-	O'Dea J.			1	
5119	-"-	Powers E.J.				
5305	-"-	Pleant				
3115	-"-	Platt E.				
5205	-"-	Peters J.				
4519	-"-	Paterson J.				
2116	L/Cpl	Rooney H.				
5308	Pte	Rock M.				
5029	-"-	Riley J.			1	
5015	-"-	Rodaway J.T.				
2809	-"-	Rye S.				
3507	-"-	Roberts J.				
5215	-"-	Rock M.				
3136	-"-	Swarbrick J.				
3693	-"-	Smyth J.				
1812	L/Cpl	Sinnott J.				
5050	Pte	Stanley J.			28	
2290	-"-	Shields J.				
2233	-"-	Saynor H.				
5323	-"-	Thomas H.				
3733	-"-	Walter G.			2	
2310	-"-	Whittaker H.				
2768	-"-	Worsley P.				
4986	-"-	Wilson J.				
3841	-"-	Webster J.				
3485	-"-	Evans H.				
	Lieut	Goodman C.R.		From Base	26.7.16	
	-"-	Rees C.R.		From Hospital	" "	
13548	Pte	Baden W.		"	20.7.16	
27063	-"-	Croft C.		"	25.7.16	
10600	-"-	Simpson J.		"	" "	
	2/Lieut	Lomas J.A.		To 98th T.M. Bty	18-6-16	
26430	Pte	Newnes J.		Transferred to RE	19-4-16	
8106	-"-	Wilson J.		To England	5.7.16	
10605	Cpl	Lloyd L.		Transferred to 1st Bn	6.7.16	
12582	Pte	Kilday E.		Transferred to RFA Base	18.7.16	
24603	L/Cpl	Kirby L.		To Base underage	" "	
8600	-"-	Graham J.		Wounded in Action	15.7.16	Gassed
14534	Pte	Briscoe J.		"	" "	

* State whether absence is of a permanent or temporary nature.

Army Form B. 213.

FIELD RETURN.

(To be furnished by all arms, services, and departments to the Base Record Office in accordance with Field Service Regulations, Part II.)

No. of Report ———— Date ————

RETURN showing numbers RATIONED by, and Transport on charge of, ———————— at ————

DETAIL.	Personnel			Animals							Transport Vehicles		Guns, carriages, and limbers, showing description	Ammunition wagons and limbers	Machine guns	REMARKS
	Officers	Other ranks	Natives	Horses			Mules		Camels	Oxen	4 Wheeled	2 Wheeled				
				Riding	Draught	Pack	Large	Small								

Effective Strength of Unit
Details, *by Arms* attached to Unit as in War Establishment:—

Total																
War Establishment																
Wanting to complete																
Surplus																
*Attached (not to include the details shown above)																
Civilians:— Employed with the Unit																
Accompanying the Unit																
TOTAL RATIONED ...																

———————————
Signature of Commander.

———————————
Date of Despatch.

* In the case of field ambulances, hospitals or depôts, the number of patients are to be included here, the names being shown in A. F. A. 36.

Forms B. 213 / 2

(51674) Wt. 2141/2190 35/000 8-09 W B & L

For information of the Officer i/c of a Base Record Office.

Officers and men who have left or joined since last report.

Place _____   Date _____

Regtl. Number	Rank	Name	Corps	Name of unit from or to which transferred	Date of being struck off or coming on the ration return	Remarks*
31246	Pte	Attwood C.		Wounded in A	18-7-16	Since reported attached 8th Bn. to 1 Lo Regt
34470	-"-	Monoghan J.W.		Missing	-"-	
8990	-"-	King J.W.		Wounded in A	-"-	
9618	-"-	O'Loughlin J.		-"-	-"-	
27416	-"-	Daley J.	King's Regt	-"-	20-7-16	
10143	-"-	McGrale J.		-"-	21-7-16	
7463	-"-	Galley J.		-"-	15-7-16	

Admittances to and Discharges from Field Ambulance

10560	Pte	Carney A.		To Field Amb	17-7-16	
13914	Cpl	Jevons A.G.		-"-	18-7-16	
27938	Pte	Devine W.		-"-	-"-	
11592	-"-	Maney J.	4th Bn	-"-	19-7-16	
34732	-"-	McNeill J.	The King's	-"-	-"-	
11013	L/Cpl	Hay J.	(Liverpool Regt)	-"-	17-7-16	
29336	Pte	Pitt J.		-"-	18-7-16	
10813	-"-	McGregor J.		-"-	7-7-16	
13631	Sgt	Christie W.		-"-	10-7-16	
29924	Pte	Devine W.		From Field Amb	20-7-16	
11592	-"-	Maney J.		-"-	21-7-16	
34732	-"-	McNeill J.		-"-	-"-	

(Sd) E.M. Beall. Lieut Col.

Comdg 4th Bn The King's (Liverpool Regt)

*State whether absence is of a permanent or temporary nature.

Army Form B. 213.

FIELD RETURN.

No. of Report _____

(To be furnished by all arms, services, and departments to the Base Record Office in accordance with Field Service Regulations, Part II.)

Date. _____

RETURN showing numbers RATIONED by, and Transport on charge of _____ at _____

DETAIL.	Personnel			Animals							Transport Vehicles		Guns, carriages, and limbers, showing description	Ammunition wagons and limbers	Machine guns	REMARKS
	Officers	Other ranks	Natives	Horses			Mules		Camels	Oxen	4 Wheeled	2 Wheeled				
				Riding	Draught	Pack	Large	Small								
Effective Strength of Unit																
Details, *by Arms* attached to Unit as in War Establishment:—																
Total																
War Establishment																
Wanting to complete																
Surplus																
*Attached (not to include the details shown above)																
Civilians:— Employed with the Unit Accompanying the Unit																
TOTAL RATIONED ...																

* In the case of field ambulances, hospitals or depôts, the number of patients are to be included here, the names being shown in A. F. A. 36.

_____ Signature of Commander.

_____ Date of Despatch.

(5.1674) Wt. 2141/2190 32000 8-09 W B & L Forms B. 213 / 2

98th Brigade.
33rd Division.

1/4th BATTALION

THE KING'S LIVERPOOL REGIMENT

AUGUST 1 9 1 6.

Army Form C. 2118.

WAR DIARY
or
INTELLIGENCE SUMMARY. 1st Bn. The King's (Liverpool Regt)

Vol 10

August 1916

(Erase heading not required.)

Place	Date	Hour	Summary of Events and Information	Remarks and references to Appendices
DERNAN-COURT	1-8-16		Fine hot - Usual training C+B Coys in wood fighting	
"	2-8-16		Fine. C of E Communion 7 a.m. - training. One man from hospital	
"	3-8-16		Fine. Battalion parade for Address by C.O. Lecture on "Contact Patrol Aeroplane" by Officer at Batt. H.Q. at 11 a.m. From 6 pm at 3½ hrs notice. 3 men from hospital	
"	4-8-16		Fine - dull - training continued.	
"	5-8-16		C.O. & Coy Commanders looking over position in MAMETZ Wood in morning - Fine day. Training continued.	
"	6-8-16		R.C. Church Service. Moved 3 p.m. Passed starting point 3.30 a.m. took over from 9th Royal Scots - Relief complete 6.30 p.m. (position in S.E. Side 7 MAMETZ WOOD) No men fell out. One man to hospital	
MAMETZ WOOD	7-8-16		1 a.m. to 5 a.m. heavily shelled by 4.2" + 5.9" - Working parties 500 men. Relieved by 16th K.R.R. Corps - Complete 2.25 p.m. moved to FRICOURT WOOD. Batt in field sundays 9/ 13000 - 13th HQ in Wood. 2 men Killed 4 Wounded and one man to hospital	
FRICOURT WOOD	8-8-16		Fine - hot - 500 men on working parties Digging communicating trenches. 4 men wounded One man to Base linebase	
"	9-8-16		Fine - hot - C.O. + Officers went to FLANMERS to demonstration near TREUX. Capt Beck awarded Military Cross - 500 men working parties. 2nd Lt. McCORKINDALE to Rawalpindi (sick) 2/21. Back to A Coy. 2 men to + one man from hospital. 3 to Base inbase.	
"	10-7-16		Wet - 500 men on working parties. One man wounded	
"	11-8-16		C.O. + Coy Commanders of 2nd Bn. R.W.F. round position	
"	12-8-16		Fine hot - 200 Working parties - 400 men working parties. 3 men wounded	
"	13-8-16		Fine - Relieved by 2nd R.W.F. - Complete 2.30 a.m. - took over front line from 16th K.R.R. from South Camps HIGH WOOD. Relief complete 7.30 a.m. 200 yds South.	

Army Form C. 2118.

WAR DIARY
or
INTELLIGENCE SUMMARY. 1/4 Bn The King's (Liverpool Regt.)

(Erase heading not required.)

August 1916.

Place	Date	Hour	Summary of Events and Information	Remarks and references to Appendices
Trenches	13-8-16		CO's conference at Bde. HQ. - Brigadier round trenches - 9.55pm to 10.30pm enemy barrage. Heavy shelling all night - 4 men killed, 11 wounded & one missing. One man from shrapnel	
BAZENTIN-LE-GRAND	14-8-16		Fine - Relieved by 4th Suffolks. Completed 9.15AM - Moved to BAZENTIN-LE-GRAND - 2 Coys in huts N.E. of village - 2 Coys in road S. of village - Working parties of 400. Heavier bombing N.E. of Wood Lane Trench. 3 men wounded and one man from shrapnel	
"	15-8-16		Fine - dull - 3 Lancs Sergt Officers + 120 men working in reserve parties - Heavier bombardment building Wood Lane Trench. 400 men working Neuralgia - 2nd Lieut Cook killed on working party. 4 killed, 21 wounded and one missing. Capt Martin to hospital	
"	16-8-16		Showery - CO round trenches - 2nd Lt GAULTER relieved by 2nd Lt REES on body dump at FRICOURT + round our Coys and 'A' Coy - 490 on working parties - Capt Mason to hospital 5 men wounded	
TRENCHES	17-8-16		Took over right ½ Coy D.4 Support line - Relief complete 9.30AM - Heavier shelling enemy's front line - Men in front line both drawn to supports - Heavy shelling all night Lt SHARPE wounded by shrapnel. 31 wounded, 3 missing	
"	18-8-16		Fine - Heavier shelling enemy's lines - Men in front line withdrawn to supports - Relay lines 2.45 p.m. - B + D Coys went one in 2 days follows by C Coy - Barrage on supports in reserve. Attack held up by enemy + falso line + machine gun fire. 20th R. Fus. came up between 6 + 8 p.m. + took over front line supports. Showers of gas Battalion came in at dusk + battalion was collected in trench behind supports. Captains SIMPRANCE + BECK wounded. 2/Lt GAULTER, NICKALLS, + REID killed. 2/Lts GOODMAN + GRAY 2 men to hospital 2/Lt YARNDELL + W.R. IRVING wounded. 45 men killed, 248 wounded, 22 missing. 1 man to base under esc. 4 men stunned by shrapnel. Battalion re-established in the huts.	
MAMETZ WOOD	19-8-16		Relieved by Y. Cameronians 12/12 Took over the whole line - Battalion moved out at 2AM to fine day - moved to Pommiers S. of FRICOURT WOOD. Bn HQ in town - in position 9.9 p.m. MAMETZ WOOD - Search party sent out to get in wounded + officers	

WAR DIARY
INTELLIGENCE SUMMARY. 4th Bn. The Kings (Liverpool Reg)

August 1916

Place	Date	Hour	Summary of Events and Information	Remarks and references to Appendices
MAMETZ WOOD	19/8/16		Search Party sent to look for official bodies – 2nd Lt. T.H. IRVING missing believes killed – 2 men wounded – one man from hospital	
FRICOURT	20.8.16		Fine – Cleaning + Washing – CO's conference at Bgde Hq at 10 a.m. 2 men to hospital. One from hospital	
WOOD	21.8.16		Fine – Gazette "Lieut" NICHOLL to be Captain – Capt. O'BRIEN took over A Coy – 200 men on working parties – Baths for men in morning. One man hospital	
"	22.8.16		Fine – Baths for men in morning – 200 men working parties. One man to hospital	
"	23.8.16		Fine – CO & C.O.'s Comdrs reconnoitred approaches to reserve defences of right reserve Brigade in Eylen Wood. POMMIERS REDOUBT + MONTAUBAN 320 men on working parties	
"	24.8.16		Relieved by 4th Suffolks – Complete 3.15pm – moved to MAMETZ WOOD – in Divnl. Reserve – 100th Bgde. Attack enemy TEA Trench – bombardment 3.45pm. working party 120 men – Enemy Shells MAMETZ Wood during night. One man wounded at from hospital
"	25.8.16		N. of BAZENTIN (le GRAND) Fine – Showery – moved to CARLTON TRENCH in position 7.15pm – in support – 1st MIDDLESEX + 2nd A&H.H. in front line – 250 men working party, digging 9ft join up gap existing between these two battalions. 1 man wounded, 1 to hospital	
CARLTON TRENCH	26.8.16		Fine – In support – Whole battalion on working parties. 3 wounded, 1 to hosp. 1 app	
"	27.8.16		Fine – OC Coys visit trenches of right battalion (1st MIDDLESEX) 1st Coy. moves up at 10.35pm Relief complete 6am (28th) 1 man died of wounds. 1 man wounded	
Front line	28.8.16		Showery – on line from LONGUEVAL – FLERS Rd to about 400 yds to North – Heavy Shelling from front line supports day & night. 9 killed. 20 wounded (3 shell shock)	

Army Form C. 2118

WAR DIARY
or
INTELLIGENCE SUMMARY 4" B" The King's (Liverpool Regt)

August 1916.

(Erase heading not required.)

Place	Date	Hour	Summary of Events and Information	Remarks and references to Appendices
Front line	29.8.16		Just before 3 officers 3 O/R of Scottish Rifles visit front line. Royal Sussex Regt. report our lines 10 men killed, 32 wounded (10 shell shock) 1 man missing	
"	30.8.16		Rel. Enemy shelling heavily - relieved by 9th Royal Sussex Regt - Guide at manor village at 5 p.m. - 2 men wounded, 2 to hospital 9 men returns per Field Ambulance.	
"	31.8.16		Relief complete 4 a.m. Lags marched to Bertrude Cross Roads. Independently - Coster per 1/2e - Battalion arrive at 7 a.m. to bivouac shack N.J. DERNANCOURT arrives 10.30 a.m. The whole day - rested. 1 men braised. 6 men to hospital via Field Ambulance.	

Ludwell Lieut. Colonel
Comdg. 4" B" The King's (Liverpool Regt)

98th Brigade.

33rd Division.

4th BATTALION

THE KING'S LIVERPOOL REGIMENT

SEPTEMBER 1 9 1 6

Army Form C. 2118

WAR DIARY
or
INTELLIGENCE SUMMARY 4th Bn. The Kings (Liverpool Regt)

(Erase heading not required.)

Vol II

September 1916

17D

Place	Date	Hour	Summary of Events and Information	Remarks and references to Appendices
DERNAN-COURT	1-9-16		Fine - Transport moved to CARDONETTE 10 A.M. - Billetting party set off 10 A.M. Bath taken by Bns. at 3 p.m. to ALLONVILLE & from there marched to CARDONETTE arriving at 6 p.m. 2 men from hospital	[initials]
CARDONETTE	2-9-16		Fine - moved to CANDAS - passed starting point 12 noon. Dinner en route at TALMAS (4 p.m. to 2.30 p.m.) arrived CANDAS 5.30 p.m. no one fell out. In billets. 1 man to hospital & 3 to ENGLAND	[initials]
CANDAS	3-9-16		Showery - men bathed. General cleaning up. 1 man to hospital - 1 to ENGLAND	[initials]
CANDAS	4-9-16		Wet - move 1 p.m. - passed starting point 4.40 p.m. Arrived BARLY 4.45 p.m. In billets - one man fell out.	[initials]
NUNCQ	5-9-16		Wet - moved 10.45 A.M. - passed starting point 11.33 A.M. Arrived NUNCQ 3.5 p.m. in billets. 3 men from hospital - 1 to Base	[initials]
"	6-9-16		Fine - warm - men washed clothing - general cleaning. 1 man to ENGLAND 12 men from Base	[initials]
"	7-9-16		Fine - C.O. inspected Coys. in full marching order - cleaning equipment in afternoon. 12 men from Base	[initials]
SUS ST LEGER	8-9-16		Fine 7.45 A.M. - passes starting point 6 A.M. Arrived SUS-ST LEGER 12.30 p.m. - no one fell out. Remainder of day resting. 1 man from hospital.	[initials]
"	9-9-16		Fine - Training - Squad drill, musketry. Lecd 5.30 p.m.	[initials]
COULLEMONT	10-9-16		Fine - moved 7 a.m. - passed starting point 7.45 A.M. - Arrived COULLEMONT R.C. Church parade 11 A.M. 10 Officers from Base	[initials]

WAR DIARY
INTELLIGENCE SUMMARY 4th Bn. The Kings (Liverpool Regt)

September 1916.

Army Form C. 2118

Place	Date	Hour	Summary of Events and Information	Remarks and references to Appendices
COULLEMONT	11-9-16		Fine - C. of E. Communion 7 A.M. - Training continued - squad drill - gas drill privately.	(MR)
"	12-9-16		Fine - Training continued. 40 Officers 740 OR from Base.	(MR)
HUMBER CAMP	13-9-16		Moved 7-45 A.M. - Busses starting point 9 A.M. - Arrived HUMBERCAMP 11.30 A.M. - in Divisional Reserve - no one fell out. One man to hospital. 19 O.R. from Base.	(MR)
"	14-9-16		Fine - Training - C. O. & Coy Commander round trenches occupied by 100th Bde.	(MR)
"	15-9-16		Fine - Brigadier inspected draft. Training Continued One man to hospital - School strength permanently attached to Inniskilling Coy. R.E. 72 O.R. from Base.	(MR)
"	16-9-16		Fine - Training - 40 men on working party. 3 men to hospital. 25 men from base.	(MR)
"	17-9-16		Fine - C. of E. Service 11 A.M. R.C. 11 A.M. 40 men working party - C.O & Coy Commanders round trenches of 98th Brigade. One man to hospital.	(MR)
"	18-9-16		Fine - Training - 2/Lt BAILEY from BASE - 1 man to Base.	(MR)
"	19-9-16		C O & Coy Commander round trenches (HEBUTERNE) - Bat - moved 2-20 p.m. arrived BAYENCOURT (South) 4-35 p.m. - relieves 16th Sherwoods in reserve billets.	(MR)
BAYENCOURT	20-9-16		Bat - took over trenches in front of HEBUTERNE - from 1/Lincolns. Specialists moved off at 2-30 p.m. Batt. moved 5 p.m. - Coys at 10 minute intervals - relief complete 9-35 p.m. arrived at hospital. A.D.S.S. Forms/C.2118. 16th K.R.R (Lost Bgde) in our right - 1/4th Middlesex on our right - the	(MR)

WAR DIARY
or
INTELLIGENCE SUMMARY   4th Bn. The King's (Liverpool Regt)

(Erase heading not required.)

September 1916.

Place	Date	Hour	Summary of Events and Information	Remarks and references to Appendices
HEBUTERNE TRENCHES	21-9-16		Fine - very quiet - cleaning trenches	
"	22-9-16		Fine - Gas alert 9-15am - Quiet - Lieut PATEY from Base - cleaning communication trenches	
"	23-9-16		Fine - Quiet - work continues	
"	24-9-16		Fine - Quiet - C.O. + Coy Commanders of 2nd A+S. H'rs round trenches	
"	25-9-16		Fine - relieved by 2nd A+S H'rs - Specialists 3-30pm - relief completed 5-55pm - Battn moved to BAYENCOURT - in Divisional reserve.	
BAYENCOURT	26-9-16		Fine - C.O. on leave - Officer visits recommences trenches 100th Inf Bgde. Capt. MATHER took over command of the Bn. 240 men from working parties. One man from hospital.	
"	27-9-16		Fine - cloudy - G.O.C. 33rd Divn. inspected Bn. 10-30am - 240 men working parties - him at baths.	
"	28-9-16		Fine - men at baths - 240 men working parties - Concert in recreation room 6pm - Divn Band played in afternoon.	
"	29-9-16		Fine - (showers) - 240 men working parties.	
"	30-9-16		First - relieved by 6th Berkshires - complete 4-30pm - arrived HUMBERCAMP 6-30pm in billets. Ernest C. Mather Capt & 4th Bn The King's Regt. Comdg 4th Bn The King's Regt.	

98th Brigade.

33rd Division.

4th BATTALION

KING's
THE LIVERPOOL REGIMENT

OCTOBER 1 9 1 6

Army Form C.2118

WAR DIARY
or
INTELLIGENCE SUMMARY
(Erase heading not required.)

4 Everker? 1231
Vol 2

18 D

Place	Date	Hour	Summary of Events and Information	Remarks and references to Appendices
BAYENCOURT	1.10.16		Fine - Bann - horse 10.20 A.m. marches to IVERGNY - dinner near COULLEMONT arrived 6.20 p.m. No one fell out. 1 man from hospital	
IVERGNY	2.10.16		Wet - general cleaning, washing - Capt. J.C.P. O'BRIEN rejoined from hospital. 2nd Lt T.Q.M. Pillington posted as R.T.O.	
"	3.10.16		Wet - Training commenced - bayonet fighting, musketry, platoon drill etc. Capt. J.C.P. O'BRIEN + 1 man from hospital	
"	4.10.16		Wet - Indoor training. Lectures. 2-30 p.m. C.O. att Coy Commanders seconded in command attended lecture by G.O.C. 33rd Divn at SUS. ST. LEGER. to men from base 1 man to Bombing School underage.	
"	5.10.16		Wet - training continues. 1 man to hospital	
"	6.10.16		Wet - training + lectures - Lt. Col. BEALL D.S.O. from leave.	
"	7.10.16		Fine - training continues. C.O. attended conference at Bge. H.Q. 2.15 p.m.	
"	8.10.16		Fine - showery. R.C. church parade 11 A.m - C.O.'s E. 11 A.m. 1 man to hospital	
"	9.10.16		Fine - training. 1500 fighting - attack on OPPY WOOD practised - Baths for men at SUS. ST. LEGER 1 man to hospital	

WAR DIARY
INTELLIGENCE SUMMARY

Volume XX

4th Bn. The King's (Liverpool Regt.)

October 1916

Army Form C. 2118

Instructions regarding War Diaries and Intelligence Summaries are contained in F. S. Regs., Part II. and the Staff Manual respectively. Title Pages will be prepared in manuscript.

(Erase heading not required.)

Place	Date	Hour	Summary of Events and Information	Remarks and references to Appendices
Iverguy	10.10.16	-	Fine. Raining. Batn practised attacks on OPPY WOOD. 2/Lt. training in Lewis Gun to England. 9 men F.1.16 Infy Base depot 5 men E.36th Infy Base depot	
"	11.10.16	-	Wet. General cleaning. 2/Lt Murdoch went to MdC Lewis Gun School. 2/Lt Coquis? returned from Corps School. 1 man to hospital	
"	12.10.16	-	Fine. Raining. Bays practised attack on OPPY WOOD. 1 man to Base Hdway	
"	13.10.16	-	Fine. Raining. Party 1st O[ffi]cers reconnoitred back & looking from SAVY – AV. BOIS to HENUTERNE front. 2/Lt Railey to Divisional Snipers School. Fine. Training. Exhibition of wire heading by Th.B. C.O inspected Boys in	
"	14.10.16	-	Marching Order. Lieut & Adjt. Staphin returned from England	
"	15.10.16	-	Fine. Church Parade Service 11.AM. Major J.F. Leader (2/8th The Kings Regt.) joined for duty. Capt NICHOLS to 3rd Army School.	
"	16.10.16	-	Brigade Practice manoeuvres near SUS ST LEGER. Lecture on "Tanks" at LUCHEUX. 4pm. Fine.	
WANQUETIN	17.10.16	-	Bn moved at 7.15AM to WANQUETIN arriving 11.45AM. Fine.	
"	18.10.16	-	Bn moved by bus back to GIVES at IVERGNY. Starting 1.15pm. arriving 4 pm. Showery. Misty.	
IVERGNY and 5 DROURS.	19.10.16	-	Bn moved from IVERGNY at 10 A.M. and went by bus to 5 DROURS. (4th Army Area). Transport Wet. moved from IVERGNY independently to TALMAS.	
"	20.10.16	-	Fine. Transport rejoined Bn at 1 P.M. 2/Lt. H.R. HUBBLE from hospital F & duty. Bn to E.13.Coy.	

Volume XX

WAR DIARY
or
INTELLIGENCE SUMMARY

Army Form C. 2118

4th Bn "The King's" Liverpool Regt.

October 1916

Place	Date	Hour	Summary of Events and Information	Remarks and references to Appendices
DAOURS to MEAULTE	21-10-16		Fine very cold. Bn moved 6.30 A.M. into tents at MEAULTE arriving 12.30 p.m.	Sketch
MEAULTE	22-10-16		Fine very cold. In tents at MEAULTE. 10 Officers per Coy to reconnoitre trenches at LES BOEUFS.	Sketch
TRONES WOOD	23-10-16		Cold & misty. Bn moved 8 A.M. Through heavy mud on route to TRONES WOOD arriving 1 P.M. Stayed night in heavy rain in shelters. 2/Lt WARING from leave & attached to G.H.Q. Brigade. O.C. Coys reconnoitre trenches.	Sketch
"	24-10-16		Wet. 2 Coys move at 1 P.M. to trenches at LES BOEUFS. (N.34.c.1.8) Bn H.Q. Bn moves 3.30 P.M. Relief complete 5 A.M. Relieved 1st KING'S own.	Sketches trenches 57c S.W. Sketch
Trenches LES BOEUFS	25-10-16		Dull. Heavy shelling of Reserve & Front Lines. 2nd Lieut. G.D. REES wounded. Heavy rain in afternoon. 3 O.R. killed & 2 wounded.	Sketch
"	26-10-16		Fine. Shelling heavy. Saw British aeroplane brought down by enemy machines. 1 O.R. wounded. 3 killed.	Sketch
"	27-10-16		Fine & dull. 5 A.M. Heavy bombardment & enemy barrage. Heavy rain evening. C.O. & two Company Commanders & 2nd Lt N.M. tree knocks. 9 men killed & 2 wounded.	Sketch
"	28-10-16		Fine. Bn attacked NEW DROP TRENCH. Zero 6 A.M. A & C Coys in front, 2nd half waves. D Coy in support in 2 lines. B Coy carrying Company for stores. 10 A.M. 2/Lt PATEY attd. 2nd Lt applied NEW DROP TRENCH captured. 2/Lt CORRIDGE in charge of bombing party. Bn attd. to JUNCTION ROAD. 5 P.M. Trench consolidated. 2nd Lt J. STEWART killed. 2nd Lt F. R. MILLIGAN & Capt J. C. P. O'BRIEN wounded. 6 O.R. killed 7 KILLS – 9 wounded.	Sketch
TRONES WOOD & Huts CARNOY	29-10-16		5 P.M. Relief by 2/STAFFS. complete. Bn moves temporarily to TRONES WOOD for break front trenches on B heels at CARNOY arriving 12.30 p.m. 2nd Lt R.H.N. MURDOCH 2nd Lt. E. BAILEY 2nd Lt S. T. EATON. JONES joining.	Sketch
	30-10-16		Wet. Huts at CARNOY. General cleaning up.	
	31-10-16		Fine Bn moves from Huts to TRONES WOOD	

Mitchell Lieut Colonel
Comdg 4th Bn The King's Ltpool Regt.

Copy of message sent to
4th Kings by G.O.C. XIV Corps.
on 28th Oct. 1916.

Series no   Day/month
BM 64.   28/10

"Following message from Major General
PINNEY begins aaa Corps Commander
LORD CAVAN sends hearty
congratulations to "LAUNCH" and
"LEAK" on capture of DEWDROP
and 100 prisoners after so many
failures by others. aaa ends.

from   LATCH (98th Brigade)
             5.50 P.M.

True ~~Exact~~ Copy

        A. Staffes Lt.
   Adjutant 4th Bn The King's
                     Lpool Regt

30-10-16.

Copy of message sent
to 4th Kings by G.O.C.
33rd Division on 29th Oct 1916.

To   COL BEALE D.S.O.
             "LAUNCH".

Senders No	Day/Month
H.D.22. - 28	-

Hearty congratulations to
yourself and "LAUNCH".

From   MAJOR-GENERAL PINNEY.
         Div. H.Q. 5.50 P.M.

     True ~~school~~ Copy

       J. L. Sumpkys Lt
    a/Adjt 4th Bn "The Kings" Lpool Regt
30 - 10 - 16.

98th Brigade.

33rd Division.

4th BATTALION

THE KING(S LIVERPOOL REGIMENT

NOVEMBER 1 9 1 6

WAR DIARY or INTELLIGENCE SUMMARY

Army Form C. 2118

Volume XXI — 4th Bn. Hastings [?] (Cinque Ports Bn.)

Vol 13

November 1916

Place	Date	Hour	Summary of Events and Information	Remarks and references to Appendices
TRONES WOOD & TRENCHES AT LES BOEUFS	1-11-16		Showers and dull. Moved to trenches at 3 P.M. in relief of 2nd R.F.H. Relief complete 12 M.N. 1 man wounded. 1 man from hospital.	Ref. ALBERT (continued sheet)
	2-11-16		Recalled by 2nd Lt. MURDOCH & 2nd Lt. BAILEY discussed. Received at N.34.c.w.7—. Very wet. 3 O.R. wounded. 2 missing.	
			Dull. Spark + 100 Bosche on our right attacked at 4 P.M. Heavy barrage on our south woods & came on camp commandant. 3 wounded 1 killed. Both bodies 9 P.M. 2 men wounded. Relief received by	
			Relief completed by 2nd R.F. 9:30 A.M. Delays by [?] gun fire. Moved into tents at Bois Quentin	
ar. BERNAFAY 4-11-16 & ROSS				
SANDPITS MEAULTE	5-11-16		9:30 A.M. moved to SANDPITS CAMP, MEAULTE — by road. Arrived at 1:30 P.M. Fine. 2 men reinforcements from base.	Fine
	6-11-16		Wet. General cleaning up. 75 men to bases. (Incl 6/63 useful section not yet strength, posted to this battalion)	Wet
	7-11-16		Wet. General cleaning + reinforcements to Camp. —	Wet
	8-11-16		Wet. Capt D.S. JONES, R.A.M.C. Capt BANGHAM + 2nd Lt. BACK on leave to England. 55 men from bases. 1 man to hospital	Wet
	9-11-16		Moved by road to DROURS at 12.30 P.M. 1 man wounded. 12 men to base.	Fine
			Fine. Transport moved to ARGOEUVES. Bn. moved at 2 P.M. to BERNANCOURT — EDGEHILL	Fine
			STATION — en route for HUPPY. Entrained at 4:30 P.M. Minimum reported BELLAHEE	
HUPPY (near ABBEVILLE)	10-11-16		at LONGPRE at 8.30 P.M. Marched via FONTAINE HERCOURT, BAILLEUL to HUPPY. Arrived in billets 3.40 A.M. Transport arrived 9 P.M. —	MARBEVILLE HUT 100 ov. BREMEN
	11-11-16		Fine. Rest in morning. General cleaning up & kit inspection. Capt A.N. BOURNEY on leave to England.	Dermas
	12-11-16		Fine. Maj Col. Bn. B'Gn'l B.Q. to Divy. St Anclis school [Senior Officer Conference] Fleeg. Adjt. —	Dermas

WAR DIARY or INTELLIGENCE SUMMARY

Army Form C. 2118

Volume XXI
4th Bn Oxf & Bucks L.I. (Duxford Coy)

November 1916

Place	Date	Hour	Summary of Events and Information	Remarks and references to Appendices
HUPPY	13-11-16		Fine. Training. Building of Training Ground for bombing etc. 2/Lt ROBERTS to T.M. Course. 2/Lt VENN to Bombing School. 2/Lt AGER to Lewis Rifle School. 2/Lt LEACH to HARROBIN? to Musical party. 61 men of Special section on Fatigue. 20 men from base.	
"	14-11-16		Fine. Training. (Squad drill musketry Bayonet fighting) 2/Lt BUCHAN & STYRING on leave to England. 2/Lt ROUTLEDGE to Rifle school (Capt PATEY and 2/Lt A. CORBRIDGE awarded M. Military Cross) 9 men to hospital. 46 men from base.	
"	15-11-16		Fine. 2/Lt HUBALE on leave to England. Training continued. 1 man to hospital	
"	16-11-16		Fine & very cold. 2/Lt FRASER to Lewis Gun School at LE TOUQUET. 2/Lt WARBURTON to Divisional Signalling School. 2/Lt KENDALL went on Tour of HUENINVILLE. 6 men from base	
"	17-11-16		Snow. 2/Lt A. CORBRIDGE to Divisional School HALLENCOURT. Training. 2/Lt FRASER to Lewis Gun School. Lt Col. LE TOUQUET. 2/Lt ROBERTS from T.M. School. 1 man to hospital. 1 man to hospital	
"	18-11-16		Cold & wet. Local training. Football match v 2/7 YXH (Rifle Coy cup Final). 1 man to hospital	
"	19-11-16		Dull. Lt-Col BELL D.S.O. rejoined from Army School at FIXECOURT. 9 men to L.G. School. 5 men from base. 1 man to hospital. Bomenil Church Parade 11 A.M.	
"	20-11-16		Dull. Training & Inspection of Companies by C.O. 2/Lt AGER from Lewis Rifle School. 1 man to hospital	
"	21-11-16		Wet. Capt. A.H. BANGHAM from leave. 2/Lt L.W.A. PACK from leave. 2/Lt ROUTLEDGE from inspection	
"	22-11-16		Dull. Local training. 2/Lt VENN from Bombing School. 63 men Gutunpol Scotland posted to 4th Bn Oxf Bucks. Draft to men from base. 1 man to hospital	
"	23-11-16		Fine. Local training. 2/Lt BUCHAN from leave. 1 man to hospital	
"	24-11-16		Fine. Local training.	
"	25-11-16		Very boisterous. Inspection of Companies by C.O. 2/Lt FRASER from Lewis Gun School. 2 men to hospital	

WAR DIARY

Army Form C. 2118

Volume XXI

INTELLIGENCE SUMMARY 4th Bn "Queen's" (Liverpool Regt)

November 1916

Place	Date	Hour	Summary of Events and Information	Remarks and references to Appendices
HUPPY	26.11.16		Sunday. Major-General PINNEY Commanding 33rd Division distributed medals to the following Officers, W.O.'s, N.C.O.'s & men. Military Medal to 11123 C.S.M. J. CARMICHAEL. 11770 C.S.M. W. FRASER. 10376 CQMS STEWART. 19225 L/Cpl A. HARN. 18033 L/c H. McKIBBIN. 9534 Pte D. BOSTOCK. 11929 Pte W. McCLOUD. 38886 Pte E. LLOYD. 14657 Pte C. CAFFERY. 14281 Pte W. FOSTER. 13180 Pte W. KENNY. 14207 Pte T. BRISLEN.	Metz
"	27.11.16		Fine. Capt. D.S. JONES. Rome for leave. Company attack practice.	Metz
"	28.11.16		Fine & misty. Night operations. Stretcher bearers to hospital. Man to hospital.	Metz
"	29.11.16		Fine. Training. 2/Lt. BUCHAN KTM School	Metz
"	30.11.16		Fine. Box Respirator (Advance & flash attack & convoy) 2/Lt H.B. TRIPP rejoined Battalion from Transport. 19A W.T.R.	Metz

Trueman Lieut-Colonel Commdg 4/70 "Queen's" R.W.S.R.(L'pool Regt)

98th Brigade.

33rd Division.

4th BATTALION

THE KING'S LIVERPOOL REGIMENT

DECEMBER 1 9 1 6

Army Form C. 2118

Volume XXII

WAR DIARY
or
INTELLIGENCE SUMMARY

(Erase heading not required.)

4 " Bn The Kings (Liverpool Regt(-)) December 1916

Oct 14

Place	Date	Hour	Summary of Events and Information	Remarks and references to Appendices
HUPPY	1-12-16		Fine. Battalion scheme from 9.30 A.M. to 1 P.M. (Avances + Flank Guard duties) 5.30 p.m. Night operation for N.C.Os.	Appx
"	2-12-16		Fine. Route march of 2 miles — 9 men transferred to M.G. Coy. 2 men to Base with age.	
"	3-12-16		Fine. Church Parade 10.20 A.M. R.C. Parade 7.30 A.M. Holy Communion 11.30 A.M. 2-Lt LASHMAR to Lewis Gun School at TOUQUET. 4 men to 178(T) Coy R.E.	Appx
"	4-12-16		Fine. Transport moved 9.30 A.M. to ARGOEUVES. 2-Lt KENDALL rejoined for duty from Tom major to HUCHENNEVILLE. 50 O.R. arrived from Base. 2 men to hospital	Appx
Outre March	5-12-16		Bn moved from HUPPY at 9 A.M. Arrived PONT REMY station 11.30 A.M. Left PONT REMY by train 4.15 p.m. Arrived MERICOURT L'ABBÉ 7.50 p.m. Marched to BILLETS at SAILLY LE SEC arriving at 9.15 p.m. Rather strenuous day; always dull.	Appx
SAILLY LE SEC	6-12-16		Dull. Major LEADER & 5 Officers + 4 O.R. visited trenches by BOUCHAVESNES — lead by the March. 2-Lt Woods rejoined from Tom major & CARNOY HUTMENTS.	Appx
Camp 112	7-12-16		Fine. Marched from SAILLY LE SEC at 10 A.M. Arrived at Camp 112 — 1 mile N of BRAY at 1.15 p.m. C.O. + 2 Officers visited trenches held by French by BOUCHAVESNES.	Appx
Camp 112 2-12-16	8-12-16		Wet. From Camp 112 at 4.15 p.m. + marched to Camp 16 — between BRAY and MARICOURT. arrived 6 p.m.	Appx
	9-12-16		Wet. C.O. and Adjutant + Coy Commanders left camp to reconnoitre trenches held by French — at 11.30 A.M. Returned 11.A.M. Bn moved from Camp 16 at 3.15 p.m. + arrived at Camp 20 — between SUZANNE + MARICOURT at 6 p.m. 1 man to hospital.	Appx

Volume XXII

WAR DIARY
or
INTELLIGENCE SUMMARY

Army Form C. 2118

4 Bn "The King's" (Liverpool Regt)

December 1916

(Erase heading not required.)

Place	Date	Hour	Summary of Events and Information	Remarks and references to Appendices
Camp 20 + huts	10-12-16		Bn. moved from Camp 20 to trenches 2 mile N of BOUCHAVESNES. Relieved 3 Coys of 19th Cheshires in front line + one Coy 2.6th Cheshires in support at AIGUILLE. Relief complete 3.10 p.m. Dr 114. Weather very bad.	Ref. full ALBERT (contoured) 1/40,000
Trenches N.E. BOUCHAVESNES	11-12-16		Wet. Bn HQrs at P.E. MORGAN. Men still extremely tired from trek. Men worked on cleaning trenches. Quiet day. 68 men from base. Arrived from Etaples. Difficult.	Ditto
"	12-12-16		Wet. Work on cleaning trenches. Quiet. Capt. A. LINDEMERE joined from England. 1 man killed. 4 men wounded.	Ditto
"	13-12-16		Bat. On Trenches. 2Lt HUBBLE from leave. 2Lt CORRIDGE from Div'l School. 1 men wounded. Relieved by 4th Suffolks. Quiet at AIGUILLE at 4.30 p.m. Relief complete. Bn moved into Brigade Reserve at PETIT BOIS.	Diitto
"	14-12-16		Complete 11.17 p.m. Bn. Lines into huts. Men very fatigued. 2 men wounded.	Diitto
PETIT BOIS	15-12-16		Men resting + general cleaning up. Special attention to feet. 34 men with trench foot. Fine. In reserve. Dug outs.	Ditto
"	16-12-16		Fine. In reserve. Lt Colonel E.M. BEALL DSO. On leave. 2 Lt WOODS to L.G. School. Major LEADER assumed temporary command of the Bn.	Ditto
"	17-12-16		Came to Base made up 7 men to hospital. Fine + mildy. Adjutant + Coy Commanders reconnoitred trenches to left Bn sector (RANCOURT) with a view to taking over later. Left Brigade laid to guide men to BETHUNE Road post R.C. of 150 men laid out line. 2 Lt ROUTLEDGE on leave.	Ditto
"	18-12-16		Morgan to front line. Relieved by 2nd Bn Worcestershire Regt at 2 p.m. Relief complete. Fine. Bn moved to Camp 17 just N of SUZANNE – 3.45 p.m.	Ditto

WAR DIARY or INTELLIGENCE SUMMARY

Army Form C. 2118

Volume XXII

1/7 Bn "The Kings" (Liverpool Regt)

December 1916

Place	Date	Hour	Summary of Events and Information	Remarks and references to Appendices
Camp 17	19-12-16		Rain & Sleet. C.O. Inspected draft of 68. 4 Officers & men recounted routes to trenches near RANCOURT. 2/Lt BUCHANNET with his Lewis gunners attacked Bn. Reserve. 2/Lt BURTON, C/Jones for duty. Party night.	pps
"	20-12-16		Fine. Cleaning up & improving Camp. Foggy night. 1 man from Base. D.T.M.	pps
"	21-12-16		Showers. G.O.C. 33d Division presented mil. ribbon to 9798 Pte A. SIMPSON - 13 men to Hospital	pps
Trenches RANCOURT	22-12-16		Fine. Moved by bus at 2 p.m. to MAUREPAS. Relieved 2nd R.W.F. in front trenches Guides at LE PRIEZ FME 5:15 p.m. Relief complete 10.45 p.m.	pps
"	23-12-16		Frost. Quiet.	pps
"	24-12-16		Frost. Intr. company relief of front line. A. relieved C. and B relieved D. 2 men wounded	pps
" MAUREPAS Ravine	25-12-16		Frost. Some shelling by our and enemy heavy artillery. Relieved by 4 Suffolk Regt. Guides 5 p.m. LE PRIEZ F/M. Relief complete 9.20 p.m. hoop into Bell Reserve at MAUREPAS Ravine. 1 man wounded. 1 man from hospital.	pps
"	26-12-16		Snowy. In Bde reserve in tents & dug-outs MAUREPAS	pps
" Camp III	27-12-16		Fine. Relieved by 19th R.W.F. at 3 p.m. Bn moved by Bus to Camp III 1 mile N of BRAY. 2/Lt. Jn. T. LASHMAR on leave.	pps
"	28-12-16		Frost. General cleaning up.	pps

WAR DIARY
or
INTELLIGENCE SUMMARY
(Erase heading not required.)

Army Form C. 2118

Place	Date	Hour	Summary of Events and Information	Remarks and references to Appendices
Camp III and BETHENCOURT ST OUEN	29-12-16		Bn moved from Camp III at 2.15 p.m. to BERNAH COURT (ALBERT Combines/Sheet). Entrained LONGPRE at 5 p.m. Arrived LONGPRE at 9.30 p.m. Marched to billets at BETHEN COURT ST OUEN arriving 1.35 AM. 30 inst. 50 men to thresh Camp PONT REMY with 2nd Lt ALLANSON. 2nd Lt BURTON + 25 men to ALLONVILLE (wood cutting party). Transport moved by road to AGOUVES at 9 A.M. Lt-Col F.M. BERLH. DSO. rejoined from leave.	Ref Ser. hop.
BETHENCOURT ST OUEN	30-12-16		In billets. General cleaning up. Transport arrived 1.15 p.m. 2nd Lt J.H. GRIME joined for duty.	
"	31-12-16		In billets. General cleaning up. Church Parade 11 A.M. 2nd Lt J.T. McCUBBIN and 2nd Lt R.B. LITTLAR joined for duty. 25 men to hospital. 2nd Lt GRIME to R.B. Lewis Gun School.	

M. Turner Lieut-Colonel
Comdg 12 Bn "The King's" (Liverpool Regt)

Volume XXIII

WAR DIARY
or
INTELLIGENCE SUMMARY
(Erase heading not required.)

4th Bn. The King's (Liverpool Regt.)

January 1917

Place	Date	Hour	Summary of Events and Information	Remarks and references to Appendices
BETHENCOURT ST OUEN	1-1-17		2nd bttlns - holding Div. and kit inspection by C.O. Cleaning up of huts. Preln. Construction of Rifle Range. #Bombproofs & Bayonet Pattern	Reference Map.
"	2-1-17		Fire Company Training. 2/Lt S. TRENBATH. 2/Lt L. MORRIDGE. 2/Lt H. BOARDMAN 2/Lt J. ROBINSON joined strength. 1 man from France. 2/Lt H.S. ROBERTS to England sick.	Orders
"	3-1-17		bttln Company training.	Orders
"	4-1-17		bttln - 2/Lt KENTISH to leave. Company training -	Orders
"	5-1-17		Bttln. Company Schemes - Night Operations. 2/Lt HUBBLE + 2/Lt NEW to Divisional School. 2/Lt VENN + 2/Lt CORBRIDGE to leave. 2/Lt ASHENDON to 33rd Div. Trench Mortar Bn. 2/Lt BURTON to hospital, Bttln. Bn Route March.	Orders
"	6-1-17		Bttln Aug.-Oct. contact patrol (aeroplane) practice arranged, but cancelled owing unfavourable weather. Officers turned over (eg) R.E. MORTIERS to instruction in bombing. Capt PATEY to leave. 1 man to hospital	Orders
"	7-1-17		Fire morning. Bttln. afternoon. 2/Lt BOARDMAN to III to IV Army Ditcher Pont School. 2/Lt FRASER to leave. Church Parade. 2/Lt FR BUCHAN to 33rd Div. Trench Mortar Bn.	Orders
"	8-1-17		Marching Order inspection. Company training. Baths.	Orders
"	9-1-17		Bttln. Company training. Night operation. 2/Lt M'CUBBIN to Bde L of School for R of English - Candidates for commissions. 2/Lt L/c HODGSON + 49250 Pte REA	Orders
"	10-1-17		Bttln. Company training. Brigade Cross Country Race, starting 1:30 p.m. (distance 4 miles.) Bn teams + Jn, officers. 1st W.I. REGT. 11th. 2/Lt. HATCH, 2/Lt KURTZ, 3/2 2/Lt WHYTE, 4th. 1 man to hospital	Orders
"	11-1-17		Bn Route March. Sleet + rain. 2/Lt BACK + 1602 to Base Bombing School 12 men for base.	Orders
"	12-1-17		Bn. Different fatigues in VIGNACOURT woods. 2/Lt LASHMAN to leave.	Orders

WAR DIARY or INTELLIGENCE SUMMARY

Volume XXIII

January 1917

4th Bn "The King's (Liverpool Regt)"

Army Form C. 2118

Place	Date	Hour	Summary of Events and Information	Remarks and references to Appendices
PETITION COURT ST OUEN	13-1-17		Dull. Lecture to 10 Officers & NCOs per Coy at Bde H.Q. by Div. Gas Officer on "New Small Box Respirator". Battalion mill.	Ref. in
"	14-1-17		Showers, some Mist. Major General PINNEY, C.B. presented M.C. ribbon to 2nd Lt F.W. HUGHES (MC) on Battalion parade. Church Parade 11 AM. 2nd Lt F. JAMES joined to duty 2nd Lt HITTLAR to XV Corps Lewis Gun School. BOUCHON, FARRELL & 9 other ranks to Corps. 2nd Lt BOARDMAN to Sniping Course - Rheumatism face. Five Company training. Major LEADER to learn.	Ref. in
"	15-1-17		Fine. Company training. Major LEADER to learn.	Ref. in
"	16-1-17		Fine. Bn attack practice - 2nd Lt WARBURTON to learn.	Ref. in
"	17-1-17		Show. 2nd Lt BAER from Bde Bomb School. Training in billets.	Ref. in
"	18-1-17		Transport moved 9 A.M. to ARBOUVES. C.O. inspected Coys & fell marching N/hr 10.15 A.M.	Ref. in
"	19-1-17		Bn marched 7 AM to LONGPRÉ. Entrained at LONGPRÉ 10 A.M. Rain departed 10.20 A.M. Arrived ACHANCOURT (ETRETIT) 1.25 PM. Marched to camp 13. 1 officer & 4 pm. Transport arrived 5.15 pm. 2nd Lt McCUBBIN from Rose L.G. School.	ALBERT Continued Sheet
"	20-1-17		In Camp 13. Cold. fine. 2nd Lt KENZER rejoined from leave.	Ref. in
"	21-1-17		In Camp 13. Cos fine. Church Parade 11 AM. 2nd Lt CORBIDGE from leave.	Ref. in
"	22-1-17		Bn moved 11 AM to JUZANNE. 6 officers reconnoitred trenches at ROAD WOOD and front line held by...	Ref. in

Army Form C. 2118

WAR DIARY
or
INTELLIGENCE SUMMARY
(Erase heading not required.)

Volume XXVII

Army: "B" Coy Kings Liverpool Regt

January 1917

Instructions regarding War Diaries and Intelligence Summaries are contained in F. S. Regs., Part II. and the Staff Manual respectively. Title Pages will be prepared in manuscript.

Place	Date	Hour	Summary of Events and Information	Remarks and references to Appendices
	23/1/17		Moved from Lugomo 3-30 pm. Junction at Luiten Rd junction at 6 p.m. Relief of 2nd Loyal N. Lancs Regt West Riding completed 12-15 am. Enemy guns 2dg front	
	24/1/17		Line front. Relieved 2nd & 6/8 S. Lancs. Guides at Road West 6-15 pm. Relief completed 10-40 pm. 2 n.c.o.'s evacuated from lines.	
	25/1/17		Sent when guns 1 dg front. 2 n.c.o. sent from base. 1 man killed	
	26/1/17		Munda - quiet. One front. 2/Lt Hughes wound in arm	
	27/1/17		Line front. Relieved by 2/Queens Regt compns 2-30 am. Moved to camp 19 Lugomo. 2/Lt Davies reported from base. Capt Parker, Lieut Russell Luttman admitted F.A.	
	28/1/17		Camp 19. Line - front.	
	29/1/17		Camp 19. Line - front. General cleaning up of camp	
	30/1/17		Camp 19. C.O. & Coy commanders went to reconnoitre ride trenches. On arrival at Lugomo cannot bomb under fire. 2/Lt Lane & 2 n.c.o.'s Lewis proceeded to the 2nd Lg School.	
	31/1/17		In Camp 19. Line - front. Camp inspected by Corps Commander. Moved at 5-0 pm on motor Lorries to the Arumba. Relieved the 2nd R.W.F. Relief complete 10-15 pm. Capt Ruszman proceeded to No 2 Pioneers of West Camp, Rikumbi. 2/Lt Routledge wounded. 2 2 men wounded from Lewis cutting Coy.	

Russell Lt.Col.
Commanding (Liverpool Regt)

WAR DIARY or INTELLIGENCE SUMMARY

4th Bn The King's (Liverpool Regt) February 1917

Place	Date	Hour	Summary of Events and Information	Remarks and references to Appendices
In trenches front line CLERY.	1-2-17		Cold + foggy. In front line trenches. - Bigger Bn, Right Subsects. CLERY SECTION - Left	62c N.W. sheets maps
	2-2-17		Cold + foggy. 15 men wounded. 3 men missing. In trenches.	Maps
	3-2-17		Frost. In trenches.	Ditto
	4-2-17		Frost. In trenches. Our artillery bombarded enemy front line. 10 AM - 4 P.M. Retaliation -	Ditto
	6-2-17		Frost. Enemy bombarded enemy front line. 1 man killed 4 men wounded by enemy retaliation.	Ditto
In Support dug outs	6-2-17		Frost. Relieved by 2/07th J.H. Relief complete 8.30 P.M. Bn moved to support in WURZEL support dug-nts, by R.C. GIRODON.	Ditto
	7-2-17		Frost. In dug-nts. 100 men to working parties enlarging dug-outs. Capt. BROWNE arrived.	Ditto
	8-2-17		Frost. In support dug-nts. O.C. Coys + C.O. went to see trenches Right Subsects. Frost. In support dug-nts. O.C. Coys + C.O. went to see trenches Right Subsects. in view to relieving 4 Suffolks. 100 men to working parties carrying dug-nts.	Ditto
In trenches Cleny.	9-2-17		Frost. In support dug-outs. Relieved 4 Suffolks. - Relief complete 7.30 P.M. 1 man wounded.	Ditto
"	10-2-17		Frost. In front trenches. Front N of SOMME. 1 man killed.	Ditto
"	11-2-17		Frost. In front trenches. Enemy artillery active. 2nd Lt. F.P. REID arrived.	Ditto
"	12-2-17		Frost. Quiet. Relieved by 4 Suffolks. Bn moved to Brigade support. R.C. GIRODON on leave.	Ditto

Army Form C. 2118

Volume XXIV

WAR DIARY
or
INTELLIGENCE SUMMARY
(Erase heading not required.)

4th Bn. The Kings (Liverpool Regt.)
February 1917

Place	Date	Hour	Summary of Events and Information	Remarks and references to Appendices
Infants School CLERY	13-2-17		Slight Snow. Quiet. Supplied 100 men working parties on enemies dug outs. Capt. BROWNE + Capt. BANGHAM. 2/Lt WHITTLAR returned from hospital.	62.C.N.W. Sheet 21
"	14-2-17		Slight snow. Quiet. Supplied 100 men R.E. working parties. 2/Lt LITTLAR to hospital. Pte BEER (A. Coy) Pte JACKSON (B. Coy) to England. Candidates for Commissions. Frost at night.	M4/21
"	15-2-17		Slight snow in morning. Lt. + Adjt. F. Ll. HUGHES rejoined from leave. 2nd R MOORE joined for duty. C.O. to Attach Machine Gun School at SUZANNE (1st Queens) 100 men for working parties.	Sheet 21
"	16-2-17		Thaw continued. Relieved by 9th H.L.I. Guides 7:30 p.m. Relief Complete 11.15 p.m. Bn. moved to Brigade Reserve in SUZANNE.	Sheet 21
SUZANNE	17-2-17		In tents + dug outs. SUZANNE. Bn. arrived 2.30 a.m. Transport arrived at Dr. Col. Cleaning up. 2/Lt A.T. BROWN joined for duty from Cadet School G.H.Q. E.H. BELL. S.S.O. assumed temp command of 98 & 9th Pde. from L.F. LEADER.	Sheet 21
"	18-2-17		Bde Reserve. Bn. Baths. Church Parade 9.45 A.M. draft of 14 O.R. from Base.	Sheet 21
"	19-2-17		Bde Reserve. Heavy rain. Specialist Training - Lecture on "Contact Aeroplane." 1/Lt F.C. to whole Bde. representatives at 6.30 p.m. & Captain of R.F.C.	M4/21
"	20-2-17		Bde Reserve. Special training of Platoons in Attack on new lines. Specialist pursued special training to specialists. Training.	M4/21
"	21-2-17		Bde Reserve. Rain. 2/Lt R. REID joined for duty direct from West Guards (where he was Sergeant)	M4/21

Volume XIV

WAR DIARY
or
INTELLIGENCE SUMMARY
(Erase heading not required.)

Army Form C. 2118

February 1917   4th Bn. Northamptonshire Regt.

Place	Date	Hour	Summary of Events and Information	Remarks and references to Appendices
SUZANNE	22/2/17		In Bde Reserve. C.O. left for Commander to take over BETHUNE ROAD Sector within relief on 24-2-17.	62 C.N.W. Ndm.
Hatherleigh Wood ROAD WOOD	23/2/17		Bn moved at 2.30 p.m. from SUZANNE. Guide at HOWITZER WOOD at 5.30 p.m. Relieved 2nd Bn R.W.F. in ROAD WOOD. Relief complete 10.30 p.m. 1 man wounded. Special post taking at SUZANNE at 7-10 A.M. Depot at FRISE BEND.	Reb/Hr
"	24/2/17		Relieved 14th Bn Cameronians in front trenches (left Bn, left subsector) BETHUNE ROAD. Guide Bn H.Q. 6 p.m. Relief complete 10.30 p.m.	Reb/Hr
Front trenches left subsector BETHUNE RD	25/2/17		Fine. Slight frost in night. Enemy retirement in neighbourhood of SERRE. Front opposite his Bn still held. Lt. Col. Beall to leave. 5 men killed + 3 wounded.	Reb/Hr
"	26/2/17		Fine. 1 man killed + 1 wounded. Relieved by 4th Suffolks. Guide 7 km Relief Complete 12.20 A.M. 27th. Bn moved to Bde Reserve HOWITZER WOOD. 1 man killed + 1 wounded.	Reb/Hr
HOWITZER WOOD	27/2/17		Fine. Raining. Special post nothing.	
"	28/2/17		Fine. Relieved 4 Suffolks in left subsector. Moved from HOWITZER WOOD at 5 p.m.	Reb/Hr

L.J. Leader Major
Comdg 4 Northants (Oxford Regt)

WAR DIARY or INTELLIGENCE SUMMARY

Army Form C. 2118

Volume XXV Vol/7
March 1917. 4th Bn. Kentrp (Oxford Regt)

Place	Date	Hour	Summary of Events and Information	Remarks and references to Appendices
LEFT SUFFOLKS PERRONNE PONKAHINES	1.3.17		In Support Ward. Relieved 4 Suffolks in Fort Kreker at night 29/-. Quiet. 4 or wounded	MWB
	2.3.17		In Fort Kreker. Relieved by 4 Suffolks. Relief complete 11.40 p.m. Bn moves into Bde Support in ROAD WOOD.	MWB
ROAD WOOD	3.3.17		Fine. Quiet. In Bde Support. 1 OR wounded. 1 OR from hospital	MWB
	4.3.17		Relieved 4 Suffolks in ROAD WOOD. Relief complete 10.60 p.m. Snow 2 OR 1 OR from hospital	MWB
	5.3.17		Quiet. Slight snow. Drafts of 58 arrived at Depot. 1 OR wounded	MWB
	6.3.17		Quiet. Fine. 2nd Bn R.R.F.D & 2nd Bn R MOORE to take Middlesex + 3rd Bn Arrived by 120" Bde	MWB
	7.3.17		Quiet. Relieved by 13 E Surrey Regt- (120 Brigade) Relief complete 11.20 p.m. Bn moved to ROAD WOOD. 3 OR wounded.	MWB
ROAD WOOD	8.3.17		Bn Relieved from ROAD WOOD by 4th Bn A.J.H. (120 Brigade) Relief complete 9.20 p.m. Bn moved to SUZANNE.	MWB
Camp 12	9.3.17	12.30 p.m.	Bn moved to Camp 12, CHIPILLY - to 2nd Corps Reserve at Bois BERNAFAY. Refused for leave. 2 Lt A.F. EDWARDS joined for duty.	MWB
	10.3.17		Cleaning up. Church Parade. Trg & R.T.	MWB
	11.3.17		Cleaning up. Church Parade 10.30 A.M. Major General PINNEY Comdg 33rd Div in attended & addressed the Battalion. Lieut A.J.P. Y.H. HOLMES to MWB	

Army Form C. 2118.

WAR DIARY
or
INTELLIGENCE SUMMARY

Volume XXV   4th Batt. The Kings (Liverpool Regt)

March 1917.

(Erase heading not required.)

Place	Date	Hour	Summary of Events and Information	Remarks and references to Appendices
Camp 12	12.3.17		Fine Baths. Armourer Sergeant inspects all rifles. Bombing & Lewis Rifle classes commence under Regtl arrangements.	W.E.O
Camp 12	13/3/17		Fine. Batt Route march about 5 miles during the morning. Platoon training in the afternoon.	W.E.O
Camp 12	14/3/17		Fine. Platoon Training. C.O. and 6 of Batty attend Conference held by C.in.C. Division followed by one by the 18th Corps Commander. 2ND LT H.R.HUBBLE to hospital (sick)	W.E.O
Camp 12	15/3/17		Fine. Batt Route march about 5 miles during the morning. Ration Training in the afternoon followed by Football match with 20th Batt. K.R.R. (lost 2 – 0)	W.E.O
Camp 12	16/3/17		Fine. Liaison Training. Boxing Competition with 20th Batt K.R.(won 4 out of 6).	W.E.O
Camp 12	17/3/17		Fine. Batt Route march about 5 miles. C.O. O.C. Coys and signalling officer attend Demonstration by Contact Aeroplane. N.C.O Brigade inspects transport. Capt A. Dinsdale to hospital (sick). Regt Labour Company arrives ex 2nd Coy	W.E.O
Camp 12	18/3/17		Fine. Church Parade 10.30. C.O. and officers carry out a Batt scheme without troops during the afternoon. 2ND LT AGER returns from Leave.	W.E.O
Camp 12	19/3/17		Fine Baths. Men Regt bounds in Bomberg & Range London commence. 2ND LT EDWARDS to hospital (sick)	W.E.O

Army Form C. 2118.

WAR DIARY
or
INTELLIGENCE SUMMARY
(Erase heading not required.)

4th Batt "The Kings" (Liverpool Regt)

Volume XXV

March 1917

Place	Date	Hour	Summary of Events and Information	Remarks and references to Appendices
Camp 12	20/3/17		Batt Route march during the morning. Platoon training in the afternoon. Received a draft 70 O.R. 2nd Lt Moore Red. R return from leave.	Appx
Camp 12	21/3/17		Company Training. Received a draft of 75 O.R.	Appx
Camp 12	22/3/17		Platoon training in the morning. Moved to SAILLY LAURETTE into billets.	Appx
Sailly Laurette	23/3/17		Company training. C.O. and all officers carry out a Batt scheme during the afternoon.	Appx
"	24/3/17		Batt Route march in the morning. O.C. and all officers attend a lecture by the Officers Cmd'g by an officer of the Army Gymnastic Staff. Received draft of 5 O.R.	Appx
"	25/3/17	10.30 AM	Church Parade. G.O.C. Bde inspects drafts.	Appx
"	26/3/17		Platoon training. Received draft of 40 O.R. 2nd Lt F.P. Reid return from hospital.	Appx
"	27/3/17		Batt scheme with troops taken for canals & drafts from H.Q. & Coys 12 for Gas Course.	Appx
"	28/3/17		Coy training. C.O. O.C. Coys & R.O. attend Gas Demonstration at Camp 13.	Appx
"	29/3/17		Batt Route March. 2nd Lt Ralton & 2nd Lt D Nicholson reinforcements & N.C.O.S return from Gas Course. Capt E. Hughes his name from Staff Class.	Appx
"	30/3/17		Coy. Training. Batt scheme without troops. Capt E. Hughes to Brigade.	Appx
"	31/3/17		Commanding Officers Parade, making all preparations for to move.	Appx

M. Brett Lieut Colonel
Commanding 4 Batt The Kings (Liverpool Regt)

Army Form C. 2118.

WAR DIARY or INTELLIGENCE SUMMARY

(Erase heading not required.)

VOLUME XXIV 4th Bn The King's (Liverpool Regt)
April 1917

Place	Date	Hour	Summary of Events and Information	Remarks and references to Appendices
SAILLY LAURETTE	1/4/17		Snow. Batt marched to billets at LAHOUSSOYE arriving there at 12-30. 6 O.R.s joing from Base.	
LAHOSSOYE	2/4/17		Batt moved by road to billets at PIERREGOT.	
PIERREGOT	3/4/17		Batt marched to billets at TALMAS. Lt Mc Crae reports for duty from 11th Cheshires.	
TALMAS	4/4/17		Batt marched to GEZAINCOURT. Bde march. 2nd Lt Cuttler from hospital, one O.R. to hospital. 10 O.R. temporarily attached to R.A.	
GEZAINCOURT	5/4/17		Batt marched to billets at POMMERA. Capt H.L. BROWNE returns from sick leave.	
POMMERA	6/4/17		Coy & Peloton training. Draining in extensive digging. 18 O.R.s to Depot Batt.	
POMMERA	7/4/17		Batt marched to COIGNEUX. 2 O.R. to hospital	
COIGNEUX	8/4/17		Batt marched to BERLES-AU-BOIS. C.O. Capt Paley & 2nd Lt Sack reconnoitred the COJEUL VALLEY	
BERLES-AU BOIS	9/4/17		Fine, all surplus kit & greatcoats stored at Bde dump. Batt under 6 hours notice to move. Capt A Lindamoor from hospital.	
	10/4/17		Very fair parade, men allowed to rest. Capt. E C Mather relieves from leave. Batt under 2 hours notice to move.	
	11/4/17		Left BERLES-AU-BOIS at 2. AM 12/4/17 billeted in dugouts & Lillies. Capt A Lindamoor to Base. 1 O.R. leave to England. At FICHEUX at 7 PM for FICHEUX. Snow all afternoon & evening. arrived at FICHEUX at 2. AM 12/4/17	

Army Form C. 2118.

WAR DIARY
or
INTELLIGENCE SUMMARY

(Erase heading not required.)

VOLUME XXIV 4th Batt "The Kings" (Liverpool Regt)
April 1917.

Place	Date	Hour	Summary of Events and Information	Remarks and references to Appendices
FICHEUX	12/4/17		Line. Relieved the 17th Manchester Regt at that Rly (FRANCE) sheet 51B, number road M3S A9C. S of MERCATEL. 5 Officers & 88 ORs to 1st line. Reinforcements. 2 OR to hospital. 2 OR to hospital	Appx
"	13/4/17		Officers reconnoitre roads to front line.	Appx
"	14/4/17		Supply working party of 400 OR. 2 OR to hospital.	Appx
"	15/4/17		Supply working party of 200 OR	Appx
"	16/4/17		C.O. & Coy visit the Line. 2 OR to hospital.	Appx
"	17/4/17		Relieve 2nd Batt ROYAL WELCH FUSILIERS in the HINDENBURG SUPPORT LINE. Map Ref 51B. S.W. N.34. 1 Company engaged on cutting wires behind line. 1 OR to hospital	Appx
HINDENBURG SUPPORT LINE MAP 51B.S.W N.34.	18/4/17		2 OR to Bde as orderlies. 3 Coys engaged on carrying bombs up to the front line.	Appx
"	19/4/17		3 Coys engaged on bomb carrying	Appx
"	20/4/17		3 Coys engaged on carrying of bombs & ammn. 2 OR wounded. Occasional bombardment by our own & enemy artillery.	Appx
"	21/4/17		CO attends G.O.C Bde Conference. 3 OR killed, 2 OR wounded. 2 OR at letter N wounded.	Appx

2449 Wt. W14957/M90 750,000 1/16 J.B.C. & A. Forms/C.2118/12.

Army Form C. 2118.

WAR DIARY
or
INTELLIGENCE SUMMARY

VOLUME XIV

4th Batt "The Kings" (Liverpool Regt)

April 1917

(Erase heading not required.)

Instructions regarding War Diaries and Intelligence Summaries are contained in F.S. Regs., Part II. and the Staff Manual respectively. Title Pages will be prepared in manuscript.

Place	Date	Hour	Summary of Events and Information	Remarks and references to Appendices
HINDENBURG SUPPORT LINE	22.4.17		Heavy bombardment by the enemy at 4 AM. 6 men wounded, 3 killed.	Col 88
MAP S1 B SW N 24	23.4.17		33rd Div taking part in a General attack Zero to 4-45 AM. Batt in Bde Reserve. A Coy attached to 1st Suffolks engaged on bombing down the HINDENBURG SUPPORT LINE all available men engaged on bomb carrying to forward Coys. 2nd Lt W.A. Pack & H.S. Callachan killed. 2nd Lt R. Reid wounded. estimated casualties 50 or so.	Col 88
"	24.4.17		Batt relieved, marched to Sunken Road. T.3.A. 2nd Lts W.A. Pack & H.S. Callachan buried at T.3a. C.H.S. men allowed to rest.	Col 88
Sunken Road T.3.A.	25.4.17		Batt marched to billets in BEAUMETZ-lez-LOGES.	Col 88
BEAUMETZ lez LOGES	26.4.17		General cleaning of baths for A Coy. 2nd Lt Habble & Edwards return from hospital. 2nd Lt Hill & 2nd Lt Parkus report for duty. 22 O.R. from Depot Batt.	Col 88
"	27.4.17		General cleaning up & refitting. Baths for B.C.D Coys.	Col 88
"	28.4.17		Regt. Lewis Rifle & Bombing Classes began. Platoon training, football during the afternoon	Col 88
"	29.4.17		4 O.R. from Depot Batt. First Bde Church Parade, followed by a Distribution of medals by the Bde commander	Col 88
"	30.4.17		Ell. Coys. Coy. Company training, football in the afternoon.	Col 88

Lie Hall Lieut Colonel
Commanding 4 "Batt "The King's Liverpool Regt"

Army Form C. 2118.

WAR DIARY or INTELLIGENCE SUMMARY

VOLUME XXV

May 1917. 4th Bn The Kings (School to Regt) Vol 19

Places	Date	Hour	Summary of Events and Information	Remarks and references to Appendices
BEAURAINS les LOGES	1/5/17		Fine. Company training. C.O. & all officers attend conference held by the Divisional General at BELLACOURT. 2nd Lt. G.R. Reid to F/A. 2 OR & F.A.	C.H.Gill
BEAUMETZ les LOGES	2/5/17		Fine. Batt moves to DOUCHY-les-AYETTE. villages in ruins. Coy's formed with centrads of billets. 5. O.R. to hospital.	G.H. Ellis
DOUCHY les AYETTE	3/5/17		Fine. Platoon training. Batt. Bombing & Lewis Gun classes formed. 36. O.R from Depot Batt. 4. O.R. to hospital.	G.H. Ellis
"	4/5/17		Fine. Platoon training. 2. O.R. to hospital.	G.H. Ellis
"	5/5/17		Fine. Platoon training. baths. 2. O.R. to hospital.	G.H. Ellis
"	6/5/17		Fine. Company training. Brigade Gymkhana at AYETTE. 3. O.R. to hospital	G.H. Ellis
"	7/5/17		Fine. Platoon training. Divisional Gymkhana	G.H. Ellis
"	8/5/17		Fine. Targets through Rain in the morning. fine during the afternoon. Platoon training.	G.H. Ellis
"	9/5/17		Fine. Company training. C.O. attends Machine Gun conference held by Division 3 O.R to hospital	G.H. Ellis
"	10/5/17		Fine. Company schemes. Regtl sports in the afternoon	G.H. Ellis

257

Army Form C. 2118.

WAR DIARY
or
INTELLIGENCE SUMMARY

(Erase heading not required.)

VOLUME XXV   4th Bn "The King's" (Lpool Regt)

May 1917.

Place	Date	Hour	Summary of Events and Information	Remarks and references to Appendices
DOUCHY by AYETTE	11/5/17		Batt moved into the line and relieved the 10th K.O.Y.L.I. in the HINDENBURG LINE, near FONTAINE-les-CROISILLES.	Appx
HINDENBURG LINE	12/5/17		Line quiet. 4 men wounded 1 killed	Appx
"	13/5/17		Line quiet	Appx
"	14/5/17		Line quiet. 1.O.R. wounded 2 O.R. to hospital	Appx
"	15/5/17		Line Bn relieved by 1st Middx Regt, now back to Lillers at BOYELLES 1 O.R. wounded.	Appx
BOYELLES	16/5/17		Baths, refitting & cleaning up.	Appx
"	17/5/17		Company training, musketry, lectures.	Appx
"	18/5/17		Platoon training, Kit inspections	Appx
"	19/5/17		Move into the trenches, HINDENBURG LINE, near FONTAINE-les-CROISILLES	Appx
HINDENBURG LINE	20/5/17		33rd Div attack along the HINDENBURG LINE. The Batt engaged on bombing down the HINDENBURG LINE in conjunction with an attack made by A & D Coys. 100 yds of Rdo, the attack was successful. Capt. Paley, 2nd Lt H.R. Hubble both wounded. A. Corbridge 2nd Lt. F. James 2nd Lt. J. Robinson killed in action, 2nd Lt Beulton wounded	Appx cont

WAR DIARY or INTELLIGENCE SUMMARY

Army Form C. 2118.

VOLUME XXV

4th Bn. The Kings (Liverpool Regt)

May 1917

Place	Date	Hour	Summary of Events and Information	Remarks and references to Appendices
HINDENBURG LINE	20/5/17		cont'd. 2/Lts Agar, 2nd Lt R. Moore wounded, remain at duty. Casualties O.R's. 15 killed, 1 missing, 79 wounded.	ditto
"	21/5/17		Batt moved back to shelters at BOYELLES.	ditto
BOYELLES	22/5/17		Time refitting & reorganising. 2nd Lt Agar to hospital. Bath.	ditto
"	23/5/17		Batt allotted swimming baths. Regtl bombing class formed.	ditto
"	24/5/17		Time platoon training. 2nd Lt Agar returns from hospital. 2nd Lt Boardman & 2/Lt Wade rejoin.	ditto
"	25/5/17		Bn moves into the line, relieves 4 Suffolks Regt. 16 O.R. to Base L Gunner 1 O.R. killed (acc)	ditto
HINDENBURG LINE FONTAINE les CROISILLES	26/5/17		Line quiet.	ditto
"	27/5/17		Line 33rd Bde. attacks the Line in front of FONTAINE les CROISILLES. Bn moves forward & captures M.G.E. on the FONTAINE - CROISILLES ROAD. Also Casualties O.R's 24.	ditto
"	28/5/17		Bn relieved by 4 Suffolks Regt & moves to camp at BOYELLES, in Bde Reserve.	ditto
BOYELLES	29/5/17		Time cleaning up & refitting. Baths & clean change.	ditto
"	30/5/17		Bn relieved by 6th Bn Bn moves to BERNEVILLE.	ditto
"	31/5/17		Platoon training Regtl Classes in Bombing & Lewis Gun	ditto

H. H. Towse Capt
Commanding 4 Kings Regt.

WAR DIARY or INTELLIGENCE SUMMARY

Army Form C. 2118.

VOLUME XXV "The King's (pool Regt.)
4th Bn The King's (pool Regt.) Vol 20
June 1917.

Place	Date	Hour	Summary of Events and Information	Remarks and references to Appendices
BLAIREVILLE	1/6/17		Fine. Platoon training. C.O. & M.O. 2nd Lieut Strong leave to England.	V.T.O.B.
"	2/6/17		Fine. Company training. Football match in the afternoon between B & C.	R.E.R.
"	3/6/17		Fine. Church Parades. Light Casualties Cleared. Minor ops and Reinforcements 52 O.R.	R.E.R.
"	4/6/17		Company training. 2nd Lieut Buchan leave to England. 2 O.R. return from leave. 7 O.R. to Div. rifle range.	R.F.R.
"	5/6/17		Company schemes of attack. 2 officers visit DOULLENS. Regt concert 10 R to hospital.	R.F.R.
"	6/6/17		Company training. Bombing & firing on the range, Corps commander inspected the Bath. 2 officers visit DOULLENS, 1 O.R. returns from leave, into Corp. T.O.W. completion in the evening.	R.F.R.
"	7/6/17		Fine. Company training. Cross country run, 60 & officers attend lecture at HQ. Lecture on Co-operation between artillery & Infantry, baths.	R.F.R.
"	8/6/17		Fine. Company training. 2nd Lt Boardman & party from service Return to England. Battalion Concert Party gave a concert See N.Q.	R.E.R.
"	9/6/17		Fine. Bn Route March. Kit inspection by C.O. Rifle completion in the afternoon 1st Bathing return from leave.	R.E.R.

Sgd S. HUTCHINGS. Lt Col. 2/c Bn 2/N King's own relieving from leave

Army Form C. 2118.

WAR DIARY
or
INTELLIGENCE SUMMARY

(Erase heading not required.)

VOLUME XXXV

4th Bn "The King's (Shrops Regt)"

June 1917

Place	Date	Hour	Summary of Events and Information	Remarks and references to Appendices
BLAIREVILLE	10/6/17		Fine. Church Parade. Football - Boxing in the afternoon. 2nd Lt Boardman "70R" returns from Lewis Gun Camp.	G.S.ell
"	11/6/17		Again. Platoon training in Camp. Firing on the range. Football match, 17 O.R. to Lewis Rifle School.	G.S.ell
"	12/6/17		Fine. Company training. Football match, 17 O.R. to B.n Bombing School. C.O. returns from leave.	G.S.ell
"	13/6/17		Fine. Coy training. Football. 2nd Lt. Kendall returns from Bde Coy School, 2nd Lt Shannon & 30 O.R. join for duty.	A2
"	14/6/17		Fine. Coy training. Comdg. Offr. & O.C. Companies witness Field Firing Exercise by students of 4th Corps School. Gamer. Compass March for Officers & N.C.O.s 10.30 p.m. - Lt. Warburton.	A2
"	15/6/17		Fine. Battalion does Field Firing Exercise on ground selected W.18.a (Pt France Sheet 51c First Bd (House) 1130 am - 1 pm. Football. Officers v N.C.O.s do Compass March by day. 2 Lt. Ager & Moore return from Paris-Plage Rest Camp. 1 O.R. to 7th Corps school. 20 O.R. to Depot Batt.	A2
"	16/6/17		Fine. Inspection of Boots by C.O. Football	A2
"	17/6/17		" Distribution of Medals by Corps Cmder, as follows:- Croix de Guerre M/c J. McCarthy 18686, Military Medal, 6/4129 Sgt Ellis, 6/29 Sgt Jackson, 13277/L Sgt Burns, 8783 Sgt Allmon, 13254 Pte Hulls, 8594 Pte Williams, 12240 Pte Coots (Sick) rebd Pte Blackburn, 14245 Cpl Burnes.	A2
"	18/6/17		Fine. Inspection of R.R. Gas Helmet & Box Respirator Drill. Finery up Battn. Battn. moved at 6.9 pm to Pte Ravine at BOYELLES T.13.E. Capt Naismith R.AMC joined. Cap. Bengough rots Lines.	A2

WAR DIARY or INTELLIGENCE SUMMARY

Army Form C. 2118.

VOLUME XXVI

(Erase heading not required.) 4th Bn. The Kings (Liverpool Regt)

June 1917

Place	Date	Hour	Summary of Events and Information	Remarks and references to Appendices
BOYELLES	19/6/17		C.O. and O.C. Companies on forthcoming tour in line. Battn. moves 9.0 p.m. to Bdl. Support. Following officers join from 3rd Plunge: 2nd Lts. F.J. BOUGHEN, J.O. ELLIOTT, G. JACKSON, E. GREENSLEY, G.H. SHAW, E.D. BURNS.	A2.
BDE. SUPPORT	20/6/17		Fine. Trench improving & strengthening by night. 2nd Lt BUCHAN to Divl. O.P. 3 O.R. to Hospital. Quiet. 2nd Lt S. Thompson joins for duty.	A2.
"	21/6/17		Fine. Carry on improving, strengthening trench by night, working party to follow. reports to R.E. Officer for work in HINDENBURG LINE. Quiet.	A2.
"	22/6/17		Showery. Hostile Artillery action between 9–11 am. We continue to strengthen improve our position. Working Party of 60 Pttes reports to R.E. for work in HINDENBURG LINE.	A2.
"	23/6/17		Fine. At night we continue working small Ports, effecting additions, improvements. Quiet. 3 O.R. Hospital.	A2.
"	24/6/17		Fine. Quiet. Battn. relieved by 1st Middlesex. Casualty 1 O.R. wounded.	A2.
BOYELLES	25/6/17		Fine. Baths, clean clothes. Inspections, cleaning up.	A2.
"	26/6/17		Fine. Baths. Platoon training. P.T. + B.F. class finish. Instructors return from base.	A2.
"	27/6/17		Fine. Coy training. P.T. + B.F. class continues. N.C.O. Coys moved to Suzzello	Here
"	28/6/17		Fine. T.G.B. 20 O.R. to hospital	
"	29/6/17		Fine. Coy training, Batt. relieved by 10th York Regt. entrained at BOYELLES for BEAUMETZ march to KILLILI in BEAUMCOURT	OrEa
"	30/6/17		Fine. Coy training, general cleaning up. 1 O.R. hospital 2nd Lt E.W. STYRING to T.M. course.	Less

Fred Bull Lieut Colonel
Commanding 4th Bn. The Kings (Liverpool Regt.)

Army Form C. 2118.

VOLUME XXVII

WAR DIARY or INTELLIGENCE SUMMARY

(Erase heading not required.)

4th Bn The King's (Liverpool Regt)

July 1917.

Vol 21

Place	Date	Hour	Summary of Events and Information	Remarks and references to Appendices
BELLACOURT	1.7.17		Divs, Bn Route March, 5 O.R. to hospital.	
"	2.7.17		Divs, Coy marches.	
"	3.7.17		Divs, Bn moved by march route to billets at ACHEUX.	
ACHEUX	4.7.17		Divs, Bn moved by march route to billets at TALMAS.	
TALMAS	5.7.17		Divs, Bn moved by march route to billets at BELLOY-SUR-SOMME.	
BELLOY-SUR-SOMME	6.7.17		Divs, Bn moved by march route to billets at ALERY.	
ALERY (PONTHIEU)	7.7.17		Divs, Improvements of billets, 2nd Lts Legge, McLellan, Dragomiroff, Divs, Improvements of billets, Capt G.H. Stewart 205 O.R. report for duty.	
			3 O.R. to England class.	
"	8.7.17		Divs, Coy & Platoon training.	
"	9.7.17		Divs, Coy & Platoon training.	
"	10.7.17		Divs, Coy & Platoon training.	
"	11.7.17		Divs, Coy & Platoon training, Cricket match in the afternoon.	
"	12.7.17		Divs, Bn Route March, 2/Lt Thompson & 2 O.R.s to P.T. course, 12 O.R. to Lewis Rifle course	
"	13.7.17		Divs, Platoon & Coy training, range firing, football match in the afternoon.	
			2nd Lt Kendall came to England.	
"	14.7.17		Divs, Coy & Platoon training, range firing.	
"	15.7.17		Divs, Church Parade, 2nd Lt Henson & 2 O.R. rejoin from firing course, 2nd Lt Frazer & 9 Divs, join from Base, 4 O.R. from hospital.	

Army Form C. 2118.

WAR DIARY or INTELLIGENCE SUMMARY

(Erase heading not required.)

VOLUME XXVII July 1917. 4th Bn. The King's (L'pool Regt.)

Place	Date	Hour	Summary of Events and Information	Remarks and references to Appendices
AVERY	16.7.17		Bn. Route march, C.E.H. Newport joined for duty, 6 O.R.'s Div. Sig. Course	G.F.E.
"	17.7.17		Coy & Platoon training, 33rd Div. Horse Show, range firing.	G.F.E.
"	18.7.17		Coy & Platoon training Army & Platoon Horse Show, 10 O.R. from Base, 2nd Lt H Jones joined for duty	G.F.E.
"	19.7.17		Coy & Platoon training, range firing, 2nd Lt. E.G. Parker selection from leave	G.F.E.
"			Rifle Coy, 2nd Lt Cyr. McCullin, Boardman return from leave	G.F.E.
"	20.7.17		Coy & Platoon training, Divisional Schemes (without troops), range firing.	G.F.E.
"	21.7.17		Coy & Platoon training, baths, 22 O.R. from Base for duty, 1 O.R. to hospital	G.F.E.
"	22.7.17		Divine Service with Bde. H.Q.'s & M, 2nd Lt P. Addison joined for duty	G.F.E.
"	23.7.17		Coy training & range firing.	G.F.E.
"	24.7.17		Bn. Route march, range firing in the afternoon, 10 O.R.'s Ble Lewis Gun School, 2nd Regt Bombing Class formed, 2nd Lt. Kindall returns from leave.	G.F.E.
"	25.7.17		Coy schemes, 2nd Lt. Puck returns from leave, Lieut Maple rejoins for duty, 6 O.R. from base.	G.F.E.
"	26.7.17		Battalion Drill, range firing in the afternoon.	G.F.E.
"	27.7.17		Platoon training, 2nd Lt. Evans returns from P.T. course	G.F.E.
"	28.7.17		Platoon training, baths.	G.F.E.

Army Form C. 2118.

WAR DIARY
or
INTELLIGENCE SUMMARY
(Erase heading not required.)

VOLUME XXVII

1/4 Bn "The King's" (Liverpool Regt)

July 1917

Place	Date	Hour	Summary of Events and Information	Remarks and references to Appendices
ALLERY	29.7.17		Church Parade. Regtl Sports & Games. Entertainment of villagers.	Ptd.(?)
"	30.7.17		Platoon training. O.O.R return from Lewis Gun Course.	Ptd.(?)
"	31.7.17		Batt entrained at PONT-RÉMY for new area at 2.55pm arrived at ADINKERKE at 1.26 A.M. 1st/8/17, marched to billets at LA PANNE. 7.O.R. to base. Classified P.B.	Ptd.(?)

Tom Small
Lieut Col.
Commanding 1/4 Batt The King's (Liverpool Regt)

Army Form C. 2118.

WAR DIARY
or
INTELLIGENCE SUMMARY

VOLUME XXVIII

4 Liverpool Reg[t]
4th Batt Th Kings Regt
Vol 22

August 1917.

Place	Date	Hour	Summary of Events and Information	Remarks and references to Appendices
LA PANNE	1.8.17		Rain, Coys engaged on cleaning of billets. 6 OR leave to England.	C.T. Ellis
"	2.8.17		Platoon training, Capt. & his C.oas leave to England from 3rd to 13th inst	W.H.G
"	3.8.17		Platoon training, 2nd Lt Frazer leave to England from 4th to 14th inst	W.H.G
"	4.8.17		Platoon & Coy training Guard Bayage Major J.H. Bowen & Capt L Bromley reconnoitre forward area, 2nd Lt Dickson & 4 OR to Gas Course.	W.H.G
"	5.8.17			
"	6.8.17		Platoon & Coy training, Commanding Officer reconnoitres front line 2nd Lt Moore & Edwards leave to England from 7th to 14th inst	C.T.E
"	7.8.17		Platoon & Coy training, range firing for A Coy. C.O, Adjutant, & two O.C Coys attend Divisional Exercise without troops on fighting in sand dunes. 10 O.R. leave to England from 8th to 18th inst	W.H.G
"	8.8.17		Platoon & Coy training, range firing on the Sands. Batt attends Demonstration of Contact Aeroplane work	W.H.G
"	9.8.17		Platoon & Coy training, range firing, Major J H Bowen & 2nd Lt Kirkwood leave to England from 10th to 20.14	W.H.G

Army Form C. 2118.

WAR DIARY
or
INTELLIGENCE SUMMARY

(Erase heading not required.)

VOLUME XXVIII

August 1917.   4th Batt. The King's (Liverpool Regt.)

Place	Date	Hour	Summary of Events and Information	Remarks and references to Appendices
LA PANNE	10/8/17		Training. Coy schemes, & range firing. 4 ORs return from HANGEST. RE Guard. 2nd Lieut Watson returned from Gas course. M.O. return from leave to England.	
"	11/8/17		Platoon & Coy training & range firing. Lieut Shayle & 1NCO to Army school.	
"	12/8/17		Church Parades & bathing.	
"	13/8/17		Company training. Capt E.C. Walker & 2nd Lt E.C. Baker leave to England from 11 to 24 inst.	
"	14/8/17		Company training & range firing. Cpl Decman to veterinary course. Capt & two Clerks relieved from leave to England.	
"	15/8/17		Company training & range firing.	
"	16/8/17		C.O. Adjt. & 4 Coy Commanders reconnoitre front line in SAINT GEORGES sector. Batt moves to OOST DUNKERKE. 3 officers & 98 O.R. to Depot. Batt at minimum strength.	
"	17/8/17		Batt relieve 15 & 2nd Lanc Fus in the Saint Georges sector. A Coy 1st section & Coy Lt section L.G. post Kentish Roads. D Coy & remaining Long of B Coy in	

Army Form C. 2113.

WAR DIARY
or
INTELLIGENCE SUMMARY

(Erase heading not required.)

VOLUME XXVIII   1/5th The King's (Liverpool Regt)

August 1917

Place	Date	Hour	Summary of Events and Information	Remarks and references to Appendices
ST GEORGES SECTOR	18/8/17		Wellington Camp. Relieved Batt on right 1st Huddie on the left. C.O.R.S. Leave to England. 2nd O.R. taken between from leave to England.	Wind
"	19/8/17		Très trenches, all quiet on Batt front. 2nd Edwards O.R. move between from Leave to England. 1 O.R. to hospital	Wind
"	20/8/17		Trenches, fine. 1 O.R. killed (seven) 7 wounded. Coys carry on with improvement of trenches.	Wind
"	21/8/17		Trenches. All quiet. 1 O.R. to hospital 2nd Ltd leave to England 21st to 30th	Wind
"	22/8/17		Trenches quiet enemy aeroplane destroyed 1 O.R. to Gas course. 10 R.	Wind
"	23/8/17		Batt relieved by 2/3rd Suffolks. Relief complete 2.35 A.M. (?) Batt moves to QUEENSLAND CAMP East of OOST DUNKERKE	Wind Hot
QUEENSLAND CAMP OOST DUNKERKE	24/8/17		Batt engaged in refitting & cleaning up. Supply working parties of 1 NCO & 40 OR in the evening 1 OR killed 7 wounded.	Wind

Army Form C. 2118.

WAR DIARY
or
INTELLIGENCE SUMMARY

VOLUME XXVIII

(Erase heading not required.)

Instructions regarding War Diaries and Intelligence Summaries are contained in F. S. Regs., Part II. and the Staff Manual respectively. Title Pages will be prepared in manuscript.

1/4 Bn The King's (Liverpool Rgt)

August 1917

Place	Date	Hour	Summary of Events and Information	Remarks and references to Appendices
QUEENSLAND CAMP	25/8/17		Gni. Clearing up.	Notes
DO57 DUNKERK				
"	26/8/17		Night marching route 8 O.R. wounded	Notes
"	27/8/17		Batt moves to LA PANNE. the whole Batt. bathe in the afternoon	Notes
LA PANNE	28/5/17		Batt move to GHYVELDE everybody billeted under cover. Sudden 70 OR save to England. Numerous rescue relieve from Depot Batt 2 off & O.R. reports for duty.	Notes
GHYVELDE	29/8/17		Batt moves to BRAY DUNES Settled in huts. 1 OR to hospital 2 off Recon't hospital. 6 off & 528 sergeant sent to England 29 & 6 8 K	Notes
BRAY DUNES	30/8/17		Commanding Officers inspection. Nation training, baths for whole Batt. 10 O.R. rejoined. Nations from army school. 8 off & 8 signing leave to England. 30 & 31 8" 4 off	Notes
"	31/8/17		Transport moves to new area by road. Car loads to England.	

A.N.E. Warburton Lt
to Major
Commanding 1/4 Kings

WAR DIARY or INTELLIGENCE SUMMARY

Army Form C. 2118

VOLUME XXIX

4th Batt. The Kings (Liverpool)

September 1917

Place	Date	Hour	Summary of Events and Information	Remarks and references to Appendices
SERQUES	1/9/17		Batt. arrived in billets at 12.45am remainder of the day spent in cleaning up.	Appx
"	2/9/17		Church Parades. 6 OR to leave, 4 OR return from leave. 4 OR to England.	Appx
"	3/9/17		Coy training. CO & Capt A.R. Humphreys to leave. 2 OR to Hill Zett. Officers from leave. Bn to Training area. Raining men.	Appx
"	4/9/17		Coy training. 3 OR leave to England.	Appx
"	5/9/17		Coy training. Regt Classes in Bombing & Lewis Gun commence. Btgn Grenadiers Talks for A&B Companys. 8 OR leave to England.	Appx
"	6/9/17		Coy training. Regimental Sporting & P.T. Class of 4 officers & 35 NCOs formed under C.S.M. Holsworth (instructor of P.T.) Battn for C in C Corps. 3 OR leave to England.	Appx
"	7/9/17		Coy training. Bttle training ground. Major Dawson (4th Welsh) has reconnoitred front in front of SANCTUARY WOOD. 1 OR leave to England.	Appx

Army Form C. 2118

Instructions regarding War Diaries and Intelligence Summaries are contained in F.S. Regs., Part II. and the Staff Manual respectively. Title Pages will be prepared in manuscript.

WAR DIARY
or
INTELLIGENCE SUMMARY

VOLUME XXIX

(Erase heading not required.) 4/Batt. the Liverpool Regt.

September 1917

Place	Date	Hour	Summary of Events and Information	Remarks and references to Appendices
SERQUES	8/9/17		Coy training. Batt. football match against 462 Syphs. Scoot 1-1. Keymate broken the afternoon.	Ohio
"	9/9/17		Field Events practice by A&D Coys. 7 O.R's to England.	Ohio
"	10/9/17		Coy training. Football match with Belg H.Q. result 3-0 for the Batt. Sgt Butterworth to England for commission. Capt D Bingham sent to Wipers from leave. 2/Lt E. Slemmon Bogger leave to England.	Ohio
"	11/9/17		Coy training. Bomb & rifle range in the afternoon. 32 N.C.O's on course of P.T. & P.T. by C.S.M. Arnecroft. Adjt., Capt. E.B. Maher, Capt. W.B. Tryhey Reconnoitre front line Corps Area. Capt. E.G. Signing to 2a. a I.O.S. for duty as instructor. Scout Squad leave for the Batt in the evening.	Ohio
"	12/9/17		Coy schemes on the training area, Capt. J.S. Langham to held ambulance sick. 2nd Lt. Knight to report to I.N.C.O. to I Corps Infy School, YOR William Ghis.	Ohio

Army Form C. 2118

WAR DIARY
or
INTELLIGENCE SUMMARY

(Erase heading not required.)

VOLUME XXIX

September 1917. "4th Batt. Th. Kings (Liverpool Regt.)"

Place	Date	Hour	Summary of Events and Information	Remarks and references to Appendices
SERQUES	8/9/17		Coys Platoon Cleaning, C & D Coys Lewis Gunners on the range, A & B Coys moving into inspection by C.O. Lieut. C.H. Haughton Cave to England. C.O.R. returns from leave	
"	14/9/17		Coys Platoon training, A & B Coys Lewis Gunners on the range. C & B Coys marching order inspection by C.O. 1 NCO to II Corps School (for Bombing course) 2 NCO's O.R. included to field Amb. sec.) 2 O.R. leave to England 7 O.R. from leave.	
"	15/9/17		Batt. moved to billets at OCHTEZEELE arriving there at 12 noon. 10 O.R. leave to England. Capt A.W. Loungsbury return from leave England	
OCHTEZEELE	16/9/17		Batt. moved to billets of STEEN VOORDE arriving there at 11 a.m. 6 O.R. return from leave 2nd Lt Atchison returns from leave. 6 O.R. leave to England	
STEENVOORDE	17/9/17		Batt. moved to billets at LE COQ de PAILLE arriving there at 11.30 a.m. 2nd Lt. E Evans leaves for England	

Army Form C. 2118

WAR DIARY
or
INTELLIGENCE SUMMARY
(Erase heading not required.)

VOLUME XXIX

1st Batt The Kings Liverpool Regt

September 1917.

Place	Date	Hour	Summary of Events and Information	Remarks and references to Appendices
LE COQ du PAILLE	18/9/17		Kit inspections. 1 O.R. from Base. 6 O.R. from leave. 8 O.R. leave to England. Lieut Col Knyge from 2d Army dry School, 2nd Lt G.O. Elliott from P.T. course.	Appx
"	19/9/17		XIII Corps circular of new attack formations. Baths for Batt. 4 men return from leave.	Appx
"	20/9/17		Batt moved to RENINGHELST. 6 O.R. return from leave.	Appx
ONTARIO CAMP RENINGHELST	21/9/17		6.0 v platoon training. Football match Batt v 99th T.M. result 3-2. 9 O.R. leave to England. 4 O.R. return	Appx
"	22/9/17		6.15 to 12 platoon training. 5 Officers & 180 O.R. to duty. 3.0 to T.M. Battery for duty. 2nd Lt Bevans returns from hospital. Football match Batt v FA result 3-0 for Batt. Batt ensue medals for football.	Appx
"	23/9/17		Batt moved to KRUISSTRAATHOEK. C.O reconnoitres front line trenches. 4 O.R. leave to England.	Appx
KRUISSTRAAT HOEK	24/9/17		Batt moved into the line relieving Batt of the 23rd Div in the KEUTELBEEK Sector. 6 O.R. missing 7 O.R. wounded. Lieuts Kitkinson & Vaughan relieves from Batt.	Appx

Army Form C. 2118

WAR DIARY or INTELLIGENCE SUMMARY

(Erase heading not required.)

VOLUME XXIX September 1917 4th Batt Hastings General Regt

Place	Date	Hour	Summary of Events and Information	Remarks and references to Appendices
NEUTELBEN (Sector)	25/9/17		Early morning about 5.30AM enemy made a big [strikethrough] attack along the 1 Sec: front. the Batt held all its frontage. The enemy made several more attempts to break through but was driven back by rifle & machine gun fire. 23 O.R killed, 18 O.R missing, 47 O.R wounded. Capt J Williams + Capt A Hodcroft killed in action.	(file)
"	26/9/17		23rd Div attack, artillery objective, ground held against all counter attacks. Capt L.D. Tryp wounded, 2nd Lt J.V. Williams killed. 9.O.R killed, 3 O.R missing, 44 O.R wounded, 10 O.R wounded, missing. Lieut E.H. Newport returned from leave.	(file)
"	27/9/17		Shelling not quite so heavy. 2nd Lt R Bolton wounded. 5.O.R killed, 6.O.R missing, 22 O.R wounded. Batt relieved by 8th Yorks 23rd Bde & proceeds to Camp near DICKEBUSCH. Divl using importation through CinC General Murray.	(file)
DICKEBUSCH	28/9/17		Batt moves by march route to OUDERDOM and on by march route to LYNDE arriving at 3.30AM 29/9/17 moves by march route from there to EBBLINGHEM	(file)

Army Form C. 2118

WAR DIARY
or
INTELLIGENCE SUMMARY

(Erase heading not required.) 4th Batt "The King's (Liverpool Regt)

VOLUME

September 1917

Place	Date	Hour	Summary of Events and Information	Remarks and references to Appendices
LYNDE	29/9/17		Coys engaged on clearing up. 2nd Lt Rycroft & Cpl Sumner to 2nd Army Inf School. 2nd Lt Crosley returns from leave. Lieut E.W. Stycring returns from Base.	
"	30/9/17		Church Parades. 2nd Lt Burns & 2/Lt to 2nd Army Infantry School. 2nd Lt Hickson to GHQ Lachois Gun School for course. 2nd Lts Co Elliott, C.M Shaw, S Thompson, E.J Hughes leave to England from 1st to 11th Oct.	R.S.V.P

Mseal
Lieut Colonel
Commanding 4 "Kings (Liverpool Regt)

WAR DIARY or INTELLIGENCE SUMMARY

Army Form C. 2418

VOLUME XXX

4TH BATTN "THE KING'S" (L'POOL REGT.)

OCTOBER 1917.

Place	Date	Hour	Summary of Events and Information	Remarks and references to Appendices
LINDE.	1/10/17		Fine - Coy training 2nd Lt. E.H.E. WARBURTON leave to England 2/10/17.	See
"	2/10/17		Fine - Coy training - talks for Batth - P.T. Class. 4 Officers 320 O.R. under Bde Instructor	See
"	3/10/17		Regtl Courses in Bombing, Lewis Gun, Signalling Commenced, 5 O.R. attached to 98th T.M. Bty 4 O.R. leave to England.	See
"	4/10/17		Fine. Batth inspected and medal distribution by Field Marshal Sir Douglas Haig G.C.B. G.C.V.O. K.C.I.E. 8 O.R. to 98th M.G. Coy for duty.	See
"			Fine. Coy training. Capt A. Fifth from hospital 2nd Lt. H.M. Cannon leave 5th to 15th.	See
"	5/10/17		Church Batth march by train to YPRES. 12 O.R. to Bgde Lewis Gun class. 5 O.R. leave to England.	See
YPRES.	6/10/17	"	Batth attached to 13th Anzac Corps and accommodated in dugouts and shelters outside EASTERN. Ramparts Ypres. Whole of Batth engaged on working parties on road Construction.	See
"	7/10/17		Rain - working parties.	See
"	8/10/17		Rain " "	See See See
"	9/10/17		Rain " "	See
"	10/10/17		Rain " "	See
"	11/10/17		Dull no rain " "	See

Army Form C. 2118

WAR DIARY
or
INTELLIGENCE SUMMARY
(Erase heading not required.)

4TH BATTN "THE KING'S" (LPOOL REGT).

OCTOBER 1917. VOLUME XXX

Place	Date	Hour	Summary of Events and Information	Remarks and references to Appendices
YPRES.	12/10/17		Line. 2nd Lt. J.N. McCUBBIN from base. - Working parties.-	Appx
"	13/10/17		Line. Working parties. Minimum Reserve of 5 officers 58 O.R. to Canteen Corner Camp. 2nd Lt. Hughes, Shaw, Thompson rejoin from leave. 2nd Lt. R. Moore rejoin from Army School. 2nd Lt. Hickson rejoins from Lewis Gun Course de Tonquet. 2nd Lt. Hughes transferred to 13th R.W.F.	Appx
"	14/10/17		Working parties continue. 2nd Lt. G.H.E Harburton rejoins from leave	Appx
"	15/10/17		Working parties. - 2nd Lt. Dawson & Hickson to leave. 2nd Lt. H.m Cannon from leave.	Appx
"	16/10/17		Working parties.	Appx
"	17/10/17		"	Appx
"	18/10/17		Line. Battn moved to NEUVE EGLISE. Minimum reserve rejoined Battn. by 'Bus.	Appx
NEUVE EGLISE.	19/10/17		Line. Battn cleaning up. H.O.R. rejoin from Bde Lewis Gun School. 2nd Lt. H Boardman to Bde as Bombing Officer. 4 o.r. to leave. 2 O.R. join from Leave.	Appx
"	20/10/17		Line. - Coy training - One officer from each Coy reconnoitre trenches near BRISTOL CASTLE. reserve. WULVERGHEM. Divis'l Band played to Battn.	Appx
"	21/10/17		Line - Working parties in forward area near WULVERGHEM. - 12 men to Bde Lewis Gun School.	Appx

Army Form C. 2118.

WAR DIARY
or
INTELLIGENCE SUMMARY.
(Erase heading not required.)

4TH BATTN THE KING'S (LPOOL REGT)

VOLUME XXX

OCTOBER 1917.

Place	Date	Hour	Summary of Events and Information	Remarks and references to Appendices
NEUVE EGLISE	23/10/17		Fine – Battn moved to <s>Neuve Eglise</s> BRISTOL CASTLE SECTOR. 1 O.R. to Second Army Signal School. Capt Triph, Lt. Ager, 2nd Lts Burns & Jones leave to England. dept.	Chas
			Bingham to U.K. Sick.	
BRISTOL CASTLE SECTOR.	23/10/17		Working parties. 1 O.R. to St. Pol. P.T. and B.F. Course. 5 O.R.s to leave. 2 O.R. wounded	Chas
"	24/10/17		Rain – dull. Working parties. 2nd Lt Nicholson to Bde Pioneer Coy.	Chas
"	25/10/17		Rain – dull. Working party. 2nd Lt McCulkin to leave.	Chas
"	26/10/17		Rain. Battn moved into Right Subsector between Trenches # Moncton. 1 O.R. to A.A. Light Course	Chas
			4 O.R. to leave.	
IN THE LINE.	27/10/17		Lull – rain – Front line trenches in bad state of repair – much water. Battn cleaning	Chas
			and repairing trenches. Casualties 1 O.R. killed 2 O.R. wounded.	
"	28/10/17		Dull – Battn cleaning and repairing trenches. 2nd Lts Davison & Hickson return from leave.	Chas
			Casualties 2 O.R. killed 2 O.R. wounded.	
"	29/10/17		Dull – Slight rain – Battn HQ came # before. Casualties. 1 O.R. wounded. Arty Subject	Chas
			to leave. 1 O.R. to Div. Anti Gas School	
"	30/10/17		Rain – Battn as before. 1 O.R. to G.H.Q. M.G. School Le Touquet. 5 O.R. to	Chas
			leave. Battn relieved by 1st Cameronians and move into billets at NEUVE EGLISE	
NEUVE EGLISE	31/10/17		Fine. Battn cleaning up. Bgde Field Engineering Course Commenced 2nd Lts Shaw Pickup Robb # Logan	Chas

Commanding 4Th Bn The Kings (LPool)

Army Form C. 2118.

WAR DIARY
or
INTELLIGENCE SUMMARY.
(Erase heading not required.)

4th Batt. The King's (Liverpool Regt.)

Vol 25

VOLUME XXXI

NOVEMBER 1917

Place	Date	Hour	Summary of Events and Information	Remarks and references to Appendices
NEUVE EGLISE	1/11/17		Line. Platoon training, 10 Officers reconnoitre defences at ARMENTIERES. 3 officers to bombing course, 2 officers & 70 R to R.E. Courses. 1 officer leave to UK.	Wea.
"	2/11/17		Line. Batt. moved to SHANKHILL CAMP NEUVE EGLISE.	Wea.
SHANKHILL CAMP NEUVE EGLISE	3/11/17		Changeable. Batt engaged in working parties making new support line. 1 officer & 7 OR came to UK.	Wea.
"	4/11/17		Fine. Batt engaged instructing as on previous day. 3 officers report for duty from base, 2 officers return from leave to UK, 1 officer return from gunnery school.	Wea.
"	5/11/17		Fine. Bombing practice. 1 officer & 1 OR leave to UK. Regt. Course on LG commenced.	Wea.
"	6/11/17		Wet. Rigging practice. 2 officers & 1 Sund Major's B. A. sick from base. 1 officer leave to UK.	Wea.

Army Form C. 2118.

WAR DIARY
or
INTELLIGENCE SUMMARY.

(Erase heading not required.) 1/4th Bn. The Kings (Liverpool Regt.)

VOLUME XXXI

NOVEMBER 1917

Instructions regarding War Diaries and Intelligence Summaries are contained in F.S. Regs., Part II. and the Staff Manual respectively. Title pages will be prepared in manuscript.

Place	Date	Hour	Summary of Events and Information	Remarks and references to Appendices
SOMEWHERE CAMP	7/11/17		Wet. Working parties. 20 O.R. from leave to U.K.	Appx
NEUVE EGLISE			Changeable. Working parties. Kept O.R. flying to VIIIth Corps T.M. School as Instructor. 1 Officer from leave to U.K.	Appx
"	8/11/17			
"	9/11/17		Fine. Working parties. 1 O.R. returns from leave.	Appx
"	10/11/17		Wet. General cleaning up & kit inspections. 1 Officer from leave to U.K.	Appx
"	11/11/17		Changeable. Church Parades. 1 Officer to hospital (injured hand.) 1 O.R. from leave to U.K.	Appx
"	12/11/17		Fine. Batt. moved to Rebels in MERRIS AREA marching via NEUVE EGLISE & BAILLEUL arriving at 12.15 p.m. 1 O.R. rejoins from leave to U.K.	Appx
MERRIS AREA	13/11/17		Fine. Coy & Platoon training, bombing & range firing. C. O. R. leave to U.K. 1 O.R. to U.K. as candidate for commission.	Appx
"	14/11/17		Dull, no rain. Representatives from each Coy & Lt. Off. reconnoitring line near PASSCHENDAELE Batho for Bn. 12 O.R. return from leave Appx	

Army Form C. 2118.

WAR DIARY
or
INTELLIGENCE SUMMARY.

VOLUME XXXL

(Erase heading not required.) 4th Bn. The King's (Shrop. Light Regt.)

NOVEMBER 1917

Instructions regarding War Diaries and Intelligence Summaries are contained in F. S. Regs., Part II. and the Staff Manual respectively. Title pages will be prepared in manuscript.

Place	Date	Hour	Summary of Events and Information	Remarks and references to Appendices
MERRIS AREA	15/11/17		Fine, dry evening. 2 officers came to U.K.	Nov
"	16/11/17		Fine, marched from billets at 7.30 a.m. to METEREN to entrain for POTIJZE AREN, detrained on road 1 mile S.W. of YPRES marched (6 Coys.) to IGA (Sheet 28) HQ YPRES arriving at 9 a.m. 5 O.R. came to U.K.	Nov
Camp I.9.A. Sheet 28	17/11/17		Fine. Coys engaged on improving Camp. 2 off & 6 o/r taken to 7 M Batt. 1 off. & 6 o/r reported from leave to U.K.	Nov
"	18/11/17		Fine, Bats move to SEINE. Relieve Batt in support on right Sect. sector. Relief completed 7 p.m. 2 Ofs, 5 D.3 WO's & 4 O.R. wounded.	Nov
SUPPORT LINE SEINE	19/11/17		Fine, Very Sunday. 20 minute duration on enemy harbour retaliation in vicinity of SEINE. 1 off. & 1 N.C.O. reconnoitred from and right subsector. Lt. B.H. NEWPORT & 10 O.R. wounded. 1 O.R. killed. work, replacement of his killed by Lieut.	Nov
	20/11/17		Fine, only morning barrage by our Artillery. Enemy retaliation heavy round SEINE, Casualties 10 killed 12 wounded. 2 Officers & 7 O.R. to Corps School. 1 off. & 60 R. came to U.K.	Nov

Army Form C. 2118.

WAR DIARY
or
INTELLIGENCE SUMMARY.
(Erase heading not required.)

1st Bn "The King's (Liverpool Regt)"

NOVEMBER 1917

Volume XXXI

Instructions regarding War Diaries and Intelligence Summaries are contained in F. S. Regs., Part II. and the Staff Manual respectively. Title pages will be prepared in manuscript.

Place	Date	Hour	Summary of Events and Information	Remarks and references to Appendices
Support line SEINE	21/11/17		Quiet 10th inst, early morning barrage by our artillery enemy retaliation not so heavy as previous day, casualties 2 O.R. wounded. 2 Officers reported for duty from base.	Offr
"	22/11/17		Fired Batt relieved 1st Hilda in trenches, high calibre relief complete 8 P.M. Casualties 1 Offr wounded from shell. 2 O.R. to hospital (sick). 2 Offr leave to U.K.	Offr
Nr Sub sector PASSCHENDAELE SECTOR	23/11/17		Fired enemy Stokes Support by causing casualties 3 killed 2 O.R. wounded.	Offr
"	24/11/17		Relieved Battn relieved by 4th Bn Scottish Rifles, relief complete 7.35 P.M. Batt moved to Camp at I.9.A. casualties 5 O.R. killed 12 O.R. wounded.	Offr
YPRES POPERINGHE	25/11/17		Changeable. Battn moved to BRANDHOEK AREA by train, entraining at JANE STN. detraining BRANDHOEK marched to TORONTO CAMP arriving there at 4 P.M. 2 O.R. leave to U.K.	Offr
TORONTO CAMP	30/11/17		Fine. Batt cleaning up. Capt H.B. Stype to Base as Gas Officer.	Offr

Army Form C. 2118.

WAR DIARY
or
INTELLIGENCE SUMMARY

Volume XXXI

4 "B" Bn. The King's (Liverpool Regt)

November 1917

Place	Date	Hour	Summary of Events and Information	Remarks and references to Appendices
TORONTO CAMP	27/11/17		Nine Oths for Bn, 107% from leave, 6 O.R. leave to U.K.	Officers
"	28/11/17		Nine, Maison training, all Box Respirators tested. Bde Com Hdrs Officers	Officers
"	29/11/17		Nine, Coy training	(Nine)
"	30/11/17		Nine, Coy training, Regtl Concert in Y.M.C.A. 6 O.R. leave to U.K.	Nine

Rushfoll W.Col
Comdg 4 Kings
1.12.17

Army Form C. 2118.

Volume XXXII

WAR DIARY
or
INTELLIGENCE SUMMARY.

(Erase heading not required.) 4th Batt. the King's (L'pool Regt.)

December 1917

Vol 26

82 D

Place	Date	Hour	Summary of Events and Information	Remarks and references to Appendices
TORONTO CAMP BRANDHOEK	1/12/17		Batt moved to POTIJZE arriving in Camp about 2p.m., 2 Offrs Robinson Joins for duty, 2 Officers return from leave from England.	View
POTIJZE	2/12/17		Batt engaged on improving the Camp, 1 Officer leave to England, 4 O.R. to Pigeon circus. 20 OR leave to U.K.	View
"	3/12/17		Batt supplies working parties.	View
"	4/12/17		Batt engaged on working parties, 2nd Lt. STEVENSON to hospital sick, 3 OR leave to U.K.	View
"	5/12/17		Batt moved to Support trenches at HAMBURG & take over from 1st Bn. the Middx Regt., relief complete 10.30pm.	View
SUPPORT HAMBURG	6/12/17		All engaged on the clearing of the area, & collecting salvage. Shells improved casualties 1 O.R. wounded.	View
"	7/12/17		Supply working parties to R.E.s for work on INVERARY TRENCH. One Coy engaged in laying trench board track from HAMBURG to CREST FARM. Work of improving area continued. 70 O.R. leave to U.K.	View

Army Form C. 2118.

Volume XXXII

WAR DIARY
or
INTELLIGENCE SUMMARY.

(Erase heading not required.) the 1/4th Bn. The King's (Liverpool Regt)

December 1917

Place	Date	Hour	Summary of Events and Information	Remarks and references to Appendices
HAMBURG	8/12/17		Supply parties to R.E., work on track continued by 1 Coy. 5 O.R. wounded.	
"	9/12/17		Work of improving shelters & trench board track continued, 4 O.R. wounded. Batt. relieved 4 Bn. the Suffolk Regt. in the Capt. Seeb sector. 11.30 p.m. relief complete.	
PASSCHENDAELE Lt. Seb sector	10/12/17		Enemy activity normal, K.O.R. wounded 3 officers rejoin from leave 3 O.R. home to U.K.	
"	11/12/17		Quiet, enemy aircraft active. 3 O.R. wounded.	
"	12/12/17		Batt. relieved by 5th Bn. Graham Light Infantry relief complete 10 p.m. 1 Officer & 10 O.R. wounded. Batt. moved to Camp at St. JEAN	
CAMP ST. JEAN	13/12/17		Batt. entrained at ST. JEAN STA. at 12.30 p.m. for EECKE AREA detrained at GODSWAERSVELDE STA. at about 2 p.m. arrived in billets about 5 p.m. 2 officers rejoin from leave.	
EECKE AREA	14/12/17		Coys. engaged on cleaning & refitting. 8 O.R. leave to U.K.	

Army Form C. 2118.

WAR DIARY
or
INTELLIGENCE SUMMARY.
(Erase heading not required.)

Volume XXXII

1st Bn. The King's (L'pool Regt)

December 1917.

Place	Date	Hour	Summary of Events and Information	Remarks and references to Appendices
EECKE AREA	15/12/17		Coys engaged in cleaning up & refitting. 1 O.R. leave to U.K.	
"	16/12/17		Church Parade. 2 O.R. leave to U.K.	
"	17/12/17		Coy & Platoon Training. Regtl Courses in Lewis Guns & Bombing commenced. 2 O.R. leave to U.K.	
"	18/12/17		2 Companies Route march. Coy & Platoon training. Lectures for all Officers by Bde Lewis Gun Officer.	
"	19/12/17		2 Companies Route march. 2 Companies Coy & Platoon training. 12 O.R. to Bde Lewis Gun Course.	
"	20/12/17		2 Companies Route march. 2 Companies Coy & Platoon training. Lecture to all Officers by G.O.C. Divn on the CAMBRAI FRONT.	
"	21/12/17		2 Companies Route march. 2 Companies Coy & Platoon training. 3 O.R. in 6 U.K. Lecture by Bde G.M.S. Officer. Football match, Officers v Sgts. Result 4-2 Officers.	
"	22/12/17		C.O. Inspection, all Coys firing on the range.	
"	23/12/17		Bridal Ribbon Presentation by G.O.C. Divn at EECKE. 1 O.R. leave to U.K.	
"	24/12/17		Bde Route march.	

Army Form C. 2118.

WAR DIARY
or
INTELLIGENCE SUMMARY.
(Erase heading not required.) H/Q 1/4 Bn The Kings (L'pool Regt.)

VOLUME XXXII
December 1917

Place	Date	Hour	Summary of Events and Information	Remarks and references to Appendices
EECKE AREA.	25/12/17		Coy football matches. Christmas Dinners to men of R+C Coys.	
"	26/12/17		Range firing by all Coys. Christmas Dinner to O+Q Coys. Lecture by R.C. Seg. Officer on "Communications".	
"	27/12/17		Lecture + Demonstration by Lt Col Leay to all Officers. Small Box Respirators tested. Christmas Dinner to HQ+A Transport. 2 O.R leave to U.K.	
"	28/12/17		Preparing to move to POPERINGHE.	
"	29/12/17		Batt less transport moved to POPERINGHE by motor lorries arriving in billets 12.30 p.m.	
"	30/12/17		3 Coys engaged on work on the CORPSLINE under R.E. supervision. 1 Coy resting. 2 O.R leave to U.K.	
"	31/12/17		3 Coys Engaged on work as on 30th inst. 1 Coy resting	

E.G. Earnshaw Capt
2nd i/c 1/4 Bn The Kings (L'pool Regt)

Army Form C. 2118.

VOLUME XXXIII. WAR DIARY or INTELLIGENCE SUMMARY.

(Erase heading not required.)

4th Batt" The King's "L'pool Regt"

JANUARY 1918

Place	Date	Hour	Summary of Events and Information	Remarks and references to Appendices
POPERINGHE	1/1/18		Fine but cold – A. C & D Coys working party on Corps Lines – B Coy and part of Hd. Artists Batts – 2nd Lt. J. F. T. BAUGHEN to leave – 5 ORs to leave R.I.M. Jones to Course of Instruction	W.D.
"	2/1/18		Cold – 3 Coys on working party as before. A Coy and Remainder Hd. Artists Batts – Capt. T. D. McKINNON R.A.M.C. rejoined from leave.	W.D.
"	3/1/18		Frosty. – H.Q.S and D Coy march to EECKE – 3 Coys on working party thro' precedes from WIELTJE to GODEWAERSVELDE thence by march route to EECKE – 2nd Lt. E. GREASLEY to leave – 2nd Lt. W. P. WILLIAMS from 4th Army Musketry School – 1 OR from leave.	W.D.
EECKE AREA	4/1/18		Fine and Frosty – Coys cleaning up – one Officer per Coy reconnoitre ST JEAN area 1 Sgt to Corps Field Punishment Cage for duty – 3 ORs to leave.	W.D.
"	5/1/18		Fine – Batn moved to ST JEAN area by bus arrived 12.30 p.m. – 2nd Lt. W. P. WILLIAMS to hospital sick – 2nd Lt. A. J. PORTER to hospital.	W.D.
"	6/1/18		B. C & D Coys working on Corps Line – 2nd Lt. F. H. DAWSON rejoined from VIII Corps Schools Intelligence Course. 2 ORs from leave – Lecture to officers by Medical Officer on the Water Cart.	W.D.
ST JEAN CAMP	7/1/18		Mild – some rain. A C & D Coys working party – Lecture on "The Organisation of Intelligence" by Intelligence Officer to officers – 5 ORs to leave.	W.D.
"	8/1/18		Snow – A B & D Coys working party. Lecture to officers on the "Travelling Cooker" by Capt E. G. MATHER – Capt E. W. STYRING from leave – R.S.M Jones from Course of Instruction	W.D.

Army Form C. 2118.

WAR DIARY
or
INTELLIGENCE SUMMARY.

(Erase heading not required.)

4th Batt. The King's (Liverpool Reg).

Instructions regarding War Diaries and Intelligence Summaries are contained in F. S. Regs., Part II. and the Staff Manual respectively. Title pages will be prepared in manuscript.

VOLUME XXXIII (CONT^D) JANUARY 1918

Place	Date	Hour	Summary of Events and Information	Remarks and references to Appendices
ST JEAN CAMP.	9/1/18		Mild. — A.B. & C Coys working party as before. 1 o.r. Rifles 2.o.R. wounded — 1 o.r. to U.K. to join Cadet Unit. — Capt. A.N. BOUMPHREY from leave — Lecture to officer on Aeroplane photographs by Intelligence Officer.	W.D.
"	10/1/18		Windy – some rain. B Coy working party. A Coy started work on MAIDEN CAMP (new) Capt Parkes lectured on PLAYFAIR CODE — 1 o.r. to U.K. to join Cadet Unit.	W.D.
"	11/1/18		A.C. & D Coys working party. B Coy work on new camp. 2nd Lt. THOMPSON lectured on 'Company Training'. — R.S.M. P.F. Jones to 4 o.r. to leave.	W.D.
"	12/1/18		Dull and rainy. A.B. & D Coys working party — Draft of 80 o.r. arrived — 4 o.r. to VIII Corps School Training Coy — 2nd Lt. MARION & CAPSTICK to Bde Lewis Gun School 5 o.r. from leave.	W.D.
"	13/1/18		Fine and clear — A.B. & C Coys working party. D Coy work on MAIDEN CAMP — Baths for Draft who were otherwise inspected by Commg Officer. 2nd Lt. S. THOMPSON to details Batln.	W.D.
"	14/1/18		B.C. & D Coys working party. — A Coy + fort. two. work in MAIDEN CAMP by A Coy. Heavy rain and wind — A.C. + D Coys working — B Coy Baths Lieut Pack 2nd Lt. JONES & Girls to VIII Corps School — 3 men to leave.	W.D.
"	15/1/18		Stormy — A.B. + D Coys working party- C Coy Baths and work on MAIDEN CAMP — 1 Sgt to 4th Army Section Anti-gas School — 1 o.R. to leave – 4 o.r. to leave.	W.D.
"	16/1/18			W.D.

Army Form C. 2118

WAR DIARY
or
INTELLIGENCE SUMMARY
(Erase heading not required.)

4th Batt. The Kings Shrops Regt.

VOLUME XXXIII
JANUARY 1918.

Place	Date	Hour	Summary of Events and Information	Remarks and references to Appendices
ST JEAN CAMP.	17/1/18		Windy - Some rain. - A B & C Coys looking party - D Coy Battn. - 3 men to leave	J.W.D.
"	18/1/18		Mild and overcast. - 2nd Lt D Coy looking party. - Battn. put through foot baths in the afternoon. - CO. and Adjt reconnoitre Support Line at HAMBURG. - 2nd Lt W.M. NELMES to 171 Tunnelling Coy for 14 days duty. - CO. held conference with Coy Commdrs.	J.W.D.
"	19/1/18		Mild and overcast. - Battn left camp at 3.45 p.m. and moved to Support Line HAMBURG. PASSCHENDAELE SECTOR. Battn HQrs at IRKSOME. Relief complete 7.05 p.m. Relieved 2nd Worcesters. - Capt E.G. MATHER to 3 days course with 21 Squadron R.F.C. - 2nd Lt J.F. MARRION and 2nd Lt E. CAPSTICK from Bgde Lewis Gun Course. - 2nd Lt S. BIRKINSHAW 2 O.R. wounded. 1 O.R. to leave.	J.W.D.
SUPPORT HAMBURG.	20/1/18		Dull - Battn provided carrying parties to front line for 2nd Worcesters. - 2nd Lt F.J. BAUGHEN and 1 O.R. from leave. - 6 O.R. to leave. - Enemy activity slight.	J.W.D.
"	21/1/18		Dull - Battn provided carrying parties to front line for 2nd Worcesters. - Battn relieved by 9th H.L.I. and moved to Right Subsector Front Line. relieved 2nd Worcesters. Battn H.Q. at HAMBURG. Relief complete 8.20 p.m. - 2nd Lt E. GREASLEY from leave. - Enemy activity slight.	J.W.D.
RIGHT SUBSECTOR	22/1/18		Fine morning - 9th H.L.I. provided carrying parties for food and R.E. material to the front lines. - Enemy activity slight.	J.W.D.
"	23/1/18		Fine day - Rain fell in the afternoon - Battn relieved by 5th Scottish Rifles - Relief complete 9.10 p.m. Battn entrained at FROST HOUSE on light railway and proceeded to ST LAWRENCE CAMP. BRANDHOEK. Battn all in camp at 2.30 A.M 24/1/18.	J.W.D.
ST LAWRENCE CAMP. BRANDHOEK	24/1/18		Fine sunny day. - MAJOR S.E. NORRIS. D.S.O. arrived and took over command of the Battn. - Battn engaged in cleaning up. - 1 O.R. proceeded to U.K. to join our O.C. Battn.	J.W.D.
BRANDHOEK	25/1/18		Fine day - Battn bathed at BRANDHOEK BATHS. - R.M. Cr. D Coy played Nelson football match. An inter-coy concert was held in the Recreation hut in the evening. - Lieut W. ASHCROFT reported for duty. - Draft of 50 O.R. arrived.	J.W.D.

Army Form C. 2118

WAR DIARY
or
INTELLIGENCE SUMMARY

4th Batt. The King's (L'pool) Regt.

(Erase heading not required.)

Army Form C. 2118

Instructions regarding War Diaries and Intelligence Summaries are contained in F.S. Regs., Part II. and the Staff Manual respectively. Title Pages will be prepared in manuscript.

VOLUME XXXIII
JANUARY 1918

Place	Date	Hour	Summary of Events and Information	Remarks and references to Appendices
ST LAWRENCE CAMP BRANDHOEK	26/1/18		Fine day. Commanding Officer addressed the Batt. on parade. – Draft of 37 O.R. arrived. Batt. football match in the afternoon.	M.D.
"	27/1/18		Fine day. – Church Services in Recreation Room in the morning. – Batt. moved to front line Right subsector Batt. HQ. at HAMBURG. – Moving by Light Railway to LOW FARM. Relief complete 8.50 p.m. – 2 O.R. killed – Moving. – 2 wounded. – Hot meals supplied and carried up by 4th Suffolks.	M.D.
RIGHT SUBSECTOR ASSCHENDAELE	28/1/18		Fine day. – 6 O.R. to leave. Enemy activity – Slight. – Meals sent up as yesterday.	M.D.
"	29/1/18		Fine day. – 2nd Lt. R.M. LUNT wounded. – Batt. relieved by 5th Northumberland Fusiliers. Relief complete 8.15 p.m. – Batt. moved by Light Railway from LOW FARM to BRANDHOEK occupying TORONTO CAMP WEST – Arrival in Camp 2 A.M. 30/1/18. – Capt. G.H.E. WARBURTON M.C. to leave.	M.D.
TORONTO CAMP WEST BRANDHOEK	30/1/18		Fine – Batt. entrained at BRANDHOEK Station 5.30 p.m. and moved to WIZERNES. Arriving 11 p.m. left WIZERNES and moved by lorries to BOISDINGHEM. – First two arrived 4.30 A.M. 31/1/18. last two arrived 7.30 A.M. 31/1/18. – 2 O.R. to leave – Draft of 5 officers 148 O.R. arrived from Kings.	M.D.
BOISDINGHEM	31/1/18		Fine – Batt. rested and started cleaning up. – Draft of 5 officers 7 O.R. to leave. 4 O.R. returned from leave.	M.D.

S.E. Moore Major
Commdg. 4th The Kings.

Army Form C. 2118

VOLUME XXXIV WAR DIARY or INTELLIGENCE SUMMARY

("Erase heading not required.) 4th Bn. "The King's" (Liverpool Regiment)

FEBRUARY 1918

Vol 28

Place	Date	Hour	Summary of Events and Information	Remarks and references to Appendices
BOISANGHEM	1/2/18		Fine. Coy. cleaning up & re-equipping. 2/Lt W.H. JONES rejoined from VIII Corps Lewis Gun School. 3 ORs to VIII Corps School - 7 ORs to leave.	G/Bde
"	2/2/18		Fine. Bn. Ceremonial parade. Football match. Bn. v 2nd A&SH, result Bn. 2 goals, 2nd A&SH 0. 2/Lt F. MAKINSON & Sgt TUNNEY to 4th Army Musketry School. 7 ORs to leave.	G/Bde
"	3/2/18		Fine. Church parades. 2/Lt E. CAPSTICK to leave. Regimental Canteen opened.	G/Bde
"	4/2/18		Fine. Coy training. A Coy inspected by C.O. 2/Lt A.F. EADES from 4th Army School. 2/Lt T. SPENCER and 10 ORs to Bde L.G. School. 6 Signallers to course of Power Buzzer amplifiers. 1 NCO to VIII Corps School.	G/Bde
"	5/2/18		Fine. 1st half. Coy training. B Coy inspected by C.O. Lt F. EAGER to leave. 8 ORs to leave.	G/Bde
"	6/2/18		Corps Gas School. 3 Lewis Gunners to course in Anti-Aircraft sights. 2 ORs to England for Commissions. Fine. Coy training. Lt W. ASHCROFT to 19th Bn. 11 ORs to 171 Tunnelling Coy. 1 OR to VIII Corps B Works Coy.	G/Bde
"	7/2/18		R.S.M. R.T. JONES to Hospital.	G/Bde
"	8/2/18		Wet. Coy training. Corps Commander visited Bn.	G/Bde
"	9/2/18		Dull - wet. A&C Coys range. B&D Coys intensive digging & wiring. 11 ORs to leave. 2/Lt W.H. JONES to leave. Capt R. McRAE and CSM TEDDY to 4th Army Infantry School	G/Bde
"	10/2/18		Fine. 1st dull. Bn. ceremonial parade.	G/Bde
"	11/2/18		Fine. Church parades. 2/Lt T. SPENCER from Bde L.G. School. 2/Lt F.T. BAUGHEN to Bde L.G. School. 10 ORs to leave.	G/Bde
"			Fine. Coy training. Final of Bde. Football Competition. Bn. v 9th A&LI - result 9th A&LI 7 Bn. O	G/Bde

34 8

Army Form C. 2118

VOLUME XXXIV

WAR DIARY or INTELLIGENCE SUMMARY

4th Bn "The King's" (Liverpool Regiment)

FEBRUARY 1918

Place	Date	Hour	Summary of Events and Information	Remarks and references to Appendices
BOISDINGHEM	12/2/18		Fine. Coy training - range - Box respirators tested. Lecture to Bn. by Div¹ Gas Officer	On Sep
"	13/2/18		Raining. Coy training. Regt¹ Bombing Class finished. Capt GHE WARBURTON M.C. from leave. 2/Lt SE BIRKINSHAW from hospital. Bde. Football Competition commenced. Bn v 1st Middlesex. Result Nil—3. A.M.2. Lecture to Bn by C.O. 11 OR's to leave. 1 OR to Veterinary Course	Ca Sep
"	14/2/18		Dull. Some rain. Coys on 30ᵗʰ range. Bde A.R.A Competition in afternoon, won by 2nd A-B-H. 2/Lt T.T. McCUBBIN M.C. to England for tour of duty.	Pt Bug
"	15/2/18		Fine. Gas demonstration. Football Match. A Coy v B Coy. 2Lt G.P. HARPER to Brit. Signaling School. 2/Lt PTBAUGHEN 4Bde LG class rejoined Bn. Regimental Boxing Contest in evening in R.F.C. Hangar	2t Sep H Sep
"	16/2/18		Fine. Bn Ceremonial Parade. Concert in evening by "Shrapnels". 2Lt F.H. DAWSON to leave.	Ct Sep Ct Sep
"	17/2/18		Fine. C.O. inspected Transport. Church Parades. 1 OR to Corps Gas School. 2/Lt W.P. WILLIAMS from Sick leave	
"	18/2/18		Fine + cold. Bn on ranges. A.B. Coys Battn. Regimental Concert in evening. 6 officers to Army Camouflage Works, WIMEREUX. 2/Lt E. CAPSTICK from leave	At Sep
"	19/2/18		Fine. Coys training + on ranges. 1 OR to leave for month. 2 OR's 9th TMB for duty. N°10 and 13 Auts. Ct Sep	Ct Sep
"	20/2/18		Fine. Aeroplane demonstration. 1 OR to England for commission. Lecture to Bn by Bvt¹ Gaz. 2/Lt RT Pick M.C. + 2/Lt G.C. GIBB from VIII Corps School. Transport left for BRANDHOEK.	Ct Sep
"	21/2/18		Fine. No parades - coys cleaning up billets etc. Lt F.C. AGER from leave. 2/Lt CR FRASER to hospital	Ct Sep
BRANDHOEK	22/2/18		Stormy. Bn left BOISDINGHEM for BRANDHOEK at 5.30 am as per order N°10 attached, arrived BRANDHOEK 12 noon. 16 OR's to leave. 2/Lt J. MARRION + 1 OR to GHQ LG School	Ct Sep

Army Form C. 2118

VOLUME XXXIV WAR DIARY or INTELLIGENCE SUMMARY

(Erase heading not required.) 4th Bn "The King's" (Liverpool Regiment)

FEBRUARY 1918

Place	Date	Hour	Summary of Events and Information	Remarks and references to Appendices
BRANDHOEK	23/2/18		Fine. Bn. left BRANDHOEK for ST JEAN arrived ST JEAN CAMP 12 noon. 2/Lt T. WAGSTAFFE & 2/Lt S.E. BIRKOMSHAW + 114 O.R.s to St Calo School 2/Lt A.O. WARD M.C. + 2/Lt F. WHEELER to leave, 10 O.R.s to leave, 2 men to Bn. Burial Officer, 17 men to C.R.E., 4 signallers to Bn. for visual work, 3 signallers to Bn. as runners. 2/Lt B. WHITLOCK to 2/2 Field Co. R.E. all for temporary attachment. 30 O.R.s to leave. 9 O.R.s to leave. 2/Lt C. NEWMAN & 2 O.R.s to R.F.C. liaison course. 1 signaller to Pigeon Course. Nil. Bn working party, 16 officers + 400 O.R.s on Cake line. 2/Lt W.R. ANDERSON to VIII Corps Gas School	
ST JEAN CAMP	24/2/18			
"	25/2/18			
	26/2/18		Fine. Bn moved to support trenches at IRKSOME starting 2.45 p.m. as per Order No. 12 attached. 1 Sergeant to Musketry Course, HAYLING ISLAND.	
SUPPORT PASSCHENDAELE SECTOR	26/2/18		Fine, quiet, supply and working parties and officers' courses carried on by 2 Coy.S.	
"	27/2/18		Changeable, wiring continued by 4 companies 2/Lt & 6 men [?] wounded. 20 O.R.s wounded, supply and carrying parties to forward Bns. 2 Lts. to colleges of 2 O.R.s Lewis Gun [?] leave to U.K.	
	28/2/18		Fine. wiring continued, supply and carrying parties to forward Bns. 15 O.R.s leave to U.K.	

S.E. Morris
Lieut Col
Commanding 4th/King's

SECRET.   4th Bn. "THE KING'S"   Order No.11.   Copy.....

Reference HAZEBROUCK S.W.
          Sheet ..

No.1.
MOVE.   The Bn will move to ST JEAN CAMP by train from
                HAZEBROUCK ?.I..B.cent. tomorrow the 3rd inst, and will
                detrain at VINNEY JUNCTION ?.4.c...3.

2.
REVEILLE.   Reveille will be at 5.30.a.m.

3.
KITS &
BLANKETS.   All Officers kits, and mens blankets rolled in bundles
                of 10) will be stacked at Q.M.Stores by 7.15.a.m.

4.
TRANSPORT.   All transport will be at Q.M.Stores by 7.30.a.m.
                to convey blankets to station.   Each Coy will detail
                I.N.C.O. and 10 men for the loading and unloading of
                blankets. These parties will move off with blankets
                and travel on the same train with them.

5.
COOK
CARTS, etc.   Cook carts, water carts, Coys M.G. limbers, medical
                cart and mess cart, will move from the present camp at
                7.45.a.m.   Cookers preparing a meal en route to be
                ready for 12.45.p.m.

6.
PARADE.   Coys will move as follows:-
                        H.qrs., A and B Coys.   12.15.a.m. under
                                                   Major F.J.H...Browne.

                        C and D Coys.   1.45.a.m. under
                                                   Capt. W.J..uther.

7.
BILLETS.   All huts must be left clean.

8.
DRESS.   DRESS. Full marching order - greatcoats, steel
                helmets, box respirators at the alert.)

9.
TRAIN
ACCOMMODATION. Train accommodation 350 each.   Truck ..

Issued at ..II...S.
2nd Feby. 17.
To O.C., and A/C, Capt. .J..uther.
   Adjt., O.C.A.B.C and D Coys,
   C.L.,Q.M.,TR....,R.....,RSM,
   Orderly..
   Guth Bde.

                                        C.Warburton
                                                ...
                                        Adjutant 4th Bn. T... KING'S.

4th Bn "THE KING'S" Order No. 19.   Copy. 14

SECRET.

REFERENCE. 1/100,000 HAZEBROUCK S.A.

No.1.
MOVE.   The Bn, less transport, will move to Toronto Camp.,
         BRANDHOEK, on 2nd Inst by train from SIZERNES.

2.
PARADE.   The Bn will parade with head of column at Bde
         Office billet, facing E., ready to march off at 5.45.a.m.
              Order of march:-
                 D Coys, M.G, C.B.A.D.
              Route. QUELMES - SETQUES - NALLINGS.

3.
REAR   O.C.D.Coy will detail one platoon as rear guard, who
GUARD.   will ensure that every man of the Battalion is in front of
         them.

4.
VALISES &   Officers valises, mess baskets and mens blankets will
BLANKETS. be stacked outside each Coy H.Qs half an hour before the Coy
         moves off, and loading party of one Sergeant and 10 men will re
         main with them, the N.C.O reporting to Capt.E.G. Mather
         immediately the Bn moves off.

5.
HANDING   Capt.E.G. Mather will be responsible for the handing
OVER.   over and obtaining receipts for all billet stores-receipts
         to be handed to Adjutant as soon as possible.

6.
TRANSPORT.   Transport present with the Bn will march under orders
         of Lieut.H.J.Kendall to arrive at SIZERNES before 5.0.a.m.,
         2nd inst.   Cooks will prepare a hot drink of tea for each
         man by the time the Bn arrives at the Station (4.in.s.a.)
              Ropes for securing horses in trucks will be carried.

7.
ENTRAINING.   Lieut.D.H.Peek M.C. will report to the entraining
         Officer at SIZERNES before 5.0.a.m. 2nd inst, to arrange
         train accommodation for the Bn.

8.
MARCH
DISCIPLINE.   O.C.Coys will remind their men that march discipline is
         to be strictly enforced, and that no N.C.O or man will, under
         any circumstance, be permitted to fall out.

9.
BILLETS.   Billets are to be left clean and tidy, and as the Bn will
         be marching off in the dark it is necessary that billets
         should be cleaned the afternoon before.

10.
MOVE.(cont).   The Bn will move from BRANDHOEK to ST JEAN CAMP by
         train at 5.0.a.m. the 3rd inst.

1/2/18.
Issued at...5.0.a.m....to
C.O. and 2/c, Capt. E.G. Mather,
Adjt, O.C.A.B.C.D.Coys, T.O.,
Q.M., Bn S.O., R.S.M., File...By   G.H.E. Warburton
                                                             Capt.
  4th Inf. Bde.   Adjutant 4th Bn "THE KING'S".

SECRET.   4th Bn "THE KING'S"   Order No.1.   Coy......A..

Reference Sheet 28.

No.1.
MOVE.   The Bn will relieve the 1st Queens Regt in Support
         on the left Brigade front, Company for Company tomorrow the
         25th inst.

2.
ADVANCE   Advance party as below, will parade at Orderly Room
PARTY.   at 11.0.a.m.   This party will take over all stores, etc.
         Bn H.Q.   2nd Lieut.W.P.Williams.
                            Signallers.
                            Cpl.H.Johnstone. (Pioneer).
         Coys.   1.Officer and 1.N.C.O per Coy.

3.
ORDER OF   D.C.B. and A Coys.   1st Platoon of D Coy will leave
MARCH.   Camp at 2.45.p.m., and will pass FROST HOUSE at 3.30.p.m.
         Succeeding platoons will leave at 10 minutes interval.
         This interval may be decreased only if visibility
decreases.
         Guides will meet the Bn at Junction of JUDAH and "K"
tracks.

4.
KITS, etc.   Puttees, blankets and Officers kits will be stacked on
         road side - site to be appointed by Q.M.

5.
RATIONS.   If rations are available, two days rations will be
         carried.

6.
PICQUETS.   A and B Coys will form INLYING PICQUETS and will be
         on duty from the time of taking over to 6.30.p.m. 26th inst.
         This duty will then be taken over by C and D Coys for
         24 hours, and so on daily, at 6.30.p.m.

7.
WORKING   Coys not on INLYING PICQUET will each provide a working
PARTY.   party of 1 Officer and 25 O.Rs.

8.
TAKING OVER.   All trench stores, defence schemes, maps, etc., will be
         taken over, receipts given and a copy forwarded to the Adjutant
         as soon as possible.

9.
S.O.S.   S.O.S. at present in use is Rifle Grenade bursting into
         two red and two green stars simultaneously

10.
RELIEF.   Completion of relief will be reported to Bn H.Q. as
         follows:-
                 "A" Coy.   Tea.   "B" Coy   Sugar.
                  C "   Milk.   D "   Spoon.
         Bn H.Q. will be at IRRSOME D.10.b.7.4.

Issued at 4.0.p.m.
24/2/18.
To C.O. 2nd 1/c, Capt.T.G.Mather,   Capt.
   Adjt, O.C.A.B.C.D.Coys., T.O.   Adjutant 4th Bn "THE KING'S"
   Q.M., Bn.S.O, R.S.M, File,
   War dy, 8th Bde.

WAR DIARY
or
INTELLIGENCE SUMMARY
(Erase heading not required.)

Army Form C. 2118

VOLUME XXXV.

4th Bn The King's (Lpool Regt)

MARCH 1918

Place	Date	Hour	Summary of Events and Information	Remarks and references to Appendices
HAMBURG (SUPPORT BN)	1/3/18		Old Line. Bn relieved by 1st Hants: relief complete 5.0 PM. Bn arrived in ST JEAN CAMP at 7.30 PM. 15 O.R. Leave to U.K.	
ST JEAN CAMP	2/3/18		Old Line. Bn on Working Parties. 8 O.R. Leave to U.K.	
"	3/3/18		Line. Baths. Church Parades.	
"	4/3/18		Line. Bn provides Working Parties. All attend Anti Trench Feet Hut in the afternoon.	
"	5/3/18		Line. Bn relieves 1st Queens in Front Line, Left Sub Sector. Order No.14 attached. 2 O.R. wounded	
"	6/3/18		Line. Quiet during day. Enemy M.G's active during the night. 4 Officers and 16 O.Rs to Leave.	
Front Line (Left)	7/3/18		Line. Enemy shells whole front with gas shells. 2 N.C.Os to England for commissions. 10 O.Rs wounded. (Gassed)	

Army Form C. 2118

WAR DIARY
or
INTELLIGENCE SUMMARY
(Erase heading not required.)

Instructions regarding War Diaries and Intelligence Summaries are contained in F.S. Regs., Part II. and the Staff Manual respectively. Title Pages will be prepared in manuscript.

Place	Date	Hour	Summary of Events and Information	Remarks and references to Appendices
Front Line Left	8/3/18		Line. 3 O.Rs wounded enemy quiet during day, little gas shelling at night. One Officer returns from leave.	Chas
"	9/3/18		Line. More gas. 9 O.Rs wounded. Bn relieved by 1st Queens Regt and moves to ST JEAN CAMP. Order No 15 attached.	Chas
ST JEAN CAMP	10/3/18		Line. Bn finds Working Parties. Baths allotted to Bn. 3 Officers and u/Os to Leave.	Chas
"	11/3/18		Line. Working Parties.	Chas
"	12/3/18		Line. 1 Officer and 80 O.Rs working party. 2 Officers to Leave. Lieut J.B. Kendle joins from 11gth Bn "The King's".	Chas
"	13/3/18		Line. Bn on Working Parties. Small Box Respirators tested. 12 O.Rs to Leave. 25 O.Rs joined from Base.	Chas
"	14/3/18		Line. Bn on Working Parties. 3 O.Rs Leave to UK. 13 O.Rs from Base.	Chas
"	15/3/18		Line. Bn relieves 1st Queens in front Line (Left Sub Sector) order No 16 attached.	Chas

Army Form C. 2118.

WAR DIARY
or
INTELLIGENCE SUMMARY
(Erase heading not required.)

Instructions regarding War Diaries and Intelligence Summaries are contained in F. S. Regs., Part II. and the Staff Manual respectively. Title Pages will be prepared in manuscript.

Place	Date	Hour	Summary of Events and Information	Remarks and references to Appendices
Trenches Left	18/3/18		Fine. All quiet. C.O. to Bde to command.	C/too
"	19/3/18		Fine. All quiet during day. Little shelling at night. Bn engaged on forward posts. 2 O.R. killed. 1 O.R. wounded.	C/too
"	19/3/18		Dull. Enemy has shelling. 13 O.R. to Leave. 5 O.R. casualties. Lieut Whitlock to England for M.G. course.	C/too
"	19/3/18		Wet. 3 Officers to Leave. 10 O.R. Officers returns from Leave. 2nd Lieut. R. Moore to England for 6 months tour of duty. Capt. R. McBee and 2nd Lieut S. Thompson from course. 10 O.R. from Base.	C/too
"	20/3/18		Wet. Enemy made a raid on Bn front (see report attached) 2 O.R. killed. 4 O.R. wounded. 2 O.R. missing. 5 O.R. to Signalling School. Capt. + R.M.A.R. JONES from Base.	C/too
"	21/3/18		Fine but cloudy. Bn relieved by 1st Hants (Order No 14 attached) Bn moved to ST LAWRENCE CAMP. 12 O.R. Leave to U.K. 1 Officer returns from Hospital. 12 O.R. to Leave.	C/too

2449 Wt. W14957/M90 750,000 1/16 J.B.C. & A. Forms/C.2118/12.

Army Form C. 2118.

WAR DIARY
or
INTELLIGENCE SUMMARY

(Erase heading not required.)

Instructions regarding War Diaries and Intelligence Summaries are contained in F. S. Regs., Part II. and the Staff Manual respectively. Title Pages will be prepared in manuscript.

Place	Date	Hour	Summary of Events and Information	Remarks and references to Appendices
ST LAWRENCE CAMP. BRANDHOEK	22/3/18		Fine. Bn engaged on cleaning up. Baths.	—
"	23/3/18		Fine. Bn engaged on Working Parties. 6 ORs to England for tour of duty.	—
"	24/3/18		Fine. Bn engaged on Working Parties. 26 ORs from Base. 1 Officer rejoins from leave.	—
"	25/3/18		Fine. Working Parties. 12 ORs to Base for transfer to H.E. 2 Officers and 16 ORs from courses.	—
"	26/3/18		Fine. Working Parties. 3 Officers from leave.	—
"	27/3/18		Fine. Working Parties. 2 ORs to T.M. Btty for duty. 10 ORs to M.G. Bn for duty.	—
"	28/3/18		Fine. Bn returns to trenches in support at HAMBURG (order No 18 attached). Very quiet day. No casualties.	—
"	29/3/18		Fine. — Batt. front line and Carrying parties for D. & T.M. Btys. and Infantry loco-nailities. —	—
"	30/3/18		Fine. — Same work as yesterday. Parties engaged on wiring front posts by night. — No casualties —	—
"	31/3/18		Fine. — Quiet — Same work as above. 2nd Lt Barritt returned from leave —	—
"	2/4/18		Fine. — Slight rain in morning. — Same work as yesterday. — Corps Commander visited Bn HQ. No casualties.	—

SS Vern Lt Col
Commdg. 1/4 Kings.

98th Infantry Brigade
33rd Division

4th Battalion
"The King's" Liverpool Regt.
APRIL 1918

WAR DIARY or INTELLIGENCE SUMMARY

Army Form C. 2118

Vol: XXXVI. 4 Nieuport Bks.

Place	Date	Hour	Summary of Events and Information	Remarks and references to Appendices
Line	1.4.18		C.O. accompanied by the M.O and Captain AGER visited "C" échelon. Arrivals:- 20 O.R. Weather:- Fine.	
"	2.4.18		Casualties:- 1 O.R. Arrivals:- 3 O.R. Weather:- Fine.	
"	3.4.18	11.30	Bn: relieved by ROYAL GUERNSEY MILITIA (29. Div). Bn: arrives in hutments, St LAWRENCE CAMP, BRANDHOEK. Arrivals 6 O.R. Bn: visits baths. Officers' conference at 6.30 P.M. Weather:- Fine.	
BRANDHOEK	4.4.18		Departures:- 6 O.R. to Home Estab: Weather: Showery.	
"	5.4.18		G.O.C. 33. Div: visits Bn: Hqrs: Billeting party under 2/Lt MARRION leave camp for AMBRINES. Weather:- Showery.	
"	6.4.18		Lt Col. E.M. BEALL visits Bn. Hqrs: Arrivals:- 1 O.R. Weather:- Showery.	
"		11.40	Divine Service Parade.	
"	7.4.18	8.55	Bn: entrains at ABEELE station.	
		12.30	" detrains at LIGNY " and marches to AMBRINES. Weather:- Raining.	
AMBRINES	8.4.18	12.30	C.O's [con]ference, all officers present. C&D. coo: march to Rifle Range. Weather:- Raining	

Army Form C. 2118

WAR DIARY
or
INTELLIGENCE SUMMARY
(Erase heading not required.)

Instructions regarding War Diaries and Intelligence Summaries are contained in F.S. Regs., Part II. and the Staff Manual respectively. Title Pages will be prepared in manuscript.

Place	Date	Hour	Summary of Events and Information	Remarks and references to Appendices
AMBRINES	9.4.18		A & B cos: march to Rifle Range – Bn: training whole day –	
		14.0	G.O.C. Div: Lectures at LIGNEVIL on "The Experiences of the Recent Fighting". Arrivals :- 13 O.R. Weather :- Raining.	
"	10.4.18		Bn: visits baths in the morning – Two cos: march to rifle range in the morning, two in the afternoon –	
		22.40	Bn: moves by train to STRAZEELE – Arrivals :- 50 O.R. Departures :- 2/Lt: C.B.ABRAHAMS. to hospital (Sick). Weather :- Showery.	98. Inf.y Bde. order No. 218 d/10.4.18 –
	11.4.18	5.30	Bn: detrained at CAESTRE Stn: and marched into bivouacs near FLÊTRE.	
		18.30	" marched to RAVELSBERG Camp and bivouaced there for the night – Casualties :- Weather :- Fine.	
RAVELSBERG	12.4.18	5.0	Bn: marches to DRANOUTRE – First reinforcement moves to billets at SHAEXKEN.	
		10.0	" " " KEMMEL HILL.	
		15.0	" " " DRANOUTRE.	
		17.0	" " " BAILLEUL aerodrome – Casualties :- 1 O.R. wounded –	

Army Form C. 2118

WAR DIARY
or
INTELLIGENCE SUMMARY
(Erase heading not required.)

Instructions regarding War Diaries and Intelligence Summaries are contained in F.S. Regs., Part II. and the Staff Manual respectively. Title Pages will be prepared in manuscript.

Place	Date	Hour	Summary of Events and Information	Remarks and references to Appendices
BAILLEUL	13.4.18	15.0	Bn: moves to METEREN in support to 19.Inf.y Bde: Casualties:- Killed 10.O.R. Wounded 10 O.R. Weather - Fine.	
METEREN	14.4.18		Bn: in support to 1.Bn: THE QUEEN'S - Casualties:- Killed - 2/Lt. F. MAKINSON. Weather - Fine	
"	15.4.18		Bn: in action (see separate report) Casualties:- Wounded. 2/Lt. F.H. DAWSON; 2/Lt. W.H. JONES; 2/Lt. E. CAPSTICK; " W.M. NELMES; " H.R. ANDERSON (remained at duty) Weather - Fine.	Appendix I
"	16.4.18		Bn: in action - (see separate report)	
"	17.4.18		Bn: in action (see separate report). Casualties:- Killed - Captain G.H.E. WARBURTON M.C.; 2/Lt: G.C. GIBB; 2/Lt: W.R. ~~GIBB~~ WILLIAMS - (Adjt: 4. THE KING'S REGT) Weather - Showery -	
"	18.4.18		Bn: in action - (see separate report) Captain A. LINDEMERE joins Bn: from Base Weather - Cold, Snow -	

WAR DIARY or INTELLIGENCE SUMMARY

Army Form C. 2118

Place	Date	Hour	Summary of Events and Information	Remarks and references to Appendices
METEREN & BOESCHEPE	19.4.18	3.0	Bn: relieved by 1. MIDDX; Regt & marches to Billets at BOESCHEPE. Captain G.H.E. WARBURTON M.C. is buried in the churchyard at BOESCHEPE, by the Revd C.E. STALEY C.F. attached 4. THE KING'S REGIMENT.	
		11.0	Bn: muster Parade. Total Casualties. Officers 20 O.R. 469. Captain F.C. AGER is appointed acting-adjutant. 2/Lt: H.F. NICHOLLS " assistant-adjutant. Weather - Cold. Snow.	
BOESCHEPE -	20.4.18	9.0	Bn: marches to Billets in BAVINCHOVE area. Weather - Fine.	
BAVINCHOVE	21.4.18	10.30	Division consisting of 4. THE KING'S - 2. A&S HIGHRS - 18. MIDDX: (PIONEERS) - R.E. & R.A.M.C. under the command of the Div: Comdr: are inspected by M. CLEMENCEAU, the French Prime minister at "LES TROIS ROIS", BAVINCHOVE. Arrivals - MAJOR J. STOPFORD TAYLOR - 2/Lt: S. PAPPA - 2/Lt: J.E. SMITH - 2/Lt: L.O. WITHER - CAPT. H.B. TRIPP rejoins the Bn: from 98. Bde: and takes over the duties of Acting Adjutant -	

WAR DIARY
or
INTELLIGENCE SUMMARY
(Erase heading not required.)

Army Form C. 2118

Place	Date	Hour	Summary of Events and Information	Remarks and references to Appendices
BAVINGHOVE	22/4/18	9.30	C.O's parade.	
		15.0	G.O.C Division inspected the Bn; and congratulated all ranks on the excellent work performed by them at METEREN, 16-18 April, 1918.	H.A. 1/4
		16.0	Bn march to STAPLE for baths.	
"	23/4/18		Football match KING'S v A.&S.H result 0-3, the Divisional Band played.	H.A. 1/5
"	24/4/18		Specialists training	H.A. 1/5
"	25/4/18		Individual training.	H.A. 1/5
"	26/4/18		Bn; moves to HONDEGHEM area. Divisional Band played in afternoon.	H.A. 1/5
HONDEGHEM	27/4/18	9.30	Divisional commander visits Bn: Hqrs. Individual training.	H.A. 1/4
		11.30	C.O. attends Brigade conference. Arrivals 50 O.R.	

Army Form C. 2118

WAR DIARY
or
INTELLIGENCE SUMMARY
(Erase heading not required.)

Instructions regarding War Diaries and Intelligence Summaries are contained in F.S. Regs., Part II. and the Staff Manual respectively. Title Pages will be prepared in manuscript.

Place	Date	Hour	Summary of Events and Information	Remarks and references to Appendices
HONDEGHEM	28/4/18		Divine Service Parade - all unemployed men and new draft fire on range at M.T. des RECOLLETS. Weather - Fine, rain at intervals.	
"	29/4/18		Bn ordered to march to BARINGHEM, move cancelled at 11.0 a.m. Football match KING'S v 99. FIELD AMB: Result loss 2-0 - Divisional Band played 5-6 p.m. Weather - Fine but cold. Arrivals :- 70 O.R.	
"	30/4/18		Musketry training. Football match KING'S v A.S.C (M.T.) result 6.2 - Weather - Fine but cold. Arrivals :- 240 O.R.	

War Diary
Appendix I

To 98th Infantry Brigade.

The following is a brief report of the action taken by the Battalion under my command (which was commanded during the first three days by Capt. G.H.E. Warburton. M.C.) in the operations around METEREN during the period 13/18th April 1918.

I regret very much, owing to very heavy casualties amongst Officers, I am not in a position to give as much detail as I would like. The Adjutant, Assistant Adjutant and Intelligence Officer became casualties.

On the afternoon of the 13th inst at 5.0.p.m the Bn left the Asylum, BAILLEUL, and proceeded to position north of METEREN in support to the 19th Infantry Brigade.

The Bn was heavily shelled and had many casualties while in the support position.

At 9.0.p.m on the 14th inst the Bn moved forward to a position lying along the road south of METEREN, approx X.2.20.b.5.0 X.21.a up to 16.c. The 5th Scottish Rifles on the right and the Tank Corps on the left.

The next 24 hours in that position were fairly quiet.

At 5.0.a.m on the 16th inst O.C. C.Coy reported to Bn Hdrs that the Tank Corps had evacuated their position in the first line on his left without letting him know. Two platoons were at once sent forward by Capt Warburton to try and fill the gap but did not succeed in reaching the position before the enemy launched his attack.

At 5.30.a.m the enemy commenced very heavily with rush bombardment and succeeded in penetrating the line taken up the gap left by the Tank Corps at 16.c. B Coy on the right stood fast and the left of the line was withdrawn and formed on line 20.b.5.0

(2)

to K.15.d. and south through the village. It was then discovered the left front Coy. (C) had practically disappeared, and the new position was taken up by two platoons of Coy.

At 11.0.a.m Officers patrol went through METEREN and discovered the enemy strongly were in it. The remainder of the day was fairly quiet and was spent in trying to clear up situation and consolidating line we were holding.

At 11.0.a.m on the 16th inst the enemy attacked the right of the Bn line at K.20.. The attack was repulsed with loss to the enemy.

At 6.0.p.m. on the 12th inst the enemy heavily attacked the line in front of farm K15.c.2.6. This attack was successful and he succeeded in occupying the farm. The French came to our assistance by counter-attacking and were entirely successful in entirelyx restoring the line. The remainder of the day was fairly quiet

At about 6.0.p.m during the attack on the farm the enemy succeeded in surrounding B.Coy Hqrs where the following Officers were holding a conference:-

    Capt.G.H.E.Warburton. .C. Adjutant
    2nd Lieut.G.C.Gibb. Int. Officer.
    Lieut.D.H.P. .C. C. Commander.
    2nd Lieut.C.F.Fraser C. Officer.
    2nd Lieut. Harrison. Lewis Gun Officer.

Capt.G.H.E.Warburton .C. and 2nd Lieut.G.C.Gibb made a desperate effort to fight their way out and I regret to say were both killed. As the other Officers have not been seen since I presume they have been captured. The death of Capt.G.H.E.Warburton .C. is particularly regretted as he had just handed over Command to Major.J.H.E.Payne prior to coming down for a rest when he went forward to B Coy Hqrs.

The remnants of B Coy were relieved at the night of 18/1..

(3)

and marched back to BOSCHEPE.

Total casualties during operations:-

20 Officers and 469 O.Rks

I will forward in due course names of certain Officers, N.C.Os and men whom I wish to bring to the notice of G.O.C for gallantry and good work during the operations.

S E Morse Lieut-Colonel
Commanding 4th Bn "The King's".

21/4/13.

SECRET.   Copy No.

98th INF. BDE. ORDER No. 218.

Ref. Map. LENS, 1/100,000.   10th April, 1918.

1. Reference Brigade Warning Order No. B.M. 702/3 dated April 10th, 33rd Division is transferred from 1st Army to 2nd Army and will move personnel by train on night April 10/11th.

2. 98th Inf. Bde. entrain at TINQUES. First train leaves at 10.40 p.m. April 10th (Route via. PENIN).

3. Units will move as follows :-

    (a) 4th King's rear to be clear of AMBRINES by 8.30 p.m.

    (b) 1st Midd'x Regt's rear to be clear of AMBRINES by 8.45 p.m.

    (c) 2nd A. & S. H. to be clear of AMBRINES by 9.30 p.m.

    (d) 212th Field Coy., 99th Field Ambulance, Bde. Headquarters and Signals, 98th Bde. Pioneer Coy., 98th T. M. Battery to be clear of AMBRINES by 10.30 p.m.

4. First Line transport will accompany Units. Orders for move of Second Line Transport by road will be issued later.

5. Blanket Lorries will be sent to TINQUES Station and blankets loaded on the train with the Unit.

6. Completion of moves will be reported to Bde. Major or representative at CAESTRE Station.

7. Divisional Report Centre will be at Town Major's office, CAESTRE, at 3.0 a.m., April 11th.

8. ACKNOWLEDGE.

                                                        Captain,
                                                    Brigade Major,
                                                98th Infantry Brigade.

Issued to all Units Bde. Group

at 8.10 p.m.

98" Bn

The following is a brief report of a RAID carried out by the enemy on the front held by the Bn under my Command at 4.30.a.m.

"The enemy opened a heavy Field Gun Barrage on front line posts and a heavy bombardment with 5.9s and 4.2s on CREST FARM and vicinity.

At 4.50.a.m. his barrage lifted off the front line posts and the enemy rushed on a frontage from No 8 post Right front Coy, to No 4 post left front Coy.

Hand-to-hand fighting took place with the nett result that a number of the enemy were killed (exact number not yet definitely known) two unwounded and two wounded prisoners were taken. So far as I can ascertain, my casualties are two killed and four wounded.

There is some doubt as to one man who may be "missing", but this cannot be confirmed until I can get out to his post tonight.

2nd Lieut. E. Capstick - who was on duty on the left front Coy - reports the enemy rushed his No 3a post, and a hand-to-hand encounter took place.

The enemy were armed with clubs, bombs and pistols, and did not carry rifles and bayonets. The strength of the party appeared to be about 30.

No Regimental Numbers or badges were being worn.

Just after 5.0.a.m. the enemy put down a Field Gun barrage along the posts, which appeared to co-incide with the withdrawal of the survivors

2nd Lieut. A.O.Ward.M.C., commanding right Coy reports that at 4.25.a.m. his reconnoitreing patrol which was working in "NO MAN'S LAND" in front of his right Coy sent in a message to say that there was something suspicious going on in front. 2nd Lieut.A.O. Ward.M.C. immediately ordered his posts to "STAND TO" and was quite ready for the enemy when he arrived. Only two men approached his No 8 post, one of whom was shot dead - the other got away.

ARTILLERY.

The S.O.S. Signal was not fired by the Coys on my front, but the barrage put down in response to the S.O.S. Signal sent up by the Bn on my left was prompt and very effective.

The 18 pdrs bursting about 50 yds in front of the posts- the 4.5s in front (about the GASOMETERS). After about 20 minutes firing the 18 pdr barrage commenced to fall short and some shells fell in line with, and in rear of my posts. Except for this the Artillery co-operation was in every way excellent.

SIGNALS.   first
The whole of the telephone lines were cut in the five minutes of the enemy barrage and the P.B. at PASSCHENDAELE was put out of order owing to his Base wires being cut. The P.B. message sent reporting the raid took considerably over an hour to reach Bn Hdrs from CREST FARM.

My Adjutant, observing from HAMBURG, states that during the whole time of the raid and enemy searchlight with a perpendicular beam was showing in the direction of MOORSLEDE. This went out just after 5.0.a.m. It is suggested that this searchlight beam was used as a signal to communicate with the raiding party.

Immediately it gets dark tonight strong patrols will be sent out to collect the bodies of the enemy killed. Any further information will be at once forwarded.

I personally was on the point of visiting my advanced posts when the raid started and took shelter from the bombardment at CREST FARM.

This position is evidently known to the enemy as the shelling was very accurate indeed

4 Liverpool Regt
4 Kings R.
Vol 31

Army Form C. 2118

WAR DIARY
or
INTELLIGENCE SUMMARY
(Erase heading not required.)

Instructions regarding War Diaries and Intelligence Summaries are contained in F.S. Regs., Part II. and the Staff Manual respectively. Title Pages will be prepared in manuscript.

Place	Date	Hour	Summary of Events and Information	Remarks and references to Appendices
HONDEGHEM	1.5.18	8.15	Bn: moves to BLARINGHEM where it is billeted. Arrivals - Lt: A.H. HOWARD - Second Lts: J.B. DOWLER - W. HESLOP - E.C. HYDE - D. KERR - A.R.B. LITTLAR - A.E. LACEY - W.D. MILLER - G.D. MELVIN - 5 other ranks. Weather - Fine.	
BLARINGHEM	2.5.18	12	G.O.C. 33 Div. inspects the Bn: and congratulates the Bn: and congratulates the following officers for good work performed at METEREN: Captain F.C. AGER - Lt: H.R. ANDERSON Captain R.D. MACKINNON, (R.A.M.C.) - and 18 other ranks.	
		17.50	Bn: embussed at EBLINGHEM and debussed at ABEELE, thence proceeded by route march to 27.L.20.a. (Bn: Hqrs: at 27.L.20.a.9.9.) Weather - Fine.	"A"
BUSSEBOOM	3.5.18		Bn: moves to BUSSEBOOM. (Bn: Hqrs: at LINDE REED FM:) Minimum Reserve moves to ABEELE area	"A"
DICKEBUSCH	4.5.18 to 6.5.18		Vide separate report attached and marked "A"	"A"

Army Form C. 2118

WAR DIARY
or
INTELLIGENCE SUMMARY
(Erase heading not required.)

Instructions regarding War Diaries and Intelligence Summaries are contained in F.S. Regs., Part II. and the Staff Manual respectively. Title Pages will be prepared in manuscript.

Place	Date	Hour	Summary of Events and Information	Remarks and references to Appendices
L.7.d.S.1.	12.5.18		Bn. in camp at 27.b.7.d.5.1. Weather - fine.	H.Q./4/1
" "	13.5.18	12	C.O. attends Brigade conference. Continued increase in number of LEWIS GUNS until each battalion has 32. Prepared to equip Aeroplanes with 2 LIGHT SIGNALS. (i) A tank bursting into a number of yellow smoke balls as a call for FLARES. (ii) A tank bursting into a number of Red smoke balls as an S.O.S. signal, denoting that the hostile infantry is forcing the tanks to the attack. (extract from O.B./1806/13/11 of May '18) Weather - Rain.	H.Q./4/1
"	14.5.18		Platoon training. New P.H. Hood Keeps to front lines after drawing tank battle "Retreat" 6/1/11 Arrivals — Lt. R.G. HAWKSLEY — 2T/S. W.J. WILSON — A.S. WATSON — R.H. WHITROD — W.H. NASON — Mr. T.H. BARNETT admitted to hospital. Weather - Fine.	H.Q./4/1
"	15.5.18	9	C.O.'s parade — Company training. B.'s under Capt. Gen F.C. AGER march to musketry camp at ROEBROUCK. Weather - Fine.	H.Q./4/1

WAR DIARY or INTELLIGENCE SUMMARY

Army Form C. 2118

Place	Date	Hour	Summary of Events and Information	Remarks and references to Appendices
27.L.d.5.1	16.6.18	9	C.O's parade. Coy Training & Special training for men likely to become N.C.O's under Captain TEMPLAR., R.F. two attached from Corps Schools. Football match – King's v. B3 M.G. Bn.; Result: 1-1. Weather – Fine.	
"	17.5.18		Coy training – A.C.D. Coy; test box respirators in gas tent. Specialist classes continued. Weather – Fine.	
Dirty Bucket Camp (28.A.30.d.1.9.)	18.5.18	5.30	Bn: marched to DIRTY BUCKET CAMP (28.A.30.d.1.9.) B.coy under Captain F. AGER rejoin Bn. from ROEBROUCK. Arrivals: Lt. T. ROTHWELL; Lt. J. WHYTE. Weather – Fine.	
"	19.5.18	10	Church parade in Church Army Hut. Sermon by Chaplain, Revd. STALEY – Band plays at service. Weather – Fine.	
"	20.5.18	9	C.O's parade – Coy training.	
		14	Presentation by C.O. of No.36 Parade, all officers & N.C.O's attend. Wire the Army Commander, Sir H.C.O PLUMER, G.C.B; G.C.M.G.; G.C.V.O. presents the military medals to 13 N.C.O's + men of the Bn. for good work in action near METEREN. Weather – Fine.	

WAR DIARY
or
INTELLIGENCE SUMMARY

(Erase heading not required.)

Army Form C. 2118

Place	Date	Hour	Summary of Events and Information	Remarks and references to Appendices
Dirty Bucket CAMP	21.5.18	9	C.O's parade. C. training. GREEN LINE (VLAMERTINGHE) and YELLOW LINE (BRANDHOEK) reconnoitred. Weather Fine.	HW/pw
"	22.5.18	9	C.O's parade	
		13.30	Inspection of 98. BDE: by ARMY COMDR: Gen: Sir H.C.O. PLUMER. G.C.B; G.C.M.G; G.C.V.O. Weather - Fine.	S.C. 0.3/4757/3 of 21.6.15 and Plan. HW/pw
"	23.5.18		Pon: leave C. on parade working party for trenches GREEN & VLAMERTINGHE lines. C. on under Major STOPFORD - TAYLOR march to ROUBROUCK for musketry Course. Weather - Fine.	HW/pw
"	24.5.18		Pon: leaves C co: on "working party". BLUE & EAST-POPERINGHE Line. Weather - Rain.	HW/pw
"	25.5.18	9.30	Bn: Scheme. C co: returned from ROUBROUCK by busses. Weather - Fine.	HW/pw
"	26.5.18	9.30	Brigade C of E. parades. Bishop of Khartoum preached. Weather - Fine.	HW/pw

Army Form C. 2118

WAR DIARY
or
INTELLIGENCE SUMMARY
(Erase heading not required.)

Instructions regarding War Diaries and Intelligence Summaries are contained in F. S. Regs., Part II. and the Staff Manual respectively. Title Pages will be prepared in manuscript.

Place	Date	Hour	Summary of Events and Information	Remarks and references to Appendices
DIRTY BUCKET CAMP	27.5.18		Bn: on "working party" BLUE LINE. Dec: battn in the forenoon. Weather - Fine.	
	28.5.18		Bn: on "working party" BLUE LINE; 2Lt: R.W. WHITROD was killed on return journey by shell, eight O.R. wounded. B & C Coys; batto. Regimental concert at 6.0 p.m. on Church Army Hut, very successful. Weather - Fine.	
	29.5.18	5	Brigade Scheme "Advance across close country to counter-attack". Ac: battle. 2Lt: R.W. WHITROD was buried at 2.30 p.m. in GWALIA military cemetery, near POPERINGHE. HONOURS - (M.C.) Captain R.D. MACKINNON R.A.M.C. ; 4/G. H.R. ANDERSON; E. CAPSTICK. Weather - Fine.	Special Idea. Narrative.
	30.5.18	5.15	Bn: marches to new area, Bn: H.qrs: at 27.D.30.d.7.7., BOIS. ST ACAIRE. Weather - Fine.	
BOIS ST ACAIRE	31.5.18		Co: Training - Musketry, L.G.S. + Rustaren practices on ranges. Weather - Fine.	

S.S. Irwine Lt. Col.
Cmdg 4/Kings Regt
31/5/18

"A"

Report on the action taken by the Battalion during the Operations in the vicinity of DICKEBUSCH LAKE and RIDGE WOOD – May 7th to 11th 1918.

On May 2nd the Bn left BLAREINGHAM by motor bus, debussing at ABEELE and marched to BUSSEBOOM AREA and bivouaced. On the 6th the Bn marched to WINGE GOED FARM.

On the night 4/5th Bn moved up to the ISLAND around DICKEBUSCH LAKE in Brigade support – 2nd Argyll & Sutherland Hdrs on the right, 1st Middlesex on the left and 4th Kings in support. On the evening of the 7th the Bn was moved back from the ISLAND to farm house at H.28.A.3.9. At 2.0 am on the 8th the enemy started heavy gas shelling of back areas. Shelling was mixed with H.E and heavy MG. Two direct hits were made on Bn one Hut bursting inside killing one and wounding [...]. The enemy attacked at 4.0 am and succeeded in driving in Amer. Bn who were holding the line on the right of the 2nd Argyll & Sutherland Hdrs, who took up a position forming line facing south of RIDGE WOOD supported by C Coy 4th Kings. A Coy of 4th Kings were in support to 1st Middlesex at SCOTTISH WOOD.

In the evening of the 8th [...] about 10 pm the 5th Scottish Rifles counter attacked on the East side of the Lake, the [...] Division on the West with a counter attack at the Scottish Rifles [...]

2.

"A"

by A. Coy 4th Kings, was completely successful and the line was restored at once. No touch was not obtained with the 1st Cameronians. A. Coy 4th Kings formed defensive flank on the right of the Scottish Rifles facing south. Later in during the evening the 2nd Queens Regt took place of 1st Cameronians, a large gap being left on the left of the Queens and the right of the Scottish Rifles - A Coy taking position in this gap and remaining there until relieved by the French in the night 11/12 th. The Brigade was relieved by 2nd Bn 60th French Regiment and marched back to camp at BUSSEBOOM. At 2.0 pm the Bn resumed march back to Area West of POPERINGHE.

Total casualties :-
1 Officer wounded.   7. O.Rs Killed.
33 O.Rs   "   " -

S.E. Norris Lieut-Col.
Commanding 4th Bn "The Kings"

4th. Bn. "The King's".
1st. Middlesex Regt.
2nd. Arg. & Suth'd. Hrs.
98th. T. M. Battery.
98th. Bde. Signal Section.
2 Coys., M. G. Battalion.
----

1. General Sir H.C.O.PLUMER, G.C.B., G.C.M.B., G.C.V.O., will inspect the Brigade and C and D Coys., M. G. Battalion on 22nd. inst. on ground 28/A.30.a.8.8. at 1.30 p.m.

2. Brigadier General J.D.H.MAITLAND, C.M.G., D.S.O., will command the parade and will give the General Salute on the arrival of the Army Commander.

3. The Brigade will be drawn up in Mass with 3 paces between ranks of platoons, in the form of a hollow square as per attached sketch.

4. Dress - Rifle, belt and sidearms, service head-dress, and with box respirator slung over the right shoulder.

5. Officers will be mounted in accordance with War Establishments.

6. Transport vehicles will not be on parade. All available transport personnel will parade dismounted.

7. Adjutants of Battalions and 1 officer per Company, M. G. Battalion and 1 officer T. M. Battery will report to the Staff Captain on the parade ground at 12.45 p.m., also one marker per Unit.

8. Units will be in position on the parade ground by 1.15 p.m.

9. The Brigade will move past the Army Commander in Column of Route, giving "Eyes Right" by platoons in the case of Battalions, and by the Officer Commanding in the case of other Units.

10. Bands will be drawn up as per sketch, and will play their own Units up to the Saluting Base where they will wheel clear of their Unit and play it past. They will stop immediately the tail of their own Unit has passed.

11. Units will not move from the parade ground until the band of the preceeding Unit has stopped playing.

12. No sticks will be carried on parade and gloves will be worn by mounted officers only.

13. The Band of the 1st. Middlesex Regt. will play during the General Salute.

14. While a Unit is being inspected, its own Band will play.

Captain,
Staff Captain,
98th Infantry Brigade.

Pipe Band

2nd A&SH

Drums

MIDD'X

T.M.D

'C' Coy
M.G. Bn

'D' Coy
M.G. Bn

15"

15"

15"

40"

30"

45"

10"

2nd KING'S

Drums

Saluting Base

R O A D

Units will march past as per dotted line

Ref. Map.
Sheet 28.

BRIGADE EXERCISE.

To exemplify - An advance across country and a
Counter-attack.

SPECIAL IDEA.

1.   After a successful attack at dawn on the front of the YSER
CANAL, the enemy advanced and attacked, at 7 a.m. the same day,
the VLAMERTINGHE - ELVERDINGHE line and succeeded in capturing
the Front and Support trenches from the railway running through
B.26.a. and b. to ELVERLINCHE (inclusive).

2.   X Infantry Brigade   formed a defensive flank from about
B.26.b.4.8. to the Support line at B.26.a.central.
    Elements of Y Infantry Brigade are reported to be holding
HOSPITAL FARM, KAIER FARM, road at B.19.b.5.6., and a party of
our troops about 50 strong is also reported at B.13.d.5.0.
    The Army on our left continue the above general line in a
northerly direction.
    X Infantry Brigade successfully repulsed the attack on their
front and are reported to be full of fight.

3.   Five German Divisions have been identified in the attack from
YPRES (exclusive) to C.7. It is believed that there are no
Divisions in reserve.

4.   The Front line of the VLAMERTINGHE line in possession of the
enemy, is reported to be, to a great extent, destroyed.

NARRATIVE.

Reference Sheet 27 N.W. 1/20,000.

1. The 98th Infantry Brigade (a Company 33rd Battalion, Machine Gun Corps attached) in a position of readiness in Square A.20., received orders at 1. 0 p.m. to counter-attack the enemy and re-capture the Front and Support lines of the VLAMERTINGHE line from B.26.b.4.8 to B.20.a.7.8.

   No attempt was to be made to re-capture the trench running through B.20.b, - East of ELVERDINGHE.

   The Army on the left to co-operate and re-capture the trench running along the Western edge of ELVERDINGHE WOOD.

2. The leading troops of both armies will cross the BRANDHOEK line at 7. 30 p.m.

3. At 7.40 p.m. a creeping barrage will be put down on the line B.26.a.2.9. - 200 yards East of KARTE FARM - B.20.a.1.9. and will remain on this line until 8.0 p.m., and will then lift on to the Support Trench of the VLAMERTINGHE line, remaining there for three minutes, after which the barrage will lift at the rate of 100 yards every three minutes, halting on a protective barrage line 300 yards East of the final objective. 4.5 Hows. will fire on the VLAMERTINGHE front line until 8.0 p.m.

4. The Brigade has ordered -

   (i) The 2nd A. & S. Highlanders to attack on the right with final objective B.26.b.4.8. to B.20.d.0.8. Left Boundary in BRANDHOEK line B.19.c.1.5. Leave A.20. at 5.30 p.m. moving S. of the line A.22.central - B.19.c.1.5.

   (ii) The 1st Middlesex Regt. to attack on the left with final objective B.20.d.0.8. to B.20.a.7.8. Right Boundary in BRANDHOEK line B.19.c.1.5. leave A.20. at 5.30 p.m. moving N. of the line A.22.central - B.19.c.1.5.

   (iii) The 4th King's Regt. will be in reserve and will reach the BRANDHOEK Support line at 7. 50 p.m. O.C. this Battalion to keep in close touch with Officers Commanding the two leading Battalions and to support their attack, if necessary, with two Companies: remaining two Companies to be in Brigade Reserve and to hold the BRANDHOEK line from railway in B.25.a to Northern Corps Boundary.

   (iv) Headquarters for all three Battalions to be established in the BRANDHOEK line.

   (v) Brigade Report Centre will be at A.24.a.3.4.

   (vi) "A" Company, 33rd Battalion, Machine Gun Corps to co-operate with overhead fire and to establish their guns in depth as soon as the final objective has been reported captured.

   (vii) Two Stokes Mortars and necessary personnel will accompany the attacking Battalions, the remaining guns 98th T. M. Battery remaining with reserve Battalion.

   (viii) Flares will be lit on reaching objective when called for by aeroplane (imaginary).

   (ix) Communication by visual to be at once established between Battalions and Brigade, when objective is reported as taken.

WAR DIARY
or
INTELLIGENCE SUMMARY
(Erase heading not required.)

Army Form C. 2118

4 Liverpool Regt

Place	Date	Hour	Summary of Events and Information	Remarks and references to Appendices
BOIS ST ACAIRE	1.6.18		Co. training. - C.O. attends demonstration in "TOPHAM" Signalling Aerodromes, 40th Squadron R.A.F. Arrivals - Revd P. WIGRAM C.F. and 97 other ranks. Weather - Fine.	
"	2.6.18	9.30	Church Parade Service. Arrivals - 30 O.R. Weather - Fine.	
EAST POPERINGHE (28.G.2.d.77.)	3.6.18	4	Bn: marches to EAST POPERINGHE in relief of 1st CAMERONIANS. MINIMUM Reserve under Captain E.G. MATHER moves to camp (27.L.8.B.1.5) Departures. Revd J.E. STALEY on completion of tour of duty. Capt & Quartermaster A.R. JONES (sick.) Weather - Fine.	
"	4.6.18	5	Bn: on working party. E. POPERINGHE, Support Line. Weather - Fine.	
"	5.6.18	5	Bn: on working party. E. POPERINGHE, Support Line.	
		12	Bn: visit Baths at HOUPOUTRE. Weather - Fine.	

Army Form C. 2118

WAR DIARY
or
INTELLIGENCE SUMMARY
(Erase heading not required.)

Instructions regarding War Diaries and Intelligence Summaries are contained in F. S. Regs., Part II. and the Staff Manual respectively. Title Pages will be prepared in manuscript.

Place	Date	Hour	Summary of Events and Information	Remarks and references to Appendices
EAST POPERINGHE	6.6.18		Bn: relieves 2. D.L.I. in Reserve (BROWN LINE) - Weather - Fine -	
"	7.6.18		Bn: in Bde: reserves. Weather, Fine -	
"	8.6.18		Co: Commanders reconnoitre front line - Arrivals - 8 O.R. - Weather - Fine -	
"	9.6.18		Bn: finds working parties for work on BROWN Line - Arrivals - 3 O.R. - Weather - Fine -	
"	10.6.18		Bn: relieves 9 H.L.I. in front line - Capt: Quartermaster A.R. JONES reporting sick from Field Amb: Weather - Fine -	
FRONT LINE Right Sub-Section	11.6.18		Bn: in front line. Capt: E.G. MATHER posted to 6. Wiltshires Reg.t - Weather. Showers at intervals.	
CANAL SECTOR	12.6.18		Bn: in front line - Commanding officer to Bethelen; MAJ. J.H.L. BROWNE G front line - Weather - Fine -	

1875 Wt. W593/826 1,000,000 4/15 J.B.C. & A. A.D.S.S./Forms/C. 2118.

Army Form C. 2118

WAR DIARY
or
INTELLIGENCE SUMMARY

(Erase heading not required.)

Instructions regarding War Diaries and Intelligence Summaries are contained in F. S. Regs., Part II. and the Staff Manual respectively. Title Pages will be prepared in manuscript.

Place	Date	Hour	Summary of Events and Information	Remarks and references to Appendices
FRONT LINE	13.6.18	3.51	Bn. in Front Lines. French on our immediate right attack RIDGE WOOD. Objectives taken.	H.D./nol
Right Sub-Sector CANAL SECTOR		9.30	Strong German counter-attack forces French back to original lines. Bn Front Line companies slightly affected by German arty & retaliation. 2/Lt H.R. ANDERSON & 4 O.R. wounded. Lt. ANDERSON remains at duty. Weather. Fine.	H.D./nol
"	14.6.18		Bn. in front lines. Quiet day. Arrivals. Captain E. ASHTON, 2/Lt. J. BULLOCK. Weather. Fine.	H.D./nol
"	15.6.18		Bn. in front lines in relieved by 2. A. & S. Highrs; . Weather. Fine.	H.D./nol
SUPPORT LINE DICKEBUSCH CANAL	16.6.18 & 17.6.18		Bn. in support. Weather. Fine.	H.D./nol

Army Form C. 2118

WAR DIARY
or
INTELLIGENCE SUMMARY
(Erase heading not required.)

Instructions regarding War Diaries and Intelligence Summaries are contained in F.S. Regs., Part II. and the Staff Manual respectively. Title Pages will be prepared in manuscript.

Place	Date	Hour	Summary of Events and Information	Remarks and references to Appendices
Support Lines	18.6.16		Bn: in Support.	
DICKEBUSCH CANAL			Departures - Lt: H.R.ANDERSON to GRANTHAM for M.G. course. Weather - Fine.	
"	19.6.16		Bn: in Support. Weather - Rain.	
"	20.6.16		Bn: in Support is relieved by 1. QUEENS. Bn: moves to BRANDHOEK in Reserve. Weather. Rain.	
BRANDHOEK	21.6.16		Commanding Officer opens joins Bn:; Major J.H.L. BROWNE to C. echelon. Accompanied by Adjt: (Capt: H.B. TRIPP). Weather. Fine.	

Army Form C. 2118

WAR DIARY
or
INTELLIGENCE SUMMARY
(Erase heading not required.)

Instructions regarding War Diaries and Intelligence Summaries are contained in F. S. Regs., Part II. and the Staff Manual respectively. Title Pages will be prepared in manuscript.

Place	Date	Hour	Summary of Events and Information	Remarks and references to Appendices
BRANDHOEK	22/6/18		Bn: in support. Officers reconnoitre new sector front line. Weather - Fine	
"	23.6.18		Bn: in support. Officers reconnoitre front line. Weather - Fine	
"	24.6.18		do.	
"	25.6.18		Bn: relieves 9. H&I. in front line. Weather - Fine.	
Front line	26.6.18		Bn: in front line - Situation normal - Weather - Fine.	
Left Sector Sector	27.6.18		Bn: in front line - Fighting patrol under Lt: WILSON cooperates with raid of Divisors on own left front - Capt: H.B. TRIPP (Adjutant) to C.C.S. (sick). Weather - Fine.	
"	28.6.18		Bn: in front line. Weather - Fine.	
"	29.6.18		Bn: in front line - One prisoner 330 Regt captured by patrol under Cpl: HIGHTON Weather - Fine.	

E. Chandler
Captain, 4/ [illegible]

4th Rifle Brigade

Army Form C. 2118.

WAR DIARY
or
INTELLIGENCE SUMMARY.
(Erase heading not required.)

Vol 33

Place	Date	Hour	Summary of Events and Information	Remarks and references to Appendices
	July 1		Weather fine. Battalion in line.	
			Relieved at night by 1.L.I.	
			1 Officer & 20 O.R. to 2nd Army Rest camp.	
			21 O.R.s from Divisional Reception Camp.	
	2		Batt. in line	
			Weather fine	
			2nd Lt. M.J. Wilson to Summer Reserve (sick)	
	3		Weather fine. Batt. in line	
			Lt. R.B. Miller 2.9.10's from course of Instruction	
			2 O.R.s to leave U.K.	
			2 O.R.s to Course of Instruction	
	4		Weather fine. Batt. in line	39 p
			Casualty: Rifmn A.R. Jones to Hospital	
			2nd Lt. W.R. Fowler to U.K. 4-7-18.	
	5		Weather fine. Batt. in line	
	6		Weather fine. Batt. in line. Batt. relieved that 1st Queen's Royal W. Surrey Rgt.	
			& proceeded to KNAPS FARM Brigade in Divisional	
			Reserve. 2 O.R's to Signal course.	

WAR DIARY or INTELLIGENCE SUMMARY.

Army Form C. 2118.

Place	Date	Hour	Summary of Events and Information	Remarks and references to Appendices
	7		Weather fine. Batt @ Knolly Farm. Holy Communion @ 9.30 AM. Working parties worked by 3 Coys. Bolia & Edwards M.C. 2nd Lt. G. Wigio offe since to PARIS. C.S.M. Cooke 60th as candidate for permanent Commission.	
	8.		Weather fine. Batt @ Knolly Farm. 4 O.R.'s to Lewis Gun Course. 2nd Lt. R.G. Nicholls rejoined from Sick Leave. 2nd Lt. W.R. Leckie & 5 O.R's from course of Instruction. Capt. H.P. Jacob M.C. to U.K. on War Office authority. Working parties Smoided by 3 Coys.	
	9.		Weather showery. Batt @ Knolly's Farm. 3 Coys working party. 1 OR leave to U.K. 1 O.R. P13T Course. Major J.R. Brown reverted SUPPORT POSITION (CANAL SECTOR)	
	10		Weather fine. Batt @ Knolly's Farm. Minimum Reserve was relieved by an equal number from the Battn. 2 O.R.'s went on leave Jean Divisional Reception Camp.	
	11.		Weather wet. Batt in billets Canal sector. Relieved 16th K.R.R.C.	

WAR DIARY
or
INTELLIGENCE SUMMARY.

(Erase heading not required.)

Army Form C. 2118.

Place	Date	Hour	Summary of Events and Information	Remarks and references to Appendices
	11.		25 O.R's to Battn. in line. 1 Officer & 30 R's to L.G. & A.A. Course. 3 O.R.s from 2nd Army Rest Camp and School.	
	12.		Weather fine. Rail in Support. 1 O.R. leave to U.K. (wounded)	
	13.		Weather showery. Rail in Support. 1 O.R. to 2nd army School. 1 O.R. from 2nd army Central School.	
	14.		Weather fine. Rail in Support. 1 O.R. killed in action. 3 O.R.s wounded in action. 1 O.R. to Gas Course. 1 O.R. from Course.	
	15.		Weather wet. Rail in Support. Cadre O.R. officer returned from leave to U.K. 1 O.R. wounded in action. 3 O.R's to army Rest Camp. 1 Officer & 15 O.R's from 2nd army Rest Camp.	
	16.		Weather fine. Rail in Support. 10 O.R.'s reinforcement from Base Depot. 8 O.R.s wounded in action. 1 O.R. leave to U.K.	
	17.		Weather showery. Rail in Support. 5-7 O.R's reinforcement from Divisional Reception Camp. 4 O.R's to Divisional Signal School. 1 O.R. to 2nd Army School of Gunnery. 1 O.R. leave to U.K. 5 O.R's to P.A.R.I.C. (Leave)	

Army Form C. 2118.

WAR DIARY
or
INTELLIGENCE SUMMARY.
(Erase heading not required.)

Instructions regarding War Diaries and Intelligence Summaries are contained in F. S. Regs., Part II. and the Staff Manual respectively. Title pages will be prepared in manuscript.

Place	Date	Hour	Summary of Events and Information	Remarks and references to Appendices
	18.		Weather fine. Review suffern. 1 OR to leave U.K.	
	19.		Weather fine. Review suffern. 9 OR's from leave of Rubicalin. Rain in afterm. 1 NCO & 12 OR's minimum Reserve working party HAPOUTRE	
	20.		Weather wet. Rain in aftern. Cpl: A.P. Edwards MC 2nd Lt. J.R. ?	
			Wayetaffe rejoined from Paris leave.	
	21.		Weather fine. Rail: @ KNOLLYS FARM. 2nd Lt: J. Waystaffe to M.G. Centre Grantham. Lieut: Matthews to U.K. candidate for temporary commission. 1 OR to U.K. leave. 2 OR's from L.G. School LE TOUQUET. Minimum Reserve Party changed over.	
	22.		Weather fine. Rail: @ KNOLLYS FARM. 4 OR's wounded. Working parties provided by 3 Coys. 3 OR's to L.G. course 2nd Army school 1 OR to L.G. course LE TOUQUET. AMB Coys deathed. 2nd Lts: H.G. Nicholls to anti-Gas school.	
	23.		Weather wet. Rail: @ KNOLLYS FARM. 1 Officer 3 OR's AA course ? c 2D coota noted.	
	24.		Weather showery. Rail: @ KNOLLYS FARM. 2 OR's 2nd looph ?	

WAR DIARY
or
INTELLIGENCE SUMMARY

Army Form C. 2118.

Place	Date	Hour	Summary of Events and Information	Remarks and references to Appendices
	24.		2 m/os leave to U.K. Lieuts C. Dixon, L.D. Walker M.C. & M.C.J.	
			M. Parkinson joined the Bn. from Divisional Reinforcements	
	25.		Weather showery. Bn @ KNOTTY'S FARM. Moved into Huts in	
			left Divisional Sector 25th/26th inst. 2 Coys H/o A.I. Regt attached	
	26.		Weather wet. Bn. in line. 1 officer & 20 O.R.s to Lewis Signal	
			Course	
	27.		Weather wet. Bn. in line. 1 O.R. to leave U.K.	
LEFT Bn:	28		Bn: in line. Training of 1/120. Regt American Infantry continues.	
LEFT Bde: SECTOR			Casualties. 1 O.R. — Weather — Showery —	
	29		Bn: in line. Training of 1/120. A.I.R. continues.	
"			Casualties. Capt: N.S. MILLICAN, O.C. "C" Coy: wounded. Weather - Fine.	
"	30		Bn: in line. Training of 1/120. A.I.R. continues.	
			Arrivals:- Lts: W.H. & O. LUCAS. P.H. PARKER. 2/Lt J. THOMPSON.	
			Lt. A.h. W. COLLINS. Weather — Fine —	

98 Inf. Bde:
Training of American
Troops. No. 5.

Army Form C. 2118.

WAR DIARY
or
INTELLIGENCE SUMMARY.
(Erase heading not required.)

Instructions regarding War Diaries and Intelligence Summaries are contained in F. S. Regs., Part II. and the Staff Manual respectively. Title pages will be prepared in manuscript.

Place	Date	Hour	Summary of Events and Information	Remarks and references to Appendices
Left Pon: Left Bde: Sector	31/8/18		Position Line. Training of 1/20 A.I.R. continues. Weather fine.	Au/ (Inf).

Signed in Command 2/9/18

4th King's (Liverpool) Regt.

Army Form C. 2118.

WAR DIARY
INTELLIGENCE SUMMARY.
(Erase heading not required.)

Place	Date	Hour	Summary of Events and Information	Remarks and references to Appendices
Left Bn.	1.8.18		Bn. in line. Weather Fine	H.Q.
Left Sub-Sector	2.8.18		— do — Weather - Showery	H.Q.
"CANAL" SECTOR	3.8.18		— do — 1 Officer and 2 O.R. carry out raid on BLAUWE POORT FARM	Appx I / H.Q.
	4.8.18		Weather Rain.	
	4.8.18		Bn. relieved by 1 QUEEN'S Regt. 2. Army Memorial Service at TERDEGHEM. Weather - Fine.	H.Q.
KNOLLYS FM	5.8.18		Bn. in Div. Reserve. Weather - Fine.	H.Q.
GREEN LINE	6.8.18		— do — C.O., one officer and 16 O.R. proceed to LA LOVIE CHATEAU for inspection by His Majesty THE KING. Weather Fine.	H.Q.
"	7.8.18		Bn. in Div. Reserve. Weather Fine.	H.Q.
"	8.8.18		— do —	H.Q.
"	9.8.18		Bn. relieved 9 H.L.I. in Right subsects CANAL SECTOR. Weather - Fine	H.Q.
Left Bn.	10.8.18		Bn. in the line. Weather - Fine	H.Q. Appx II
Right Sub-Sector	11.8.18		— do — Special Parade Service at TERDEGHEM. Weather - Fine	H.Q.
"CANAL SECTOR"	12.8.18		— do — Weather - Fine	H.Q.

Army Form C. 2118.

WAR DIARY
or
INTELLIGENCE SUMMARY.
(Erase heading not required.)

Instructions regarding War Diaries and Intelligence Summaries are contained in F. S. Regs., Part II. and the Staff Manual respectively. Title pages will be prepared in manuscript.

Place	Date	Hour	Summary of Events and Information	Remarks and references to Appendices
Left Bau: Right Sub-Sector "CANAL" SECTOR	13.8.18		Bn. in line. Weather Fine.	
	14.8.18		— do — — do —	
	15.8.18		— do — — do —	
	16.8.18		Bn. relieved by 2/1/9 G.L.R. on relief Bn. moved by rail to REMY SIDING thence by road to ROAD CAMP. ST JAN TER BIEZEN. Weather Fine	
ST JAN-TER-BIEZEN	17.8.18		Bn. at ROAD CAMP. Weather Fine.	
"	18.8.18		Bn. at ROAD CAMP. Arrivals: Lt.Col. E.M. BEALL; A.M.G.; D.S.O. and assumed command of 4. THE KING'S Regt. Departures: Lt.Col. S.E. NORRIS D.S.O. Weather Fine.	
"	19.8.18		Bn. at ROAD CAMP. Bn. Transport proceeded to hut area at MENTQUE by road. Weather Fine.	
"	20.8.18	13.30	Bn. entrained at PROVEN for WATTEN thence by route march to MENTQUE. Weather Fine	
MENTQUE	21.8.18		Bn. in Billets at MENTQUE. Weather Fine.	
"	22.8.18		Lecture by C.O. to all Officers, W.O.s and N.C.O.s. Weather Fine	

Army Form C. 2118.

WAR DIARY
or
INTELLIGENCE SUMMARY.
(Erase heading not required.)

Instructions regarding War Diaries and Intelligence Summaries are contained in F. S. Regs., Part II. and the Staff Manual respectively. Title pages will be prepared in manuscript.

Place	Date	Hour	Summary of Events and Information	Remarks and references to Appendices
MENTQUE	23.8.18		Platoon and Section training — Platoon demonstration by "Training Staff" at NORTLEULINGHEM all officers attended. Arrivals :- Captain A.R. NICHOLS. Lt. W.A. BARTON. 2 Lt. H. CRYAN. F.P. ARTHUR. Weather Fine.	HK/1404
"	24.8.18	9.30	G.O.C. 33 Division presents medal ribands at a ceremonial parade at NORTLEULINGHEM. Re-ord Sec. training — Recreational training in afternoon Weather Fine + Showery.	HK/1404
"	25.8.18		Church parades. Weather Fine. 2 Lt J. THOMSON M.C. leaves U.K. 2 Lt W. AMASON, 2/Lt W.C. MARSHALL and 2.O.to attend Corps School of Instruction.	HK/SN
"	26.8.18		Company training — Recreational training in the afternoon. Weather Fine.	HK/SN
"	27.8.18		Company training — preparation for move to new area — 2 Lt A.S. WATSON to U.K. for transfer to R.A.F. Weather showery.	HK/SN
MENTQUE	28.8.18		Bn. move from MENTQUE to GROUCHES. Entrained St OMER 6.0 A.M. GROUCHES detrained DOULLENS 4 PM marched to GROUCHES arriving in billets 6.30 PM weather wet.	HK/SN
GROUCHES	29.8.18		General cleaning up — weather fine.	HK/SN

Army Form C. 2118.

WAR DIARY
or
INTELLIGENCE SUMMARY.
(Erase heading not required.)

Instructions regarding War Diaries and Intelligence Summaries are contained in F. S. Regs., Part II. and the Staff Manual respectively. Title pages will be prepared in manuscript.

Place	Date	Hour	Summary of Events and Information	Remarks and references to Appendices
GROUCHES	30.8.18		Company training - Lieut. A.P.Dixon and one O.R. to course of instruction. Weather fine	B.Gall
GROUCHES	31.8.18		Battalion training - new formations - Bn bathes in afternoon - weather showery.	B.Gall

Rudsdell Lt Col
Comndg W. Kings.

17

Army Form C. 2118

WAR DIARY
or
INTELLIGENCE SUMMARY
(Erase heading not required.)

VOLUME XXXXI

SEPTEMBER 1918.

Place	Date	Hour	Summary of Events and Information	Remarks and references to Appendices
GROUCHES.	1/9/18		Fine weather – Church parade – Baths. Sports – 3 O.R. to Base for substitution	
"	2/9/18		Fine weather. – Coys. at field firing – 2Lt. ROTHFIELD. 2Lt. HYDE 2Lt. J.P. WINDLE rejoined Baths – 2.O.R. leave to U.K.	
"	3/9/18		Showery weather. – Coys. at field firing – Lt. R.G. HAWKSLEY and 2Lt. J. BULLOCK rejoined the Bath. – 10 R. leave to U.K.	
"	4/9/18		Fine weather – Bath Scheme with aeroplanes and tanks (dummies).	
"	5/9/18		Fine weather – Commdg. Officer inspects R.S.B. Coys – Coys firing on ranges 2 O.R. leave to U.K.	
"	6/9/18		Fine weather – Bath Scheme. – 2 O.R. leave to U.K.	
"	7/9/18		Wet – Bath scheme – Concert held in evening 1 O.R. leave to U.K.	
"	8/9/18.		Wet – Church services held – Lt. BROUGH rejoined Bath. from hospital – Major HEMERYK joined the Bath.	
"	9/9/18.		Wet – Training and lectures carried on in Bath – 2nd Lt. J.E. SMITH and 1.O.R. rejoined from course – 2nd Lt. F.J. BAUGHEN leave to U.K.	
"	10/9/18		Wet. – Coy training and Range practice carried on. – 2.O.R. leave to U.K.	
"	11/9/18.		Wet – Bath School Closed Coys. went to join Bn. – Coy training carried on. P.S.U.3 Instructors Battn. Coys. Lt. HOOPER Bath. S.O. Officer returned to Coys.	

Army Form C. 2118

WAR DIARY
or
INTELLIGENCE SUMMARY
(Erase heading not required.)

SEPTEMBER 1918. Volume Cont'd.

Instructions regarding War Diaries and Intelligence Summaries are contained in F. S. Regs., Part II. and the Staff Manual respectively. Title Pages will be prepared in manuscript.

Place	Date	Hour	Summary of Events and Information	Remarks and references to Appendices
GROUCHES	12/9/18		Showery weather. – Schemes carried out by A, C, & D Coys. – B Coy carries out Bullet & Bayonet training practices. – R.S.C. Division lecture to C.B. officers, N.C.Os. – 10 O.R. leave to U.K.	M.O.
	13/9/18		Fine weather. – Training in Coy area. – Preparation to move to new area. – 4 O.R. leave.	M.O.
			to U.K. – 33 O.R. rejoined from 212 Field Coy R.E.	M.O.
	14/9/18		Fine weather. – Batt. standing by for move. Advance party to new Coy area carried out.	M.O.
LES BOEUFS	15/9/18		Fine weather. – Batt. entrained for LES BOEUFS at 7.45 p.m. arrived about 3.30 a.m. 16.9.18.	M.O.
	16/9/18		Changeable weather – Batt. arrived LES BOEUFS 3.30 a.m. – 3 O.R. leave to U.K.	M.O.
LES BOEUFS	17/9/18		Fine weather. – Batt. left LES BOEUFS at 6.15 p.m. for LECHELLE by march route arrived	M.O.
		11.15 p.m.	– Minimum Reserve remained at LES BOEUFS. – 2 N.C.Os. to G.H.Q. L.S. School. – 1 O.R. leave to U.K.	M.O.
LECHELLE	18/9/18		Wet. – Batt. left LECHELLE at 5.15 for EQUANCOURT. – B Echelon at LECHELLE – 5 men to Army Rest Camp. Batt. take up position at FINS RIDGE.	M.O.
EQUANCOURT FINS RIDGE	19/9/18		Fine weather. – Batt. started at 8 p.m. for trenches infront of VILLERS GUISLAIN. – Relieved 9th KORLI. – Relief complete 1 a.m. – 2nd Lt. MARSHALL & MASON from Army School. 3 O.R. to leave.	M.O.
TRENCHES NEAR VILLERS GUISLAIN	20/9/18		Fine. – Casualties 5 killed 7 wounded. 6 O.R. leave to U.K.	M.O.
"	21/9/18		Fine – Battn sends forward fighting patrols to assist attack made by 2 a.s. Wks. – Casualties 1 killed 6 wounded 4 missing. – 3 O.R. leave to U.K.	M.O.

WAR DIARY
or
INTELLIGENCE SUMMARY

Army Form C. 2118

VOLUME.
(CONT⁰.)

SEPTEMBER 1918

Place	Date	Hour	Summary of Events and Information	Remarks and references to Appendices
TRENCHES NEAR VILLERS GUISLAIN	22/9/18		Changeable. Some rain. Casualties 3 killed 20 wounded 6 missing - 2nd Lt. H. CRYAN to hospital sick. 1 O.R. leave to U.K.	
"	23/9/18		Rain throughout day. - Casualties 1 killed 3 wounded. - Capt. SPIRING and Lieut. WHYTE rejoined from leave. - 1 man leave to U.K.	
"	24/9/18		Showery. - Casualties 1 killed 7 wounded 4 men leave to U.K.	
"	25/9/18		Fine but cold - Casualties 2 killed 4 wounded - 5 O.R. leave to U.K.	
"	26/9/18		Fine. - Casualties 1 killed 2 wounded - "B" Echelon move to EQUANCOURT. - 2nd Lt. E. CAPSTICK joined Batt. from Base. - 2 O.R. leave to U.K.	
"	27/9/18		Fine day but cold early morning & evening. - Casualties 2 O.R. wounded. - 2 Lt. E.W. BELL joined Batt. from the Base.	
"	28/9/18		Same as yesterday. - Casualties 2 wounded.	
"	29/9/18		Fine - Batt. attacked VILLERS GUISLAIN at 3.30 a.m. in conjunction with 2nd S.Wh. on the Right. Sharp fight put up by enemy - Prisoners taken by Batt. 30 Officers and other ranks. Casualties 2 Lt. S. G.P. HARPER and W.C. MARSHALL and 19 O.R. killed 2 Lt. R.H. PARKER and 55 O.R. wounded & 9 O.R. missing	
"	30/9/18		Fine. - Little act. during the night. - Enemy evacuated VILLERS GUISLAIN - line moved forward in Bde. Frontier in position and became Batt. in Bde. Reserve.	

2nd C. F.H. DAWSON forces Batt. from Base

WAR DIARY or INTELLIGENCE SUMMARY

Army Form C. 2118.

Volume XXXII

1/6 7th King (L'pool) Reg.

Vol. 36

Place	Date	Hour	Summary of Events and Information	Remarks and references to Appendices
VILLERS GUISLAIN	1/10/18		Fine weather - 2/Lt. H. BOARDMAN M.C. to U.K. on leave - reconnoitring parties	
"	2/10/18		sent forward to Canal De L'ESCAUT	
"			Fine weather - Bn in Bde reserve - Lt. D.H.S. REOUGH from leave to U.K.	
"			2/Lt. M. PARKINSON from hospital -	
"	3/10/18		Fine weather. Bn reorganizing. Capt. K.A.F. EDWARDS M.C. to U.K. on leave	
"			- do - - do - 3 O.Rs. to leave. wounded	
"	4/10/18		Bn moved to PIGEON QUARRY. 2 O.Rs & 2 horses killed.	
PIGEON QUARRY 5/10/18			Capt. F.W.S. TYLING to hospital - 2 O.Rs to M.H.Q Lewis gun school - 2 O.Rs	
			to U.K on leave. Lt. W.A. BAYSTON to T.H.Q. 1st Echelon for duty.	
"	4/10/18		Fine weather. 3 O.Rs to leave.	
"	5/10/18		Fine weather. 2/Lt. T.B. WADDLE to U.K on leave. 2 O.Rs to U.K on leave	
"			Reinforcements 76 O.Rs. joined from Base.	
HONNECOURT 6/10/18			Showery weather. Bn. moved to line E. of HONNECOURT in evening.	
			Previous occupiers hardly changed out. Lt. A.P. DIXON and R.S.M. SHUTER rejoined	
			from leave & instruction.	

42 B

Army Form C. 2118.

WAR DIARY
or
INTELLIGENCE SUMMARY.
(Erase heading not required.)

VOLUME XXXII (cont).

Place	Date	Hour	Summary of Events and Information	Remarks and references to Appendices
HONNECOURT CLARY	9/9/18		Fine weather. Bn moved from HONNECOURT to CLARY - took place in line. Enemy line held here slightly.	
CLARY TROISVILLES R.SELLE	10/10/18		Fine weather. Bn moved to R.SELLE - enemy put up strong opposition. Lt NOUGHTON MM wounded in action.	
R.SELLE	11/10/18		Showery weather. Bn in line banks of R.SELLE. RSM GRIFFIN killed in action.	
TROISVILLES	12/10/18		Bn relieved and moved back to CLARY arriving 15.00hrs.	
CLARY	13/10/18		Church parade. Bn at baths.	
"	14/10/18		Fine weather. Bn at baths. Major J.H.R.GOWNE to Whn leave - H.Q.C. to have comd of Bn. Major J.STOPFORD TAYLOR rejoined from leave & took charge. Numerous inspects.	
"	15/10/18		Wet weather. G.O.C. Division inspects Bn - 3. O.Cs & M.O on leave.	
"	16/10/18		Foden delivers to us at Bn - Scheme with Tanks Rifle for Coy Commanders. L. OCs & Nth on leave.	
"	17/10/18		Showery weather. Bn scheme with Tanks.	
"	18/10/18		Lewis gun training.	

Army Form C. 2118.

WAR DIARY
or
INTELLIGENCE SUMMARY. VOLUME XXXII (cont)

(Erase heading not required.)

Instructions regarding War Diaries and Intelligence Summaries are contained in F. S. Regs., Part II. and the Staff Manual respectively. Title pages will be prepared in manuscript.

Place	Date	Hour	Summary of Events and Information	Remarks and references to Appendices
CLARY.	19/9/18		Showery weather. Rfts. Ens. N.C.O. &olrs. R.w. S.R.Bn. L/S Hickney, 2 O.R.s to camp. Major J. STOPFORD TAYNOR to hospital.	
" "	20/9/18		Wet weather. Church parade. Musquit rocket demonstration to all officers and N.C.Os. 2/Lt. F.E. SMITH to U.K. on leave. 2 O.R.s to leave.	
CLARY to CROISILLES	21/9/18		Wet weather. Bn. moved from CLARY to TROISVILLES. Lt-Col. E.W. BEALL CMG DSO to T.N.2 Small Arms school CAMIERS. Capt. K.F. ASHTON, Lt. A.B. CLOTHIAR and 2/Lt. D.H. KEER L.U.K. on leave. 2/Lt. H. BOARDMAN MC from leave to U.K.	
TROISVILLES	22/9/18		Wet weather. C.O. and adjutant reconnoitred front area. Bn. moved to assembly place prior to attack on FOREST. 2/Lt. E.G. HYDE to U.K. on leave.	
MONTAY AREA	23/9/18		1 O.R. from Third Army Rest camp. Fine weather. Bn. attacked and moved thro' FOREST to CROIX. Capt. A.R. NICHOLLS killed. Lt. A.P. DIXON wounded.	
CROIX	24/9/18		Fine weather. Bn. continued in attack towards ENGLEFONTAIN. Lt. J. ROTHFIELD - 2/Lt. F.J. BAUGHEN - 2/Lt. E.W. BEALL - 2/Lt. F.P. ARTHUR wounded in action. 2/Lt. W.H. MASON to hospital.	
LA FAUCETTE	25/9/18		Fine weather. Bn. continued in operation.	

A6945 Wt. W11422/M1100 350,000 12/16 D. D. & L. Forms/C./2118/14.

Army Form C. 2118.

WAR DIARY
or
INTELLIGENCE SUMMARY. Volume XXXX II (cont.)
(Erase heading not required.)

Instructions regarding War Diaries and Intelligence Summaries are contained in F. S. Regs., Part II. and the Staff Manual respectively. Title pages will be prepared in manuscript.

Place	Date	Hour	Summary of Events and Information	Remarks and references to Appendices
ENGLEFONT- AIN.	28/10/18		Fine weather. Bn attacked ENGLEFONTAIN - capture completed. 2/Lt. H.O.BOARDMAN m.c. Wounded. 6320 L/SGT. SHUTER Wounded. Bn relieved and returned to billets MONTAY arriving 18.00 hrs.	
MONTAY	29/10/18		Fine weather. Bn at baths and cleaning up generally. 2/Lt. T.G.WINDLE Bn turns and retired to billets MONTAY arriving 18.00 hrs. 2/Lt. W.H.O.LUCAS M.C. & 2/Lt. B.G. HAWKSLEY to UK on leave. 2 O.R.s to Corps M.K.	
"	30/10/18		- do - Bn cleaning up. Lt.Col E.M. REALE C.M.G.D.S.O. returned from CAMIERS	
"	30/10/18		Fine weather. G.O.C inspects Bn turn-to inspection by G.O.C Division 2 O.R.s Ham - do - G.O.C Division inspects Bn and presents medal ribbons 1 O.R. to leave. 2/Lt. T.B.WINDLE to hospital.	
"	31/10/18		Showery weather. S.B.R. inspection. L.G. firing. Reinforcements 80 O.R. joined from base. Bn concert held in evening.	

Lloyd Lt.Col
A.O.B "The Kings Regt

WAR DIARY or INTELLIGENCE SUMMARY

Army Form C. 2118

4 Kings (L'pool) R.

VOLUME XXXVIII

NOVEMBER 1918

Place	Date	Hour	Summary of Events and Information	Remarks and references to Appendices
MONTAY.	1 Nov.		Weather fine – Bn. carried out Lewis gun training at the range. Coys at distance of Coy Commander for Platoon training near Range. Draft which arrived two days ago bathed and inspected by Commanding Officer.	WP
	2nd		Parson – Bath. Carried out Lewis Gun & grenade training at the range – Major Whitehouse T.M.L. OSBORNE rejoined Bn from leave to U.K.	WP
	3rd		Hot afternoon training Stanley – Church Service in the open (C of E) R.C. service in village Church.	WP
	4th		Fine – Bn moved through FOREST and thence by tracks to ENGLEFONTAINE – Bn. has fought over greater portion of this from a week ago. Good billets in ENGLEFONTAINE. Coy Commanders and others reconnoitred route for advance tomorrow. No hostile Shelling.	WP
ENGLEFONTAINE	5th		Misty morning settling to heavy rain from noon. Batt'n march from ENGLEFONTAINE via ROUTE DHECQ to LOCQUIGNOL (FORET DE MORMAL), arriving about 07.30 hrs. Orders arrived to advance towards SAMBRE RIVER through remainder of FORET DE MORMAL. About 1130 hours Bn clear of forest and moving towards SASSEGNIES which was entered at noon. In front, in touch on right with 50th Division. A & C Coys pushed on to Western bank of SAMBRE River and took up line along railway. B & C Coys in support. A Coy on right were troubled with enemy snipers but these were engaged with rifle grenades with excellent results. Bn H.Q. situated in SASSEGNIES. At 1900 hours 2nd WORCESTERS commenced taking over line from Bn.	WP

438

WAR DIARY or INTELLIGENCE SUMMARY

Army Form C. 2118

November 1918

Place	Date	Hour	Summary of Events and Information	Remarks and references to Appendices
SASSEGNIES	5th		Relief complete midnight. Battn. moved to billets in SART-BARA.	YD
SART-BARA.	6th		Wet – Rested till afternoon at 1600 hours Battn. moved across R. SAMBRE and billeted in factories EAST of AULNOYE – Comfortable night – No hostile activity.	YD YD YD
"	7th		Showery. Battn. moved in column of route through AULNOYE to POT DE VIN. from this point Battn. pushed through 1st Cameronians on a one Coy front. A, B, C & D Coys and after overcoming slight resistance by enemy Snipers + M.Gs. reached AVESNES – MAUBERGE road. This position was held till midnight when Division was relieved by 38th Division. Battn. moved back in early hours of 8th November to AULNOYE. – Total Casualties for the fighting to last 3 days 2 killed 2 died of wounds 15 wounded. At 0900 hours Battn. moved by march route to SASSEGNIES to billets.	YD
AULNOYE.	8th			YD
SASSEGNIES	9th		Weather fine – Bn. devoted the day to cleaning up and improvements in billeting area.	YD YD
"	10th		Fine – Church parade in field near Battn HQ. afternoon informing billets. Major D. Alkinson joined Bn.	YD
"	11th		Fine. News received that an Armistice had be signed with Germany. As from 1100 hours. The news was received very quietly in the Batt. In the morning was devoted to taking of small box respirators. In the afternoon a draft of 5 offrs + 65 O.R. arrived. Lieut. Stevenson M.C. 2nd Lts. Greensley, Snoddon, Rowland + W.J. Elliott. 2nd Lts D. Kerr. + J.E. Smith returned from leave.	YD

Army Form C. 2118.

Volume XXXXIII (continued) WAR DIARY or INTELLIGENCE SUMMARY.

(Erase heading not required.)

Place	Date	Hour	Summary of Events and Information	Remarks and references to Appendices
SASSEGNIES	1/11/18		Weather fine. Bath. reorganization. 11 O.R. (Band) from V. Corps Threshing School	BH
"	2/11/18		Weather fine. Company training in morning. Football during afternoon. 5 O.R. to Div. Burial officer. 4 O.R. from Div. Burial officer.	BH
			Divl Band played in village.	
"	3/11/18		Weather fine. Route march in morning. Lecture by 2/Lt McLAREN - ASSt "Investigation of British Army in the field" attended by 10 Officers 40 NCOs.	BH
VENDEGIES aux BOIS	4/11/18		Weather fine. Bn moved from SASSEGNIES to VENDEGIE au BOIS leaving 08 behind. Arriving 14.00 hours. 2/Lt. E.C. HYDE from leave to U.K.	BH
			MAJOR. I.H. BROWNE from base hospital. 3 O.R. to leave.	
CAULLERY	6/11/18		Weather fine. Bn moved from VENDEGIE au BOIS to CAULLERY arriving 14 hours. Lieut W.H. to LUCAS Mc Lieut R.S. HAWKSLEY from leave to U.K.	BH
"	7/11/18		Weather fine. Church service. Bathing parade.	BH
"	8/11/18		Weather fine. Company training. 2/Lt R. MOORE joins Bn.	BH
"	9/11/18		Weather fine. C.O. inspects A and C Companies. Lieut H.F. BURTON joined Bn. 2/Lieut R.I. TURNER M.C. from leave.	BH

Army Form C. 2118.

Volume XXXIII (Continued) WAR DIARY or INTELLIGENCE SUMMARY.

3

Instructions regarding War Diaries and Intelligence Summaries are contained in F. S. Regs., Part II. and the Staff Manual respectively. Title pages will be prepared in manuscript.

(Erase heading not required.)

Place	Date	Hour	Summary of Events and Information	Remarks and references to Appendices
CHULLERY	20/11/8		Weather mild. Morning Maurie M.S.M.G.M. Companies being refitted. Football match Arts Coy. v C+D Coy 72.	H.
"	21/11/8		Weather fine. G.O.C. inspection 11 o'clock. Drew full marching order. Pte. Mc GREAVEY reported 13.00 hours from "Desertin".	H.
"	22/11/8		Weather fine. Company training – P+BF McGREAVEY rejoined Bn. 2/Lieut H CRYAN rejoined from hospital. C.O. inspected Lewis Guns.	H.
"	23/11/8		Bn Concert 17.30 hours. Billeting Party left for CORBIE area. Weather fine – wet – cleaning part of Divisional area of Salvage. Major P. PILKINGTON to hospital. Lieut R.G. HAWKSLEY to hospital.	H.
"	24/11/8		Weather fine – Church Parades.	H.
"	25/11/8		Weather dull. Bn carried on with Salvage work. Games in afternoon.	H.
"	26/11/8		Weather dull. Bn Drill followed by Route march – 2h. G. ATACK, 2/Lieuts J.H. BUTTRISS – v. BIRTWISTLE – J.H. CARKETT – S. COOKSEY – H.D. HARLING – W.E. TANSER – H.R. WILDMORE and 11 O.R. reinforcements from base. Lectures on "Demobilization" by Rev. Stuart Kennedy at CLARY.	H.

Volume XXXVII (Continues)

WAR DIARY
or
INTELLIGENCE SUMMARY.
(Erase heading not required.)

Army Form C. 2118.

Place	Date	Hour	Summary of Events and Information	Remarks and references to Appendices
CAULLERY.	27/11/18		weather wet	
"	28/11/18		Company training and salvage work. Pt.B# Institutes relieving B.n work finished	
"	29/11/18		L.G. training on range. Concert in the Brigade Recreational room.	
"	30/11/18		Weather wet - Company training. B.n Bathed - Brigade Concert in Recreation. Room	
			Weather wet - Company training - C+D Coy. on range - afternoon	
			Sports - football - Possibles v Probables. - D Coy cross country run	

J.H. Watted
Comnd 4th Kings

WAR DIARY or INTELLIGENCE SUMMARY

Army Form C. 2118.

4 Liverpool R
Volume XXXIV Part II
VII 38

Place	Date	Hour	Summary of Events and Information	Remarks and references to Appendices
CAULLERY	1/12/18		Weather fine. Church services.	
do	2/12/18		Weather fine - Company training - Football matches in afternoon - Commanding Officer's leave (PARIS). Capt A.N. DUMPHREY leave (1 month)	
do	3/12/18		Weather wet - Company training - Recreational training in afternoon	
do	4/12/18		Weather wet - Bn paraded for visit of Him the King - Recreational training in the afternoon	
do	5/12/18		Weather wet - Bn Ceremonial drill - Bn football team played Divisional team - winning 1-0.	
do	6/12/18		Weather showery - Bn route march - football in afternoon.	
do	7/12/18		Weather wet - Bn ceremonial drill - baths - football Bn football team beat Brigade 6-2.	
do	8/12/18		Weather fine. Church services. Brigade Cross Country run. Capt F.H DUNCAN M.C. second place. Names: (1) Middlesex Regt (2) 2" A+SH. (3) 4" Kings	

44¢

WAR DIARY
or
INTELLIGENCE SUMMARY.

Army Form C. 2118.

Volume XXXIV Continued

Place	Date	Hour	Summary of Events and Information	Remarks and references to Appendices
CAULLERY	9/11/18		weather fine. Platoon singing competition - Bn packed up ready to move to new Area - Capt F H Davison MC to Brigade HQ - Captain R McCRAE returned Bn from Base. Commanding officer from leave	B.F.
—	10/11/18		weather showery - Bn left CAULLERY for HANNOT area - first day's march to MASNIERES - 4 O.R. to leave. 5 O.R. from leave	B.F.
MASNIERES	11/11/18		march continued to PAY RUN - weather showery	B.F.
PAY RUN				B.F.
BAPAUME	12/11/18		weather showery - march continued to BAPAUME.	B.F.
ALBERT	13/11/18		weather fine - do - to ALBERT	B.F.
ALLONVILLE	14/11/18		weather fine - march to ALLONVILLE - 4 O.R. to PARIS for Concerts	B.F.
AILLY-SUR-SOMME	15/11/18		Heavy repair shops weather fine - march to AILLY-SUR-SOMME	B.F.
CAMP. EN. AMIENOIS	16/11/18		weather wet - march to CAMP. EN AMIENOIS	B.F.
DROMESNIL	17/11/18		weather wet - march to DROMESNIL	B.F.
do	18/11/18		weather cool - Bn cleaning up - 20 r GALLAGHER from Base	B.F.
do	19/11/18		weather wet - Cleaning up & improvement of billets - Lt Gen W COLLINS - to leave	B.F.

WAR DIARY
INTELLIGENCE SUMMARY

Volume XXXIV Continued

Army Form C. 2118.

Place	Date	Hour	Summary of Events and Information	Remarks and references to Appendices
INCHEVILLE	20/1/18		Batt. rest. Platoon training. Recreational training in afternoon.	Bt.
do	21/1/18		Weather wet. Company training. 2/Lt H.G. NICHOLLS to leave. MAJOR T. STOPFORD-TAYLOR from leave.	Bt.
do	22/1/18		Weather wet. Company training - blow bad return.	Bt.
do	23/1/18		Weather wet. Church Service. Football match v RAMC lost 2-1. Batt. rest. A.C.D. hope route march. 'B' Coy on duty - 2 Officers & O.R. Attended lecture on Machine Gunnery. Capt F.H. DAWSON ret. from Brigade. Commanding Officer to Brigade as acting Brigadier. 'A' Coy train during.	Bt.
do	24/1/18		Weather fine. Church Parade. Football Officers v Sergts 3-3.	Bt.
do	25/1/18		'C' Company dinner.	Bt.
do	26/1/18		Weather wet. Route march for A.B.D. Coys. - 'B' Company dinner. Football match v 2nd A.&S.H. Regt lost 4-0.	Bt.
do	27/1/18		Weather wet. Company training. Boys Army v Byegones Lot 4-3. 2/Lt R.J. TURNER A.C. Shaw	Bt.
do	28/1/18		Weather wet. Company training. Football in afternoon.	Bt.
do	29/1/18		Weather wet. Church Service. Medical inspection by G.O.C. Division. 2/Lt M. PARKINSON from leave.	Bt.

Army Form C. 2118.

WAR DIARY
or
INTELLIGENCE SUMMARY.

Volume XXXIV Continued

(Erase heading not required.)

Place	Date	Hour	Summary of Events and Information	Remarks and references to Appendices
D/ROMESNIL	30/1/18		Weather wet. - Company training. football in afternoon	
to -	31/1/18		Weather wet. - Bn Route march - 2 Lt SNOWDEN to leave.	

M Newnes Major
Commanding 4" Bn "The King's" Regt

Army Form C. 2118.

WAR DIARY
or
INTELLIGENCE SUMMARY
(Erase heading not required.)

VOLUME 33

JANUARY 1919

4 Liverpool Regt

F↑F

45.8

Place	Date	Hour	Summary of Events and Information	Remarks and references to Appendices
TROMESNIL	1-1-19		Weather fine - Bn Drill - Recreation in the afternoon	
"	2-1-19		Weather fine. Bn left Tromesnil for POIX-du-NORD 10.30 am by road rail. Arrived POIX-du-NORD 14.00 hrs.	
POIX-du-NORD	3-1-19		Weather fine. Bn left POIX-du-NORD for LE HAVRE by rail 10.30 hrs. Arrived LE HAVRE 0300 hrs	
LE HAVRE CAMP 14 HARFLEUR	4-1-19		Bn at LE HAVRE (Harfleur, Camp - 14) B.9.B.D. Weather fine. Bn rested after journey. RE & QM Calling reported from leave.	
CAMP 14 HARFLEUR LE HAVRE	5-1-19		Weather fine. Battalion at Camp 14 HARFLEUR, preparing to take over camps to form Despatch Division. No 2 Embarkation Camp.	
"	6-1-19		Weather fine. A & C Coys and 40 other Ranks of D Coy proceeded to SANVIC Despatch Camp for instruction in the running and working of a Despatch Division. A Coy at Camp 1. C Coy and 40 other Ranks of D Coy at Camp 2 SANVIC.	
"	7-1-19		Weather fine. B.N. Headquarters at Camp 14 HARFLEUR. also 1st Coys. Preparing Camps for a Despatch Division and building NISSEN Huts.	

WAR DIARY or INTELLIGENCE SUMMARY

Army Form C. 2118.

(Erase heading not required.)

Place	Date	Hour	Summary of Events and Information	Remarks and references to Appendices
HARFLEUR	8-1-19		Weather Fine. Work on Camp continued.	
"	9-1-19		Weather Fine. Work on Camp continued	
"	10-1-19		Weather Fine. Work on Camps continued.	
"	11-1-19		Weather Fine. Work on Camps continued. Lt. G.H. NICHOLLS returned from leave.	
"	12-1-19		Weather Fine. 2d Corps rejoined BN HQ from SANVIC. Church service.	
"	13-1-19		Battalion working on Camps & building Huts. Weather fine. Recreational training by Coys in their turn.	
"	14-1-19		Weather Fine. Work & Recreational Training continued. Bath transport inspected by (acting) Brigadier General.	
"	15-1-19		Weather Fine. Work etc continued.	

WAR DIARY or INTELLIGENCE SUMMARY

Army Form C. 2118.

Place	Date	Hour	Summary of Events and Information	Remarks and references to Appendices
HARFLEUR CAMP 14.	16-1-19		Weather fine. B.C.D. Coys Route March. A Coy work on Huts. Lt Col E.M. BEALL CMG DSO, rejoined Battalion from B again HQ.	
"	17-1-19		Weather wet. Bn Work on Camp & Huts.	
"	18-1-19		Weather fine. Bn work on Huts etc and Recreational training.	
"	19-1-19		Weather wet. Work on Huts continued. Afternoon, Bn Football match V. 1st QUEENS R.W. SURREYS. Result. 0 — 1.	
HARFLEUR CAMP 15	20-1-19		Weather wet. Battalion on Camp 15. Battalion HQ moved to "B" 93RD HQrs. Coys working on Huts.	
HARFLEUR CAMP 15	21-1-19		Weather fine. Work continued.	

WAR DIARY
or
INTELLIGENCE SUMMARY

Army Form C. 2118.

Place	Date	Hour	Summary of Events and Information	Remarks and references to Appendices
HARFLEUR CAMP 15.	22.1.19		Weather fine. Work on 'Huts' continued. Lt P.H.L. BROUGH M.C. rejoined Battn from French Army. Battalion concert in the evening.	
"	23.1.19		Weather fine. Work continued. Lt L. STEVENSON M.C. } Released to civil employment. 2LT. C.F. GALLAGHER	
"	24.1.19		Weather fine Work on Huts, preparing for opening of No 2 Embarkation Camp. Despatch Division.	
"	25.1.19		Weather fine. Work continued. Lt H.F. BUCHAN released to civil employment.	
"	26.1.19		Weather wet. Camp - Church parade.	
"	27.1.19		Weather wet, some snow. Work on Huts continued. Battalion now known as N° 2 Embarkation Camp. Despatch Division.	

Army Form C. 2118.

WAR DIARY
or
INTELLIGENCE SUMMARY

(Erase heading not required.)

Place	Date	Hour	Summary of Events and Information	Remarks and references to Appendices
HARFLEUR	28/1/19		Weather fine. Camp divided into 3 Wings. No 1 Wing - A Coy No 2 " - C Coy No 3 " - D Coy B Coy form reserve and emergency wing. Wings in operation. First Troops for demobilization arrive in Camp.	
"	29-1-19		Weather Frosty, but dry. Battalion at work despatching Troops.	
"	30-1-19		Weather Frosty. Bn Despatching Troops.	
"	31-1-19		Weather Frosty. "	

Marshall Lt Col
Comdg.
4th Bn "The King's (Liverpool Regt.)

Volume 46.

4 Liverpool

WAR DIARY
or
INTELLIGENCE SUMMARY.

Army Form C. 2118.

Place	Date 1919	Hour	Summary of Events and Information	Remarks and references to Appendices
HARFLEUR	Feb. 1		The work of Demobilizing 1st Army Troops continued. 24 Officers 906 ORs passed through non-Combatants Camp Bedford Division.	fine
			Bn demobilized 2 ORs. Received 2 reinforcements from Base. Weather wet.	fine
	2		57 Officers 1524 ORs passed thro'	fine
	3		2 ORs sent to England – 10 ORs to Hospital – Received 1 OR from Base	fine
			2 Officers to Hospital. 18 Officers 7+6 ORs passed thro'. Wet.	fine
	4		Bn demobilized 1 Officer and 4 ORs. 8 ORs demobilized to England in leave.	fine
			3 ORs sent to England. No boat sailed. Wet.	fine
	5		Received 1 OR from Base. Lieut. P. GREASLEY Leave (Special) to England.	fine
			11 Officers 1184 ORs passed thro'. Fine.	fine
	6		Bn demobilized 12 ORs. 27 Officers 1180 ORs passed thro'. Wet.	fine
	7		2 ORs sent to England. 9 ORs Hospital. 20 Officers 535 ORs	fine
			passed thro'. Wet.	fine
	8		Bn demobilized 10 ORs. 1 OR sent to England. 11 Officers 645 ORs	fine
			Receipts of 1st Army Troops for demob. finished. Wet.	fine

Army Form C. 2118.

WAR DIARY
or
INTELLIGENCE SUMMARY.
(Erase heading not required.)

Place	Date	Hour	Summary of Events and Information	Remarks and references to Appendices
HARFLEUR	Feb 9		Batt. demobilized 11 O.Rs. Received 1 O.R. from Hospital. No 94350 Pte. A. YATES died from pneumonia at No 40. Sta. Hosp.	fine
	10		No troops passed thro. Fine	fine
			3 O.Rs. from the EAST arrived for demob. Frost.	hard
	11		Batt. demobilized 1 O.R. 3 O.Rs. leave to England. 27 officers 967 O.Rs. passed thro. FROST.	hard frost
	12		11 O.Rs. to Hospital. 39 officers 1279 O.Rs. passed thro FROST.	frost
	13		1 O.R. leave to England. 34 officers 1475 O.Rs. passed thro. Wet.	hard
	14		Batt. demobilised 7 O.Rs. 146 O.Rs. leave to England. 30 officers 1005 O.Rs. passed thro. Fine	fine
	15		Batt. demobilised 4 O.Rs. 1 officer to Hosp. 51208 Pte White died at No 40 Stationary Hosp. pneumonia. Draft of 10 officers 268 O.Rs. received from 12 Div. Walking from near DOULLENS. 46 officers 1041 O.Rs. passed thro. Wet.	hard wet
	16		Batt. demobilised 12 O.Rs. 10 O.Rs leave to England. 2nd Lt. E. CAPSTICK M.C. to assistant adjutant. 79 officers 1773 O.Rs. passed thro. Wet.	hard wet
	17		Batt. demobilised 12 O.Rs. 12 O.Rs. sent to England. 1 O.R. from Hospital. 69 officers 940 O.Rs. passed thro. wet.	

WAR DIARY or INTELLIGENCE SUMMARY

Army Form C. 2118.

Place	Date	Hour	Summary of Events and Information	Remarks and references to Appendices
HARFLEUR	FEB 18		Batt. demobilized 7 O.Rs. 10 O.Rs leave to England. 49 officers 1578 O.Rs from tur. het.	Fine
	19		— 5 — 7 — — — 30 — 1093 —	Fine
			Major S. TAYLOR evacuated sick to England. Capt & Adjt F.H. Dawson lab. leave to England.	Fine
	20		Batt. demobilized 2 O.Rs. 2 O.Rs leave to England (Special) 17 officers 1363 O.Rs from tur. het. Wet	wet
	21		— 5 — 2 officers — — (Conducting) 12 — 740 —	Fine
			Regt. E. Stephen leave to England	fine
	22		Batt. demobilized 11 O.Rs. 38 officers 898 O.Rs from tur. wet.	wet
	23		— 5 — 38 — 1329 —	fine
	24		— 4 — 23 — 687 — — — 6 O.Rs leave to England	fine
	25		— 15 — 60 — 1692 — — — 9 —	fine
	26		— 9 — 56 — 1204 — — — 10 officers 6 —	fine
	27		1 officer — 16 — 56 — 1711 — — — 6 O.Rs	fine
	28		— 11 — 26 — 946 — — — 1 —	fine
				fine 7
			No. 406622 Pte J. Atterton buried 22 cmy "Abour"	
			During the month Batt. cleared 804 officers and 28521 other Ranks.	
			Lieut Colonel W. L. Cameron 4th Bn. Northumberland Regt	

WAR DIARY or INTELLIGENCE SUMMARY

Army Form C. 2118.

4 Suff. Regt
Vol 41

Place	Date 1919	Hour	Summary of Events and Information	Remarks and references to Appendices
HARFLEUR	MARCH 1st		The bent of demobilization of troops from SALONICA and the EAST Cont. – 69 offs and 1059 O.R. passed through No 2 Despatch Camp. Br demobilizes 9 O.R. – 6 men leave to U.K. – Fine but windy.	
	2nd		52 offs 1024 O.R. passed through Camp. – 2nd/Lt W.E. TANSER wit draft to U.K. 14 days leave – 1 O.R. to leave – 10 men demobilizes from Batt. – Fine.	
	3.		37 offs 1465 O.R. passed through Camp. Batt. demobilized 2 O.R. – 1 O.R. joined Batt. from Hospital.	
	4.		51 offs 1976 O.R. passed through Camp. – Batt. demobilizes 14 O.R. – 1 man leave to U.K. – Wet.	
	5.		12 men demobilizes from Batt. – 9 O.R. to recruitment furlough – 22 offs 893 O.R. passed through Camp. – Changeable.	
	6.		5 men demobilizes from Batt. – 5 O.R. to recruitment furlough. – 6 offs 108 O.R. passed through Camp.	
	7		42 offs 1258 O.R. passed through Camp. – 8 men demobilizes from Batt. – 1 man to U.K. recruitment furlough. – 1 man joined Batt. from 78th T.M.B. – Capt F.H. DAWSON M.C. rejoined leave to U.K.	
	8		28 offs 1065 O.R. passed through Camp. – 10 men demobilized from Batt. – 1 man from Hospital	

A6945 Wt. W11422/M1160 350,000 12/16 D.D. & L. Forms/C/2118/14.

WAR DIARY
or
INTELLIGENCE SUMMARY.
(Erase heading not required.)

Army Form C. 2118.

Place	Date	Hour	Summary of Events and Information	Remarks and references to Appendices
HARFLEUR	MARCH 1919		Cont^d	
	8		1 man leave to U.K. - Draft of 7 offrs 172 O.R. from 1/7 Batt. The Kings (Liverpool Reg) joined Batt^n - Fine.	
	9.		20 offrs 528 O.R. passed through Camp - 1 man joined from Base - 1 man from Hospital. Lieut D. WATSON M.C. and Lieut L.C. TAYLOR to U.K. with drafts. Lieut TAYLOR to 14 days leave on completion of duty. - Fine.	
	10.		26 offrs and 1095 O.R. passed through Camp. - 2 men demobilized from Batt^n - 2nd Lt T.R. KENSHOLE on leave to U.K. after conducting duty - 2 O.R. leave to U.K. het.	
	11.		19 offrs and 1086 O.R. passed through Camp - 6 men from Batt^n for demobilization - 2 men to re-enlistment furloughs - 1 man joined from Hospital - 2 O.R. to leave. Fine.	
	12.		33 offrs 1397 O.R. passed through Camp - 7 men from leave ex 1/7 Batt. The Kings (Lpool Reg) Lieut & Q.M. COLLINS to Hospital (sick) 2nd Lt W.J. ELLIOTT leave to U.K. after conducting duty - 3 O.R. leave to U.K.	
	13.		Lieut J. WHYTE to conducting duty - 35 offrs 1966 O.R. passed through the Camp. 4 men demobilized from Batt^n - Fine.	
	14.		19 offrs 905 O.R. passed through the Camp. - 1 man from leave ex 1/7 B. The Kings (Lpool Reg) 6 men demobilized from Batt^n - 3 men to leave - Fine.	

Army Form C. 2118.

WAR DIARY
or
INTELLIGENCE SUMMARY
(Erase heading not required.)

Instructions regarding War Diaries and Intelligence Summaries are contained in F.S. Regs., Part II. and the Staff Manual respectively. Title Pages will be prepared in manuscript.

Place	Date	Hour	Summary of Events and Information	Remarks and references to Appendices
HARFLEUR	1919 MARCH 15		89 off. 7554 O.Rs. passed through Camp. 3 men to leave. 6 O.Rs. from Battalion for demobilization.	JCR
	16		82 off. 1393 ORs passed through Camp. 6 men from leave ex 1/7th Bn. The Kings (Liverpool Regt). 1 O.R. from Batt. for demobilization. 1 O.R. to re-enlistment furlough.	JCR
	17		20 off. 864 ORs passed through Camp. 5 O.R. from leave ex 1/7th Bn. the Kings (Liverpool Regt).	JCR
	18		Lt D. WATSON M.C. and Lt J. WHYTE to demobilization. 2 O.R. from Bn. for demobilization. 2 O.R. to WATFORD DETAILS. 3 O.R. from Bn. to leave.	JCR
	19		21 off. 963 ORs passed through the Camp. 3 O.R. from leave ex 1/7th Bn. the Kings (L'pool Regt). 1 O.R. from Batt. 6 O.R. from Batter to leave.	JCR
	20		45 off. 1295 O.Rs. passed through the Camp. 2 O.R. from leave for demobilization.	JCR

2449 Wt. W14957/M90 750,000 1/16 J.B.C. & A. Forms/C.2118/12.

WAR DIARY
or
INTELLIGENCE SUMMARY.
(Erase heading not required.)

Army Form C. 2118.

Place	Date	Hour	Summary of Events and Information	Remarks and references to Appendices
HARFLEUR MCH	1919			
	20	onto	1 x 1/7th Bn The Kings (Liverpool Regt). Lt R. MOORE and 3 O.Rs from Battn for demobilisation. 1 O.R. to re-enlistment furlough – 6 O.R. from Bn to leave.	MR
	21		30 Offrs. 934 O.Rs passed through the Camp. Draft of 1 Offr. 29 O.Rs from 18th (LHY) Bn The Kings (Lpool Regt) joined the Bn. 6 O.R. from Bn to leave – 3 O.R. from Bn to demobilization – 2 O.R. from Bn to Re-enlistment furlough. 7 O.R. from leave to 1/7th Bn The Kings (Lpool Regt).	MR
	22		30 Offrs. 2321 O.Rs passed through the Camp. 2/Lt J.E. SMITH and 2/Lt J.H. BUTTRISS to U.K. on draft conducting duty. 4 O.Rs from Bn for demobilisation – 5 O.R. to leave	MR
	23		84 Offrs. 1327 O.Rs passed through the Camp. 2 men from leave to 1/7th Bn The Kings (Lpool Regt). 1 O.R. from military Prison	MR
	24		48 Offrs. 904 O.Rs passed through the Camp. 7 O.R. to leave 2 O.R. from leave to 1/7 Bn The Kings (Lpool Regt).	MR

WAR DIARY
or
INTELLIGENCE SUMMARY.

Army Form C. 2118.

Place	Date 1919	Hour	Summary of Events and Information	Remarks and references to Appendices
HARFLEUR	MRCH 25		20 offs. 1321 ORs passed through the Camp. 2/Lt D. KERR M.C. and 3 ORs for demobilisation. 1 OR. to re-enlistment furlough. 5 OR. from leave ex 1/17 Bn The Kings (L'pool Regt). 6 OR to leave.	
	26		60 ORs 1664 ORs passed through the Camp. 2 O.R. from leave ex 1/17th Bn The Kings (Liverpool Regt). 1 O.R. to Home Establishment. 6 O.R. to leave.	
	27		8 offs. 396 ORs passed through the Camp. 2 OR to re-enlistment furlough. 6 OR to leave. 2 OR from leave ex 1/17 Bn The Kings (L'pool Regt).	
	28		23 offs. 557 ORs passed through the Camp. 1 OR to Demobilization. 2 OR to re-enlistment furlough. 3 OR to leave.	
	29		49 offs. 643 ORs passed through the Camp. Lt. A.S. LIGHTBOWN from 1/17 Bn The Kings (L'pool Regt) joined Bn. Draft of 2 offs. 163 ORs joined Bn from 10th Bn LANCASHIRE FUSILIERS. 3 OR to re-enlistment furlough. 6 OR to leave	

WAR DIARY
or
INTELLIGENCE SUMMARY

Army Form C. 2118

Place	Date	Hour	Summary of Events and Information	Remarks and references to Appendices
HARFLEUR/MCH	1919 29		CNTD. 1 O.R. to Hospital.	W.R.
	30		44 Offs. 1551 O.Rs passed through the Camp. 4 O.R. to re-enrolment furlough. 5 O.R. to leave.	W.R.
	31		59 Offs. 1201 O.Rs passed through the Camp. LT W.H.O LUCAS M.C. to U.K. for Repatriation. 2 O.R. from Bn for demobilisation. 1 O.R. to re-enrolment furlough. 5 O.R. to leave. 1 O.R. to hospital. 1 O.R. from leave ex 10th Bn Lancashire Fusiliers.	W.R.
			Note - during the month of March 1048 officers and 34,255 other ranks passed through No 2 Despatch Camp. Total passed through since 29.1.19. 2017 officers and 64441. O.R.	W.R.

Marshall Lt Col
Commdg No 45 No 2 Desp

Army Form C. 2118.

WAR DIARY
or
INTELLIGENCE SUMMARY

(Erase heading not required.)

Instructions regarding War Diaries and Intelligence Summaries are contained in F.S. Regs., Part II. and the Staff Manual respectively. Title Pages will be prepared in manuscript.

4 Liverpool   M42

Place	Date	Hour	Summary of Events and Information	Remarks and references to Appendices
Harfleur.	1/4/19.	Weather Fine.	3 Officers and 166 O.Rs passed through Camp.-No.2 Dispatch-Capt.R.McCrae to"Demobilization".	Y/P.
	2/4/19.	Weather Fine.	52 Officers 1308 O.Rs passed through Camp. 6 O.Rs to leave-U.K.	Y/P.
	3/4/19.	Weather Fine.	71 Officers 1339 O.Rs passed through Camp. 1 O.R to U.K for re-enlistment furlough. 6 O.Rs to leave.	Y/P.
	4/4/19.	Weather Fine.	52 Officers 1513 O.Rs passed through Camp. 2nd Lieut.J.H.Buttriss and 2nd Lieut.S.Cooksey to U.K. for demobilization. 6 O.Rs to leave.	Y/P.
	5/4/19.	Weather Fine.	51 Officers. 2021 O.Rs passed through Camp. The following Officers to U.K for demobilization:- 2nd Lieut.J.E.Smith, 2nd Lieut.E.G.Hyde, 2nd Lieut.G.Atack. 6 O.Rs to leave.	Y/P.
	6/4/19.	Weather Fine.	46 Officers 1842 O.Rs passed through Camp. 6 O.Rs to leave. Church Services at Church Hut Camp 15 Harfleur.	Y/P.
	7/4/19.	Weather Fine.	47 Officers. 2020 O.Rs passed through Camp. 2nd Lieut.H.R.Wilshire to U.K. for leave. Major J.H.L.Browne from Draft Conducting duties.	Y/P.
	8/4/19.	Weather Fine.	8 Officers 830 O.Rs passed through Camp. The following officers proceeded to the 52nd Bn. the King's Regt.(Armies of Occupation) 6 O.Rs to leave.	Y/P.
	9/4/19.	Weather Fine.	55 Officers 830 O.Rs passed through Camp. 6 O.Rs to leave.	Y/P.
	10/4/19.	Weather Fine.	49 Officers 1620 O.Rs passed through Camp.	Y/P.
	11/4/19.	Weather Fine.	45 Officers. 1346 O.Rs passed through Camp. The following Officers proceeded to 52nd Bn "The King's" Regt (Armies of Occupation). Lieut.W.E.Long, Lieut.D.J.Johnson, 2nd Lieut.D.J.Caldwell,2nd Lieut.F.Stott, 2nd Lieut.A.S.Rigby.	Y/P.

WAR DIARY or INTELLIGENCE SUMMARY

April 1919.

Army Form C. 2118.

(Erase heading not required.)

Instructions regarding War Diaries and Intelligence Summaries are contained in F.S. Regs., Part II. and the Staff Manual respectively. Title Pages will be prepared in manuscript.

Place	Date	Hour	Summary of Events and Information	Remarks and references to Appendices
Harfleur	12/4/19.	Weather Fine.	36 Officers. 1388 O.Rs passed through Camp. Capt.F.G.Ager from Draft Conducting duty. Lieut.P.H.L.Brough.M.C. from leave to U.K. 1 O.R to U.K. to join Home Establishment (Compassionate case)	W.D.
	13/4/19.	Weather Fine.	7 Officers. 313 O.Rs passed through Camp. 10 O.Rs to leave.	W.D.
	14/4/19.	Weather Fine.	6 Officers. 632 O.Rs passed through Camp. 10 O.Rs to leave.	W.D.
	15/4/19.	Weather Wet.	13 Officers. 839 O.Rs passed through Camp. 2 O.Rs re-enlisted. 10 O.Rs to leave.	W.D.
	16/4/19.	Weather Fine.	14 Officers. 274 O.Rs passed through Camp. 2 O.Rs re-enlisted. Capt.F.R.Skillen to 175 P of W Coy. 10 O.Rs to leave.	W.D.
	17/4/19.	Weather Fine.	6 Officers. 417 O.Rs passed through Camp. 10 O.Rs to leave.	W.D.
	18/4/19.	Weather Fine.	Good Friday. 14 Officers. 419 O.Rs passed through Camp. 10 O.Rs to leave Football Match. Officers versus Sergeants. result Offs.4. Sgts.2.	W.D.
	19/4/19.	Weather Fine.	12 Officers. 462 O.Rs passed through Camp. 10 O.Rs to leave. Football Match versus 1st Queens. Result. Bn 3. Queens 1.	W.D.
	20/4/19.	Weather Fine.	6 Officers. 332 O.Rs passed through Camp. 10 O.Rs to leave. Divine Services.	W.D.
	21/4/19.	Weather Fine.	7 Officers. 538 O.Rs passed through Camp. 10 O.Rs to leave.	W.D.
	22/4/19.	Weather Fine.	9 Officers. 534 O.Rs passed through Camp. 10 O.Rs to leave. 2nd Lieut. W.H.Leckie.M.C. to U.K. for demobilization.	W.D.
	23/4/19.	Weather Fine.	12 Officers. 625 O.Rs. 10 O.Rs to leave.	W.D.
	24/4/19.	Weather Fine.	No Sailing. 10 O.Rs to leave. Band Concert in Y.M.C.A.	W.D.
	25/4/19.	Weather Fine.	35 Officers. 647 O.Rs passed through Camp. 10 O.Rs to leave. ANZAC DAY Sports at Australian Depot. 40 O.Rs of Bn competed.	W.D.

Army Form C. 2118.

WAR DIARY
or
INTELLIGENCE SUMMARY

(*Erase heading not required.*)

April 1919.

Place	Date	Hour	Summary of Events and Information	Remarks and references to Appendices
Harfleur.	26/4/19.		Weather Fine. 10 Officers. 134 O.Rs passed through Camp. 10 O.Rs to leave. Football Match Bn versus "G.B.D". Result :0-0: C.O³' Conference at 98th Inf.Bde Hqrs. 12 O.Rs to 33rd Divisional School of Instruction.	
	27/4/19.		Weather Wet. 1 Officer. 47 O.Rs passed through Camp. 10 O.Rs to leave. Divine Services.	
	28/4/19.		Weather Wet. No sailing. 10. O.Rs to leave. 5 O.Rs to 33rd Divisional. M.T. Coy	
	29/4/19.		Weather Wet. 10 Officers. 179 O.Rs passed through Camp. 10 O.Rs to leave. 2 O.Rs to Chinese Labour Depot, Noyelles.	
	30/4/19.		Weather Wet. No sailing. 10 O.Rs to leave. Major J.H.L.Browne transferred to U.K.(Regular soldier officer). 2 Re-inforcements joined from 7th King's.	
			During the month of April training was carried out daily by 1 per platoon per Coy. On the 29th April No. 1 Wing, No.2 Dispatch Camp was closed down and A Coy(No.1 Wing) commenced Coy training The following numbers passed through No.2 Dispatch Camp during the month. 734 Offs. 22846 O.Rs. Total Number passed through Camp since January 1919. 2975 Offs. 88142 O.Rs.	
	May 1st 1919.		Commanding 4th Bn "The King's" Regiment. Lieut⁰ Colonel.	

WAR DIARY or INTELLIGENCE SUMMARY

Army Form C. 2118.

4 Liverpool Regt

Place	Date	Hour	Summary of Events and Information	Remarks and references to Appendices
HARFLEUR	1919 MAY 1		The work of Demobilisation of local troops and 1st & 3rd ARMY CADRES continued. 1 Off. & 1 O.R. passed thro' H.Q. Embarkation Camp. Dispatch Drivers. 9 O.R. leave to U.K. this date.	
	2.		29 Officers 427 O.R. passed thro'. LIEUT LEWIS AEB Draft Conducting 10 O.R. leave to O.K.	
	3.		4 Officers 59 O.R. passed thro'. 10. O.R leave to U.K.	
	4.		10 O.R. leave to U.K. No troops for dispersal passed thro'.	
	5.		Lts Delmers. M.C; J.S. Tolly; F.C.S Harrison. 2nd Lts C.H Frearson; J. Ashcroft; A. Partridge and F.H Ellissen. joined the Battalion from the Rhine Army.	
			10. O.R's leave to U.K.	
	6.		10. O.R's leave to U.K. 30 Officers 321 O.R passed thro' this	
	7.		10. O.R leave to U.K. 3 Officers 11 O.R passed thro'. the	
	8.		H.Q. Embarkation Camp. SANVIC closed down. This cup. to take all local personnel dispersal. 10. O.R's leave to U.K. 10 O.R's passed thro' this	
	9.		10. O.R's leave to U.K. 40 Officers 365 O.R passed thro'. this	
	10.		2nd Lieuts C. DANCER. M.C; W.R. WINSHIRE demobilised 2nd Lieut H.H Jennings. D M.O.T. 11th B. Leicester Regt Army of the RHINE. 10 O.R's leave to O.K. joined the Battalion from	
			3 Officers 107 O.R's passed thro' this	
	11.		10 O.R's leave to U.K. 2 Officers 63 O.R passed thro'. the 40 O.R's passed thro the	
	12.		LIEUT. F.N. BRITTNEH. M.C 100. leave to O.K. 23 Off 23 Off 9 officers 91 O.R passed thro the	
			LIEUT - C. GIRVAH. demobilised 10 O.R leave to O.K.	

Army Form C. 2118.

WAR DIARY
or
INTELLIGENCE SUMMARY

(Erase heading not required.)

Instructions regarding War Diaries and Intelligence Summaries are contained in F. S. Regs., Part II. and the Staff Manual respectively. Title Pages will be prepared in manuscript.

Place	Date	Hour	Summary of Events and Information	Remarks and references to Appendices
HARFLEUR	1919 MAY 15		10 ORs to leave to U.K. 20 Officers 30 8 OR passed thro' here.	
	16		10 ORs leave to U.K. 3 Officers 85 OR passed thro' here	
	17		Battalion Sports. 2 Officers bateau to France. 100R leave to UK. 3 Officers 100R passed thro'	
	18		12 ORs leave to U.K. 19 Officers 284 ORs passed thro'. here.	
	19		Bn. Platoon Competition won by No 13 Platoon D Coy. 16 Officers 243 OR passed thro'	
	20		H.O. Cpl TWIST tried by F.G.C.M. for "Absence" Advance party of 2/5 Gloucesters	
			1/3 OR's leave to U.K. 3 Officers 300R passed thro H.O.	
	21		Arrival. 2Lt J.H. CARKEET demobilised. 26 Officers 520 OR passed thro' H.O.	
			Lt R.C. STEPHENS & 10 ORs leave to U.K. the morning rain mess at	
	22		2 ORs leave O.K. 14 Officers 12q OR passed thro' the 4 ORs despatched for re-embarkt furlough	
	23		2Lt G.J. PEARCE. 3 9 ORs leave to U.K. 2 Officers 850R passed thro' here.	
	24		4 Officers 53 OR passed thro' here	
			1 Officer to leave to France. 5 ORs leave to U.K. No sailing	
	25		4 ORs leave to U.K. here.	
	26		6 ORs leave to U.K. 23 Officers 419 OR passed thro' here. 5 Officers 60 ORs	
	27		Lt L.S. FORSTER. 2nd Lt M. PARKINSON and 11 ORs leave to U.K. passed thro' here.	

Army Form C. 2118.

WAR DIARY
or
INTELLIGENCE SUMMARY.
(Erase heading not required.)

Place	Date 1918	Hour	Summary of Events and Information	Remarks and references to Appendices
MARLEUR	MAY 28		H.Q. & Battalion Cadre Sketch Division taken over by 2/5 Gloucesters. Total number Borne this is date 3,287 Officers 92, 383 Other Ranks	Sle
	2		1 Officer to leave & have 10 ORis leave to U.K. 2nd Lt YA PARTRIDGE admitted to hospital this AM Better. Sons at 11 am	Sle
	29		10 OR leave to U.K. the	Sle
	30		2 Lt H.D. HARDING + 9 OR. leave U.O.K. the	Sle
	31		5 OR leave to U.K. slight thunderstorm.	Sle

Arthur Lieut Colonel
Commdg 4th Bn The Kings Regt.

33

4 Liverpool R

508

Army Form C. 2118.

WAR DIARY
or
INTELLIGENCE SUMMARY.
(Erase heading not required.)

Instructions regarding War Diaries and Intelligence Summaries are contained in F. S. Regs., Part II. and the Staff Manual respectively. Title pages will be prepared in manuscript.

Place	Date	Hour	Summary of Events and Information	Remarks and references to Appendices
	JUNE			
HAVRE	1		Divine Service – 250 ORs on parade. – Weather fine	
	2		2/Lt ACKLAND & 14 ORs to 33rd Divisional School – Weather fine – 4 ORs to leave U.K.	
	3		3 ORs leave to UK – Weather fine	
	4		4 ORs leave to UK – Weather fine	
	5		2/Lt N.C. BULMER & 12 ORs leave to UK – Weather fine	
	6		9 ORs leave to UK – Weather fine	
	7		Battalion preparing for move – 9 ORs leave to UK – Weather fine	
	8		Battalion standing by to move to DUISANS – 10 ORs to leave U.K. – Weather fine	
	9		Battalion entrained for DUISANS. 21.45 hour – 20 ORs to leave U.K. – Weather fine	
	10		Battalion detrained at ACQ at 19.00 hrs marched to DUISANS, arriving at "Y" Hutments at 2 cookhouse – Weather fine	
DUISANS	11		Clearing up camp – 2 Companies guided towns at Chinese Compound, ARRAS. 1 NCO & 4 men as escort to NOYELLES. – 1 Officer & a platoon remained as guard.	
	12		Cleaning up camp – Guard from Chinese Compound returns – 6 ORs to leave U.K.	
	13		Preparing of detachment – 14 ORs to leave U.K. – Weather fine	
	14		6 ORs to leave U.K. – Weather fine	

WAR DIARY
or
INTELLIGENCE SUMMARY.

(Erase heading not required.)

Army Form C. 2118.

Instructions regarding War Diaries and Intelligence Summaries are contained in F. S. Regs., Part II. and the Staff Manual respectively. Title pages will be prepared in manuscript.

Place	Date	Hour	Summary of Events and Information	Remarks and references to Appendices
DUISANS	JUNE 15		LIEUT FORSTER from leave - 6 ORs to leave - U.K. - weather fine	
	16		Detachments went to various Stations in the I. area - weather fine	
	17		Battalion H.Q. & Company details leave DUISANS at 18.00 hr. Arrive DOUAI 21.00 hr. Located. CASERNE DE CAUX. - weather fine	
DOUAI	18		Cleaning barracks. - 2 ORs to leave - weather fine	
	19		Commanding Officer rode to MONTIGNY visiting posts. - "B" Company H.Q. move to MONS - 4 ORs to leave - weather fine	
	20		Pos. weather fine	
	21		Commanding Officer visited DENAIN and all "C" Company with "C" Coy. - 3 ORs to leave - weather fine	
	22		2/Lt. N.C. BULMER & 2/Lt. M. PARKINSON from leave - 1 OR to leave - weather fine. Commanding Officer & Adjutant rode to SOMAIN visited "A" Company's guard.	
	23		Commanding Officer at VALENCIENNES - 1 OR to leave - weather fine	
	24		Lieut. H.N. SPRECKLEY demobilised - 2/Lt. HARLING from leave - weather showery	
	25		Commanding Officer visits VALENCIENNES by 09.30 hr train, thence car to MONS, BINCHE and all "B" Coy's posts. - 2/Lt. E.H. RYAN to leave - weather showery.	

WAR DIARY or INTELLIGENCE SUMMARY.

Army Form C. 2118.

Place	Date	Hour	Summary of Events and Information	Remarks and references to Appendices
DOUAI	JUNE. 26		Commanding Officer & Adjutant rode to SAINS LE MARQUIEN & visited detachment. 5 O.R.s to leave - weather showery	
	27		G-O-C 98th Brigade & Brigade Major visited Battalion Headquarters. - 2 O.R.s to leave - weather showery mainly.	
	28		Commanding Officer visits posts at LENS, VERQUIGNEUL, BETHUNE, HESDIGNEUL, BARLIN, COUPIGNY, BOYEFFLES, GRAND SERVIN and STUART CAMP (ARRAS) - 2 O.R.s to leave - weather showery.	
	29		Commanding Officer rode to TEMPLEUVE and visited posts - 2 O.R.s to leave - weather showery	
	30		Commanding Officer visited CASERNE DE RUTTE, DOUAI. - Lieut H.G. NICHOLLS & 7 O.R.s to leave. weather showery.	
			The Batt.n was relieved at No 2 Despatch Riders Embarkation Camp, HARFLEUR, on the 28th of June, by the 2/5 B.n The Gloucestershire Regt. The Batt.n then came to No1 Area. Staying for a few days at DUISANS afterwards moving to DOUAI. No1 Area is divided into four subareas with their H.Q. at the following places BETHUNE SUBAREA at HERSIN COUPIGNY - DOUAI SUBAREA ARRAS SUBAREA 42 at DUISANS	

WAR DIARY
or
INTELLIGENCE SUMMARY.
(Erase heading not required.)

Army Form C. 2118.

Place	Date	Hour	Summary of Events and Information	Remarks and references to Appendices
at VALENCIENNES			— MONS SUBAREA at MONS. The chief work of these Subareas is the clearing up of the country and the collection of war material. Large dumps of ammunition are therefore necessary as the work of sending material to the base ports in Engr. Nevertheless the breaking up of these dumps and similar duties in No.1 Area are carried out by the Bn. The location of the Bn. HQ. is now:—	
			Bn.H.Q. administered by DOUAI SUBAREA. located at CASERNE DURUTTE DOUAI.	
			A. Coy. " ARRAS SUBAREA " STUART CAMP Nr ARRAS.	
			B " MONS SUBAREA " MONS.	
			C " DOUAI SUBAREA " CASERNE DURUTTE DOUAI.	
			D " BETHUNE SUBAREA " BARLIN.	

M Mall Lt.Col.
Commanding 4"B" The Kings Liverpool Regt.

Army Form C. 2118.

WAR DIARY
or
INTELLIGENCE SUMMARY
(Erase heading not required.)

Instructions regarding War Diaries and Intelligence Summaries are contained in F. S. Regs., Part II. and the Staff Manual respectively. Title Pages will be prepared in manuscript.

Place	Date	Hour	Summary of Events and Information	Remarks and references to Appendices
DOUAI	JULY 1		Battalion move from CASERNE DE CAUX, DOUAI to CASERNE DURUTTE, DOUAI. Weather Hot.	N.T.
	2		Commanding Officer visits detachments at MASNY. Weather Hot. Heavy storm in evening. 11 ORs to leave. 9 ORs rejoin from leave. 2/Lt. TURNER M.C. & 2/Lt. E. SNOWDEN struck off strength "Pending Demobilization" vide ORs 5994.	N.T.
	3		Lt. Taylor i.e. assumes command of C Coy. 2 ORs to leave. 7 ORs rejoin from leave. Weather Stormy.	N.T.
	4		Commanding Officer rides to DENAIN, visits guard at BESSENER DUMP. 2 ORs to leave. 6 ORs rejoin from leave.	N.T.
	5		Commanding Officer visits detachment at MONCHECOURT. AT BROUGH ME & Lt. CARTER to Civil Employment. 2 ORs to leave. 2 ORs rejoin from leave. Weather Showery.	N.T.
	6		Commanding Officer rides to TEMPLEUVE visits detachment. 2 ORs to leave U.K. 3 ORs rejoin from leave.	N.T.
	7		3 ORs to leave U.K. 2 ORs rejoin from leave.	N.T.
	8		Commanding Officer visits detachment at DAINVILLE, CAMBLAIN L'ABBE, ST. POL, & BARLIN. Car breakdown near BARLIN - Returned 03.30 hrs 9.7.1919. 1 OR. to leave - 2 ORs rejoin from leave.	N.T.
	9		Commanding Officer rides to SANS LE MARAVIEN visits detachment there. 2 O.R. to leave. 2 O.R. rejoin from leave.	N.T.
	10		2 ORs to leave - 3 ORs rejoin from leave - Weather fine.	N.T.
	11		Commanding Officer visits MONS, TEMPLEUVE, TOURNAI detachments. 1 OR to leave, 1 OR rejoin from leave.	N.T.

WAR DIARY
or
INTELLIGENCE SUMMARY
(Erase heading not required.)

Army Form C. 2118.

Place	Date	Hour	Summary of Events and Information	Remarks and references to Appendices
DOUAI	JULY 12		Commanding Officer visits to SOMAIN & ANICHE & visits detachments. Football team to Valenciennes. 3 O.Rs rejoin from leave.	N.S.
	13		Football match at VALENCIENNES versus 18th French Infantry Regiment. Result Kings 5 goals - French 4 goals. Party of Sixty (60) men on lorries to VALENCIENNES return same night. 2 O.Rs to leave. 3 O.Rs rejoin from leave.	N.S.
	14		French Push celebrations. Review of party of "King's" Chener troops by Commandant d'Armes, Douai.	N.S.
	15		Commanding Officer & Adjutant ride to TEMPLEUVE & visit detachment. 4 O.Rs to leave.	N.S.
	16		Commanding Officer rides to MONCHICOURT & visits detachment. Lt NICHOLL & 3 O.Rs rejoin from leave. Capt A.F.EDWARDS, 2/Lt J.ASHCROFT & 2 O.Rs to leave.	N.S.
	17		2 O.Rs to leave. V.K. 6 O.Rs rejoin from leave.	N.S.
	18		Commanding Officer & Lt Col DANZEY (A.A.G.) visit V Hutments, DUISANS. 6 NCOs to 59th Divn School. 2 O.Rs to leave V.K. 2 O.Rs rejoin from leave.	N.S.
	19		British Peace Celebration. Regimental Band gives performance in PLACE CARNOT - DOUAI. Football match 'KINGS' versus FRENCH CIVILIANS. Result Kings six goals, French nil. — 2/Lt RYAN rejoins from leave. 2 O.Rs to leave.	N.S.
	20		Church Parade. Attendance — 60. - 2 O.Rs to leave - 2 O.Rs rejoin from leave.	N.S.
	21		Brigadier General WYATT visits Battalion. 2 O.Rs to leave. 32 O.Rs join Bn.	N.S.

WAR DIARY
or
INTELLIGENCE SUMMARY.
(Erase heading not required)

Army Form C. 2118.

Place	Date	Hour	Summary of Events and Information	Remarks and references to Appendices
DOUAI	JULY 22		Commanding Officer went MONS & DENAIN - 3 ORs to leave	ASY
	23		Bearing rallying parties to A & D Coys. - 2 ORs to leave - 1 OR rejoin from leave	ASY
	24		Arrival of A Coy at 20.00 hrs from ARRAS. - Major PILKINGTON struck off strength - England	ASY
			2 ORs to leave - 11 ORs rejoin from leave	ASY
	25		Arrival of D Coy at 21.00 hrs from BETHUNE - 2 ORs to leave - 4 ORs rejoin from leave	ASY
	26		Commanding Officer inspects A Coy Transport - General BIDWORTH visits Battn. Lieut Sg.Lt major	ASY
			D Coy draws new equipment &c., - 2 ORs to leave - 11 ORs rejoin from leave	ASY
	27		Open air Church services at 10.00 hrs. - Commanding Officer rode to MONCHECOURT	ASY
			ANICHE SOMAIN EMERCHICOURT	
	28		Brigadier General WYATT & Commanding Officer visit posts at SOMAIN & MONCHECOURT	ASY
			5 ORs to leave - 18 NCOs rejoin from 6th Divn School. - 5 ORs rejoin from leave	ASY
			Commanding the 9 OR Boys visit new training grounds. - Training 9.45 Inspection	
	29		PART SEVEN RATION Company NewDay River - 2 ORs to leave - 9/15 ASHCROFT	ASY
			rejoins from leave.	ASY
	30		Recupies training as on 29th. - Training grounds allotted to A & D Companies	

Army Form C. 2118

WAR DIARY
or
INTELLIGENCE SUMMARY
(Erase heading not required.)

Instructions regarding War Diaries and Intelligence Summaries are contained in F. S. Regs., Part II. and the Staff Manual respectively. Title Pages will be prepared in manuscript.

Place	Date	Hour	Summary of Events and Information	Remarks and references to Appendices
DOUAI	JULY 31		Companies training — P & RT — Bioscope dine — March discipline. Football match "A" V "D" — Result "D" 1 goal "A" nil. H. O/Rs to leave. 2 O/Rs rejoin from leave.	WSJ

Ainsdale Lieut. Colonel.
Comdg 4th Bttn. Kings (Liverpool) Regt.

Army Form C. 2118.

WAR DIARY
or
INTELLIGENCE SUMMARY.
(Erase heading not required.)

1st Bn. The King's (Liverpool Regt.)

August 1919

WAR DIARY
or
INTELLIGENCE SUMMARY

AUGUST 1919

Army Form C. 2118

Place	Date	Hour	Summary of Events and Information	Remarks and references to Appendices
DOUAI	AUGUST 1		Two Companies carried out training. - Lieut O.G. Lewis and 2 O.R.s. leave to U.K.	W.D.
	2		Commanding Officer and Adjutant by car to MONS and HOUDENG to visit detachment (B Coy) at those places. - A & D Coys balled at DOUAI - 10 O.R.s. to leave - 2 O.R.s. from leave.	W.D.
	3.		Open air Divine Service in Barracks DOUAI. - Commanding Officer visited MONCHECOURT and ANICHE - Capt. A.F. Edwards MC. and 3 O.R.s. from leave to U.K. - 10 O.R.s. to leave.	W.D.
	4.		Bank Holiday - Football Match in evening Result D Coy 5 goals - A Coy nil - Capt & Adjt J.H. Dawson M.C. leave to U.K. - 3 O.R.s. returned from leave.	W.D.
	5.		A & D Coys - Company & Platoon training - Commanding Officer visits Somain detachments (C Coy) - 2 O.R.s. from leave to U.K.	W.D.
	6.		Training continued - Commanding Officer visits MONTIGNY detachments (C Coy).	W.D.
	7.		Training continued. - 10 O.R.s. leave to U.K. - 2 O.R.s from leave.	W.D.

Army Form C. 2118

WAR DIARY
or
INTELLIGENCE SUMMARY

AUGUST 1919. PAGE 2.

(Erase heading not required.)

Instructions regarding War Diaries and Intelligence Summaries are contained in F. S. Regs., Part II. and the Staff Manual respectively. Title Pages will be prepared in manuscript.

Place	Date	Hour	Summary of Events and Information	Remarks and references to Appendices
DOUAI.	August 8.		Fine — A. + B. Coys. Continue training. — Preparations for relief of Mons detachment (B Coy) by A + B Platoons D Coy Commence. — 10 o.r.s. to leave to-nite. — 2 o.r.s. from leave.	Y.P.D.
	9		Fine — A + B Coys. battled and inspected in readiness to move to Mons. 10 o.r.s. leave to U.K.	Y.P.D.
	10.		Fine — Roy Ht. — Chaplain divine service at Barracks Douai. — Afternoon french held training competition — Band rendered selections — Country officer won 1st prize. — 2 o.r.s. to leave.	Y.P.D.
	11		Fine. — Commanding officers visits Mons — A Coy and 3 Platoons D Coy move to Mons by rail in relief of B Coy — 10 o.r.s. to leave.	Y.P.D.
	12		Fine. — Major General Sir J. Capper K.C.B. (G.O.C. Nº I AREA) visits Battn. — 1 o.r. leave to U.K. — 1 o.r. from leave.	Y.P.D.

WAR DIARY
or
INTELLIGENCE SUMMARY.
(Erase heading not required.)

Army Form C. 2118.

Instructions regarding War Diaries and Intelligence Summaries are contained in F.S. Regs., Part II. and the Staff Manual respectively. Title pages will be prepared in manuscript.

Place	Date	Hour	Summary of Events and Information	Remarks and references to Appendices
DOUAI.	AUGUST 13.	Fine.	Brig Gen R.J. Wyatt DSO Commanding 98th Inf Bde visits Battn. - B Coy arrive from Mons. - Lieut G Delmer M.C. to hospital - 3 ors. from leave.	M.D.
	14	Fine.	Commanding Officer inspects detachments at MASNY and LEWARDE (C Coy) Capt C.R. NICKELS leave to the Rhine from Mons. - 3 ors from leave.	M.D.
	15.	Fine.	B Coy refitting and cleaning up stores etc. - 6 ors leave to UK.	M.D.
	16.	Dull.	Detachment at LEWARDE (C Coy) withdrawn - Comdg Officer inspects B. Coy - 5 ors. to leave - 3 ors from leave.	M.D.
	17.	Fine.	Given an Ecienne Service at Barracks Denain - Comdg Officer took detachment at AMIENS (C Coy) - 6 ors. from leave.	M.D.
	18.	Fine.	B Coy training. - 5 ors. to leave 3 ors from leave.	M.D.
	19.	Fine.	Major General Sir J. CAPPER KCB Cmd (G.O.C. No1 Area) inspects B Cy and Transport afternoon final inspection - Lieut G. DELMER M.C. from Hospital.	M.D.

Army Form C. 2118.

WAR DIARY
or
INTELLIGENCE SUMMARY.
(Erase heading not required.)

Instructions regarding War Diaries and Intelligence Summaries are contained in F. S. Regs., Part II. and the Staff Manual respectively. Title pages will be prepared in manuscript.

Place	Date	Hour	Summary of Events and Information	Remarks and references to Appendices
DOUAI.	AUGUST 20.	—	Fine — B Coy Training — 5 ORs to leave	MD
	21.	—	Fine — Cunning Officers took VALENCIENNES — CONDE and MONS — B Coy on Rifle Range — 5 ORs leave to UK — Capt + Adjt F.H. Dawson MC, Lieut A.E. LEWIS and 1 OR from leave	MD
	22.	—	Fine — B Coy Training (P.P.R.D. lectys to drill etc) — Capt C.R. NICCOLLS reported from leave to Rhine area — 3 ORs to leave — 9 ORs from leave	MD
	23.	—	Fine — B Coy Training (Platoon drill — P.P.R.D. etc) Lieut F.J. McWHINNIE reported from N.O. Coy — 33 NCOs from HAVRE — 3 ORs to leave — 5 ORs from leave	MD
	24	—	Fine during morning — Raining in afternoon — No 1 Green Remount Squadron had Gymkhana at TRAGNONVILLE — Band played selections — Major Gen Sir J. CAPPER K.C.B. handed prizes — Battn took following prizes Officers Jumping — 2nd prize — 2/Lt E.W. Beall Cmy OTD Officers Bending — 2nd prize — 2/Lt A.D. Harding 1 Mile Race — 1st prize — Pte Howard (H) (Transport Section) 2nd prize — Pte Young B Coy 1st prize — Sgt Gaspard B Coy	MD

Army Form C. 2118.

WAR DIARY
or
INTELLIGENCE SUMMARY.
(Erase heading not required.)

Instructions regarding War Diaries and Intelligence Summaries are contained in F. S. Regs., Part II. and the Staff Manual respectively. Title pages will be prepared in manuscript.

Place	Date	Hour	Summary of Events and Information	Remarks and references to Appendices
	AUGUST 24	8 p.m.	Lieut. D.B. Cummins OC. leave to U.K. from MONS – 3 ors. to leave 10 ors. from leave.	W.D.
	25.		Drill – B Coy Training 4 ors. to leave. 3 ors. from leave.	W.D.
	26.		B Coy training (musketry) – 3 ors. to leave ? – 2nd Lieut. Ackland and 4 ors. from leave.	W.D.
	27.		Fine. B Cy on Rifle range = Commanding Officer = President of Audit Board.	W.D.
	28.		Fine – B Coy training (P. + R.D. Infantry, Lewis Gun Drill). 3 ors. to leave. 5 o.r. from leave. – Commanding Officer to VALENCIENNES as a 27th inst.	W.D.
	29.		Fine. B Cy training (Lewis Gun drill + P+R.D.) 4 ors. to leave. Commanding Officer to VALENCIENNES as on 27th inst.	W.D.
	30.		Fine. – B Cy. Bathing and kit inspection. – 4 ors. leave to U.K. 4 ors. from leave.	W.D.

Army Form C. 2118.

WAR DIARY
or
INTELLIGENCE SUMMARY.
(Erase heading not required.)

Instructions regarding War Diaries and Intelligence Summaries are contained in F. S. Regs., Part II. and the Staff Manual respectively. Title pages will be prepared in manuscript.

Place	Date	Hour	Summary of Events and Information	Remarks and references to Appendices
	August 30		Commanding Officer proceeded to VALENCIENNES to attend Bgde Horse to 9th Inf. Bde H.Q. - CROIX	M.D.
	31.		Xmas Mail - Divine service held indoors – 5 men to leave – 4 men from leave	M.D.

M. Lund Lt Col.
Commdg. 4th Bn. The King's (Liverpool Regt.)

4th Liverpool 9/3/19

WAR DIARY
or
INTELLIGENCE SUMMARY.
(Erase heading not required.)

Army Form C. 2118.

Sep 1919

Place	Date	Hour	Summary of Events and Information	Remarks and references to Appendices
DOUAI	Sept 1.		B Coy training (P&RY) Games (Hockey) - 5 ORs to leave & ORs from leave. Weather fine.	
	2.		do — Commanding Officer rode to ANICHE & SOMAIN	
	3.		Our winter detachment there. 3 ORs to leave. 3 ORs from leave. Weather fine. B Coy training. Commanding officer inspected detachments at MONS. 4 ORs leave	
	4.		4 ORs from leave. Weather showery. B Coy on range. Lieut R.C. STEPHENS & 2/Lt Mc BURMER from leave to PARIS. 4 ORs to leave. 5 ORs from leave. Weather fine.	
	5.		On NVHEAN. N.H. fired by 2/2 Coy. 4 ORs to ARSENOE Serious economy - repairing of barracks - 5 ORs to leave - 6 ORs from leave weather fine	
	6.		Bathing Kit Equipment inspections. 48 "DERBY" MEN & SOMAIN concentration. backups for disposal. 6 ORs to leave. 6 ORs from leave. Weather fine	
	7.		Open air divine service in barrack square. - 4 ORs to leave. - 5 ORs from leave weather fine.	
	8.		Q Coy training (P&RY) Games. Revive Patrolling Duties 4 ORs to leave weather showery	
	9.		Brigadier Gener WYATT Cmdg 98th Inf Bde visited Battalion. Lieut G. DELMER M.O. 4 ORs to leave. 3 ORs from leave. Weather fine	
	10.		Coy training. Commanding officer visited VALENCIENNES regarding DOUAI evacuation. 4 ORs to leave. Weather fine	
	11.		B Coy on range. Brigadier General WYATT visited Battn. - 46 ORs to SOMAIN Concentration camp for disposal. - 4 ORs to leave. - 7 ORs from leave - weather fine	
	12.		Serious economy - repairing of barracks &c. - 4 ORs to leave. - 3 ORs from leave - weather fine	
	13.		Kit equipment inspection. Bathing &c. - 4 ORs to leave - 5 ORs from leave - weather clear	

Army Form C. 2118.

WAR DIARY
or
INTELLIGENCE SUMMARY.
(Erase heading not required.)

Instructions regarding War Diaries and Intelligence Summaries are contained in F.S. Regs., Part II. and the Staff Manual respectively. Title pages will be prepared in manuscript.

Place	Date	Hour	Summary of Events and Information	Remarks and references to Appendices
DOUAI	Sept 14		PRESIDENT POINCARÉ visits DOUAI. Various Reps. of town. H.R. Rate. The King (Nicol) Rct. provides Guard of Honour. 4 Officer 7.33 O.Rs. to LOMAIN Concentration Camp for dispersal to O.Rs. + leave. 1 O.Reg. from leave - Weather Dull.	
	15.		"B" Coy 9.RRT games Parametry. Commanding Officer visited detachments at MONS. 2 ORs + leave. 1 O.R. from leave - Weather fine.	
	16		"B" Coy on range - 2 ORs + leave - Weather Showery	
	17		Commanding Officer visits to LOMAIN, visited detachments at ORs + leave. 13 ORs from leave. Weather cold.	
	18.		Lieut. R.C. TAYLOR & 2/Lt. MUIR + leave. Weather fine - each. 5 ORs + leave.	
	19		Interior economy, cleaning, refitting of transport. Weather cold. 2 ORs + leave.	
	20		- do - . Kit equipment inspection. Nutrition. CAPT CP NICKELLS YAT WT ELLIOT + hospital. Weather fine. 8 ORs from leave - NO leave train to CALAIS.	
	21.		Divine Service in Barracks - Weather cold. 4 ORs + leave	
	22		"B" Coy training. 39 ORs to LOMAIN Concentration Camp for dispersal. 5 ORs + leave. 3 ORs + Leave. Weather cool.	
	23		"B" Coy preparing for move to ARRAS	
	24		- do - Inst of Pte MEADOWS. C by Officer for ABSENCE. Weather cool. 2 ORs + leave. 6 ORs + leave	
	25.		"B" Coy move to ARRAS. Various detachments for SAINS LE MAROEUIL, FREMICOURT, BETHUNE, AGNIET & MAROEUIL. Headquarters at STUART CAMP, ARRAS. 2 O.R. + leave. 46 O.Rs from leave.	AT Q' BELMER W.E

Army Form C. 2118.

WAR DIARY
or
INTELLIGENCE SUMMARY.
(Erase heading not required.)

Instructions regarding War Diaries and Intelligence Summaries are contained in F. S. Regs., Part II. and the Staff Manual respectively. Title pages will be prepared in manuscript.

Place	Date	Hour	Summary of Events and Information	Remarks and references to Appendices
	Sept.			
DOUAI	26		Interior economy - reinburying of Armenek - 80 ORs to ARRAS concentration camp for dispersal. 2 ORs to leave - weather fine	
	27		Brigadier General WYATT inspected Battalion - 5 ORs for leave - no leave train to CALAIS. Weather cold & showery	
	28		All leave & demobilization concerns owing to railway strike in England - 50 ORs disposal concerned. Weather very showery.	
	29		Details - interior economy - clothing & kit equipment inspection. Weather changy.	
	30		Lieut. N.T. ELLIOTT rejoined from hospital - weather fine.	

M.W. Hall Lieutenant Colonel
Comg 1st Bn The King's (Liverpool) Regiment.

Army Form C. 2118.

4 Kings

WAR DIARY
or
INTELLIGENCE SUMMARY.
(Erase heading not required.)

Instructions regarding War Diaries and Intelligence Summaries are contained in F. S. Regs., Part II. and the Staff Manual respectively. Title pages will be prepared in manuscript.

Place	Date	Hour	Summary of Events and Information	Remarks and references to Appendices
DOUAI.	OCTOBER			
	1		Battalion Paper Strength 24 Officers & 612 ORs	
			Commanding Officer visited Somain detachment. — 3 ORs reinforcements — Interior economy	
	2		Weather showery — Interior economy — 2 ORs reinforcements — 2 ORs to Hospˡ — 2 ORs from Hospital.	
	3		Weather fine — Inspection & Training (P.R.J. Gunnery) — 1 OR Rheumatism Cry — Pte Meadows	
			Reverser to go days I.P. Hosp for G.O.C.M for ABSENCE — 7 dropatched & Field Equipment Company	
	4		Commanding Officer visited MONS detachments — Bathing & Kit Inspections — 2 ORs from Hospˡ	
	5		Divine Service in Barracks — Weather cool — 1 OR to Hospˡ — 1 OR from Hospˡ — Capt Chase	
			in afternoon.	
	6		Company training — weather fine cold — R. G. DELMER M.C to 69ᵗʰ A.P.L.U. — 2 ORs reinforcements	
	7		Company training — (P.R.J. Gunnery) — weather fine cold — 1 OR to Hospital	
	8		Weather wet — Interior economy — (Training of Barrack fig.)	
	9		Rugby Union WYATT visited Battalion — Lieut OR NICKELLS & 2/Lt. M.D HARLING	
			Hospital — Pte L.C. TAYLOR from Base — Battalion football match v. Go Labour Groups. Bn Wn	
			3 — 1 — weather fine cool — Training	
	10		Company Training — (P.R.J. Gunner) — 2 ORs from Hospital weather fine	
	11		Kit Inspections & Bathing — Weather fine — 1 OR to Hospital.	

548

Army Form C. 2118.

WAR DIARY
or
INTELLIGENCE SUMMARY.
(Erase heading not required.)

Instructions regarding War Diaries and Intelligence Summaries are contained in F. S. Regs., Part II. and the Staff Manual respectively. Title pages will be prepared in manuscript.

Place	Date	Hour	Summary of Events and Information	Remarks and references to Appendices
DOUAI	OCTOBER 12.		Divine Service in Barracks – 2/Lt. F.K. ELLISSEN to Divl. Employ – 2 O.Rs to Hospital.	
			Paper chase in afternoon – weather fine-cold.	
	13.		Training – Capts F.H. DANSON D.L.C. & Lt. A.E. LEWIS to Divl. Employ – Commanding Officer visited MONTIGNY detachment.	
	14.		Commanding Officer visited SOMAIN detachment – Training – weather fine-cold.	
			C.S.M. ROBSON to Record Office.	
	15.		Commanding Officer visited detachments at FREMICOURT, ACHIET & ARRAS –	
			Weather fine – 7 O.Rs from leave.	
	16.		Training for Inspection – 1/2 O.Rs to Divl. Employ – 7 O.Rs from leave – weather fine.	
	17.		Divine Parade – (Rev Shepherd Ye) – 9 O.Rs from leave – 2 O.Rs to Hospital.	
			2 O.Rs from Hospital – 1 O.R. Reinforcement – weather fine – All DOUAI guards relieved.	
	18.		Battn. inspected by Generals – 2 O.Rs to leave – weather fine.	
	19.		Divine Service in Barracks – weather fine – 2 O.Rs to leave – Paper Chase in afternoon.	
	20.		Training – Lt. S.P. FORSTER to O.Rs & leave – 7 O.Rs from leave – weather fine-cold.	
	21.		3 O.Rs to Divl. Employ – SOMAIN detachment withdrawn – Lt. R.C. STEPHENS & 3 O.Rs to leave	
			3 O.Rs from leave – weather fine.	

WAR DIARY
or
INTELLIGENCE SUMMARY.
(Erase heading not required.)

Army Form C. 2118.

Place	Date	Hour	Summary of Events and Information	Remarks and references to Appendices
	OCTOBER			
DOURI	22		B. 2 Companies found Escorts at DOURI. 2 Sidings at FREMICOURT, MARQUIN.	
			"FLAKOFF" DUMP & SANS LE MARQUIEN relieved by 90th Labour Group. – 3 ORs from leave. –	
	23		2 ORs to leave – 2 ORs to hospital – weather fine.	
			Weather fine – Inspection of B v D Companies – Footbne match B v D. Latter coy winning. –	
			2 ORs to leave – 1 OR from leave	
	24		Lt. TULLY & 2/Lt ACKLAND 2 ORs to leave. – 1 OR from hospital – weather warm.	
	25		2 Coy join Battalion at DOURI – all guards & detachments at MONS relieved –	
			B Coy cleaning up – 2 ORs to leave – 1 OR from leave. weather cold	
	26		2/Lt DAVIS & 119 ORs to leave. Employed Prim. Course in Rouen. – 2/Lt 12th HCRO Cpl k	
			2/Lt HARKING to Paris. Leave – Pips. Show in afternoon – weather very cold – Evening –	
	27		Loss Labour Training – QM CULBERT (106y. JP4O2) & QA ELMER (88 cy. JP No 2) A	
			2d Company ARRAS – Vacancy – 2 ORs to leave.	
	28		Weather not good – Vacancy	
	29		Weather cold – 2 ORs to leave – Ad 19130 Pte ROSE. T informed annulment	
			10 days about.	
	30		2/Lt SASHCROFT & HARKING from PARIS – 2 ORs to leave – 6 ORs from leave – weather cold	

WAR DIARY
or
INTELLIGENCE SUMMARY.
(Erase heading not required.)

Army Form C. 2118.

Place	Date	Hour	Summary of Events and Information	Remarks and references to Appendices
DOUAI	OCTOBER 31st		Brigadier General WYATT visited Battalion - ACHIET detachment relieved - nearly over. 20 O.Rs to Divn Employment. 1 Officer + 15 O.Rs remain at AUCHEL - all other detachments withdrawn.	

M. Hill
Lieutenant Colonel
Comdg 1st Bn The King's (Liverpool) Regt.

WAR DIARY or INTELLIGENCE SUMMARY.

(Erase heading not required.)

Army Form C. 2118.

Instructions regarding War Diaries and Intelligence Summaries are contained in F.S. Regs., Part II. and the Staff Manual respectively. Title pages will be prepared in manuscript.

Place	Date	Hour	Summary of Events and Information	Remarks and references to Appendices
DOUAI.	NOVEMBER 1		Battalion (Paps) Strength 21 Officers, 282 O.R. Battalion preparing for move – Cleaning of equipment re – Kinetogyne – even – 1 O.R. from Hospital – O.R. Special Service down.	A.S.
	2		Battalion preparing for move – 1 O.R. to Civil Employment – 1 O.R. from leave – Weather cold – Rutter.	A.S.
	3		Battalion preparing for move – Loading of Limbers – Returns se – 1 O.R. to Hospital – Weather cold – rain.	A.S.
	4		Battalion entrains at Burl St Eloi, Douai at 12.45 hrs. (Strength 13 officers + 180 O.R.) 3 O.R. from leave – Weather cool.	A.S.
BOULOGNE.	5		Battalion arrives at Boulogne at 02.30 hrs & detrains at Bassin Loubet at 08.30 hrs. Accommodated in No. H. Rest Camp. Henriville – Major D. Gardiner, M.C. 13th KRRc Posted to Bn as 2nd in Command – Lieut. L.S. Forster from leave – Commanding Officer visits Base Commandant, Boulogne & returns to Cadre Strength. Boulogne – Battalion returns to Cadre Strength at once – Weather cold + showery	A.S.
	6		Preparing for induction to Cadre Strength – Handing in of stores – 21 O.R. to Civil Employment – 4 O.R. from leave – Weather showery	A.S.
	7		33 O.R. to Civil Employment – Handing in of stores – 8 H.D. Horses, 11 L.D. Horses, 15 L.D. Mules & 3 Chargers handed in – 3 O.R. from leave – Weather showery.	A.S.
	8		76 O.R. to Civil Employment – Lieuts: Forster, Elliott, Cumming, Stephens & Bulmer & 2/Lieuts: Ashcroft & Pearse to Civil Employment – 2 Chargers & 6 H.D. Horses handed in – Weather fine – cold.	A.S.
	9		25 O.R. to Civil Employment – 2 O.R. from leave to Civil Employment – Major D. Gardiner, M.C. Assumes H.Q. Strength – (Authority APG Boulogne Dismet)	A.S.

Army Form C. 2118.

WAR DIARY
or
INTELLIGENCE SUMMARY.
(Erase heading not required.)

Instructions regarding War Diaries and Intelligence Summaries are contained in F. S. Regs., Part II. and the Staff Manual respectively. Title pages will be prepared in manuscript.

Place	Date	Hour	Summary of Events and Information	Remarks and references to Appendices
BOULOGNE	NOVEMBER			
	10.		LIEUTS. TAYLOR, M^cKINNIE & NICHOLLS & 5 O.Rs to Civil Employment – 2 Lieut. Irving posted to & joined unit for Army of Occupation dispatched to COLVIN CAMP reporting (Authority A.C.I. R1/5231/3) – weather showery – Handing in Stores.	NA
	11.		LIEUT. M. PARKINSON 1th Cam – 11 ORs from Cam – 6 ORs to Civil Employment – 1 O.R. to G.H.Q. FORWARD AREA GROUP – Anniversary of ARMISTICE DAY – Cws numerer Silence – weather showery – Handing in Stores.	NA
	12.		11 ORs from leave – 9 ORs to Civil Employment – One percent parade of CADRE – Inspection & Cleaning up of Camps – weather cold – sun – Handing in Stores	NA
	13.		1 OR from leave – Lieut. M. PARKINSON Joined HARKING & 5 OR. to Civil Employment – Bathing parade for Personnel of CADRE – weather cold – sun. Handing in stores	NA
	14.		5 ORs from leave to Civil Employment – 2 H.D. men arrived in – weather cold – sun – One percent parade of Personnel of "CADRE" – Cleaning of equipment	NA
	15.		All percent parade – Cleaning up – Pers. COLBERT & BOYLE arm from Civil Employment – Company. ARRAS & dispatched to 13th NORFOLK REGT – weather fine – snowing all day	NA
	16.		A.F.B. 213 to Base A/O. Ruth. orange of Officers 9 R. ORs (Estab 5 & 32. Command 3 & 39. Leave 4 ORs – awaiting demob. 1 Officer) – weather cold – sun.	NA
	17.		First marching over Parade of CADRE – 1 OR from leave dispatched to 13th R. NORFOLK REGT for demob – weather cold – sun rain.	NA
	18.		Lieut. C. RNICKELS to Civil Employment – Notificat. in of reinft. to CADRE to A.A.G. BOULOGNE. – Some recruitment to D.A.Q.M.G. – weather fine	NA

(Apr23). Wt. W13591/M1293. 750,000. 1/17. D. D. & L., Ltd. Forms/C.2118/14

Army Form C. 2118.

WAR DIARY
or
INTELLIGENCE SUMMARY.
(Erase heading not required.)

Instructions regarding War Diaries and Intelligence Summaries are contained in F.S. Regs., Part II. and the Staff Manual respectively. Title pages will be prepared in manuscript.

Place	Date	Hour	Summary of Events and Information	Remarks and references to Appendices
BOULOGNE	NOVEMBER			
	19.		All present Parade CADRE – Bathing Parade – Interior economy – 3 O.Rs from leave to Civil Employment – 3 O.Rs Civil on leave – weather very showery	NT
	20.		1 O.R. (CADRE) to Civil Employment on "Compassionate Bus." – "All present" Parade – weather fine – windy.	NT
	21.		2 O.Rs from leave to Civil Employment – Notification of move to ENGLAND on Sunday 23 NOVBR – All present Parade – Preparing for move – weather fine.	NT
	22.		"All Present" Parade – Preparing for move to ENGLAND – weather cold & showery.	NT
	23.		Battalion embarks for ENGLAND from BOULOGNE at 08.30 hrs.	NT

M. Noll
Lieutenant Colonel
Comdg 4th Bn. "The King's" (Liverpool) Regiment.

www.ingramcontent.com/pod-product-compliance
Lightning Source LLC
Chambersburg PA
CBHW080809010526
44113CB00013B/2351